CORE

Java™ Web Server

ISBN 0-13-080559-9

90000

9 780130 805591

PRENTICE HALL PTR
CORE SERIES

CORE
Java™ Web Server

Chris Taylor & Tim Kimmet

Prentice Hall PTR, Upper Saddle River, NJ 07458
http://www.phptr.com

Editorial/Production Supervision: Joe Czerwinski
Acquisitions Editor: Greg Doench
Editorial Assistant: Mary Treacy
Development Editor: Jim Markham
Technical Editor: Cameron Laird
Marketing Manager: Kaylie Smith
Manufacturing Manager: Alexis Heydt
Cover Design: Design Source
Cover Design Direction: Jerry Votta
Art Director: Gail Cocker-Bogusz

© 1999 Prentice Hall PTR
Prentice-Hall, Inc.
A Simon & Schuster Company
Upper Saddle River, NJ 07458

Printed in the United States of America

10 9 8 7 6 5 4 3 2 1

ISBN 0-13-080559-9

Prentice-Hall International (UK) Limited, London
Prentice-Hall of Australia Pty. Limited, Sydney
Prentice-Hall Canada Inc., Toronto
Prentice-Hall Hispanoamericana, S.A., Mexico
Prentice-Hall of India Private Limited, New Delhi
Prentice-Hall of Japan, Inc., Tokyo
Simon & Schuster Asia Pte. Ltd., Singapore
Editora Prentice-Hall do Brasil, Ltda., Rio de Janeiro

Contents

3   ALTERNATE LIFESTYLES FOR THE JAVA WEB SERVER 56

4   ADMINISTRATING THE JAVA WEB SERVER 86

APPENDIX

Preface

All of this started in the Spring of 1997 when we took a Java programming course at San Jose State University, taught by the Java God himself, Dr. Cay Horstmann. As a term project, we were given the task of writing a client/server application in Java. As fortune would have it, the Java Web Server made its public beta debut only weeks before the class project teams formed. Our team quickly moved through the developer documentation and example programs, set up our own RMI/JDBC data server, wrote several servlets using that data server, and had the entire system up and running within two weeks.

By the way, we got an "A+" for the project.

So what is this anecdote doing in the introduction to our book on the Java Web Server? First, it gives you, as the reader, an idea of our own experience with the Java Web Server. As you'll find in the chapters to come, we approach topics with the attitude of "show me, don't tell me", using numerous code examples and experimental tricks to dig into topics ranging from web security to the popular JSP scripting language. We won't "forget to tell you" about problems we've encountered; instead, we walk you through repeating the same (non-trivial!) mistakes we made when we first developed with the servlet API. This candid view of the "darker side" of servlet development is worth the price of the book alone (at least, it would have been to us when we took that course; half of our time was spent head-scratching over "Document contains no data" messages coming from the Java Web Server)!

The last two words of our anecdote, "two weeks," should open some eyes to another exciting benefit with the Java Web Server: rapid server-side application development. By building on the expertise of the developers at JavaSoft, our team was free to focus on the problem at hand: how to get student resumes from a backend database into the web browsers of prospective employers. All of this coolness was made possible by the Java platform's promise of "make the simple things easy, and make the difficult things possible," which clearly shows through in the design of the servlet API.

Putting the religion aside for a moment, consider how the introduction of Java applets sparked an explosion on the Web; documents became living, breathing entities, adding interactive capabilities atop a non-interactive protocol like HTTP.

Servlets promise the same breakthroughs on the server side.

Like their applet cousins, servlets can be compiled once and run on any servlet-compatible system. The servlet API separates the idiosyncrasies of a particular web server from the task of "getting the user's requests processed to send back proper results". If you're anything like us that's all you wanted to accomplish anyway (who wants to become an expert on a particular web server just to write some server-side scripts?).

That's where this book comes in. It acts as a tour guide, taking you past the paved roads of the API documentation and deep into the jungle of undocumented programming territory.

Who Should Read This Book?

That's a good question. The most obvious audience is programmers who want to write applications with the Java Web Server. And even if you aren't writing servlets just for the JWS, the knowledge you'll take away from reading this book applies to any servlet-enabled web server, whether it be Apache, Netscape Enterprise Server, or Microsoft's Internet Information Server (just to name a few).

Of course, we don't expect you to have a strong knowledge of web servers or servlet programming before reading this book. This book was written with this third group in mind, the Java programmers who want to break out onto the web and write some really cool stuff, but don't know how to make it happen. Hopefully, you'll find everything you need to know about web servers and how to extend them with Java between these covers.

Good luck!

What You'll Need

You'll need a Java-compatible operating system. Personally, we like Windows NT (the entire book, except for certain installation chapters, was written on Windows NT), with its native threading support and responsive GUI. Windows 95 works too, but it's not very stable (especially when things go wrong—can you say "GPF?") If you're a Unix fan, Solaris or Linux would be a good choice.

As for software, most of it can be found on the CD-ROM (see the section "About the CD-ROM" for more info). We've included the latest JDK (1.1.6) for Win32 and Solaris platforms, but you'll want to check the JavaSoft web site (`www.javasoft.com`) for the latest and greatest version. You'll also need a copy of the Java Web Server. As we're big proponents of "try before you buy", we've included a trial version of the Java Web Server (with the JSP extensions) on the CD-ROM.

So, to reiterate, you'll need:

- Java-compatible O/S
- Java Development Kit compatible with JDK 1.1
- Java Web Server

How This Book Is Organized

Just as any developer should know the underlying operating system for which he develops programs, we feel that you should know the Java Web Server Web server inside and out before you actually attempt to extend its features. This requires that you know what features are offered through the web server as well as how to administer its capabilities. In the first part of this book, we introduce you to features and show you how to administer the Java Web Server. Chapter 1 explains many of the features offered under the Java Web Server as well as its underlying architecture. Chapter 2 shows you how to install the Java Web Server on different platforms, including Windows NT, Windows 95, Solaris, and Linux. Even though Chapter 4 reads "Administering The Java Web Server", the administration really begins in Chapter 3, "Alternative Lifestyles For The Java Web Server," where we show you how to configure the JWS to use different virtual machines. Finally, in Chapter 4 we show you how to configure JWS by walking you through different scenarios in the Admin Applet.

In the second part of the book, we show you how to extend the JWS. In order to extend the features of the Java Web Server, you'll need to get comfortable with the Java Servlet API, which allows you to write server-side programs that run in the Java Web Server. Chapters 5 and 6 introduce you to the Mother of all Servlets, the `GenericServlet` class. We cover the API as well as pinpoint some of the problems that we've encountered while developing our own applications. In order to be effective on the Web, you'll need to get familiar with the HTTP-specific Servlet classes offered by the Servlet API. What is HTTP? Glad you asked! Chapter 7 introduces you to HTTP and gives you a clear understanding of all the HTTP 1.1 methods, so that you'll be ready for Chapter 8, where you'll learn about HTTP-specific Servlet development. In Chapter 9, we focus on the differences between CGI and Servlets and show the CGI developer how easy it can be to make the transition from CGI to the more efficient Servlet alternative. Chapters 10 and 11 show you how to implement more advanced features of HTTP, including caching and session management. Chapter 12 gives an introduction to the JWS component model, which is very similar to the JavaBeans component model. Chapter 13 introduces you to JavaServer Pages, which is the latest technology introduced by the Java Web Server team. Finally, in Chapter 14, we provide extensive coverage of the security features under JWS. The fun does not end with Chapter 14, however! Appendix A gives extensive coverage to topics that make JWS even more powerful, namely SGML, XML, and HTML. In our (not-so!) humble opinion, the XML coverage in this chapter is better than most complete references we've seen!

Conventions Used in This Book

We've tried to stay away from fancy sidebars and shaded areas throughout the book, mainly because we put all of the meaty stuff you'd find in those places in the text itself! When we did use sidebars, they were for a special reason. That reason is apparent from the title of the sidebar. *Notes* are for providing additional information on a topic without requiring an illustrating example. *Design Patterns* explain certain portions of the software architecture by comparing them to well-known software patterns, like those found in pattern catalogs like the G4 text (Design Patterns, Gamma et al.). *Bugs* describe inconsistencies we've found between the printed documentation and reality. Bugs should be taken in context, as they might be ironed out in a later release of Java Web Server. *Alerts* are like Bugs, except that we've included a suitable workaround for the problem we encountered.

About the CD-ROM

The CD-ROM contains all of the source code examples in the book (organized by chapter), the latest version of the Java Developer's Kit, and trial versions of the Java Web Server for both Solaris and Win32 systems. In addition, we've put some "goodies" on the disc, like Tim's favorite editor (med), the coolest HTML editor on the planet (DreamWeaver), two XML parsers written in Java, third-party servlet runners (JRun and ServletExec), various standards documents for RFC's referenced in the book, and the latest Java Foundation Classes from JavaSoft.

Foreword

I f you are a Web programmer, or you are thinking of becoming one, you want to learn about servlets. Servlets are so much better than other Web server extension mechanisms that they are sure to become the method of choice for server-side processing. CGI scripts in Perl are fine for small jobs, but servlets use Java—a real programming language with rich support libraries, including convenient database access via JDBC. And most importantly, servlets are a lot more efficient than CGI scripts, because you don't pay for the overhead of spawning a new process for every invocation. NSAPI and ISAPI are proprietary mechanisms that lock you into a single vendor and, with the latter, into a single platform. The same is true for LiveWire and active server pages. Servlets give you the freedom to choose vendors and platforms. They are supported by the Java Web Server (AKA Jeeves), Netscape, Apache and others. Basic servlet programming is easy—the subset of Java that you need to get started is a lot simpler than the cryptic Perl syntax. And servlets easily scale up to heavy-duty processing tasks.

The servlet programming skills that you learn in this book will serve you well, no matter which Web server you run. This book does delve further into the Java Web Server, a fine Web server that has been proven in the field and that has some unique properties. Among them are Java Server Pages, an automated way for generating HTML on the fly with genuine Java, not some unstable scripting language. And, of course, since the Java Web Server was written in Java, it will run on any platform that supports a Java virtual machine.

This book teaches you all you need to know to get started programming servlets and running the Java Web server. The examples are great. In the spirit of the Core series, the book is technically accurate. There is a large amount of behind-the-scenes detail that obviously took the authors a lot of time to flush out. Most importantly, the book is fun to read. I take particular pride in the fact that the authors were two of my star students at the Computer Science Department of San Jose State University, the training ground for many of Silicon Valley's professionals. I hope that you enjoy this book as much as I did, and that you will find it useful for your Web development.

Cay Horstmann
VP Technology, Preview Systems
Professor for Computer Science, San Jose State University

Acknowledgments

Writing a book is not a solitary ordeal. When the dust settles, only our names show up on the front cover to take responsibility for its content, yet without the help of a whole group of people the book would never have been completed. Some of them reviewed chapters, some of them work at Prentice Hall where all of the magic happens, and some of them patiently put up with our regular absences!

Among all of these wonderful people is Dr. Cay Horstmann. It's no surprise that our first book would be a part of his Core series; he was our professor at San Jose State University. He helped open the door for us at Prentice Hall, pushed for us to get the contract, reviewed some of our chapters, and even found the time to write our foreword. Thanks, Cay!

Greg Doench, Prentice Hall's executive editor, took a chance on us (although we're sure that Cay's recommendation helped a lot!) and gave us a contract to write this book. Thanks for giving two college students a chance, Greg!

We also had the luck of working with one of the best technical reviewers in the business, Cameron Laird. Although we never met him face to face, his technical guidance improved the book's quality far beyond our expectations. He also made sure to tell us when things were good, too! Thanks, Cameron!

And then there is Jim Markham. Jim was our development editor, and he had the unenviable job of keeping track of deadlines, reviews, and our personal schedules. If you're reading this right now, you know how good he is! Thanks, Jim!

We also got extra help reviewing from a great group of people at Tandem Computers and Seagull Technology. Everyone was enthusiastic about the book.

A special thanks goes out to Juan J. Gutierrez, Shoushan Farhad, Curtis Carter, Barbara Thomas, Jeanne Pawluk, and George Hunter for lending a hand!

Finally, we'd like to thank the friends and family that helped us cope with writing a 600+ page book. A special thanks goes out to Chris' mother, Dixie Taylor, for all of those years helping him learn to properly use the English language. Thanks to Tim's mother and father, Pam and Chuck, for all their support through college and the writing of this book—Tim's portion is dedicated to the both of you! We'd also like to thank Rie Tajitsu and her brother Toyofumi for the kind words and the friendly company. Donna Weniger gets a big "thanks!" for keeping us in shape while we were in the final stages of writing (Chris is never going rock climbing again!). Aaron Corrie, a longtime friend, kept our hand-eye reflexes sharp with numerous networked computer games like GTA and Quake II. Pete Ziatek, the Java God of Silicon Graphics, deserves double thanks for reviewing chapters and being an original member of the San Jose State programming team that started this whole thing off! Paul Tero, our friend across the Pond, deserves thanks for reviewing several of the programming chapters. Finally, we'd like to thank Chris' good friend and ex-coworker, Benjamin Hyatt, for reviewing several chapters. Thanks Moms, Dad, George, Rie, Donna, Ton, Aaron, Pete, Paul, and Ben!

CORE
Java™ Web Server

THE JAVA™ WEB SERVER

Topics in This Chapter

- Java Web Server defined
- What are its components?
- How does it work?
- Why choose the Java Web Server over other Web servers?

Chapter

Welcome to *Core Java™ Web Server*! Because you're reading this book, we're guessing that you've heard of JavaSoft's Servlet API, or you've seen Duke (the Java mascot) serving up pages on a "Powered by Java Web Server" banner, or you're interested in Java programming in general. That's how *we* got into the Java Web Server in the first place.

After reading this first chapter, we hope you'll come away with an excitement about servlets, together with a high-level understanding of how the Java Web Server operates and a basic knowledge of the features it provides.

What this chapter *won't* provide are code examples with servlets (that's a topic filling the latter half of this book!), an elemental breakdown of how each piece works, or an introduction to Java programming.

With that said, onward to the Java Web Server.

What Is the Java Web Server?

For starters, the Java Web Server is a fully HTTP 1.1 compliant Web server. It comes with all of the following standard HTTP 1.1 features:

- Virtual host support
- CGI mapping
- Imagemap services
- Extensive logging capabilities

- SSL services
- Proxy services
- Resource security settings

To refresh your memory, we've described these features in Table 1-1.

Table I-I   Standard HTTP I.I Features

Feature	*Description*
Virtual host support	This allows a server to handle multiple domains. For example, if you wanted to host http://www.coolsite.com and http://www.italian-dinners-to-go on the same Web server, you would use virtual hosting to accomplish this task.
CGI mapping	The "original" way to extend a Web server's capabilities, the Common Gateway Interface delegates a request to an external program for processing. For example, you may have seen guestbooks on Web sites you've visited; these guestbooks are usually controlled via a CGI program.
Imagemap services	They say a picture is worth a thousand words. An Imagemap gives clients a graphical navigation system, allowing them to browse a site by clicking regions of a graphic instead of reading hyperlinked text.
Logging capabilities	No server would be complete without some log files to wade through. Besides the standard file-based logs, the Java Web Server provides interfaces for plugging in your own customized logging objects.
SSL services	The Secure Sockets Layer is the lingua franca of electronic commerce on the Web. When SSL is in use, all communication is encrypted (so that bad guys can't swipe your credit card number during a transaction!).
Proxy services	Proxy servers improve network performance by caching HTTP responses from clients. They also play a role in site security.
Security	Sometimes you want to set aside parts of your server for certain users. A good security system lets you specify who can and who can't access certain areas of your site.

In addition, the Java Web Server supports the servlet API. This API provides a way to add customized extensions, called servlets, using the Java programming language (see Figure 1-1). These extensions work just like Java applets, except that they run on the server instead of the client. (More information on how to write servlets begins in Chapter 5, "Generic Servlets.")

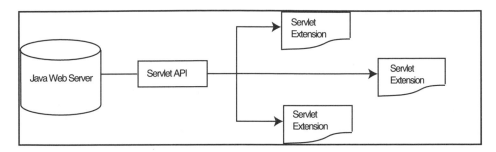

Figure 1-1   Servlets are server-side extensions of the Java Web Server.

However, the Java Web Server isn't the only servlet API host in town. Figure 1-2 shows the interaction of *servlet runners,* which are able to operate beneath the covers of other popular Web servers like Microsoft Internet Information Server, Netscape Enterprise Server, and Apache. Parts of these servers are mapped to the servlet API, providing a portable way to interact and extend a Web server without knowing the gory details of Web-server-specific data structures and methods.

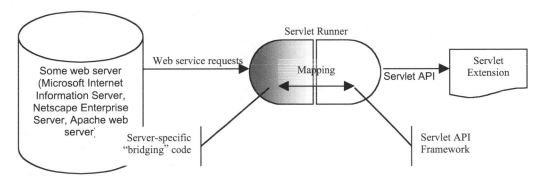

Figure 1-2   Alternative servlet hosts.

The Java Web Server itself is a Java Server Toolkit (JST) application. The JST is a framework for writing server programs in Java, just as the `java.applet` and `java.awt` packages provide a structure for writing client-side applications. The design team at JavaSoft noticed that programmers wrote most servers from scratch, replicating the same set of functionality for each server they wrote. The team has provided the JST to free developers from the drudgery of writing the plumbing of the server, thereby freeing them to concentrate on improving their product. Another benefit is that using tested code in a project reduces the number of bugs introduced. By using the JST as the foundation of a server, then, you'll get better results in less time.

Java Web Server Components?

Above and beyond the standard Web services, the Java Web Server distinguishes itself by providing the following group of handy tools for creating snazzy Web sites:

- Servlet API
- HTML templates
- Page compilation
- Servlet beans
- Java Server pages
- Session management

Servlet API

As mentioned earlier, the Java Web Server offers built-in support for the servlet API. Furthermore, all of the services provided by the Java Web Server are servlets themselves. Figure 1-3 shows how this layering approach leverages the existing code provided by the JST.

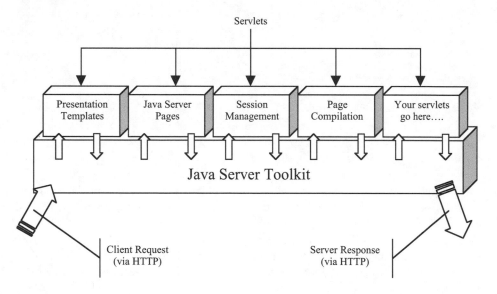

Figure 1-3   Services in the Java Web Server.

Did you notice the box labeled "Your servlets go here" in Figure 1-3? Your servlets act as server extensions, just like those that come with the Java Web Server. In addition, you can replace the stock servlets with your own. For example, you might want to replace the stock CGI servlet, as it only handles executable programs and perl scripts. If you were running the Java Web Server on the Macintosh, you might want to support Apple Script through CGI. By extending the class `com.sun.server.Webserver.CgiServlet`, you could add this functionality, and then make the Java Web Server use your new class by adding it to the system with the admin tool (fully covered in Chapter 4, "Administering the Java Web Server").

You'll typically write your own extensions using two packages from the Servlet API:

```
javax.servlet
javax.servlet.http
```

More information on these Java packages and servlet programming can be found in Chapter 5.

HTML Templates

For us, what separates a "cool" Web site from the rest lies in the presentation. Cool sites use a consistent navigation system, a standardized set of fonts and colors, and a judicious display of lightweight images. Furthermore, a cool site provides a "theme," something unique that sticks in the mind. Later, when you see something similar, you'll recognize it: "Hey! That looks just like the xyz site!"

There is a handful of different ways to put style information into your Web site, although some have limitations and drawbacks. You could take advantage of W3's Cascading Style Sheets, except that they are only supported in Internet Explorer (version 3.0 and later) and Netscape (version 4.0 and later). You could piggyback your changes inside a server-side-include document (a page that's built on-the-fly by the server when it is accessed), except that you'd be using precious server resources to continuously build this file. You could use search-and-replace scripts that run through an entire Web site and "fix up" the style information in those documents, except that you could end up with clients running through the rubble of half-changed sites (an attribute of a *non*-cool site!). Also, you might forget to run the scripts after you made a change, because there isn't a connection between the updated style and its affected documents.

What you need is an automatic solution that runs on the server side without using too many resources. Fortunately, the Java Web Server has a solution: HTML templates.

HTML template processing is provided by a special servlet that combines template information found in a special file called a *template file* with your own Web content ,as shown in Figure 1-4. (More information about template file processing is given in Chapter 14 "JSP, Page Compilation, and Template Processing.")

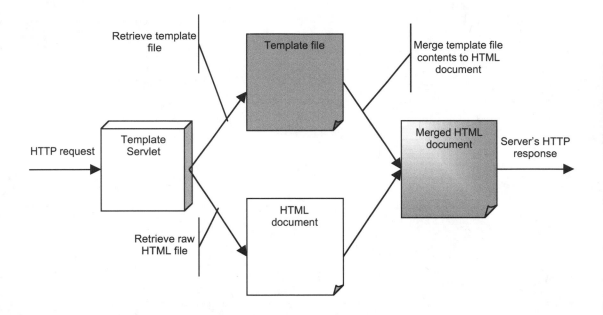

Figure 1-4   Template files and the template servlet.

Page Compilation

How many times have you heard, "It'd be a whole lot easier if we did it in Java?" At times we've wished we could stick some Java code directly into our HTML to perform some tricky task. A special extension to the Java Web Server called the "page compiler" allows you to do just this. You can stick pieces of Java code directly into an HTML file as if it were just another HTML tag. The process is very simple, but you must use a special HTML tag:

```
<java> ...code... </java>
```

These page-compilation files are processed because they have special names, so you'll need to save them with a .jhtml extension. When these files are requested for the first time, a Java servlet (the PageCompileServlet) is used to load and compile the source code found in the JHTML file. This compilation process (shown in Figure 1-5) is done only once, resulting in a dynamic servlet that is used to handle the current request and subsequent requests as well (more information about page compilation is given in Chapter 14).

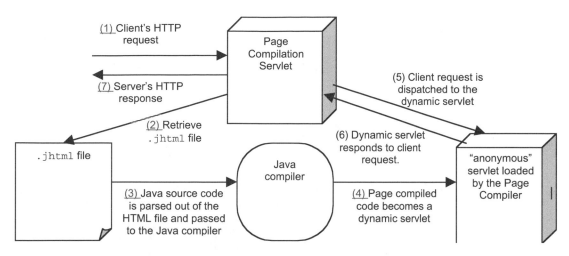

Figure 1-5 Java servlet is used to load and compile code.

Servlet Beans: The Java Web Server's Component Model

The latest in object-oriented development tips and tricks is a piece of software called a *component*. A component provides a set of services to a user, but its internal structure is hidden. While this sounds like a fancy new name for *object*, there *is* a subtle difference. Components can provide a set of services usually produced by several different classes interacting together. Components provide an *interface* to these internal objects, so a user may make a single request that may end up becoming a lengthy dialog between objects (Figure 1-6).

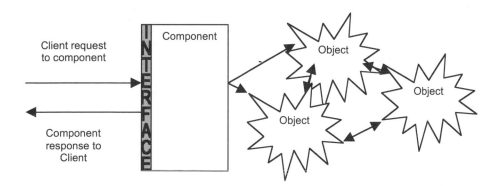

Figure 1-6 Conceptual model of a component.

The Java Web Server supports a type of component called a *servlet bean*. Servlet beans are based on the Java beans specification (more information is available at http://www.javasoft.com/beans). Servlet beans operate as reusable pieces of code that can be invoked in page compilation scripts or JavaServer Page documents (which leads us into our next topic).

JavaServer Pages

The JavaServer Pages API is one of the newest additions to the Java Web Server. Rob Clark, project leader for the Java Web Server at JavaSoft, describes JSP as "Page Compilation: The Next Generation," because it borrows heavily from the work they did on page compilation. JSP cleans up the syntax for writing HTML/Java hybrid documents and adds a new tag called a *bean* tag. The bean tag is used to invoke a servlet bean from HTML. This tag helps to separate programmers who write components from Web developers who use them. It allows the Web developers to concentrate on the style of the site rather than all of the gritty details of programming. (More information is given in Chapter 14.)

Session Management: The Stateless Become Stateful

Electronic commerce applications are the raison d'être for companies on the Web. More and more corporations are offering electronic storefronts, which allow Web surfers to purchase items from the corporation's site. More business is being handled over the Web, so site differentiation is a primary goal for companies providing these services. As a Web developer, you need a hefty bag of tricks to support those corporation's needs.

HTTP is the protocol of the Web, so all Web-based electronic commerce applications use it. Unfortunately, HTTP presents a complex problem for electronic commerce applications—how do you maintain a context for your users over a protocol that has no built-in state mechanisms? In simpler terms, how can we coordinate a customer's shopping experience so that everything runs smoothly from browsing to checkout?

Again, the Java Web Server addresses this problem by providing a framework for writing session-based applications. A session is simply a group of requests from a client brought together under a single transaction. Imagine a real-life parallel, where you walk into a supermarket, find the items you want, place them in a basket, take them up to the counter, pay for them, and walk out. In this sense, the session exists as your physical body moving about the store. We all can't really *go* to these virtual stores on the Internet, so we need some sort of body to represent us in the store. This body, shown in Figure 1-7, is called a *session*.

Session management is a fairly complex topic. It is covered in more detail in Chapter 11.

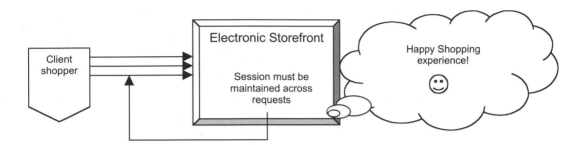

Figure 1-7   Session model in action.

Why Java Web Server Rules

Perhaps the most powerful advantage of the Java Web Server is its ability to support Java servlets. As compared with the Common Gateway Interface (CGI), servlets offer superior performance, platform independence, and the power of a well-developed object-oriented programming language. JavaSoft claims that servlets are much more efficient than traditional CGI, offering 10- to 15-fold speed increases. (For more information visit `http://java.sun.com/pr/1997/dec/pr971203.html`.)

Move out of CGI and into Servlets

CGI can be written in just about any language, but none offers the *write-once run-anywhere* freedom Java promises. Switching to Java Web Server does not mean that you have to throw away your existing CGI code. The Java Web Server supports CGI, allowing you to run your current scripts while you port them to a more efficient servlet equivalent. In addition, the transition from CGI and servlets should be easy, since they are both based on similar theory.

Persistence Is Quick and Easy

Mastering the art of *persistence* in Java gives you the power to turn your Web site into an on-line data warehouse.

There are multiple ways to make Java objects persistent. You can use flat files, the Java Database Connectivity (JDBC) API coupled with a relational database management system (RDBMS), or an object-oriented database like Object Design's Persistent Storage Engine (PSE) product. To store small amounts of data on a low-impact site you can use object serialization—a Java technique that flattens your objects, writing their states to an output stream. Object serialization is an attractive approach because it's simple to use and it is included with the JDK (i.e., free). The obvious disadvantage of serialization is that it can be inefficient if a large number of objects are reachable from the object being written.

Core Note

When an object is reachable from another object, the law of transitivity applies. For example, if object A is connected to object B, and object B is connected to object C, then C is reachable from A. Transitivity applies to serialization as well, so if you write object A to a stream, objects B and C will be written, too.

Sites that require random access to objects should use a database instead. The JDBC API gives the developer freedom to access virtually any relational database. This is an attractive solution for companies with an existing database system in place.

Of course, relational databases don't map well to objects. Rows and columns don't fit easily into fields and superclasses. This is where an object-oriented database fills the gap. Beyond the simplified interface, OODBs are generally more efficient than their relational cousins because there is no overhead required to map the object-oriented structure of Java onto an unrelated table-driven database.

With Java you have the flexibility to meet your persistence needs, and, as extensions to the Java Web Server are written in Java, your JWS projects receive the same benefits.

Rapid Application Development

If you are a seasoned Java programmer who has retired from C++, we don't have to explain why the Java Web Server offers such quick development time. It combines a powerful programming language (Java) with the Web, resulting in a ubiquitous application platform that can run anywhere. Developing complex applications is a snap with built-in multithreading support and automatic memory management. In addition, Java's object-oriented features can be used to support large-scale applications. Where code reuse is desperately needed in order to make a deadline, these projects can be easily divided among a group of developers.

Remote-Control Interface

Administering the Java Web Server is simple and can be accomplished from remote locations from within the office or home, or even while relaxing at the beach. (Okay, technically if you are administrating the Java Web Server at the beach, you aren't *really* relaxing. But it beats being in a cubicle.) The Java Web Server comes packaged with an Administration applet (the Admin applet) that allows you to customize everything from Web service to access control lists (ACLs). (You'll find more information on how to use the Admin applet in Chapter 4, "Administrating the Java Web Server.")

It's a Better Design

The Java Web Server supports many features offered by competing Web servers. It also has some unique features which differentiate it from the rest, as summarized in Table 1-2.

Table 1-2 Superior Features Offered by the Java Web Server	
Feature	*Short Description*
Admin Applet	Allows you to remote-control the Web server
Native servlet support	Has native support for the servlet technology
More stable	Is less likely to crash
Dynamic server extension	Can dynamically extend the Java Web Server
Portable	Supports a portable scripting language (servlets)

No other Web server offers the power of the Admin applet (introduced earlier in this chapter) that is packaged with the Java Web Server. Others offer remote-control capability through HTML forms, which is limited, because HTML cannot assist the developer through constraints and visual cues. By using an applet, the Java Web Server is able to provide a remote-control interface with the power of an application.

The Java Web Server has native support for Java servlets. Other servers support a style of API called a Binary Gateway Interface (BGI). For example, Netscape Enterprise Server supports NSAPI (Netscape Server API). BGI applications are typically written as dynamically linked libraries in C or C++ that run *in-process* with the Web server. A BGI application can alter the behavior of the Web server because it is running inside it. Figure 1-8 displays this tight coupling between the server and its extensions, giving the designer the power to develop a scaleable server that was not possible within the traditional CGI architecture.

Of course, being written in C or C++ limits a BGI program's portability. An effort is required to port it if the service needs to run on a different hardware platform. Furthermore, C++ has no built-in security checks or enforced exception handling, leading to some interesting situations if a BGI program writes to memory where it shouldn't. As a result, there are situations when a crashing extension can bring down the whole Web server. If a servlet running in the Java Web Server encounters a problem, however, the thread handling the request that hit the problem dies, but the Java Web Server continues to run.

Another aspect of the BGI system is that it requires a server to shut down in order to update a previously loaded extension. Seeing this as a big limitation, Sun's Java Web Server development team took a different approach. The Java Web Server allows for dynamic loading and updating of servlets on the fly without requiring a shut down and restart of the Web server.

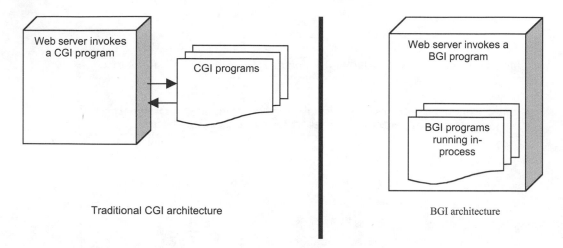

Figure 1-8   Notice the tight fit.

Summary

The Java Web Server is a robust one that can support all of your client/server applications on the intranet and Internet. In this chapter we have given you a quick tour of the Java Web Server. Starting with its underlying Web server engine, we walked you through its main features, then explained some of its unique components. Of course, in order take full advantage of the Java Web Server and learn its many features, you will have to keep on reading! The next chapter shows you how to install the Java Web Server, and the following two show you how to efficiently run and administer it.

INSTALLING THE JAVA WEB SERVER

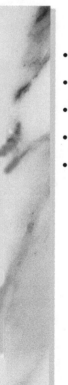

Topics in This Chapter

- Installing the Java Web Server on different platforms
- Controlling the JavaWebServer Service
- Manually running the Java Web Server
- Validating installation
- Uninstalling the Java Web Server

Chapter 2

An early requirement in any book on a specific software product like the Java Web Server is a chapter on how to install it. For one thing, all of the latter chapters expect the server to be working properly. You'll need a working JWS to run any of the sample programs listed.

Some texts focus on a single operating system. For products that aren't offered over many platforms, that isn't a problem. However, with a cross-platform product like the Java Web Server, concentrating on a single operating system (whether it be Windows or Solaris or Linux or whatever) isn't sufficient.

We don't cover *all* of the Java-compatible operating systems out there, and in fact we hardly scratch the surface of possibilities. Instead, we concentrate on the systems we've had experience with: Windows NT, Windows 95, Solaris, and Linux. The NT, 95, and Solaris installations are specialized because they contain native executables and libraries. Fortunately, you aren't required to use this native code for basic Web services, as the Linux installation will prove. Similarly, if you are planning to install the Java Web Server on a different platform, you should follow the Linux installation instructions—the steps are the same for any platform not previously listed here.

And so, without further ado, let's install the Java Web Server!

Installing the Java Web Server on Windows NT

Owing to its flexibility, affordability, and ease of maintenance, Windows NT is among the most popular operating systems that supports the Java Web Server. In this section we show you how to install Java Web Server on the Windows NT operating system. We introduce you to some key concepts which you should know in advance. Then we walk you through the complete installation, placing emphasis on the Windows NT operating system.

The Windows NT Resource Kit

Programming requires that a person know both the specific language and the operating system in which the applications will be deployed. Therefore, programmers writing software on or for the Windows NT operating system should be intimately familiar with its internals. If you are looking for more information on the Windows NT operating system, the Microsoft *Windows NT Resource Kit*—a series of three volumes published by the Microsoft Press—is a good place to start. It provides information on NT (some of which is not included in the operating-system documentation) and includes a CD with utilities for Windows NT Server and Windows NT Workstation. These utilities will save you time and grief as you attempt to administer parts of NT.

Windows NT Services

Windows NT gives the *administrator* the option of running programs as services. The administrator is anyone having an account that has administrator privileges (that is, his or her account must be in the Administrators group). See the user manager in the administrative tools group for more information.

Each time NT boots, programs that are configured to run as services can be started automatically. If you take a look, you will notice that many services are already running. These are the default services. A few examples are Remote Procedure Call (RPC), Workstation, and EventLog.

The Service Life Cycle

Windows NT was designed to handle multiple users, each with his or her own user account. As in other multiuser operating systems, applications started during a session will be closed when you log off. For example, if you are cruising the Web in

Netscape and you decide to log off, NT will magically shut down the browser first. This works because your session owns these processes. In contrast, a Windows NT service operates beyond the confines of a log-on session. That is, it keeps running even if users come and go. Regardless of which user is currently logged on, a service will happily chug along handling incoming requests. This is the key to understanding the service concept—a program configured to run as a Windows NT service maintains availability. With that in mind, we strongly recommend that you run the Java Web Server as a service.

Managing Services in Windows NT

Windows NT comes packaged with more ways to manage services than you can shake a stick at. There are two varieties: *command-line programs* for the DOS freaks and *GUI-driven wizards* for those of you who have carpal tunnel. Some of our favorites are shown in Table 2-1.

Table 2-1   Programs That Can Be Used to Administer NT Services

Program	Description
NET START	Lists all services that were started
Services icon (in the Control Panel)	A GUI used to view/manage installed services
INSTSRV	Installs/removes services
SCLIST	Lists information on all installed services
SRVINSTW	A wizard that allows you to install/remove services

The first two programs come with Windows NT and the latter three are included with the Resource Kit. Not all of the programs are used only for services. For example, you will find the NET command very useful, given a variety of networking applications—type NET HELP and you will get a list of commands that can be used with NET. You can view the current list of started services on your NT machine by typing *net start* at the command prompt (see Figure 2-1).

The services icon in the Control Panel allows you to view and manage services that have already been installed. It does not, however, give you the ability to add and remove services. If you don't have the Resource Kit, you may find yourself resorting to hacking away at the registry, trying to perform some task which could have been easily resolved, given a utility provided by the Resource Kit.

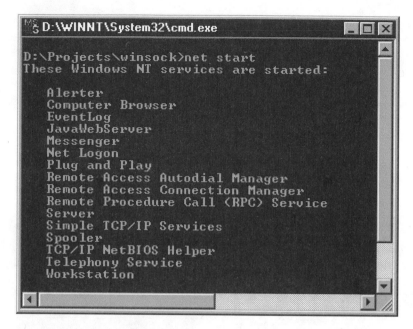

```
D:\WINNT\System32\cmd.exe                    _ □ ×

D:\Projects\winsock>net start
These Windows NT services are started:

   Alerter
   Computer Browser
   EventLog
   JavaWebServer
   Messenger
   Net Logon
   Plug and Play
   Remote Access Autodial Manager
   Remote Access Connection Manager
   Remote Procedure Call (RPC) Service
   Server
   Simple TCP/IP Services
   Spooler
   TCP/IP NetBIOS Helper
   Telephony Service
   Workstation
```

Figure 2-1   NET START in action.

Core Alert

Microsoft documentation prefaces every mention of registry editing with a warning about the possible consequences of making a mistake. In a nutshell, the registry is a database of configuration information used by the operating system. Erasing this data with an editing tool could make Windows NT unhappy. Personally, we hack around the registry all the time, but only if there isn't any other way (because registry editing can be a tedious process).

Hardware Requirements

Table 2-2 displays the hardware you need before running the Java Web Server.

Table 2-2 Windows NT Hardware Requirements	
Description	*Memory Required*
Hard disk space	Almost 14 megabytes (13,847,942 bytes)
Memory	32 megabytes (64 or more recommended)

If you plan to run the Java Web Server for serious applications, you should stock up on as much memory as possible. Most of our development on the Java Web Server was done on machines containing 128 megabytes of memory. In addition to the hardware requirements, you will need a Java virtual machine to run the server. The Java Web Server ships with a stripped-down version of the JDK called the Java Runtime Environment (JRE). Supported on Windows NT, Windows 95, and Solaris, the JRE provides a "runs right out of the box" configuration for the Java Web Server. However, you aren't forced to use the JRE. With a few configuration changes, any third-party virtual machine can be hooked up to the Java Web Server. (For details see Chapter 3, "Alternative Lifestyles for the Java Web Server.")

Preparing Windows NT to Run Java Web Server

In order to run the Java Web Server, you will need to properly configure Windows NT's networking facilities. Windows NT uses a layered network framework, in which each layer provides specific functionality for others. It is the combination of these layers that allows for communication between two or more computers on a network.

The bottom two layers of this framework consist of network adapter software (or network drivers) and network interface cards. Upper layers use the network adapter software to interface with the network card. The network card provides a means for connecting computers together over a network. In order to run Java Web Server on Windows NT you need to make sure that you have properly configured your network adapter software.

So what should you do if you are running the Java Web Server on a machine that does not have a network card? Wait—a Web server on a machine without a network card? What's the point? Well, if you're developing servlets, you might not need to be connected to a LAN, especially if you roaming about with your laptop. You can use the MS Loopback Adapter provided with NT as a substitute for a real network card. The MS Loopback Adapter fools the NT operating system into thinking that you have a network card installed.

The following steps can be used to configure the MS Loopback Adapter:

1. From the Control Panel, select the Network icon.
2. Click on the Adapters tab, then select Add and move to add an adapter
3. Scroll down and double-click on the MS Loopback Adapter.
4. Choose the frame type that corresponds to the protocol you are using.
5. Follow the instructions given by the wizard to complete the installation.

Installing the Java Web Server

Now that the networking part of the install is behind us, we're ready to begin the software installation of the Java Web Server. If you haven't already purchased the Java Web Server from Sun, you can use the thirty-day trial version included on the CD-ROM in the back of the book. (By the time you read this, a newer version of the trial may be available on the Sun Web site (http://jserv.java.sun.com), so check it out.) After you've located the server package you want to install, you can begin the installation by invoking the self-extracting executable file.

At this point InstallShield will take over and walk you through the installation. First, a dialog box will appear asking if you want to continue installing Java Web Server 1.1. As soon as you choose to continue, InstallShield will begin extracting the files that are needed to run the installation. Next, a Choose Destination Location dialog box should appear, prompting you to choose the destination directory, or a default directory, in which to install the Java Web Server. Usually the default directory is good enough. Choosing OK will cause InstallShield to begin copying files to your hard disk, as shown in Figure 2-2.

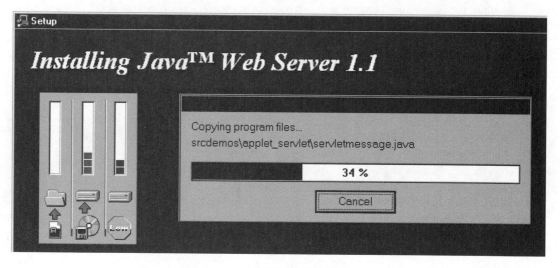

Figure 2-2   InstallShield in action: copying files to disk.

The last couple of steps in the installation process involve installing the Java Web Server as an NT service (see the "Windows NT Servicing" section earlier in this chapter). You will be prompted with a Question dialog box asking if you want to install NT Service (see Figure 2-3). This dialog box is a little misleading. By choosing Yes you are not actually installing NT Service; you are adding the Java Web Server as an NT service! If you choose Yes, then InstallShield will attempt to add Java Web Server into the list of services in NT.

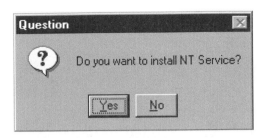

Figure 2-3   Installing JavaWebServer as a service.

When you choose Yes here, an Information dialog box should appear, notifying you that NT service will be installed (see Figure 2-4).

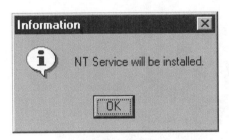

Figure 2-4   Dialog box informing you that NT service will be installed.

The Java Web Server installation is now complete. If you chose Yes to install the NT service during installation, the Java Web Server should start each time you reboot NT. Otherwise, if you want to make the server available, you will need to start the Java Web Server manually each time you log on.

Shucks, I Forgot to Install the Service!

Wait! Don't start hacking away at that registry yet! If you want to install Java Web Server as an NT service because you didn't do so during installation, you can use a program written by Javasoft to add it for you. At the command prompt, type:

```
jservsvc JavaWebServer install
```

and Java Web Server will be added to the current list of NT services. Similarly, you can remove the service by using the following command:

```
jservsvc JavaWebServer remove
```

Core Note

You must have administrator privileges in order to install or remove services in NT.

Controlling the JavaWebServer Service

On occasion, you will want to manually stop or start the Java Web Server. You can start/stop the Java Web Server either as an NT service or as a separate process. This section will show you how to start and stop the JavaWebServer service.

If Java Web Server is running as an NT service, you can quickly stop the service by using the NET STOP command (see Figure2-5):

```
net stop javawebserver
```

where javawebserver is the name of the service that is mapped to the Java Web Server.

Figure 2-5   Using NET STOP to stop the Java Web Server service.

You can restart the Java Web Server as a service by using the NET START command:

```
net start javawebserver
```

Manually Running the Java Web Server

To start the Java Web Server manually (without running it as an NT service) you can use the `httpd.exe` or `httpdnojre.exe` programs that are packaged with it. These programs are located in the bin directory of the Web Server root directory (usually JavaWebServer1.1). The `httpdnojre` uses the Java Runtime that is on your local system, rather than the one packaged with the Java Web Server. As you will see in future chapters, `httpdnojre` can be very useful when debugging Java Servlets.

Core Alert

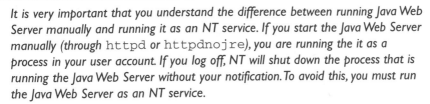

It is very important that you understand the difference between running Java Web Server manually and running it as an NT service. If you start the Java Web Server manually (through `httpd` *or* `httpdnojre`*), you are running the it as a process in your user account. If you log off, NT will shut down the process that is running the Java Web Server without your notification. To avoid this, you must run the Java Web Server as an NT service.*

Validating Installation

You can validate your installation by visiting `http://localhost:8080/`. Java Web Server should respond by sending you the default index.html Web page (see Figure 2-6).

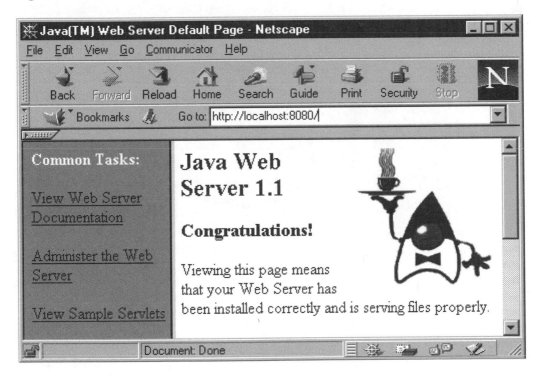

Figure 2-6 Validating the Java Web Sever installation.

Uninstalling the Java Web Server

Uninstalling the Java Web Server is an easy three-step process:

1. Shut down the JavaWebServer if it is running.
2. Remove the JavaWebServer service from NT.
3. Delete the Java Web Server root directory.

If you configured NT to run Java Web Server as an NT service, you must remove the service by using the jservsvc program provided with the Java Web Server:

```
jservsvc JavaWebServer remove
```

Next, you will need to remove related files from your hard disk. You can have NT automatically remove programs that are listed in the Programs Properties dialog box. In NT 4.0 this dialog box lives in the Control Panel in the Add/Remove Programs icon (see Figure 2-7). NT 3.5.1 users can find an uninstall program in the Java Web Server program group.

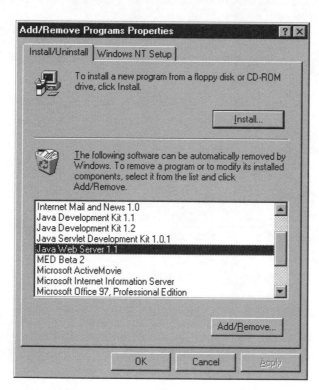

Figure 2-7   Removing programs in NT.

After choosing OK, UninstallShield will begin deleting files from your hard disk. As it is near completion, UninstallShield will begin checking off entities that have been removed, such as program folders, program directories, and program registry entries. Now you are done—right? Wrong! The UninstallShield does not always remove all of the files (in fact, it never did for us), so you should check to make sure it did not leave any files on your hard disk.

Troubleshooting

Installing the Java Web Server is not entirely trivial. The Java Web Server relies on the fact that your operating system is network ready and in a healthy state. Just because the installation went well does not mean that Java Web Server is magically ready for operation. This section addresses some common problems that could cause it to run improperly.

No Response

If the Java Web Server is not running properly, then your browser will most likely display a message similar to the one shown in Figure 2-8.

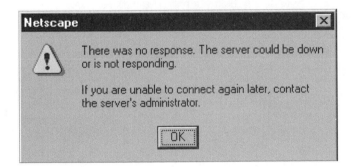

Figure 2-8   No response.

If this problem is haunting you, a couple of quick checks should get you up and running quickly.

Default Port Settings

When you visit `http://localhost/` you are actually telling your browser to visit `http://localhost:80/index.html`, where `80` is the port number and `index.html` the default Web page. If the Java Web Server is not running, or you have entered an invalid URL, your browser will wait for a couple of seconds and then complain, saying that it didn't get a response from the server. This is shown in Figure 2-8. Java Web Server comes preconfigured to run on port 8080. Therefore, if you have just installed it, you should visit `http://localhost:8080/`. To change port 8080 to port 80 see Chapter 4, "Administering the Java Web Server."

Is Java Web Server Running?

If you have just installed the Java Web Server, then most likely it is not running (unless you've rebooted). Even though Install Shield added the Java Web Server as a service, it did not start the Java Web Server. First, make sure the server is running by viewing the processes in the task manager (or, for you DOS gurus, by entering TLIST at the command line). Make sure that jserv.exe is among the processes in the process list. You can quickly bring up the task manager by pressing [CTRL+SHIFT+ESC]. If jserv.exe is not in the list of processes, then go to the command prompt and NET START the Java Web Server:

```
net start javawebserver
```

Core Note

The NET START command will work only if you installed Java Web Server as an NT service. If you did not choose to do this, then you must manually start the JavaWebServer using httpd *or* httpdnojre. *See the section "Manually Running the Java Web Server" earlier in this chapter.*

Problems with httpdnojre

In order to run Java Web Server using httpdnojre, you need to either set your JAVA_HOME environment variable, or use httpdnojre -javahome. Having an improperly set JAVA_HOME variable (or none at all) will result in a reaction similar to the one shown in Figure 2-9.

If you are at the command prompt, you can check the current value of the JAVA_HOME environment variable by using the SET command:

```
SET JAVA_HOME
```

You can set the JAVA_HOME environment variable permanently through the system properties, using the following steps:

1.   Right-click on the *My Computer* icon on your desktop.
2.   Click on Properties to bring up the System Properties dialog box.
3.   Click on the properties tab and set the JAVA_HOME variable to your

JDK directory (Figure 2-10).

4. Click the Set button and then apply to set the environment variable.

5. Click OK to close the System Properties dialog box.

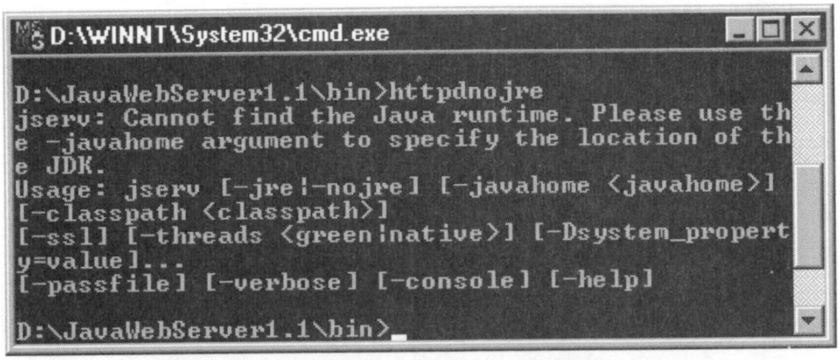

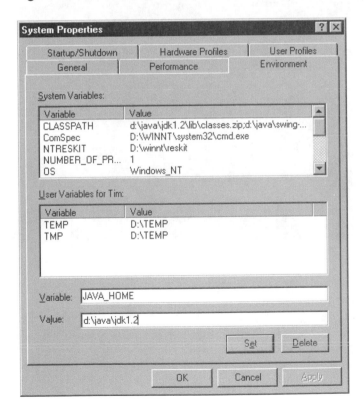

Figure 2-9 The JAVA_HOME environment variable.

Figure 2-10 Setting the JAVA_HOME variable.

You will need to start a new DOS prompt in order for the changes to take effect. If you don't want to set the JAVA_HOME environment variable permanently, you can use the javahome switch to specify your Java home directory:

```
httpdnojre -javahome d:\java\jdk1.2
```

Having to use the javahome switch each time you use `httpdnojre` can get old real fast! Alternatively, you can set the JAVA_HOME environment for the life of your DOS prompt session:

```
set JAVA_HOME=d:\java\jdk1.2
```

If the Java Web Server Does Not Start...

If the Java Web Server does not start, make sure that port 8080 is not in use. When starting, the Web service portion of Java Web Server will attempt to connect to port 8080 (by default) and listen for incoming requests. In addition, the Admin Service binds to port 9090. If port 8080 (or port 9090) is in use by another process, an attempt to start the Java Web Server will fail. This problem is easily recognized if you attempt to start the Java Web Server using `httpd`. For example, Figure 2-11 shows an error message printed by `httpd.exe` when we attempted to start Java Web Server on port 80, which was being used by another process at the time.

Figure 2-11   Attempting to start the Java Web Server on a port that is in use.

This concludes the discussion on installing the Java Web Server on the Windows NT operating system. With the right tools, the installation should be a snap.

Of course, running Windows NT incurs some heavy hardware requirements. You might want to consider using Windows 95 for your servlet development instead, especially if your machine is low on memory.

Installing the Java Web Server on Windows 95

Although Microsoft doesn't support it as a server platform, Windows 95 can be a programmer's best friend for developing servlets. It is the only 32-bit Windows-based operating system that shows acceptable performance on low-memory systems such as laptops. In fact, Windows 95 was designed for these systems, operating efficiently with as low as 16 megabytes of memory. As notebooks mean freedom from office-bound workstations, Windows 95 lets you take your development away from the workplace and out to the beach where it belongs.

Core Note

Installing the Java Web Server on the Windows 98 operating system follows the same procedure as for Windows 95.

With this in mind, you'll want to install the Java Web Server *before* you leave for the boardwalk. Even though both Windows 95 and Windows NT support the Win32 API, there are significant differences between the two platforms, and these differences are most apparent during the initial installation process.

Hardware Requirements

The minimum requirements for Java software development under Windows 95 are 16 megabytes of memory and a 486/33-MHz processor. Table 2-3 provides a more comprehensive list of requirements. As with any other program, more memory and CPU mean faster execution times for the VM and larger heap space, so you should stock up as much RAM and chip as you can afford.

Table 2-3   Windows 95 Requirements

CPU	*Memory*	*Performance*
486/33 MHz	16 MB	Slug
486/100 MHz	32 MB	Lazy Sunday
Pentium/133 MHz	32 MB	Brisk walk
Pentium/233 MHz w/MMX	128 MB	Screaming demon

Besides the regular components, you'll also need a network card, as Windows 95 doesn't have a loopback adapter to fake out the networking software. Since the Java Web Server makes extensive use of the Windows networking facilities, a network card is a necessity. Fortunately, you can pick up a cheap ISA network adapter for about $40. Laptop users aren't quite as lucky, as the cheapest PCMCIA network adapters start at around $80.

Software Requirements

According to the Javasoft installation documentation, running the Java Web Server on Windows 95 requires Winsock 2 to be installed.

Core Note

We found this to be not entirely true. The Java Web Server runs on a Winsock 1.1 version of Windows 95, but it's a good idea to install the latest Winsock for other reasons (there was a serious socket memory leak with the stock Winsock).

But before you go and install Winsock 2 on your machine, you should test for its existence on your system. Doing so is as simple as running one of the utility programs we've included on the CD-ROM, `ws2test.exe`. The test program has three possible responses, as shown in Table 2-4.

Table 2-4   Responses from the Test Program

Response	Meaning
"Error finding Winsock Information"	Networking and TCP/IP support has not been installed on this machine.
"This Windows doesn't support Winsock 2"	A Winsock was found on the system, but it is an earlier version (1.1 or 1.0). You should upgrade this system to Winsock 2.
"This Windows supports Winsock 2"	Winsock 2 was found on the system. No upgrade is necessary.

For readers who haven't thrown all of their C++ compilers into the garbage, Listing 2-1 provides the test program's source code for your review. A Visual C++ makefile is included on the CD-ROM with the C++ source code, because an extra library (wsock32.lib) is required during compilation. Savvy Visual C++ users can simply add the wsock32.lib library to their projects via the Settings->Link property page. See the Visual C++ documentation for more information.

Listing 2-1   Detecting the Version of Your Winsock in C++

```cpp
#include <windows.h>
#include <iostream.h>

main ()
{
  WORD version = MAKEWORD(2,0);
  WSAData data;
  int err = WSAStartup(version,&data);
  if (err != 0)
  {
    cout << "Error finding Winsock information."
        <<  " Perhaps networking is not installed" << endl;
  }
  else
  {
    if ( LOBYTE( data.wVersion ) != 2 ||
       HIBYTE( data.wVersion ) != 0 )
    {
      cout << "This Windows doesn't support Winsock 2"
              << endl;
      WSACleanup( );
    }
    else
    {
      cout << "This Windows supports Winsock 2 " << endl;
      WSACleanup();
    }
  }
  return 0;
}
```

The meat of the code lies in the call to WSAStartup. The first parameter of the call specifies the version of the Winsock libraries to load, while the second receives the Winsock version currently available. Since you've specified 2.0 (from the MAKEWORD macro call) as the desired Winsock version, the system will attempt to locate and load a compatible Winsock. The test program's response depends on the version number returned from the WSAStartup function call. You won't have to worry whether a newer version of Winsock will break this test program or the Java Web Server, because Winsocks are meant to be backward compatible.

If your system is reporting an earlier Winsock version, you'll need to grab the Winsock 2 update from the Winsock 2 Software Development Kit at http://www.microsoft.com/win32dev/netwrk/winsock2/ws295sdk.html.

After you download the SDK, upgrading to Winsock 2 is a two-part process: (1) install the SDK, then (2) install the Winsock 2 libraries.

Installing the Winsock SDK

After you've downloaded the SDK from Microsoft's Web site, double-click on the ws295sdk.exe icon and review Microsoft's license agreement (shown in Figure 2-12).

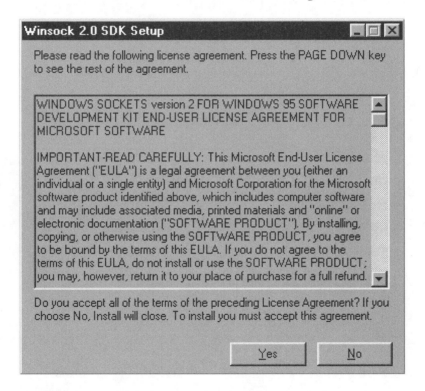

Figure 2-12   The Microsoft License Agreement.

Four cups of coffee and 11 pages later (if you agree to the demands), click on the Yes button to start the installation process. Next, you'll be prompted for the SDK's destination directory, as shown in Figure 2-13.

Choose where you want the SDK, or simply accept the defaults by pressing the Save button. After that, the installation program takes over and plops all of the SDK files in the chosen directory, which completes the first part of the Winsock installation.

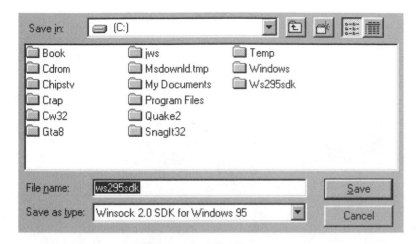

Figure 2-13   Deciding where to install the Winsock SDK.

Upgrading to Winsock 2

Now that the SDK is installed, you'll want to update your Winsock with the SDK version. Along with the C/C++ header files and libraries comes a configuration program for updating the Winsock. This program, named ws2setup.exe, is in the setup subdirectory of the SDK. When you run this program, don't expect much in response other than the final "I'm Done!" message, as shown in Figure 2-14.

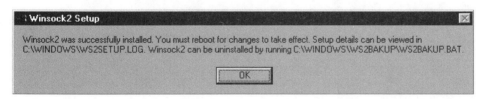

Figure 2-14   "I'm Done!"

Since the Winsock libraries were in use during the installation, ws2setup needs to restart the machine so the system changes can take effect. Take the screen's advice and reboot your Windows 95 machine. When the machine comes back up, run the ws2test.exe program again. If all went well, your machine will be Winsock 2 compatible.

Starting the Java Web Server Installation

Now that you've got the necessary hardware and software requirements out of the way, you'll want to get the Java Web Server installed. Start by executing the setup program (either from the Windows Explorer or from the command line). InstallShield will ask you to confirm your installation before continuing, as shown in Figure 2-15.

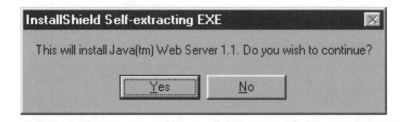

Figure 2-15   Confirming the installation.

After a series of initial "just click next" screens, you'll be asked where you want to install the Java Web Server. The program defaults to "`c:\javawebserver1.1`", which mercifully can be changed to something shorter like "`jws`" (Figure 2-16).

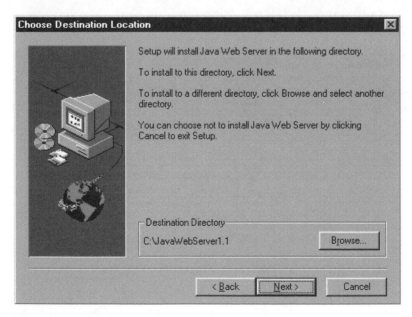

Figure 2-16   Choosing the destination directory.

There isn't much more to the Windows 95 installation beyond the question of a destination directory. However, if you've installed the Java Web Server on Windows NT, you remember the "Install the NT Service" dialog at the end of the installation. Since Windows 95 doesn't support services, the installation program skips the question completely.

What are you missing by not having the Java Web Server run as a service? In a nutshell, an NT service lets a program run beyond the logon session of one user. When a user logs off, all of the programs in that session are shut down, including the Java Web Server. Since Windows 95 doesn't support NT's service facilities, using the Java Web Server on Windows 95 becomes more difficult—it won't be automatically started until someone logs on.

Automatically Starting the Java Web Server

Actually, there *is* a "servicelike" capability in Windows 95 for running programs without a logon session. When Windows 95 starts, it reads a special key in the system registry like a checklist. Each value in this key corresponds to a program that should be started *before* any logon takes place. This special registry key is found at `HKEY_LOCAL_MACHINE\Software\Microsoft\Windows\CurrentVersion\RunServices`. For example, if we wanted to start the System Monitor utility at startup, we would use the registry editor (`regedit.exe`) to make a "String" value entry under the `RunServices` called "SYSMON" with the value "C:\Windows\SYSMON.EXE". The next time the computer boots into Windows 95, the system monitor should pop up before anyone has logged on.

Core Note

Making arbitrary changes to the system registry is not recommended unless you already feel comfortable with the consequences. On Windows 95, you can back up the registry by copying the hidden files `user.da0` *and* `system.da0` *to a floppy disk. Also, if you use the /e switch with* `RegEdit` *(the registry editing program), you can force a backup copy of the registry to be made named* `file.reg`*.*

Following the same logic, you can make the Java Web Server start automatically by creating another value called "JEEVES" in the registry. (The name is irrelevant. We could have picked "Blue Horseshoe" for the same effect.) This shown in Figure 2-17.

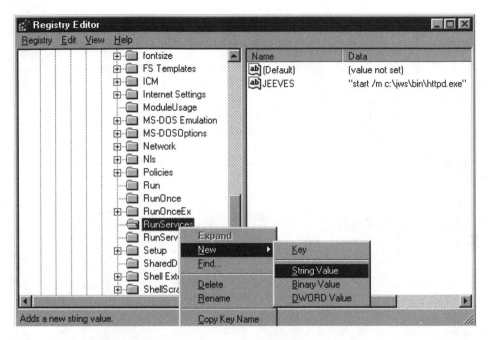

Figure 2-17   Making the Java Web Server a "RunService."

Unfortunately, the Java Web Server has the annoying habit of starting a console window in the center of the screen. Since this console screen has nothing important to say, it would be a convenience to have it start minimized. You can use the `Start` program to run the Java Web Server in a minimized window. `Start` supports the parameters listed in Table 2-5.

Table 2-5   Parameters Supported by `Start`

Parameter Switch	*Description*
/m	Minimized
/max	Maximized
/r	Restored (use previous size settings)
/w	Wait until program has finished

By wrapping our **JEEVES** entry with a start call (`start /m c:\jws\bin\ httpd.exe`), the Java Web Server starts in the minimized state.

Problems with Using the RunServices Hack

Granted, using the RunServices registry key is a great way to get programs to *start* automatically, but how about handling shutdowns? When a user logs on to Windows 95, programs started via the RunServices method are assigned to that user. This doesn't pose a serious problem until the user attempts to log off. At that point, the shell terminates all of the running programs, including the Java Web Server. This is where the "service-like" features of RunServices differ most sharply from true Windows NT-based services.

In Windows NT, services exist before any user logs in, as they are unaffected by user sessions. Like UNIX, the NT service facility ignores users as they enter and exit the system, and these services will continue running until they are shut down either by an administrator or by Windows NT when the computer is restarted. On the other hand, Windows 95 is still a single-user operating system, without support for user sessions and background *daemon* processes. All of these facts point out that the name *RunServices* is a misnomer, and that a more appropriate title for the registry key would have been *RunAtBoot*.

Starting the Java Web Server by Hand

With all of these problems in autostarting the Java Web Server on Windows 95, it's no wonder that Javasoft doesn't recommend it as a server platform. We've given you some undocumented options for running it as your Web server, but it is more trouble than its worth. If you plan to run the Java Web Server on a Windows platform, you'd be better off with Windows NT. Contrary to popular belief, you won't break the bank building a machine that supports Windows NT, and the added stability is worth the extra cost.

Windows 95 is more appropriate for *writing* servlets, and you can test your creations under the Java Web Server running as a user program on Windows 95. Like most network services, the Java Web Server is a console-mode program that reads, processes, and writes data back to a client. The main program that runs the server is httpd.exe, which is found in the Java Web Server's bin subdirectory. A GUI program works as well as a console-mode program. Since most servers operate as detached processes under Windows NT, having an integrated GUI doesn't make as much sense.

You would start the server just as you would a command shell, either by using a shortcut icon or by executing httpd directly, as shown in Figure 2-18.

The Java Web Server is made up of three running services: the properties service, the administrative service, and the Web page service. The Web page service is set to run on port 8080 during the installation process, and the administrative service runs on port 9090. With the server running, you should test to see if everything is running

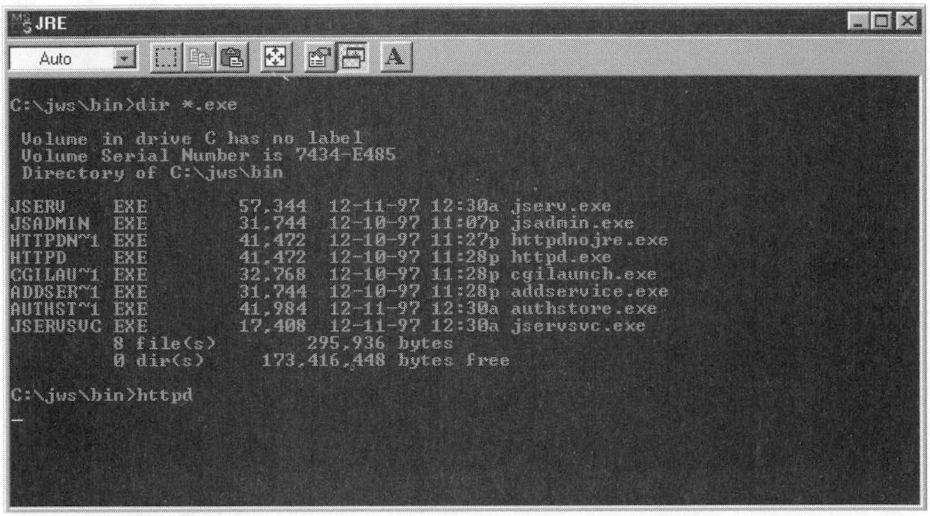

Figure 2-18   Running the Java Web Server from the console.

properly. Open your Web browser and connect to the server with the URL `http://localhost:8080/` shown in Figure 2-19.

Figure 2-19   Hello, Java Web Server!

If you see a smiling Duke waiting for you, then everything went according to plan, and the installation was a success. However, there must have been a problem if you receive the dreaded "can't connect to server" message shown in Figure 2-20.

Figure 2-20   Gads! I can't connect!

Troubleshooting the Installation on Windows 95

Every piece of software has its inconsistencies, and Windows 95 and the Java Web Server are no exception. Most of the issues with Windows 95, as well as general troubleshooting tips for the Java Web Server on Windows platforms, were covered earlier in this chapter. Windows 95 does add one more problem to the list. When the Java Web Server is shut down using the CTRL-C key combination, the jserv and jrew processes fail to terminate. See Figures 2-21 and 2-22.

The next time you try to start the Java Web Server, you'll receive the message: "Cannot start service, port already in use," as shown in Figure 2-23.

Since the Java Runtime Environment (jrew) hasn't gone away, it is still hanging onto the ports used by the Java Web Server. To stop these two rogue processes, just press CTRL-ALT-DEL and use the End Task option on the Close Program dialog.

Figure 2-21   Shutting down the server using Ctrl-c.

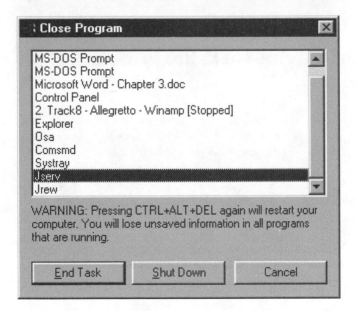

Figure 2-22   The task list still shows `jserv` and `jrew` processes.

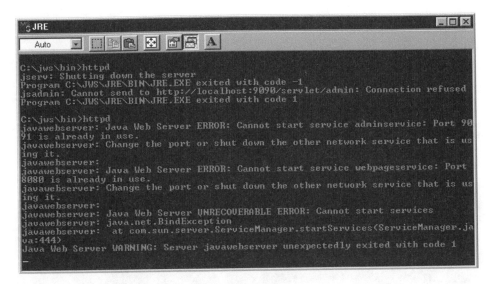

Figure 2-23   Port, port, who's got the port?

Uninstalling the Java Web Server on Windows 95

Removing the Java Web Server from Windows 95 can become an involved process. You can make it easier on yourself by following these simple steps:

1. Shut down the Java Web Server.
2. Run the "Remove Programs" control panel.
3. Uninstall the Java Web Server 1.1.
4. Erase the Java Web Server directory on the hard disk.
5. Remove any RunServices registry entries.

Shutting Down the Java Web Server

Locate the console window used by the Java Web Server, and tell it to shut down with a CTRL-C keystroke combination. If your installation is using the Java Runtime Environment, open up the task list and kill the remaining two processes: jserv and jrew. Erring on the side of caution, open up a Web browser and try to connect to the Java Web Server's administrative service with the URL `http://localhost:9090/`. Here, 9090 is the default port for the Java Web Server's admin service. Your installation may differ, depending on whether you changed this setting. If you receive the "could not connect to host" error dialog, you have successfully shut down the Java Web Server.

Run the "Remove Programs" Control Panel

Once you have the Web server stopped, open up the Windows 95 control panel window from the Start menu as shown in Figure 2-24.

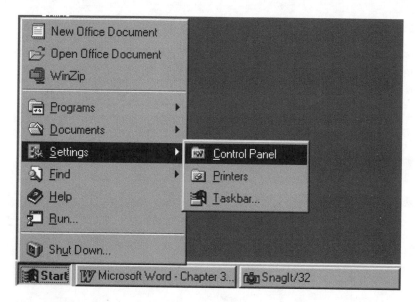

Figure 2-24   Control panel.

From there you'll want to open the Add/Remove Programs control applet. (This is an unfortunate choice of names: these programs have nothing to do with Java applets.) This program uninstalls Windows applications safely from your system. For most applications, support DLL files are loaded into the windows\system directory. If the DLL is private to the application being uninstalled, it can be removed without interfering with other programs.

Windows keeps a reference count with each program installation, incrementing the count for each application that needs a specific DLL. When the count reaches zero, the DLL can be safely removed. Accomplishing this task requires programs to be installed into the system and removed using the Add/Remove Programs facility. Failing to do so can create incorrect reference counts, potentially wasting disk space with DLL files that will never be used again.

Since the Java Web Server was installed properly into Windows, it is a good idea to remove it properly. In the Add/Remove Programs dialog, find the entry "Java Web Server 1.1" (Figure 2-25).

With the Java Web Server entry selected, press the Add/Remove button on the dialog. Next, as shown in Figure 2-26, Windows should give you a last-chance opportunity to back out of the uninstallation.

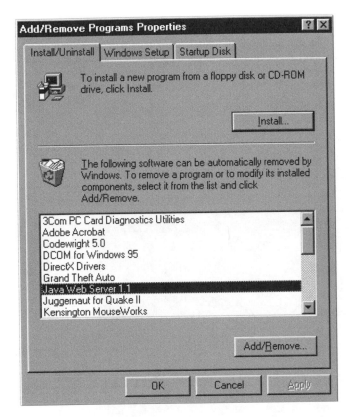

Figure 2-25   Add/Remove Programs from Windows 95.

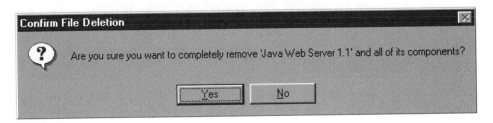

Figure 2-26   "Are you really sure?"

Press yes if you still want to uninstall the Java Web Server. The rest of the process is automated, with only a final message to tell you it has successfully finished (Figure 2-27).

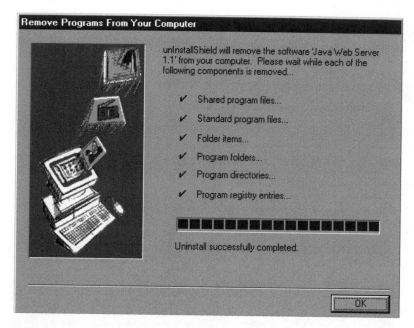

Figure 2-27   "I'm done!"

Erase the Java Web Server Directory on the Hard Disk

Unfortunately, the uninstallation process doesn't do anything on Windows 95. You can prove that by taking a quick look in the root directory of the Java Web Server (a directory that should have been erased by the uninstaller), and you'll see all of your old files. Getting rid of these files is as easy as dragging the Java Web Server folder to the recycle bin, but remember to empty the recycle bin to reclaim the used disk space.

Remove any RunServices Registry Entries

If you took our earlier advice and configured the Java Web Server to start automatically via the RunServices registry key, you'll want to remove the entry you made. All you need to do is remove the value you made (our example value was called JEEVES). Failing to remove this value entry doesn't produce any errors when Windows 95 boots, but it is a good practice to completely clean out any changes you've made to your system.

Installing the Java Web Server on Solaris

Unlike the flashy Windows installations, getting the Java Web Server onto a Solaris machine is an uneventful process. You'll need to place the compressed tar file containing the server files in some directory. Once you have the file on the server, uncompress it using the UNIX uncompress command:

```
uncompress jws11-try-solaris2-sparc-gl-ssl_tar.Z
```

When the uncompress command finishes, you'll want to untar the archive:

```
tar xvpf jws11-try-solaris2-sparc-gl-ssl_tar
```

At this point, you should see a directory named JavaWebServer1.1. Navigate into this directory and then down into its bin subdirectory. From there, start the Java Web Server with the httpd command:

```
cd JavaWebServer1.1/bin
./httpd
```

With the Web server running, open up a browser and navigate to your Solaris machine on port 8080 (the default port for the Java Web Server).

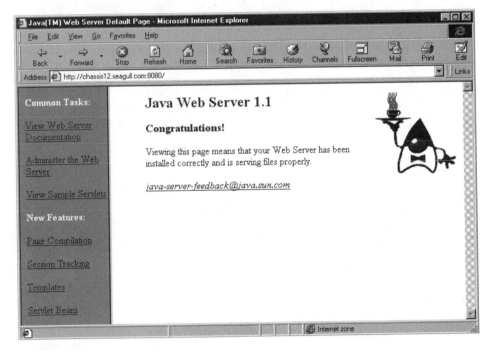

Figure 2-28   Verifying the Solaris installation.

Congratulations! You've got the Java Web Server running successfully on your Solaris machine.

Beyond the Initial Installation

After the installation euphoria washes away, you should be realizing that you're not done yet. For example, the JWS doesn't automatically start, it runs with the user account of whoever installed it, and it listens on port 8080 instead of the default Web port of 80. All of these issues need to be addressed.

Starting with the last, the Java Web Server starts on port 8080 by default due to UNIX security restrictions. No program may listen on a port less than 1024 unless it is running with `root` privileges. Since we've installed the Java Web Server on our own user account, the Javasoft developers knew that this would cause a problem with security if the server automatically tried to bind to port 80. You can change the default port with the administrative tool (covered in the next chapter on Administration), but only after you've configured the server to run with root privileges.

Getting the Java Web Server to start automatically requires root access to the machine. Once you are root, you'll want to put JWS somewhere less conspicuous than in your home directory. Our suggestion is to put it in your `/opt` directory.

```
mv JavaWebServer1.1 /opt
```

Now you'll need to change the security on those files from your old user account over to root. Move over to the `opt` directory:

```
cd /opt
```

Execute a recursive change owner and change group command to give control over to `root`:

```
chown -R root JavaWebServer1.1
chgrp -R root JavaWebServer1.1
```

With the Java Web Server in the right place, the time has come to make it start automatically at boot time. In the `etc` subdirectory of the JWS is a file called `java-server.startup`. It is an `init.d`-style script file, and it should be moved to the `/etc/rc3.d` directory. From there, rename the file `S42jserv`, give it executable privileges, and create a symbolic link to it with the name `K42jserv`:

```
mv java-server.startup S42jserv
chmod u+x S42jserv
ln -s S42jserv K42jserv
```

Now, open the `S42jserv` file with your favorite text editor. Scroll down to the section marked "START OF STUFF YOU NEED TO CONFIGURE". From there, the changes are simple, since a Solaris-compatible Java Runtime Environment comes bundled with the Java Web Server:

```
JSERV_HOME=/opt/JavaWebServer1.1
USE_JRE=jre
THREADS_TYPE=native
```

Of course, if you installed the Java Web Server to a different directory on your system, you should reflect that change in the JSERV_HOME variable. Also, if you want to use green threads (software threads) instead of kernel threads, you can make this change by changing the value of THREADS_TYPE :

```
THREADS_TYPE=green
```

Using the Linux Platform

Linux is a powerful, UNIXlike operating system that runs efficiently on less-expensive hardware. Owing to its attractive pricing (i.e., free) Linux makes an excellent choice to run a Web server like the Java Web Server. This section provides a cursory look at how Linux is configured to run a Java-based Web server, including:

- Installing the JDK
- Installing the Java Web Server
- Modifying the Java Web Server's configuration script

Although certain features of the Java Web Server aren't available on the Linux platform (such as SSL support), the main requirement to serve HTTP requests and maintain Servlets is preserved.

If you're considering loading Linux onto your computer, we suggest using RedHat Linux (www.redhat.com). RedHat is available for purchase on CD-ROM or as a free download from their FTP site (ftp.redhat.com). Even with a moderately fast network connection (128 kbps+), you can install Linux via FTP in less than a half-hour. More information on installing Linux can be found on the Web or at your local computer bookstore.

Hardware Requirements

Linux runs comfortably on 8 megabytes of memory without X-Windows support, and the Java Web Server uses about another 8 megabytes during heavy loads, so the minimum safe amount of memory is 16 megabytes. However, just as with Windows NT, more memory never hurts, since Linux uses all available memory as a large disk cache.

You need network support, through either a real network adapter or a *fake* adapter using a loopback driver or the dummy driver. More information about setting up these and other network devices under Linux exists in the Ethernet HOWTO.

Core Note

This and all other Linux HOWTO documents are available at the Sunsite ftp site (ftp://sunsite.unc.edu/LDP/HOWTO/Ethernet-HOWTO.html).

Software Requirements

Besides a working version of Linux, you'll need two other pieces of software: the Solaris version of the Java Web Server, and a Linux version of the 1.1 JDK. Since only two versions of the Java Web Server are available from Javasoft (a Windows version and a Solaris version), you can use the Solaris version as a "Pure Java" implementation of the Java Web Server on any platform, including Linux. Unfortunately, certain features such as SSL support aren't written in Java, and these operating-system-dependent pieces are unavailable on non-Solaris platforms. Also, since the Solaris version of the Java Web Server ships with the Solaris Java Runtime Environment (JRE), you'll need a version of either the JDK or the JRE for Linux. Several different ports of the Java Developer's Kit are available for Linux, and a list of these JDK ports is kept on JavaSoft's Web site at

```
http://www.javasoft.com/cgi-bin/java-ports.cgi
```

For our installation, we used the Java-Linux Porting Project's release of the Sun JDK, downloaded from

```
http://www.blackdown.org/java-linux.html
```

What It Means to Be Root

Before going any further with any installations, you need to understand an important Linux concept. Every Linux machine has several different user accounts. Every account but one has certain access privileges that limit their use of parts of the operating system (files permissions, special operations, quotas, etc.). A special user that has no solid restrictions in the system is *root*, or the *SuperUser*, which acts as part of the operating system.

All of the installation examples implicitly assume you are running as the root user. Certain operations (such as making changes to init.d scripts—a topic covered later) can be accomplished only by root.

However, along with the privileges of root access come the terrible consequences of a mistake. For example, as root you can erase the entire file system in one swift blow by incorrectly using the `rm` command. Therefore, unless your Linux machine is expendable, *please* make a backup of any critical data before assuming root.

With that said, onward to installation.

Installing the JDK

At the time this chapter was written, the latest available JDK from the JLPP was version 1.1.3. Using an FTP client, navigate to the nearest mirror site (a list of mirror sites is kept on the Blackdown Web server) and retrieve the file linux-

`jdk.1.1.3-v2.tar.gz`. A JRE is also available with a reduced footprint, but as we wanted to do Java development on Linux, we spent the extra disk space and installed the JDK instead. Next, you'll want to open up the archive with the `tar` utility:

```
tar -xzf linux-jdk.1.1.3-v2.tar.gz
```

After a few moments of disk churning, you'll have an opened Java directory with the complete distribution contained inside. You can put this directory anywhere you wish, but we moved it to the `/usr/local/java` directory.

Starting the Installation

With the JDK successfully installed, the next step is to load the Java Web Server onto your Linux machine. For our installation, we used the trial version (which operates for thirty days after it is installed) of the server, which is distributed as a tar file: `jws11-try-solaris2-sparc-gl-ssl_tar.Z`. You can open the tar file with:

```
tar -xzf jws11-try-solaris2-sparc-gl-ssl_tar.Z
```

When the `tar` program is finished, you should be left with a `JavaWebServer1.1` directory holding the contents of the Java Web Server, as shown in Figure 2-29.

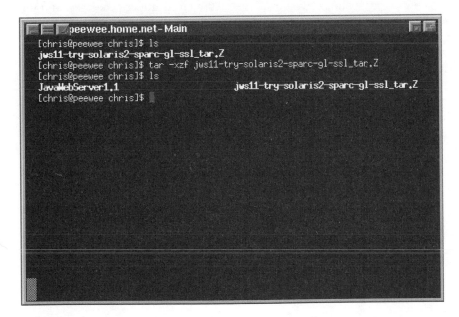

Figure 2-29 Java Web Server uncompressed.

You'll most likely want to move the Java Web Server installation out of your home directory. As an example, we moved it underneath `/usr/local`:

```
mv JavaWebServer1.1 /usr/local
```

Core Note

Using the `mv` *command to shift directories around the file system has some interesting security implications. For instance, when any file is moved, it keeps its original permission bits instead of inheriting the security attributes of its new parent. If this isn't a desirable result, you may want to copy the directory tree instead:*

```
cp -R JavaWebServer1.1 /usr/local
```

An `mv` *command will also fail if your source and destination directories are on different disk partitions.*

Automatically Starting the Java Web Server

Most Web servers are configured to run as background daemon processes, and the Java Web Server is no exception. Linux executes a special set of scripts during the boot sequence, and each of these scripts is responsible for a different server process. These scripts are stored in the `/etc/rc.d/init.d` directory, with topics ranging from Ethernet adapter configuration settings to anonymous FTP server options.

Fortunately, the Java Web Server developers didn't want to waste our time by forcing us to create our own script for their product. They thoughtfully placed a sample script in the `etc` subdirectory of the installation. You'll want to place this script into the `/etc/rc.d/init.d directory` with the rest of the startup scripts, making it executable by changing the permission bits:

```
cp JavaWebServer1.1/etc/java-server.startup /etc/rc.d/init.d/jws
chmod u+x /etc/rc.d/init.d/jws
```

Configuring the Startup Script

The startup script has several options that need to be configured before the server will work right. These options are found near the top of the script in a section marked "START OF STUFF YOU NEED TO CONFIGURE."

```
JSERV_HOME
```

```
USE_JRE
JAVA_HOME
CLASSPATH
THREADS_TYPE
SSL_HOME
```

JSERV_HOME

The JSERV_HOME variable should be set to the home directory of the Java Web Server. Following our example, JSERV_HOME would be set to "/usr/local/JavaWebServer1.1":

```
JSERV_HOME=/usr/local/JavaWebServer1.1
```

USE_JRE

USE_JRE is a boolean flag that switches between the built-in Java Runtime Environment or another Java virtual machine to run the Java Web Server on. Since the Java Web Server installation comes with the Solaris JRE, which is useless under Linux, you will want to set this variable to "nojre":

```
USE_JRE=nojre
```

JAVA_HOME

Once you've decided to use an external virtual machine, the startup script needs to know where to find it. The JAVA_HOME variable lists the directory of the JDK. Again, following the previous examples, you'd set the JAVA_HOME to:

```
JAVA_HOME=/usr/local/java
```

This variable is ignored if the USE_JRE variable is set to "jre".

CLASSPATH

If any of your servlets want to take advantage of other APIs, such as JavaMail or JNDI, you'll need to include their respective jar files in your CLASSPATH. Using this variable, you can specify these files without placing them in the global environment. For example, if you wanted to use the JavaMail API with the Java Web Server, and JavaMail had been installed to /usr/local/java-mail, you could make your CLASSPATH:

```
CLASSPATH=/usr/local/java/java-mail/mail.jar
```

THREADS_TYPE

Sun has released a *Native Threads Pack* for their Solaris version of the JDK. Since Linux doesn't support this Solaris-native code, you'll need to specify the default green (software) threads instead:

```
THREADS_TYPE=green
```

SSL_HOME

The Java Web Server comes with an SSL implementation. Unfortunately, this implementation requires some native code, which is already compiled for Solaris. Since you won't be using any SSL, it's safe to leave this variable blank. In the future, if someone produces a Linux-compatible SSL distribution, you can return and add the correct path to enable SSL.

Linking It All Together

All that is left to do is create two symbolic links to our configured jws startup script. These scripts are used to automatically start and shut down the Java Web Server, depending on the runlevel.

Core Note

Runlevels are used by UNIX systems to signify what mode the computer is in. The runlevels mean different things to different UNIX variants. On Linux, runlevel 3 is used to start all network services, while runlevel 6 is used for shutting down the entire system.

Create a link called S99jws in the rc3.d directory to the jws script you edited in the init.d directory:

```
pwd
/etc/rc.d/rc3.d
ln -s /etc/rc.d/init.d/jws S99jws
```

The S in the name S99jws tells the script to run the "start" portion of the jws script, while the high number means "run this last."

To make the accompanying shutdown entry, create a link to the jws script from the rc6.d directory:

```
pwd
/etc/rc.d/rc6.d
ln -s /etc/rc.d/init.d/jws K00jws
```

Voila! You now have the Java Web Server automatically starting on Linux.

Uninstalling the Java Web Server

The Linux installation is a snap to remove from your system. Just follow these three steps:

1. Shut down the Java Web Server.
2. Remove the startup script links.
3. Erase the Java Web Server.

Shut Down the Java Web Server

If that Java Web Server is already running, you'll need to shut it down by issuing a `./jws stop` in the `init.d` subdirectory. You will experience strange behavior when trying to uninstall files that are already in use.

Removing the Startup Scripts

Once the Web server is down, go back into the `rc3.d` subdirectory and remove the `S99jws` file. Next, navigate to the `rc6.d` directory and kill the `K00jws` file as well.

Erasing the Java Web Server

All you'll need to do is to run a `rm -rf` on the Java Web Server directory to get rid of the unwanted files:

```
pwd
/usr/local/JavaWebServer1.1
cd ..
rm -rf JavaWebServer1.1
```

Summary

Amazing, isn't it? The Java Web Server truly is a testament to the Java creed "write once, run anywhere," since you just installed the same Java files on four different operating systems. The installation process for the platform of your choice is the only system-dependent operation related to JWS.

Now, before you jump head first into configuring the Java Web Server, we thought you'd like to know how to run the Java Web Server with other virtual machines, and why doing this is a good idea. The next chapter might seem off topic for a book about Web servers, but an efficient Java virtual machine is the key for achieving good performance with any Java program.

ALTERNATIVE LIFESTYLES FOR THE JAVA WEB SERVER

Topics in This Chapter

- Why use other virtual machines?
- The basics of a virtual machine
- Hooking up other virtual machines to the Java Web Server
- Performance testing and benchmarking

Chapter

3

Virtual machines (VMs) are a complex subject about which entire books have
been written. Here we provide a quick overview of how a VM operates in the
context of the Java Web Server, and why its capabilities can drastically change
the performance of your Java applications.

Both of us can remember when we first started programming in Java. We ran our
"Hello World" applications with this mysterious program named `java.exe`, which
was described in the accompanying documentation as a "virtual machine." Neither of
us knew anything about virtual machines or garbage collection when we started coding in Java, except that both were cool features that made Java a powerful language.

Perhaps you had the same introductory experience to Java, where the virtual
machine ran quietly in the background of your mind as you wrote your programs.
Memory was to be used whenever you needed it, and you could add threading to your
program just by creating new thread objects. You never had memory-corruption
errors, pointer problems, or memory leaks. Protecting resources from multiple concurrent accesses was as simple as marking an activity `synchronized`. How all this
magic worked was blissfully hidden inside `java.exe`.

After a brief presentation of theory, we'll walk you through some benchmark tests
of different vendors' virtual-machine offerings. Only a fraction of those available
were tested here, but you could apply the same principles to any VM you wanted to
test. Our biggest goal for the performance-testing section is to inculcate a distrust of
any benchmark that claims to have all the answers, because a little research into its
structure can reveal flaws that affect the outcome.

Finally, you'll configure the Java Web Server to use different virtual machines, and you'll learn about the `jserv` program and how you can modify its source code to meet you own particular needs.

Why Be Flexible?

When you install software on your computer, you expect it to run straight out of the box. The Java Web Server is no exception, and it accomplishes this feat on the Solaris and Windows platforms because it comes bundled with JavaSoft's Java Runtime Environment (commonly referred to as the JRE).

Core Note

The JRE is a stripped-down version of the Java Developer's Kit (JDK), containing only the necessary components for running Java applications (i.e., no compilers, no debuggers, no demonstration programs, etc.)

While this "Instant-Server" capability is convenient, the Java Web Server development team knew that their customers would want the flexibility to replace the JRE with the virtual machine of their choice. Here are two reasons why you'd want to use a different virtual machine:

- Better performance
- No JRE available for your platform

Better Performance

Java is getting faster—not only faster than previous Java implementations, but just plain *fast!*

Skeptical? Check out Java performance-related articles at the JavaWorld Web site (`http://www.javaworld.com`). One company, Volano LLC, created a benchmarking program to test the capabilities of server-side virtual machines. VolanoMark, their benchmarking program, is available for download from their Web site at `http://www.volano.com`.

Armed with VolanoMark, we ran our own battery of tests against both the stock JDK 1.1.5 and Microsoft's Java 2.0 SDK, and found the two virtual machines evenly matched. (More information on these tests appears later in the chapter.) Just for fun, we tested the JDK 1.1.5 against the older JDK 1.0.2 and realized an eightfold performance increase. (This was a repeat of the tests Volano LLC ran between the Microsoft Java SDK 2.0 and the JDK 1.0.2.)

You can use VolanoMark to check out how your favorite virtual machine compares to other virtual machines on the same platform. Knowing how the VMs stack up can help you decide which one to use with the Java Web Server or any other Java programs you want to run. However, while a faster virtual machine usually means faster performance, some third-party implementations come with certain caveats. For example, the Microsoft Java SDK isn't compatible with the Java standard, and programs that need to use RMI (Remote Method Invocation) or JFC (Java Foundation Classes) won't run properly (if at all).

No JRE Available for Your Platform?

While speed freaks will be interested in wringing the most performance out of the Java Web Server, most of us are happy when we get it up and running. If you're using Windows or Solaris, then you're in luck, as a compatible JRE comes standard with the Java Web Server installation. However, if you aren't running either of these operating systems, then you must install an external virtual machine to use with the Java Web Server. The only requirement of the virtual machine is that it be JDK 1.1 compatible. (Compatible virtual machines are listed on the JavaSoft Web site at `http://www.javasoft.com/cgi-bin/java-ports.cgi`).

Before considering installation of third-party virtual machines, you probably should know what a virtual machine actually does for a Java program. Armed with this knowledge, you can decide better where any bottlenecks exist and how your code can affect overall performance.

The Basics of a Virtual Machine

Although most Java developers know an interpreter is executing their programs, we'd bet many of them haven't investigated exactly how the magic works. For programmers to be ignorant of the system and still produce excellent programs illustrates one of Java's strengths over micro-managed languages like C++. Yet, we think that every Java programmer should know how the Java interpreter provides important features like platform independence, automatic memory management, and simple network access, not only to enrich their understanding of Java, but also to make them aware of issues such as garbage collection, thread scheduling, and portability constraints.

In a nutshell, a virtual machine provides a bridge between your Java program and the physical computer the interpreter is running on, as shown in Figure 3-1.

Notice how the virtual machine is split into two pieces: the top half provides the platform-independent facilities to a Java program, while the lower half implements the platform-dependent pieces required to make the virtual machine function. This diagram may look strangely familiar to computer scientists, because with a few name changes it is identical to how the UNIX operating system was designed. In comparison, the top portion of the UNIX kernel is written in C, providing source-independence, while portions of the bottom are written in machine-specific assembler to support features such as context switching and memory management (mileage may vary depending on the UNIX in question).

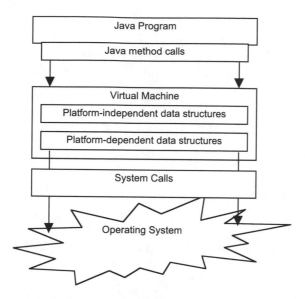

Figure 3-1   The virtual machine bridge.

Another way to look at the virtual machine is shown in Figure 3-2.

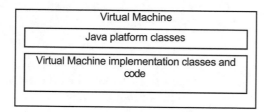

Figure 3-2   A second look at the virtual
machine.

The top half acts as a well-known interface for Java programs through the body of the standard Java classes (classes found in the `java.*` packages), while the bottom half consists of virtual machine-specific Java classes and native code that provide the underlying support for the platform. By restricting a Java programmer to the standard Java classes (the 100% Pure Java Initiative), platform independence is guaranteed, because every virtual machine is required to implement them.

Of course, this hasn't stopped companies like Microsoft from pick-and-choosing which parts of the JDK they decide to implement. At the time of this writing, Sun, in an effort to keep Java portable, has filed suit against Microsoft. More information can be found at the JavaSoft Web site.

So, while the upper portion of the virtual machine provides support for platform independence, it is the bottom piece that implements automatic memory management and thread scheduling. In our opinion, the better you understand the mechanics of how these features are provided in the lower half of the virtual machine, the better you'll know how they impact the performance of your Java code.

So without further ado, on to memory management and thread scheduling.

Memory Management

The Java platform features a garbage-collection system by which memory is automatically released when it is no longer needed. In order to make this work, the Java language can't give a developer direct access to memory. As an illustration, take the C programming language that gives a programmer the capability to massage (massacre?) memory through its pointer types. For example, you can declare a *pointer* variable of some type and then assign any number you want as the "address" of that data:

```
char * some_string;
some_string = (char *)(0x1000);
```

Now you can write some data to that memory using one of the standard C library functions, memcpy:

```
memcpy (some_string,"SOME DATA",strlen("SOME DATA"));
```

This is a handy trick for writing device drivers, because you can access data when it is found at some specific memory address. However, when was the last time you wrote a device driver? Most of the developers we know write applications and don't enjoy the bit-twiddling nature of pointers, *yet they continue to write programs as if they were coding for hardware!*

So why are pointers found littering numerous C and C++ application programs? The reason is that they fill an important need for *dynamic memory allocation*. With pointers, you can allocate memory when you need it from the heap using the malloc function, then release that memory when you no longer need it with the free function:

```
struct some_struct * my_pointer;
my_pointer = (struct some_struct*)malloc(sizeof(struct some_struct));
/* some nonessential code for this example*/
free(my_pointer);
```

Everything looks okay so far. Now, tucked away in that nonessential code area is a simple variable assignment:

```
struct some_struct * another_pointer = my_pointer;
```

But there isn't anything wrong with this code—or is there? Imagine that somewhere after the call to free on my_pointer, someone accesses another_pointer's data. Since the memory where that information was kept had already been sent back to the heap, you have an unpredictable problem on your hands. If any calls had been made to the heap between the free and the use of another_pointer's data, that memory could belong to another variable. What happens next depends on who owns the memory, resulting in bugs that appear for no logical reason. Even worse, the programmers assigned to fix this bug will waste valuable effort looking over code at the crash site and not at where the data was corrupted by the previously freed memory.

So you can see that the fragility of pointers goes hand in hand with the ability to release memory. Fortunately, the Java designers understood this problem. Their solution was to deny programmers the ability to release memory once they allocated it, which at first glance sounds like the cure that killed the patient! Even with memory at rock-bottom prices, any process that runs for a lengthy period of time is destined to exhaust all available memory.

This is where garbage collection comes into play. A garbage collector walks through allocated memory and releases whatever isn't being referenced any more. Without the ability to declare pointer types or massage memory addresses, the developer can't create problems for the garbage collector.

Well, you know that there is this "thing" called a garbage collector, but how does it work in a virtual machine? There isn't a simple answer, because the implementation is left up to the virtual-machine designers, making the "gc" (the Java name for the garbage collector) implementation virtual-machine-specific. All that a Java developer needs to know about the garbage collector is:

- Objects can be created, but not explicitly destroyed.
- The garbage collector frees objects when no more references to it exist.
- The garbage collector runs when memory is low.

Since the garbage collector's job is to reclaim wasted memory, it needs to run whenever memory availability reaches a low threshold. Valuable time for running the application is consumed as the garbage collector walks through the heap structures. The amount of time wasted depends on the size of the heap, but the need to garbage collect is completely a function of the program's memory consumption. This provides us with a perfect segue into a performance tip:

Core Note

Constantly creating objects can dramatically slow the performance of your Java code. More memory use means more CPU time spent cleaning it up, which results in less time for your code to execute. Of course, some memory use is inevitable, but you shouldn't feel that you must allocate all available memory to solve a problem!

So how does all of this talk about garbage collection relate to choosing a virtual machine for the Java Web Server? Since the Java Web Server is a long-running process that consumes a fair amount of memory, it will undergo several garbage-collection cycles in its lifetime. This will impact server performance, so using a virtual machine that implements a fast garbage-collection algorithm can alleviate some congestion.

Core Note

This is especially important on Java implementations under UNIX that don't have native thread support (a topic coming up next), because the garbage collector will pause the application as it makes its run.

For example, when an object is created in the stock virtual machine from Sun, memory gets allocated from the heap, and a reference to that memory is stored in the system handle table. The user receives a reference to that handle-table entry which points to the object. This process, shown in Figure 3-3, is sometimes referred to as *double indirection*.

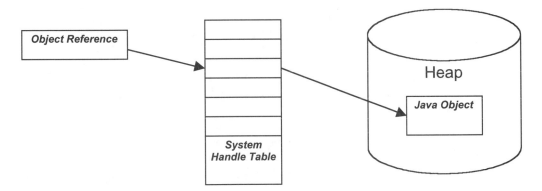

Figure 3-3 Here is double indirection.

When memory runs low in the heap, the garbage collector will walk through the object-reference variables on all of the thread stacks. Each time it crosses a variable that is "connected," it marks it as "used" and continues processing. When the entire system has been processed, all of the objects that haven't been marked are swept away as garbage and their memory is reclaimed.

In terms of their lifetimes, objects can be broken down into two types: (1) temporary *calculation* objects that have a short life span, and (2) longer-living *application* objects that represent the program as a set of interconnected objects, possibly existing for the entire life of the program. To illustrate this distinction, imagine that we have a class `SayHello` with a single static method `Hi` that takes one String variable containing the name of the person the object should greet:

```
public class SayHello
{
  public static void Hi (String name)
  {
    System.out.println ("Hi "+name);
  }
}
```

Underneath the covers of the VM, a `StringBuffer` object is created to concatenate the Strings `"Hi "` and `name` in the `println` call. This `StringBuffer` is a temporary object with a lifetime of one statement, and its memory can be garbage collected during the next collection cycle.

In comparison, the `out` variable of the `System` class exists for the entire life of the Java program, so its memory will never be reclaimed during garbage collection. It is a long-term "application" object.

Most nontrivial programs contain a large group of objects like the `System.out` variable. Since the simple garbage-collection scheme used by the stock VM doesn't recognize this distinction, it will process these variables during every collection cycle. They will not be released, resulting in the garbage collector's squandering precious processor time that could have been used by the program.

This isn't a good thing.

Fortunately, a more sophisticated garbage-collection technique is employed in the Microsoft `jview` VM and the upcoming "HotSpot" VM from Sun Microsystems. Both of these virtual machines have a "generation" garbage collector that separates objects into our two groups (long-term and short-term). In short, all objects are created in a special "short-term" heap. If these objects survive several garbage-collection cycles, they get promoted to a long-term heap that is collected less frequently. The generational garbage collector shows better performance, because it can restrict itself to a small number of objects in the "short-term" heap.

The moral of the story is to find out who is taking out your garbage, because your program's performance depends on it.

Thread Management

Multithreading is another popular Java feature that doesn't naturally exist in either C or C++. In Java, threads are first-class objects, and they can be manipulated through method calls. When they are active, threads can execute concurrently by timesharing all available processors.

The most attractive feature of Java threads is their simplicity. For example, creating a thread is a simple, two-step operation

```
Thread some_thread = new Thread();
some_thread.start();
```

where the thread object is constructed on the first line and then started on the second line.

This makes life easy for the application programmer, but at a cost to the virtual-machine designer. One big problem to solve is this: How does the virtual machine provide threadlike behavior on platforms that don't support threads natively in the operating system? Essentially, there are two kinds of virtual machines:

- Those that use native threads if the operating system supports them.
- Those that use software thread libraries if the operating system doesn't support threads.

The Natives Are Restless

Native-thread support is typically implemented by manipulating operating-system-dependent thread structures in that lower portion of the virtual machine. Most of the Java platforms have some form of native-thread capability. For example, both the Sun JDK and the Microsoft Java SDK support threads natively under Windows 95 and Windows NT. The "Native Threads Pack" released by JavaSoft gives Java programs on the Solaris platform an extra boost by utilizing kernel threads in the virtual machine.

Put simply, the use of operating-system threads lets the virtual machine take more processing time away from other programs. As threads are the only schedulable entities in most operating systems, all processor time is shared among those currently in the runnable state. As a result, most thread schedulers aren't "fair," giving more time to Java execution as the virtual machine has "spread out" over several schedulable threads.

Another benefit of using native threads concerns blocking I/O calls. When a program issues a read to a file, it will block (the operating system removes it from the "runnable" list of threads) until the file can be read and the data brought into memory. Simple calls like `fread` in C will cause a program to stop executing. This is typically the behavior you expect, as you want to return from the call after data has been read.

But in the case of having "software" threads mapped to one native thread, a careless virtual-machine implementation could cause a group of Java threads to stop running because one of them issued a blocking call. Blocking calls must be replaced with asynchronous versions so that the virtual machine can continue processing without stopping for I/O.

In any event, sophisticated programming techniques must be employed to gain adequate performance for multithreaded Java applications on nonnative threaded virtual machines. Knowing whether the virtual machine you are planning to use supports native threads can result in a huge performance win when using it with a heavily threaded program like the Java Web Server.

Beating the 80/20 Rule

Contrary to public opinion, Java isn't a completely interpreted language. Java source code is turned into bytecodes by a Java compiler. These bytecodes are targeted for the native instruction set of a Java virtual machine. As the JVM reads the bytecodes, it executes them as a real chip would execute instructions. Of course, the stock JDK doesn't have registers, and it executes all instructions on an operand stack. More information can be found in the Java Virtual Machine Specification, which is available from Sun Microsystems. A good way to think about this procedure is that the Java compiler performs 80% of the work involved in getting the instructions into executable code, while the virtual machine finishes the last 20% at run time.

Even though 80% of the work has already been done, repeating the interpretation process over and over again impacts performance. Why not translate the bytecode into native instructions once during the lifetime of the program, therefore improving performance for heavily trafficked subroutines? This process is called *just-in-time (JIT) compiling*, a feature that exists in most (but not all) virtual machines. JIT compilers can boost Java runtime performance up to ten times that of the stock JDK. This performance benefit is especially pronounced in programs that run for a long time, as the extra amount of work spent compiling the code into native instructions is negligible compared to the time saved executing that native code. Server programs, like the Java Web Server, are a class of software that typically runs for an extended period of time.

Obviously, if a JIT-enabled virtual machine is available for your platform, you should use it with the Java Web Server.

Hooking Up with a Third-Party Virtual Machine

So the virtual machine you use with the Java Web Server *does* affect its performance, but how do you hook up with another vendor's faster VM? A good place to start looking would be the Java Web Server itself, because it already talks to an external VM called the JRE. In essence, all VMs are external to the Java Web Server, but the server comes with some special *glue* code to automatically use the JRE if no other VMs are available.

If you've assimilated the section on "Installing the Java Web Server on Linux" back in Chapter 2, then hooking up another VM should be a snap. As a quick review for those of you who shamefully skipped that section, we found that the Java Web Server is a *Pure Java* program that can run on any JDK 1.1 compatible VM, but only after a little tweaking to the system environment. For those of you who read the section on Linux, you'll be happy to know that we explain the *why* behind the installation procedure here.

Not Quite an Alien Autopsy, But...

When the Java Web Server starts, a special *wrapper* program is executed to monitor and control it. This program is called jserv, and it is either a shell script on UNIX or a Win32 executable on the Windows platform. Fortunately, the Java Web Server comes with the source code for this program (it's located in the bin subdirectory). With the source in hand, it's easier to follow what's going on.

When we used a debugger to walk through the jserv executable, we found that its behavior changes depending on the values of environment variables and command-line parameters. Instead of boring you with C snippets from the jserv source code, we extracted all of the useful information from it and present it to you in a handy table.

Command-Line Arguments

The command-line arguments to jserv are parsed in the parse_arguments helper function in jserv.c as shown in Table 3-1.

Table 3-1 Command-Line Arguments for jserv

Argument	Description
-[no]jre	[Don't] Use the Java Runtime Environment to run the Java Web Server. If this argument isn't specified, jserv uses the environment variable JAVA_HOME to decide whether to use the JRE or not.
-console	If set, error messages are printed out to the console. This option makes sense only if the Java Web Server is started in a shell (not as a service) using the JRE. (Using a third-party VM always prints out the error messages.)
-verbose	Same as -console, except initialization settings are displayed as the server starts. Also, a system property is set (-Dserver.verbose) which doesn't do anything at the present.
-help	Print out the documented command-line options and their usage, then exit.
-norestart	If the Java Web Server crashes, the typical response is to automatically restart it. If this argument is used, the server will not automatically be restarted.
-start_server [server name]	This option and its value are used to start a specific service. Typically, you won't use this option. The admin-server (the default server started by jserv) uses this command-line argument when starting the other servers.

continued

Table 3-1 Command-Line Arguments for `jserv` *(continued)*

Argument	Description
-java_home [path-to-java-directory]	Use this option to tell jserv where to look for a Java VM (including the JRE). If this variable isn't set, jserv uses the environment variable JAVA_HOME to find the directory for the VM, or it defaults to "C:\java" if neither the command-line argument nor the environment variable exists.
-classpath	Additional CLASSPATH settings. Directory paths and jar files added here will be loaded by the system class loader.
-threads [green | native]	Sets whether to use software (green) or operating-system (native) threads in the virtual machine. The difference between green and native threads was covered earlier in this chapter. This setting currently doesn't do anything on the Windows platform (all threads are native).
-main_class [class name]	Package-qualified class name that jserv passes to the VM. If this argument isn't specified, the default class is com.sun.server.ServerProcess. This is an "undocumented" argument.
-login_class [class name]	Package-qualified class name that jserv uses to retrieve a passphrase. This passphrase is used to decrypt the file keys in the Java Web Server's home directory. The SSL libraries decrypt incoming service requests using these keys. You can use this option to provide custom authentication procedures (hardware tokens, M (N secret-sharing, etc …).
-serverroot [path-to-JWS]	The home directory of the Java Web Server. If this option isn't specified, the default is "..\" taken from the path of the jserv program (i.e., e:\javawebserver1.1\bin\.."").
-jsthome [path-to-JST]	Path to the Java Server Toolkit classes. The Java Web Server is a JST application. You only need to use this argument if you have an updated version of the JST that you want to use with the Java Web Server, as the JST classes are bundled with JWS in the jws.jar file in the lib subdirectory. This is an "undocumented" argument.
-jsdkhome [path-to-JSDK]	Path to the Java servlet Development Kit classes. These files are also included with the Java Server Toolkit. Like the ñjsthome argument, you'll want to specify this argument if you have an updated set of classes for javax.servlet.° and sun.servlet.° packages.
-ssl	Turns on the use of SSL in the Java Web Server. You'll need to specify this argument if you've installed a different key-management system than the default file-based mechanism.

Argument	Description
-passfile	Pull the passphrase out of a text file named keys.passphrase in the JWS home directory. Warning: This is a possible security hole, depending on who has access to this file.
-sslhome [path-to-SSL libraries]	Path to the Secure Socket Layer classes. These files are included in the domestic version of the Java Server Toolkit. Like the –jsthome and –jsdkhome options, this makes sense only if you want to run JWS with a newer set of classes from an updated JST installation.
-vmargs [arguments]	Optional arguments passed into the Java Web Server through the system property server.vmargs and at the command-line to the virtual machine. For example, you could increase the starting size of the heap by adding the argument –vmargs –ms32m to the jserv command.
-ntservice	Set when the program executes as a Windows NT service. You shouldn't need to set this flag, because the jservsvc program (a wrapper program that handles Windows NT service-request calls and directs them down into the jserv process) sets it for you.

Some of these command-line options look for more information from the system environment. These environment variables are listed in Table 3-2.

Table 3-2   Environment Variables for `jserv`

Environment Variable	Description
JAVA_HOME	Points to the home directory for the virtual machine running the Java Web Server. If this variable is not defined, jserv may not be able to find a suitable VM to use with JWS. If the –jre command-line option is used and the JAVA_HOME variable is absent, jserv uses the JRE bundled with the Java Web Server (located in the jre subdirectory).
JAVA_EXE	Names the virtual-machine executable. You'll need to define this variable if you want to use third-party virtual machines such as Microsoft's jview or the Jolt Project's kaffe.
JSERV_HOME	Points to the home directory for the Java Web Server. If this environment variable and the command-line argument –serverroot are specified, the command-line argument takes precedence.

Wow! From the look of these tables, the Java Web Server team designed an open interface in order to utilize any vendor's virtual machine with JWS. Yet, how well does it work in practice? A simple test would be to get the Java Web Server to run using Microsoft's VM, `jview`. What you need to do is create an environment variable JAVA_EXE and set its value to `%SystemRoot%\jview.exe`:

```
set JAVA_EXE=%systemroot%\jview.exe
```

Restart the Java Web Server. Did you see what we found in Figure 3-4?

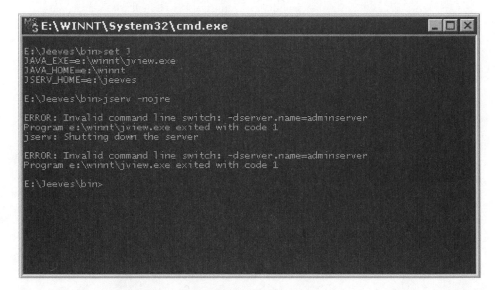

Figure 3-4   Problems between jview and jserv.

What went wrong? It seems that `jview` doesn't like system properties sent with the "-D" prefix used by the JDK virtual machine. Instead, `jview` wants them formatted with the prefix "/d:". If you quickly scan over `jserv.c`, you'll find over a dozen places where the development team hard-coded system properties with the prefix "-D", instead of doing some kind of runtime check.

For the sake of brevity, we've chosen the quick-and-dirty route, leaving the clean solution as a reader exercise. What we've done is wrap system-property definitions in a macro call that prepends either "-D" or "/d:" depending on the state of a `#define`:

```
#ifdef JVIEW
#define SYSPROP(PROPERTY)  "/d:"##PROPERTY
#else
#define SYSPROP(PROPERTY)  "-D"##PROPERTY
#endif
```

If your favorite virtual machine handles system properties in a different way, you'll need to add another type of SYSPROP macro customized for it.

After a quick compile in Visual C++, we end up with a `jserv.exe` that works with `jview`. This is shown in Figure 3-5.

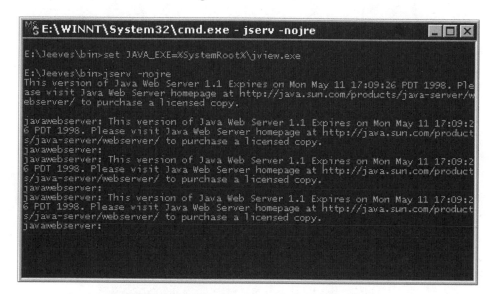

```
E:\WINNT\System32\cmd.exe - jserv -nojre

E:\Jeeves\bin>set JAVA_EXE=%SystemRoot%\jview.exe

E:\Jeeves\bin>jserv -nojre
This version of Java Web Server 1.1 Expires on Mon May 11 17:09:26 PDT 1998. Ple
ase visit Java Web Server homepage at http://java.sun.com/products/java-server/w
ebserver/ to purchase a licensed copy.

javawebserver: This version of Java Web Server 1.1 Expires on Mon May 11 17:09:2
6 PDT 1998. Please visit Java Web Server homepage at http://java.sun.com/product
s/java-server/webserver/ to purchase a licensed copy.
javawebserver:
javawebserver: This version of Java Web Server 1.1 Expires on Mon May 11 17:09:2
6 PDT 1998. Please visit Java Web Server homepage at http://java.sun.com/product
s/java-server/webserver/ to purchase a licensed copy.
javawebserver:
javawebserver: This version of Java Web Server 1.1 Expires on Mon May 11 17:09:2
6 PDT 1998. Please visit Java Web Server homepage at http://java.sun.com/product
s/java-server/webserver/ to purchase a licensed copy.
javawebserver:
```

Figure 3-5   A Modified jserv in action.

We put the modified `jserv.exe` program on the CD-ROM, so you don't have to rebuild it yourself to get it to work with `jview`. According to the Sun licensing agreement, we can't reprint the source code here, so you'll have to make the modifications yourself with the macro replacement with your own copy of `jserv.c`.

The Java Web Server team also included two convenience programs along with `jserv` to make it easier to run JWS from the command line: `httpd` and `httpdnojre`. `httpd` runs the Java Web Server with the built-in Java Runtime Environment, while `httpdnojre` uses an external virtual machine (like the Sun JDK or the Microsoft Java SDK). Both of these programs just call `jserv` with certain parameters set.

King of the VM Hill

As we've said before, the Java Web Server can be configured to run atop any JDK 1.1 compatible virtual machine. So, which vendor's VM should you be using? Making a decision like this depends on several factors:

- Price
- Features
- Performance

The price is a budget matter, so we won't discuss that here. Different vendors pack an array of features along with their VM offerings, some of which (such as JIT compiling) impact the performance of your applications.

Although it's listed last, we believe that questions of performance should guide your virtual-machine choice. So which VM is the best performer? That depends on what kind of performance you're looking for. We've come up with three ways to judge performance:

- Read the marketing reports.
- Use someone else's benchmark results.
- Do your own benchmarking.

Read the Marketing Reports

Are you kidding? These things are always stacked to give back the desired results. We strongly discourage you from using these reports in making a decision on virtual-machine performance for the Java Web Server.

Use Someone Else's Benchmark Results

You've probably heard the quote that in the computer industry, there are "lies, damn lies, and benchmarks!" The results of someone else's benchmarking are always suspect, unless you either know how the test was conducted or can repeat the tests yourself.

Fortunately, Volano LLC, a company selling Chat servers written in Java, put together a Java Virtual Machine performance test suite called `VolanoMark` and made it available for download from their Web site at `http://www.volano.com`.

`VolanoMark` attaches several clients to a test server, sends network packets, records the latency time for a response, then displays the results. Unlike previous benchmarking programs such as `CaffeineMark` (the first client-side Java benchmark program, discussed in detail at `http://www.pendragon-software.com`), `VolanoMark` was designed for server-side Java. The results from this test should be representative of the overall performance of a specific virtual machine.

However, `VolanoMark` doesn't provide all of the information required to make an educated decision on performance. A benchmark that is geared for the problem being solved by the server program should be used for *visible* performance. In a nutshell, what we're looking for is *Java Web Server performance*, not *virtual-machine performance*. As the Java Web Server provides Web services to clients, a benchmark program designed to flex a Web server can provide this information.

Do Your Own Benchmarking

Finally, it never hurts to write your own benchmarking tests. It's satisfying to get results from something you've written, especially if they match up with those from other test suites. Conversely, if your results differ greatly from those of another benchmark test, you might want to reconsider the validity of either test's results.

Meet the Challengers!

Just to illustrate how you'd go about testing JWS performance on your platform, we've put six virtual-machine configurations through three tests. The test machine is a Dual Pentium-II 300-MHz system with 128 MB of memory, using a disk subsystem of a single Seagate Cheetah 10,000-rpm UW-SCSI drive and an Adaptec 2940UW SCSI controller. Windows NT 4.0 with Service Pack 3 is the operating system for running the test.

The six VM configurations are:

- JDK 1.1.5 no JIT
- JDK 1.1.5 JIT
- JDK 1.2beta3 no JIT
- JDK 1.2beta3 JIT
- Microsoft Jview 2.0 no JIT
- Microsoft Jview 2.0 JIT

The three tests are:

- VolanoMark
- Ziff-Davis Web Bench 2.0
- Our own custom test

And now, without further ado, the contenders for the crown.

VolanoMark

`VolanoMark` is a simple, client/server test program. Unfortunately, the free edition runs on only one machine, which skews the results, since you have two virtual machines (one for the client, one for the server) competing for a single CPU resource. It is been our experience that server programs typically perform better across a network than running locally. However, until we ran `VolanoMark` our-selves, we weren't aware of the "single-machine" limitation they placed on their benchmark, as it wasn't documented in any of their published results.

Running the `VolanoMark` test yourself is a three-step process:

1. Install the `VolanoMark` package.
2. Start the Volano Server program.
3. Start the Volano Benchmark client.

Installing the VolanoMark Package

The `VolanoMark` benchmark comes as an installable Java class file (it's packaged with InstallShield Java Edition). You start the installation by running the `vmark10.class` file through the Java interpreter:

```
java vmark10
```

At this point, you should be greeted with a license-approval screen as shown in Figure 3-6.

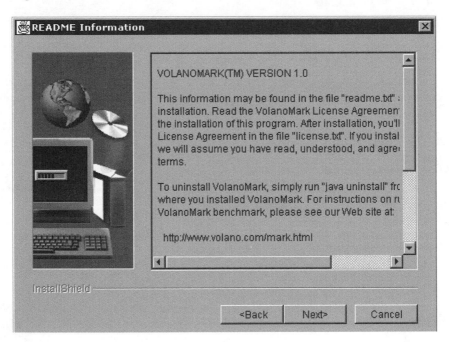

Figure 3-6 License approval for VolanoMark.

Read the brief license agreement and decide if you agree with the licensing restrictions. If you agree, continue on past the next screen (which is another licensing dialog) and choose where you want to install the test classes (Figure 3-7).

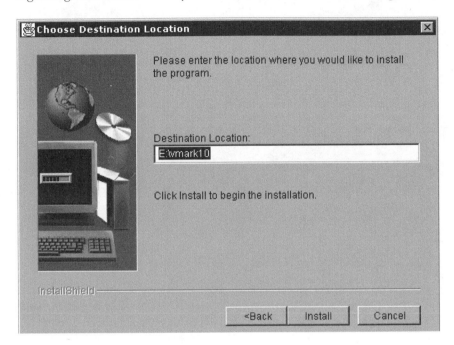

Figure 3-7   Choose the installation directory.

Press the install button, and the files will be unpacked and dropped in the target directory. The installation of VolanoMark is complete.

Starting the VolanoMark Server Program

Open up a command window and navigate to where you installed the VolanoMark software. In our case, we installed it to e:\vmark10. Once you are in the directory, you can start the server with the virtual machine of your choice. For example, to use the Sun JDK to run the server, use:

```
java -classpath %classpath%;. COM.volano.Main
```

But to use the Microsoft J++ VM (jview), you would type:

```
jview /cp:a ;. COM.volano.Main
```

In either case, you should see the output shown in Figure 3-8 after you start the server.

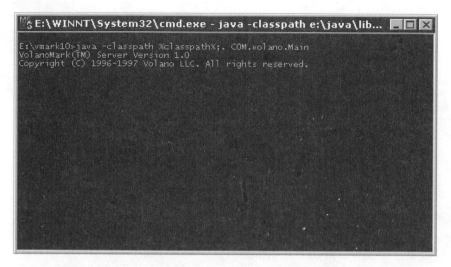

Figure 3-8   The VolanoMark server is running.

Starting the VolanoMark Benchmark Client

Open up a second command window and navigate to where you installed the VolanoMark software. Once you are there, you need to run the client program with the virtual machine of your choice. For example, to use the Sun JDK to run the client, use:

```
java –classpath %classpath%;. COM.volano.Mark
```

And to use the Microsoft J++ VM (jview), you would type:

```
jview /cp:a ;. COM.volano.Mark
```

Once the client starts, the benchmark begins. The test runs for approximately one minute. At the end of the test, the command window should look like Figure 3-9.

The Verdict Is In...

Remember when we mentioned that we were surprised by the single-machine limitation on `VolanoMark`, and how it wasn't mentioned in the published results? (See the JavaWorld article at `http://www.javaworld.com/jw-12-1997/jw-12-volanomark.html`.) If you've read the published results, you might be surprised to see the numbers we came up with (Figure 3-10).

Figure 3-9   The VolanoMark benchmark is complete.

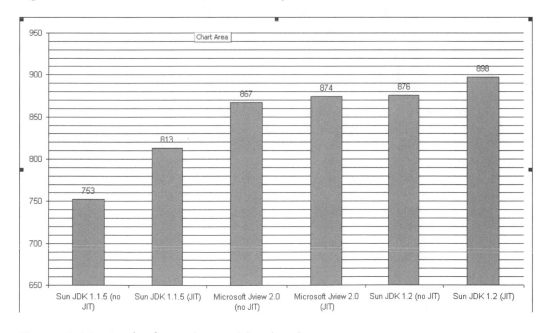

Figure 3-10   Results of our VolanoMark benchmark tests.

These results paint a much different picture concerning Microsoft's VM performance over the stock Sun JDK. Unlike the supposed "2-to-1" performance difference between JIT-enabled Sun and Microsoft VMs, our results showed a mere 7% difference between the two VMs. Of course, the printed benchmarks were run against JDK 1.1.4 from Sun, so the two tests are not the same. This discrepancy brings up another important point:

Don't use old benchmarks for current decisions.

Software, like everything else, changes, so rerun your benchmarks with every release as it is made available. You might be surprised with the results!

Validity of VolanoMark

As we mentioned at the beginning of the section on benchmarking, the results from the `VolanoMark` test suite may not give an accurate reading of VM performance. `VolanoMark` is a client/server test that runs on one machine. Since the entire idea of client/server programming is to separate processing across a network, results taken from `VolanoMark` should be interpreted accordingly.

So why bother presenting the `VolanoMark` results at all? Well, even partially flawed benchmarks illustrate the relative performance between different virtual machines. Additionally, the `VolanoMark` tests were touted as the "first JVM server benchmark," and a large number (authors included) of Java developers were affected by this article. Our opinions of the numbers changed, once we spent some time playing with the `VolanoMark` tests.

WebBench

To make a better test than `VolanoMark` you should separate clients onto different machines, reproducing the real case of external clients making requests to your server. Furthermore, the test should exercise what your server program is trying to accomplish, such as providing Web services in the case of the Java Web Server. Fortunately, you can use a program like WebBench from Ziff-Davis to gather statistics on JWS performance.

Once again, the server side of the test will run on our dual-processor PII system. However, two more systems are also needed: the *client* to make requests to the server and the *controller* to orchestrate what tests the client will run. As a picture, the testing layout looks like that in Figure 3-11.

Since there are more machines involved in the WebBench tests, we've put the machine descriptions in Table 3-3.

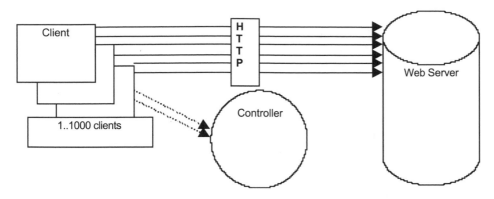

Figure 3-11 WebBench testing layout.

Table 3-3	Machines Participating in the WebBench Test

Role	*Machine Description*
Controller	Pentium 75 MHz, 64 MB RAM, 6 GB EIDE HD, Number Nine Imagine 128 video card, 3Com 3c905 100BT Ethernet Controller, Windows NT 4.0 Server w/SP3
Client	Pentium 233 MHz w/MMX, 128 MB RAM, 3 GB EIDE HD, Chips & Technology video card, 3Com 3c575 PCMCIA 100BT Ethernet Controller, Windows NT 4.0 Workstation w/SP3
Server	Dual Pentium II 300 MHz, 128 MB RAM, 9 GB Seagate Cheetah 10,000-rpm UW-SCSI drive, Adaptec 2940UW SCSI controller, Matrox Millennium II video card, Windows NT 4.0 Workstation w/SP3

Since this test is actually running across a network, knowing which network cards are being used is an important factor that can affect the outcome. Both the server and the controller are running "Vortex" 3Com 3C905 100Base-T adapters, and the laptop has a 3C575 100Base-T PCMCIA adapter, all of which are hooked into a LinkSys 100Base-T hub.

Getting WebBench

You can get the WebBench programs from the Ziff-Davis Web site at `http://www1.zdnet.com/zdbop/webbench/webbench.html`.

The WebBench test suite is a set of three programs, one for each role in the test procedure. `we20cl.exe` installs the client's files and `we20co.exe` installs the controller's files. There is a wide selection of files, depending on the hardware platform for the server role of the test. Since our server runs Windows NT, we retrieved `nt_x86.exe` from the Ziff-Davis Web site.

Installing the WebBench Client

After you've downloaded the `we20cl.exe` file from the Web, you'll want to execute it on your client machine. The file is a self-extracting archive containing the necessary files for installing the client. Start the installation process by running the `setup` program. The installation asks you to pick a destination directory. Next, you should be prompted for a "unique client ID," which is a number between 1 and 1000 (Figure 3-12). This ID must be unique among all of your client machines. Since our test uses one client, we used the ID "1" for our installation.

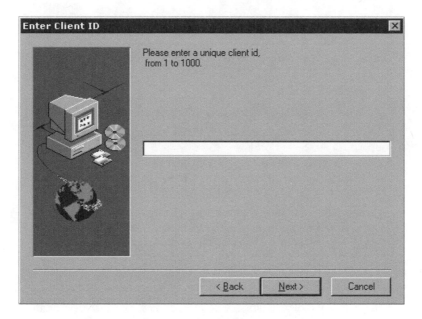

Figure 3-12   Choosing the client ID.

Once the software is installed, you'll need to make two new entries into the client's `hosts` file. The `hosts` file is used to convert easy-to-read machine names into network-friendly IP addresses. On Windows NT, the `hosts` file is found in the `winnt\system32\drivers\etc` directory. The two entries are for the controller and the server, and in our case the controller has the IP address 192.168.50.150 and the server has the IP address 192.168.50.151. With this information, the `hosts` file would look like:

```
192.168.50.150 controller
192.168.50.151 server
```

According to the WebBench documentation, you must use the name *controller* for the actual controller machine. More information can be found at the Ziff-Davis Web site and in the WebBench documentation.

Installing the WebBench Controller

The controller files are stored in the self-extracting archive `we20co.exe`. You start the installation by activating the setup executable. Unlike the client installation, the controller install only asks for a destination directory before it drops its files.

After the controller is installed, you can use its main control panel to edit, run, or review tests, as shown in Figure 3-13.

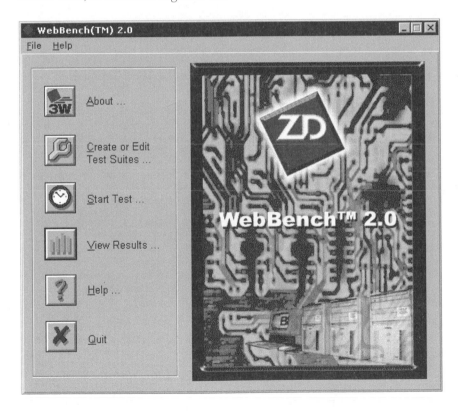

Figure 3-13　Controlling the WebBench test.

Installing the Server Test Files

With both the controller and the client installations completed, all that remains is to install the necessary server files. These server files contain static Web page content, the same type of content that you'd be served out on the Internet. WebBench uses this content in its standard `zd_static_v20.tst` benchmark, a battery of prewritten tests useful for stress-testing your Web server.

Just open up the self-extracting archive in your Java Web Server's `public_html` directory, and everything should be ready to go.

Running the WebBench

Stress-testing your Web server using the desired virtual machine is a simple, three-step process.

1. Start the controller.
2. Start the clients.
3. Run the test from the controller once all of the clients have connected.

When we ran our tests with the Java Web Server, we received roughly the same results that we got from the `VolanoMark` tests. We leave your own benchmarking with WebBench up to you; the framework it provides gives a tester a flexible structure for generating tests aimed at specific goals, such as timely content delivery and dynamic application scalability. More information on writing your own tests with WebBench can be found in the documentation accompanying the package or on the Ziff-Davis Web site.

Rolling Your Own Tests

Using someone else's testing tools is always a great time saver, but sometimes these general-use programs don't provide everything you need. For example, you may want to compare performance results on a servlet that you've written using HTTP and RMI. WebBench only gets you half of the information, as it doesn't have a mechanism for testing across the RMI protocol. It's these special cases that warrant writing your own tests.

Consider the example of a servlet handling a Web site's guest book. We wanted to test its performance under a moderate request load, so that our users wouldn't receive embarrassing error messages. To accomplish this goal, we put together a simple GUI that makes requests to the guest book via an HTTP POST and times the results.

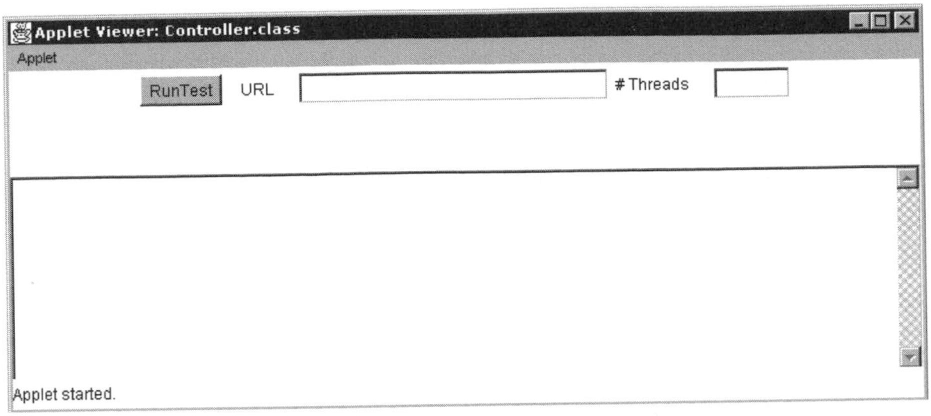

Figure 3-14   Simple testing GUI.

The GUI collects user-supplied information about the destination URL for testing and the number of concurrent threads that should make requests to that destination. In Listing 3-1, we've created a subclass of java.lang.Thread named TimedThread that tracks the time spent in its run method.

Listing 3-1   TimedThread.java

```java
public class TimedThread extends Thread
{
  private long delta = 0L;

  public TimedThread(Runnable r, String name)
  {
    super(r, name);
  }

  public void run ()
  {
    long start = System.currentTimeMillis();
    super.run();
    long stop  = System.currentTimeMillis();
    delta = stop - start;
  }

  public long getDelta ()
  {
    return delta;
  }
}
```

TimedThreads don't do any real work on their own. They need a Runnable object (passed through the constructor) to provide the meat of the testing process. In Listing 3-2, we created the WorkerThread class, which implements the Runnable interface, to provide the correct behavior.

Listing 3-2   WorkerThread.java

```java
import java.awt.*;
import java.net.*;
import java.io.*;

class WorkerThread implements Runnable
{
  private URL theURL;
  private String postData;

  public WorkerThread(URL theURL)
  {
    this.theURL = theURL;
  }

  public void run ()
  {
    String postData = "name=" +
                      Thread.currentThread().getName() +
                      "&email=" +
                      Thread.currentThread().getName()
                      + "@javasoft.com";
    int contentLength = doPOST(theURL, postData);
  }

  public int doPOST(URL theURL, String postData)
  {
      try
    {
      URLConnection conn = theURL.openConnection();
      conn.setDoOutput(true);
      conn.setUseCaches(false);
      PrintWriter pw = new
        PrintWriter(conn.getOutputStream());
      pw.println(postData);
      pw.flush();
      pw.close();

      conn.getContent();
```

```
    return 0;
  }
  catch(Exception e)
  {
    e.printStackTrace();
  }
  return 0;
  }
}
```

You might wonder why we didn't combine the two capabilities into a single TimedWorkerThread class, since an instance of the java.lang.Thread class is already a Runnable object. We separated them owing to a second design goal, because in the process of stress testing our servlet we wanted to end up with a framework that we could reuse for different applications. Since a TimedThread has no idea about the code that it is executing, it can be reused with any Runnable object.

Now, if you have any experience with professional-quality testing tools, you should notice that our architecture is a bit oversimplified. For starters, we create *way* too many threads for each atom of work accomplished. A better design would multiplex multiple requests on a single thread. Fortunately, with some minor adjustments to WorkerThread, you could have it run multiple requests without affecting any other part of the framework.

A second problem arises around the idea of time. With possibly thousands of threads contending for a single processor resource, each thread will artificially take longer to complete, skewing the timing results. Currently, Java threads don't have a portable way to retrieve anything but this *wall-clock* time, which makes it difficult to take accurate timing readings. Although, even with this ability, HTTP requests could receive better scores because the thread making the request won't get charged for the time if it isn't running. All of these issues need to be thought out when running your own benchmarks.

Summary

Now that you've finished reading this chapter, we hope you have a better sense for how the virtual machine works. Furthermore, you've ventured into the mad world of performance testing, yet you've (hopefully) developed a healthy disrespect for benchmarks in general.

Finally, you've learned the basics of administrating the Java Web Server. Although configuring virtual machines is only one small part of the administrative pie, it's an important piece to know. More administrative duties can be found in the next chapter, "Administrating the Java Web Server."

ADMINISTRATING THE JAVA WEB SERVER

Topics in This Chapter

- Defining How Web Servers Are Administrated
- Java Web Server Secrets and Shortcuts
- Utilizing the Admin Servlet

Chapter 4

Web servers, like any other complex program, require a certain amount of configuration in order to run. Options such as "what port should the server run on" and "where is the document root" come preconfigured, but these default values may not be right for your needs. Just to complicate matters for administrators, each Web server has its own particular method of administration, and the Java Web Server is no different. All administration tasks with the JWS are handled through a special Java applet called the Admin applet.

Our aim in this chapter is to ease the pain of administrating the Java Web Server by providing side notes and hints to common duties and tasks. Most of these little tidbits were gleaned from our hands-on work with the Java Web Server, and a few were tucked away within the accompanying HTML documentation.

How Are Web Servers Administrated?

Historically, we've seen two different styles of Web server administration. Older, UNIX-based freeware servers like NCSA and CERN read text files when they start up. These text files contain name/value pairs that are used to configure certain options in the server. When a configuration change is made, the server needs to be informed of the change, which in UNIX is typically accomplished with a "kill –SIGHUP [*pid of the server process*]".

Using text files for configuration is a mixed blessing. In its favor, text files are easy to manipulate with scripting languages like Perl, making it a snap to automate the configuration of multiple servers. A negative aspect is that any changes made to a configuration won't show up until the server is restarted, making configuration a trial-and-error task of "try this change and see if it works." Administrators would be better served if a program could assist with configuration tasks, which leads to the second style of Web server administration.

Newer, commercially sold servers like Netscape Enterprise Server and Microsoft Internet Information Server present administrators with a GUI program for making their configuration changes. A properly written GUI program can provide assistance when making such changes, reducing the learning curve for administration. In addition, these tools provide checks on the values entered by an administrator, so the server is guaranteed to start after the changes are made. On the other hand, it is more difficult to automate GUI tools than making changes to text files. Furthermore, these servers also need to be alerted explicitly when reconfigured; this is generally done by stopping and restarting their operation.

The engineers at JavaSoft combined the two administration approaches when they designed the Java Web Server. They wanted to offer a GUI tool for configuring the server, but one that would utilize text files to store the configuration changes. The text files themselves are of a special kind called a Properties file, which appears pervasively in Java.

Properties Files

A Properties file is a "frozen" copy of a Properties object, which itself is an instance of the class `java.util.Properties`. The Properties class is derived from the `Hashtable` class, so it can map keys to target values like its parent, with one exception. Instead of using arbitrary classes for the key and its associated value, a Properties object's keys are restricted to Java String objects. This "String to String" mapping makes it easy to change the "frozen" version of the object using common text-manipulation utilities like awk and Perl.

Creating a Properties object is a simple matter of making a new instance of the class, storing the appropriate values inside, and then "freezing" the object to a file. Listing 4-1 demonstrates this.

Listing 4-1   Playing with Properties

```
import java.io.*;
import java.util.*;

public class PropertiesTest
{
  public static void main (String[] args)
  {
    try
    {
```

```
   Properties p = new Properties();
   p.put("Book.Title","Core Java Web Server");
   p.put("Book.Author","Chris Taylor,Tim Kimmet");
   FileOutputStream fos =
    new FileOutputStream("book.props");
   p.save(fos,null);
   fos.close();
     }
     catch (IOException ioe)
     {
         ioe.printStackTrace();
     }
   }
 }
```

In this short example a Properties object was created with two stored values. The first is named "Book.Title" and has the value "Core Java Web Server". The second +is "Book.Author" and has the value "Chris Taylor, Tim Kimmet". Once the values have been stored in the Properties object, you can save the contents to a file called "book.props" using the save method.

Core Note

Notice how the key names can be ordered into hierarchies by using periods as separators. This technique is employed extensively by Java to create logical name-spaces for groups of properties (e.g., java.security.* for configuring parts of the Java security modules, AWT.* for configuring parts of the Abstract Windowing Toolkit, etc.).

There should be a file named "book.props" in the directory where you ran the example after compiling and executing the program. Use your favorite text editor (e.g., notepad on Windows or vi on UNIX) and open up that file for viewing.

```
#Thu May 07 01:17:18 PDT 1998
Book.Title=Core Java Web Server
Book.Author=Chris Taylor,Tim Kimmet
```

If you're familiar with UNIX configuration files or Windows INI files, you should recognize the tell-tale "name=value" pairs. Programs can ask for the value of a specific property by using the getProperty method:

```
Properties p = new Properties();
...
String myHomeDirectory = p.getProperty("home.dir");
```

Now let's go the other way and load the contents of the file into a Properties object. To make things more interesting, rearrange the author names in the "book.props" file in the following manner:

```
Book.Author=Chris Baylor, Tim Bimmet
```

Now let's read these properties in and see if the changes get registered, as shown in Listing 4-2.

Listing 4-2   Even More Properties Fun

```java
import java.io.*;
import java.util.*;

public class PropertiesTest2
{
  public static void main (String[] args)
  {
    try
    {
    FileInputStream fis =
    new FileInputStream("book.props");
    Properties p = new Properties();
    p.load(fis);
    p.list(System.out);
    }
    catch (IOException ioe)
    {
        ioe.printStackTrace();
    }
  }
}
```

Running this program should list two entries in the properties file loaded from the FileInputStream:

```
- listing properties -
Book.Title=Core Java Web Server
Book.Author=Chris Baylor, Tim Bimmet
```

Since a picture is worth a thousand lines of code, Figure 4-1 presents a pictorial representation of an application using a Properties object.

Now you can see why applications like the Java Web Server use Properties files, as they provide a "poor-man's database" for storing configuration information. The Java Web Server has a specific directory structure for where it puts its configuration files. They are kept in a subdirectory called "properties" off the server root. Underneath

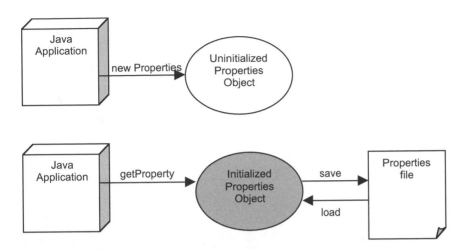

Figure 4-1   Using a Properties object.

the properties directory is another directory called "server." This is where all of the configuration settings for your entire server are kept. Underneath the server directory lies a directory for each individual server (javawebserver, adminserver). This way you run multiple servers (HTTP, SMTP, NNTP, etc...) from the same installation directory.

As we are interested in the Java Web Server, we'll spend most of our configuration time in the `javawebserver` subdirectory. Beneath the server directory are all of the services (webpageservice, proxyservice, secureservice, etc...). When we start discussing configuration settings using the Admin applet later in this chapter, we'll show you how to accomplish the same configuration task by manipulating the appropriate Properties files directly.

Don't let all of these code examples scare you into thinking that you'll have to program to make configuration changes to the Java Web Server. A GUI tool will handle all of this messiness for you.

Speaking of the GUI tool...

The Admin Applet:
A JWS Administrator's Best Friend

Remember when we said the Java Web Server was a 100% Pure Java product? That goes for its configuration GUI as well, since it is a Java applet. Furthermore, the Java Web Server team realized that the majority of Java-enabled Web browsers support JDK 1.0.2, so the Admin applet is written to that API. As a result, you can configure the Java Web Server from any Java-capable Web browser.

When you installed the Java Web Server in Chapter 2, you used your Web browser to test if the installation was successful. Let's do the same thing again, except this time use the URL `http://localhost:9090`.

Once your browser finishes loading the Admin applet, you should see a prompt for a logon name and password, as shown in Figure 4-2.

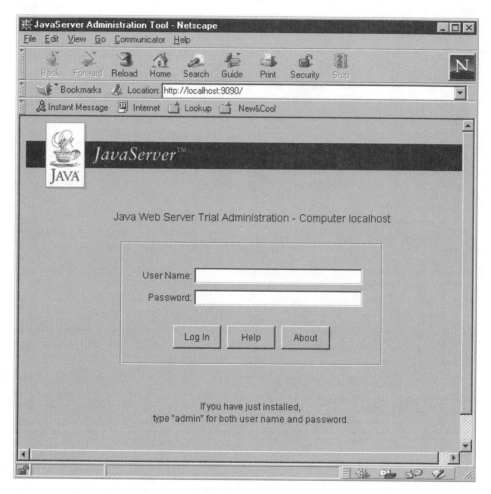

Figure 4-2   Login to the Admin applet.

As this is the first time you've logged in, you should use the name `"admin"` and password `"admin"` suggested by the text beneath the login panel. If you make a mistake logging in, the applet will complain, as in Figure 4-3.

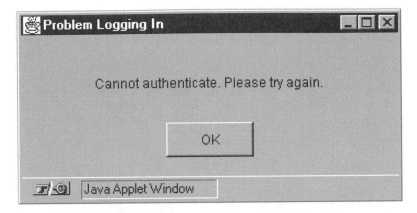

Figure 4-3   Oops! Login problem.

Once you are logged in, you'll be greeted by the service overview panel.

On it, you should see three services: Web Service, Secure Web Service, and Proxy Service. Of the three, only the Web Service should be in the running state.

The next most important after the status field is the version field. Knowing the version of the software you are running is extremely helpful when you are trying to locate the source of possible bugs in your system. You should periodically check the Java Web Server Web site at http://www.javasoft.com/jserv for updates and bug fixes. Some of your problems could be attributed to the version of the Java Web Server you are running, which you'll know by reading the updated bug list.

Core Alert

This happened to us while we were writing this book. Java Web Server v1.1 had a
problem with spurious servlet creation that was fixed in the v1.1.1 release.

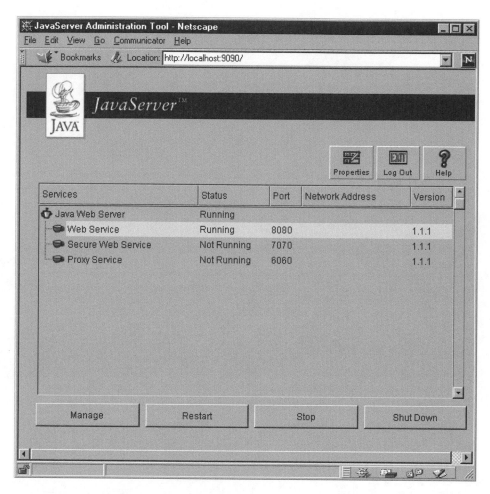

Figure 4-4   The service overview panel.

Beneath the list of services is the button panel. There should be four buttons listed: `Manage`, `Restart`, `Stop`, and `Shutdown`. Their functions are listed in Table 4-1.

The only option that requires further exploration is the manage function. Select the "Web Service" and click on the `Manage` button to invoke the service management panel, as shown in Figure 4-5.

Core Tip

You can double-click on the service name to invoke the service management panel as well.

Table 4-1	Functions of Service Overview Panel

Function	Description
Manage	Open up the service management panel for the selected service. This panel is customized for the service being administered.
Restart	Shut down the selected service. Once the service is shut down, restart it.
Stop	Shut down the selected service.
Shut down	This selection shouldn't be in the same area as the other three, as it applies to all of the services. When selected, all of the running services will be shut down, and then the main server will quit. This is the best way to perform a clean shutdown of the system.

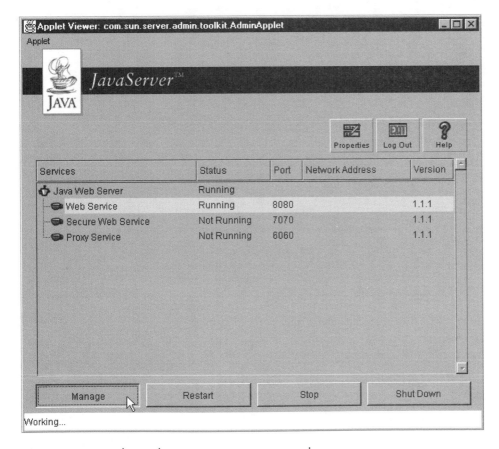

Figure 4-5   Exploring the service management panel.

The service management panel is where you'll spend a majority of your time configuring the server. The panel contains a main task bar with four icons (`Setup`, `Monitor`, `Security`, and `Servlets`), a tree control listing all of the configurable sections for this task, and a view area for the currently selected section.

Before we go on to various administrative tasks, we'd like to show you what's happening beneath the covers of the Admin applet as you navigate through the various configuration options. The applet is only the client portion of a special client/server pair designed for configuration tasks. On the server side is a special program called the Admin servlet. Owing to the network restrictions created by firewalls, the designers at JavaSoft decided that the only reliable transport for passing configuration information from the client to the server and back is HTTP. All changes to the system are encapsulated in HTTP POST requests (like a form submission on a Web page) sent by the Admin applet, and the results of the update are couched in an HTTP response message sent back from the Admin servlet, as seen in Figure 4-6.

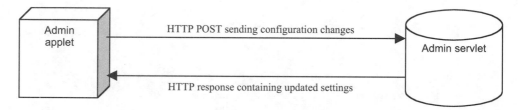

Figure 4-6   Admin applet and servlet communicating.

Requests and responses are protected using the Digest security scheme (which is a one-way hash function that guarantees data hasn't been tampered with after transmission).

Core Note

More details on how the Admin applet and Admin servlet work together can be found in the Java Server Toolkit documentation (check out `http://jserv.javasoft.com` *for more details).*

Now that you've got a handle on how the Admin applet works to configure the Java Web Server, it is time to try your hand at some typical administrative tasks.

Changing the Admin Password

Once you've successfully logged into the Admin applet, the very first thing you'll want to do is change the administrator's password. You can change the password from the Service Overview Panel. Click on the button labeled `Properties` in the upper right-hand corner, as shown in Figure 4-7.

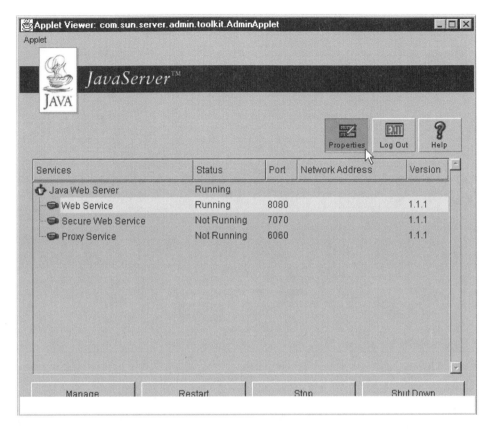

Figure 4-7   Clicking on the Properties button.

Next you should see a dialog titled "JavaServer Administration Tool—Properties." This dialog contains a three-tabbed panel. Select the tab labeled "Admin Password." This is where you can change the administrator's password. Just type your new password twice, once per text field, and press the "OK" button. You can see this in action in Figure 4-8.

Changing the Document Root

When a Web server gets a request for a Web page, it needs to look somewhere on the hard disk for the target file. Instead of using the root directory of the file system, you can configure the Web server to use some other directory as the "virtual" root directory for the search. This directory is called the *document root*. When the Java Web Server is first installed, it creates a subdirectory named `public_html` as the initial document root.

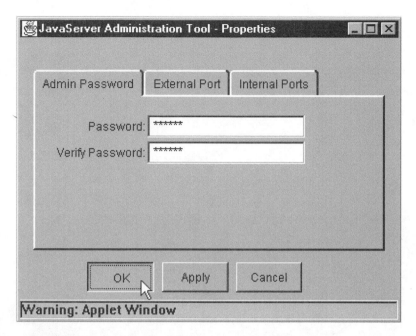

Figure 4-8   Changing the administrator's password.

You might want to change the document root for any of the following reasons:

- You want to share Web pages with another server that already has a document root.
- You want the Web pages to load from a different disk than the Java Web Server.
- You want the Web pages to load from across the network.

Whatever your reasons, changing the document root begins by opening up the service configuration panel. Navigate through the interface to the `site` setup option in the tree control, and then you should see the site configuration panel in the view area (Figure 4-9).

As you can see, we've changed our document root to `e:\web_pages`. After editing the field, click the save button to make your change permanent.

You aren't restricted to using an absolute directory path. All relative directory paths (such as `public_html`) are resolved as starting beneath the Java Web Server installation directory (a.k.a *server_root*). So, if you made a directory called `foo_pages` beneath the *server_root*, the document root would be `foo_pages`.

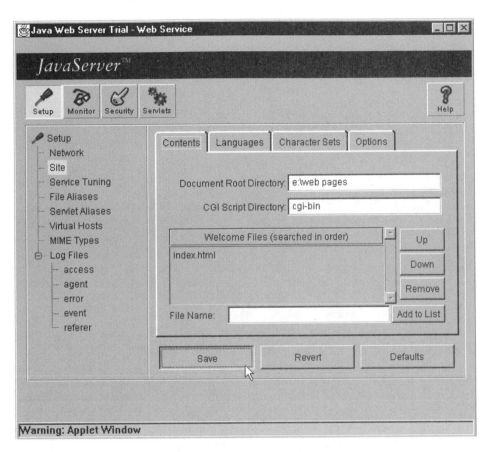

Figure 4-9   Changing the document root.

Core Note

When you make a change to the document root, the Java Web Server doesn't verify whether the document root directory exists until you actually try and access it. If you've misconfigured these settings, a client browser will receive an HTTP/1.1 403 Forbidden *error (you're forbidden to get anything from a directory that doesn't exist).*

The document root value is stored in the Properties file doc.properties, which is stored in the *server_root*\server\javawebserver\ webpageservice directory:

    doc.root=e:\web pages

If you modify the value for doc.root, restart the Java Web Server for it to take effect.

Changing the Port and IP Address of the Server

When the Java Web Server is run for the first time, it binds to all of the available network interfaces on TCP port 8080. If you want JWS to be your primary Web server, you'll want to change it to the default Web port of 80.

Core Note

On UNIX systems, only privileged processes running as root may bind to a port less than 1024. This is one of the big reasons why the Java Web Server is preconfigured to start on port 8080. You'll need to be root to make this change on a UNIX machine.

To make the change, navigate to the `network` entry in the tree control, and the network control panel should appear in the view area. You should see a field labeled "Port" with the value of 8080. Change that number to 80 (or to whatever number you want the server to run on), then press the `restart` button. This change is illustrated in Figure 4-10.

If you've got several network cards (including a modem connection), the *provide service on* setting gives you some added flexibility. Like we said earlier, the Java Web Server binds to all of the available network interfaces when it starts. In some situations you may only want to run on one of those interfaces, restricting Web access to a single subnet. For example, if your machine is acting as a gateway between your network and someone else's network, you'll want your JWS-based intranet to be visible only to you. In this case, you'll want to change the network address settings from "All Network Addresses" to "Network Address" and fill in the text field with the host name or the IP address of the network interface you want the server to use. Figure 4-11 illustrates this configuration setup.

Core Note

Currently, the only endpoint options available with JWS are binding to all interfaces or binding to one interface only.

In the graphical example, you'd want to bind to IP address 192.168.50.1 and *not* 192.168.51.1. By specifying the desired IP address in the text field and saving those changes, you'll provide service only to the one subnet (192.168.50.X). You can see this change made in Figure 4-12.

Web developers may want to change the IP address to the localhost interface (127.0.0.1). Using the localhost interface will permit only programs running on the same machine as the Java Web Server to access its services (i.e., Netscape Communicator for testing, etc.), which is an excellent way to restrict other people from browsing your site before it's ready.

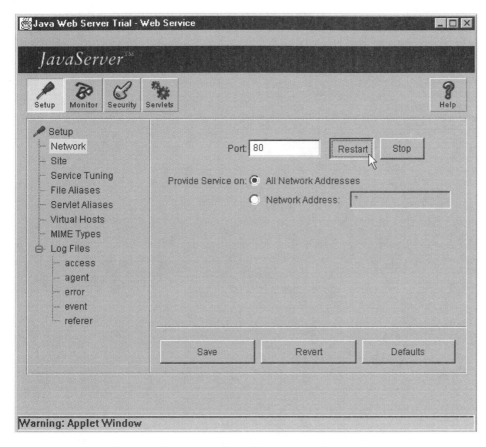

Figure 4-10   Changing the port number of the Java Web Server..

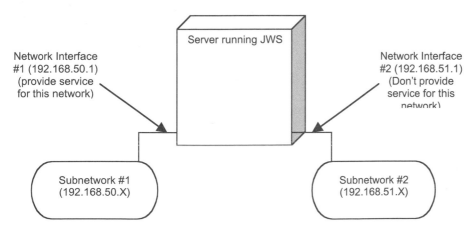

Figure 4-11   A dual-homed host running JWS.

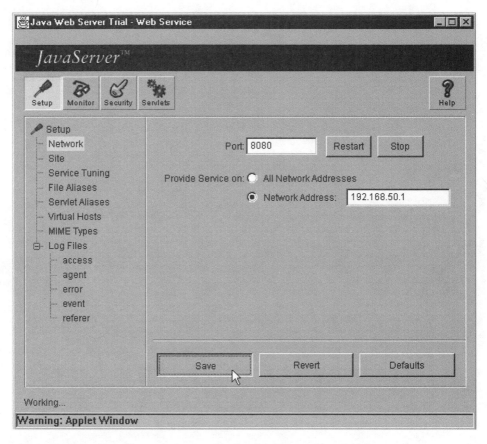

Figure 4-12 Configuration options for binding to a single IP address.

You can also hand-edit the special Properties file `endpoint.properties` to get the same configuration results. This file is stored at *server_root*\server\ `javawebserver`\`webpageservice` directory, and contains two lines for you to change:

```
endpoint.main.interface=* // Change to the IP address or hostname of
                           // your choice
```

```
endpoint.main.port=8080  // Change to the port of your choice (80)
```

Once you've made the changes, save the files and restart the Java Web Server to verify the results.

Configuring Virtual Directories

Most of you don't have the luxury of having a T-1 (a high-speed network connection) piped into your homes. Strapped with the bandwidth problems that come with a 33.6K modem, you'll typically have your ISP (Internet Service Provider—AOL, Netcom, Flashnet, etc.) host your Web sites on their Web server (which should *hopefully* be connected to a T-3).

So, while you may not host your Web site on your home machine, a lot of you (especially those running small businesses) have your own *domain names*.

Core Note

microsoft.com, javasoft.com, and ibm.com are all examples of domain names. A special protocol called DNS (Domain Name Services) makes these names available to programs like Web browsers for location purposes ("where is www.foo-software.com?")

When prospective clients want to access your Web site to find out more about you, you'd like them to type:

```
http://www.your-company.com
```

But if your site is housed on a shared server at your ISP, this name must map their name to your ISP's Web server IP address. In this shared situation, how can the Web server differentiate requests for

```
http://www.isp.com
```

and

```
http://www.your-company.com
```

if they exist on the same machine? Does a Web browser tell the server what host they're looking for?

The answer is: yes and no. Before the introduction of HTTP/1.1, when a Web browser made a request, it didn't say which host it was looking for. The only portion of the request that the server could use to separate Web sites was the server's IP address and port number. Using different port numbers was out of the question, since no one wanted to have their site's URL be:

```
http://www.your-company.com:8000
```

leaving the IP address as the only differentiating factor. Under this scheme, an ISP was forced to waste an entire IP address for each domain name. A machine could literally have tens of IP addresses mapped to a single network interface just for this purpose. There had to be a better way! Figure 4-13 shows this dilemma in graphic detail.

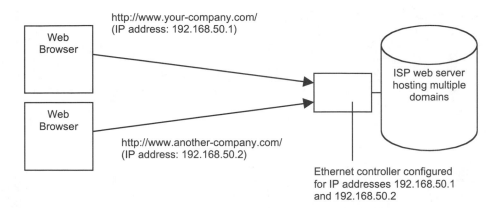

Figure 4-13   Handling multiple domains the old-fashioned way.

When the W3 (`http://www.w3.org`, where all Web-related standards are maintained) and contributing members started to work on HTTP/1.1, they realized that this IP Address-for-each-domain-name hack needed to be fixed. They addressed the problem by introducing a special HTTP header (see the chapter on HTTP for more information on the HTTP protocol) called "host," which would carry the destination Web site's hostname in the request. Web servers that were HTTP/1.1-compliant could use this header to know which domain should handle the request. This technique is known as *virtual hosting*, and you can see it in action in Figure 4-14.

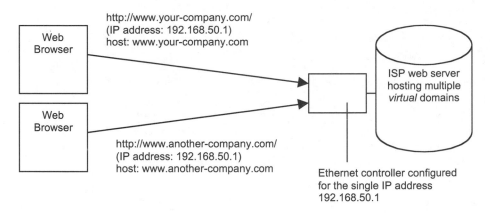

Figure 4-14   Using the host HTTP header to handle multiple domains.

The Java Web Server, because it complies with the HTTP/1.1 protocol, supports virtual hosting. Configuring multiple domains for a Web server is a three-step process:

1. Register the domain name with the IP address of the Web server (DNS).
2. Create a directory to host the site's Web pages.
3. Add the virtual host to the Java Web Server.

Register the Domain Name

Registering the domain name is something you should ask your ISP to handle for you (if they are already the administrative authority for your domain), or if you are handling your own domain you'll need to make an ADDRESS record (A record) in your DNS map (administrating the DNS protocol is beyond the scope of this book, but a good primer to check out is O'Reilly's *DNS and Bind*).

Create a Directory for the Site

You'll need to make a directory to store the site's Web content. You can make the directory as a subdirectory of the Java Web Server installation, or as a separate directory all together (follow the same rules that apply to the previous section on *changing the document root*).

Core Note

Each site must share the Java Web Server's CGI-bin directory (`server_root`\cgi-bin).

Add the Virtual Host to the Java Web Server

With the domain name mapped to the server's IP address and the content directory prepared, open up the Admin applet and navigate to the `virtual hosts` node in the service configuration panel's tree control. Select the add button at the bottom of the panel, and then type in the domain name of the virtual host (i.e., `www.your-company.com`). In the Document Root column put the directory that you created in the previous step (i.e., `e:\web pages`). Check out Figure 4-15 for a visual.

In our example, we've mapped the virtual host `flobee` to the directory `d:\flobee`. The final step is to test that the installation was successful. Open up your Web browser and access your virtual host's domain name (i.e., `http://flobee`). If the right content appears, you were successful!

You can also hand-edit the special Properties file `doc.properties` to get the same configuration results. This file is stored at the *server_root*\server\ javawebserver\webpageservice directory. To add a virtual host, just add a line that says:

```
doc.root.[hostname]=[directory]
```

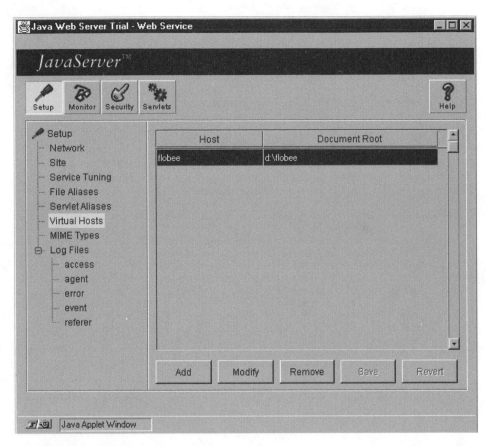

Figure 4-15   Adding a virtual host.

So, our example would be:

```
doc.root.flobee=d:\flobee
```

After saving the file, restart the Java Web Server for the changes to take effect.

Configuring File Aliases

If you've hosted your Web pages on a UNIX machine before, you've probably noticed that in your home directory (the directory where all of your files are kept) is a file named `public_html`. Sometimes that file is a symbolic link (a special UNIX file that points to another file) to a directory in the Web server's content tree (i.e., beneath `public_html` in the Java Web Server's installation directory), but other times it is a "real" directory. Often you'll access your site using a URL like `http://www.isp.com/~cstaylor` or `http://www.isp.com/users/tkimmet`.

How does the Web server know to look beneath your home directory instead of under the document root? In the case of the Java Web Server, it keeps a special list of URL-to-directory mappings called `file aliases`.

Imagine that you had a large number of Java applets that you wanted to serve to your clients. Instead of placing those files in the main content tree, you wanted to put them in a special directory somewhere else on the disk. First, make a directory to store your applet code (for example, `d:\java-applets`). Next, open up the Admin applet and navigate to the `file aliases` tree entry in the service configuration panel. Click on the `add` button to add a blank entry. The `column alias pathname` field holds the Web *resource location* of the directory. Edit the column `alias pathname`, and enter the path `/java`. In the `full pathname` column put `d:\java-applets`, and save your changes so they can take effect. This procedure is illustrated in Figure 4-16.

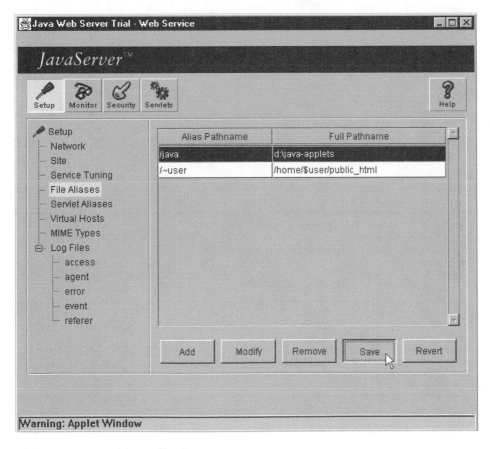

Figure 4-16 Adding a file alias.

To test our example, we've put together in Listing 4-3 an *extremely* simple applet, called `AliasTester`.

Listing 4-3   The AliasTester applet

```java
import java.applet.*;
import java.awt.*;

public class AliasTester extends Applet
{
  public void paint (Graphics g)
  {
    Font f = g.getFont();
    FontMetrics fm = getFontMetrics(f);
    String text = "Java is Rad!";
    Rectangle rect = bounds();
    int draw_x = rect.width/2  - fm.stringWidth(text)/2;
  int draw_y = rect.height/2 - fm.getHeight()/2;
    g.drawString(text,draw_x,draw_y);
  }

}
```

After compiling this source code, place the resulting class file in the `d:\java-applets` directory. Next, make a Web page named `AliasTester.html` to load the applet, as shown in Listing 4-4.

Listing 4-4   AliasTester.html

```html
<html>
<head>
<title>AliasTester</title>
<body>
<applet code="AliasTester.class" codebase="/java"
 width=300 height=200>
</applet>
</body>
</html>
```

Notice the added `codebase` attribute to the `applet` tag. This will tell the Web browser to look for our `AliasTester` applet at `http://localhost/java` instead of the same document base as this Web page (`http://localhost/`).

Finally, place this HTML file into `public_html` beneath the Java Web Server installation directory.

Now for the test! We opened up Netscape Communicator and pointed it at `http://localhost/AliasTester.html`. The evidence is laid out clearly in Figure 4-17.

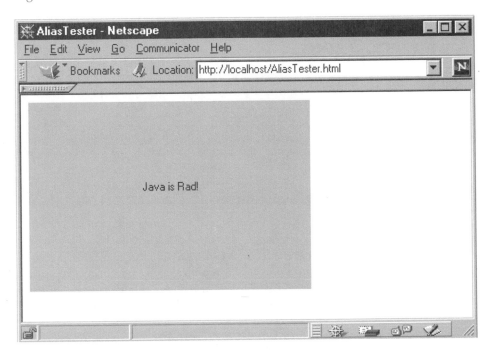

Figure 4-17 The file alias worked!

What just happened here? First off, the browser downloaded the file `AliasTester.html`. While rendering the page, it ran across the `applet` tag, so it needed to find the class file `AliasTester.class`. By specifying the `codebase` attribute in the applet tag, the browser downloaded the class file from `http://localhost/java`. When the request for the file `/java/AliasTester.class` was received by the Java Web Server, it looked to see if any file aliases would correspond to that URL. It found the mapping `/java->d:\java-applets`, so it looked in the directory `d:\java-applets` for the `AliasTester` class.

Core Note

File mappings are always checked before searching the hard disk. Therefore, if you had made a directory beneath `server_root`*public_html called java, the Web server would have ignored it completely, owing to the existing file alias.*

File aliases are stored in the file `aliases.properties`. You'd add an alias like the one in our example by adding the line:

```
/java=d:\java-applets
```

The syntax is `[virtual path]=[physical path]`. Once you've made your changes, save the file and restart the server for it to take effect.

Configuring Servlets

Most of your administrative duties will surround servlet configuration. As the next chapter details, servlets are Java objects that extend the functionality of the Java Web Server. They're similar to CGI scripts, as they add dynamic capabilities to a Web server, but they do it without a loss of performance. When you receive (or develop) a servlet, it comes "packaged" in one of two ways: plain servlets or configured servlet beans.

Installing, Configuring, and Removing Plain Servlets

Any Java class that implements the `javax.servlet.Servlet` interface can be called a *plain servlet*. Unlike a servlet bean (which is discussed later), a plain servlet is a class without some stored instance data. As an administrator, it is your responsibility to give the servlet the appropriate information it needs to get properly instantiated. Imagine that a plain servlet is like a cookie cutter—it provides the basic shape of the servlet, but it's up to the administrator to provide the sprinkles and frosting! You can decorate your servlets using the service configuration panel's `servlets` toolbar button (see Figure 4-18 for more details).

Notice that the tree control has a large list of servlets already installed into the system. Some of these servlets are essential to the Java Web Server. For example, the `File` servlet retrieves files from the hard disk and sends them to the client. It also caches the data so it can achieve better response times in the future. The `Invoker` servlet acts as a dispatcher for activating other servlets when a request comes in. In all, six "essential" servlets come with the Java Web Server:

- CGI
- Imagemap
- File
- Invoker
- SSInclude
- Admin

These servlets work together to make the Java Web Server work.

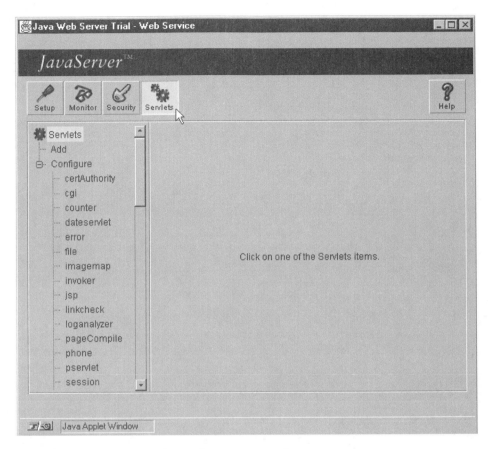

Figure 4-18   Inspecting the servlets.

Besides these essential servlets, some "extra" servlets supply extended capabilities. For example, the `pageCompile` servlet lets a Web developer embed Java code inside of a Web page for processing during a request. The `jsp` servlet is the "next-generation page-compiler" servlet, with newer features like servlet-bean support within HTML. While neither of these two features is required for standard Web activities, they make life easier for the developer.

Finally, beyond the essential servlets and the extras, there are a number of demonstration servlets for learning purposes. Each of these demos illustrates a different Web-related problem to be solved. Since these servlets aren't required by the Java Web Server to work correctly, you can use them to experiment with servlet administration.

Let's start playing with the `counter` servlet, which is one of the demonstration servlets. The `counter` servlet shows a simple example of how to utilize HTTP cookies. You can see the `counter` in action by opening your Web browser to `http://localhost/servlet/counter` (Figure 4-19).

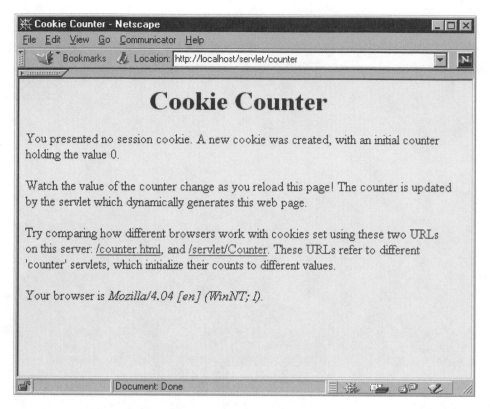

Figure 4-19   The cookie counter.

Now let's play with its settings. Open up the service configuration panel and navigate to the servlet section. You should find the tree-control entry for counter right below the `cgi` entry and above the `dataservlet` entry (the servlets are listed in alphabetical order). Figure 4-20 shows this tree control.

Once you click on the `counter` servlet's entry, there should be a two-tabbed display in the view area. The first tab is labeled `configuration`, and the second is labeled `properties`. The `configuration` tab is used to describe where and when a specific servlet should be loaded. Once you've got that squared away, you can use the `properties` tab to spread those sprinkles and frosting on a servlet instance.

Since the `counter` servlet has already been installed, you can look at its existing configuration settings. The configuration panel is split into two areas: the "when" area at the top and the "where" area within the frame labeled "Load Servlet Class Remotely" at the bottom. The configuration panel is shown in Figure 4-21.

Almost all of the settings are editable, with the name field being the sole exception.

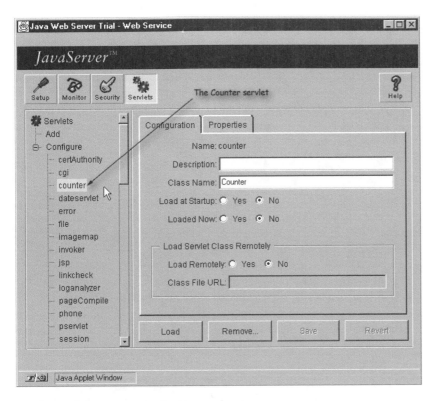

Figure 4-20   Inspecting the counter servlet.

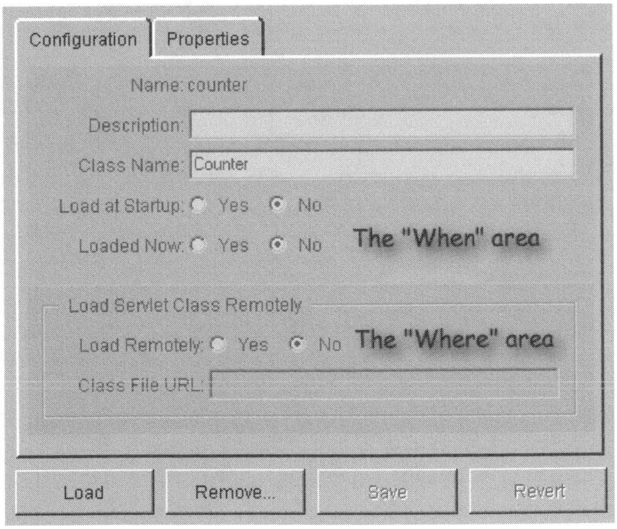

Figure 4-21   The configuration panel split between "when" and "where."

Core Note

The only way to rename a servlet is to delete the current entry and create a new one with the new name.

There are four fields to configure in the "when" area:

- Description
- Class name
- Load at startup
- Loaded now

You can add a comment about a servlet in the `description` field. It's not used for any purposes beyond documentation, so most of the time it is left blank (as in the `counter` example). The class-name field contains the fully qualified Java class name of the servlet. The counter servlet resides in the default package, so its class name is Counter. Other servlets such as the File servlet exist in packages. When you add a servlet that is in a package, use the complete name for the class-name entry (e.g., if the package name is `com.servlets` and the class name is `TestServlet`, use the string `com.servlets.TestServlet` as the value for the class-name field).

Core Note

The Java Web Server uses a ClassLoader to load its servlets. Servlets are loaded by name using the `Class.forName(String)` *static method, and this call requires the complete name of the class (package name + class name).*

Servlet instances are created either at Web server startup time ("eager initialization") or when they are first accessed ("lazy initialization"). The `load at startup` field lets an administrator control when a servlet gets created. We suggest that your servlets be lazy and start only when they are needed—for two reasons:

- No memory is wasted with servlets that aren't being used.
- Startup time for the Java Web Server is faster.

The `loaded now` radio box plays a double role as a view of the current state of the servlet and a control to change that state. It's like a light switch on your bedroom wall. You know by looking at the switch if power isn't being sent to the lights, and you can toggle the switch to turn them on. If we look at the counter servlet through the Admin applet, we can see if it's a lazy servlet *and* if it's loaded into memory (Figure 4-22).

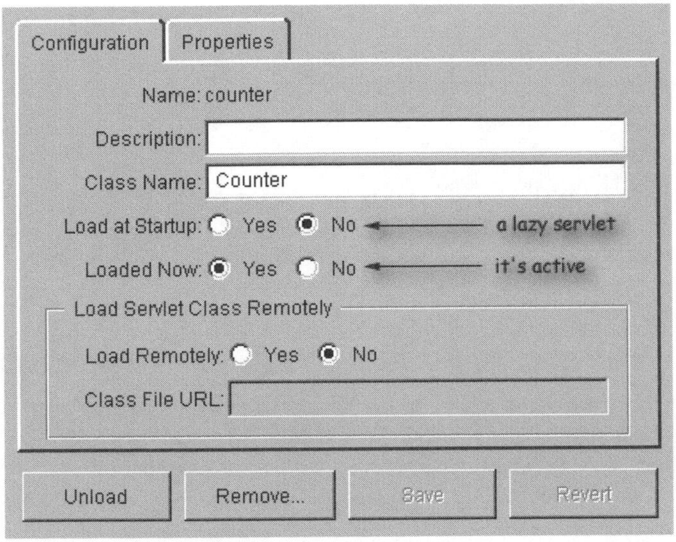

Configuration | Properties

Name: counter

Description: [   ]

Class Name: [Counter   ]

Load at Startup: ○ Yes ◉ No ◄———— *a lazy servlet*

Loaded Now: ◉ Yes ○ No ◄———— *it's active*

Load Servlet Class Remotely

Load Remotely: ○ Yes ◉ No

Class File URL: [   ]

[Unload] [Remove...] [Save] [Revert]

Figure 4-22   Reading the blinking lights on a servlet's dashboard.

Core Note

You can also use the `Load/Unload` *button beneath the configuration panel to view/change the state of a servlet.*

So what's with the "where" portion of the `configuration` panel? Servlets can be loaded locally from the same machine that the Java Web Server is running on, or they can be loaded remotely from another machine across the HTTP protocol.

Core Note

Yes, Virginia, just like applets.

Of course, servlet classes that are loaded remotely are subject to security restrictions, just like their applet cousins. More information on security within the Java Web Server follows later on in the chapter.

So, if you had wanted to load the counter class from another machine, you would specify that the counter servlet was remotely loaded, and then you would put the URL (including the trailing slash) of the server. For example, if the counter servlet on my machine were stored on *timbo* (Tim's laptop) underneath his `java_classes` directory, the proper configuration would be as shown in Figure 4-23.

We could think of only two reasons for using this remote servlet loading feature:

- Centralized distribution
- License management

All we mean by centralizing distribution is to place all of your servlet code on one Web server and have all of the other Web servers download servlets from the master. Having an entire fleet of servers pulling their servlets from one place makes upgrading a snap. Furthermore, you can keep track of which machines are using your servlets by parsing the distribution server's access log.

Core Note

The Java Web Server has a set of logs for tracking accesses to Web resources, errors, and system events. You can read more about logging later in the chapter.

Once you've got everyone pulling servlet code down from one machine, you can protect access to the code, maintaining the proper licensing agreements. In short, licensing means everyone who should get paid, does. You can track the servers that are using particular servlets by trapping requests for the class files. We've put together a special class named `LicenseServlet` to act as the trap, and this trap is visualized in Figure 4-24.

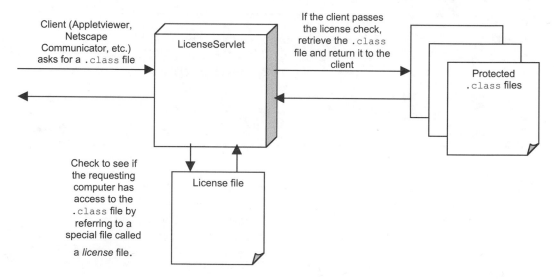

Figure 4-24   Trapping requests for .class files for licensing purposes.

Core Note

The LicenseServlet's _source code is on the CD-ROM._

Before moving on to customizing servlets, we neglected to mention how a servlet gets invoked in the first place. Take a second look at the URL you used to check out the counter servlet:

```
http://localhost/servlet/counter
```

The /servlet path prefix tells the Java Web Server that you're asking for a servlet to handle this request. When a request beginning with /servlet is received by the Java Web Server, it passes the request on to the Invoker servlet. So the next logical question is, "How does the Java Web Server know to pass these requests on to the Invoker servlet?" That decision is based on "servlet aliasing," which is the topic of the next section.

Now, back to customizing a servlet. Click on the properties tab on the servlet configuration panel, and you should be presented with a screen similar to that found in Figure 4-25.

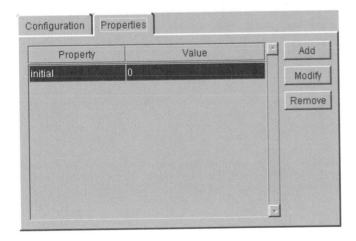

Figure 4-25   Customizing a servlet.

There is a table control in the center of the panel, and it contains two columns. The first is marked "Property" and the second, "Value". When a servlet is created by the Java Web Server, it can access these properties through a call to getInitParameter(String). (More information about this and other servlet programming APIs is given in the Chapter 5, "Generic Servlets.")

Looking at the table control, you can see that the counter servlet has a single parameter defined for it in the properties panel. This parameter is named initial, and it has the value "0.' What could the counter servlet be using this parameter for?

Remember when you accessed the servlet through the Netscape browser? It mentioned something about "initial value," and then it said you had accessed the servlet "0" times. This "initial value" came from the property! To test the theory, change the value of the property (Figure 4-26) to "5", toggle the servlet's loaded now light switch, and reconnect with the Web browser. Once connected, you should see something like the picture in Figure 4-27.

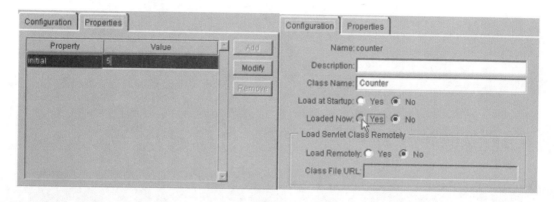

Figure 4-26   Changing the initial counter and restarting the servlet.

Core Note

To change a property, you can select the value field and then press the Modify *button, or you can simply double-click the value field directly. You know you are in editing mode when the blue background on the text field turns a brighter shade of blue.*

Success! You've configured your first servlet! Well, not quite. You *changed* the configuration of an *existing* servlet.

It's time to learn how to add a new servlet to the Java Web Server.

Looking back at the servlet configuration panel, you should see at the top of the tree control a special branch labeled Add. Click on the Add entry, and a new panel should appear in the view area (Figure 4-28).

This panel is split into two pieces. At the top you create the name for the servlet and its corresponding Java class. At the bottom is a separate area used for servlet beans, which you'll ignore for right now. Since you don't have a new servlet to install, why not do the next best thing and create a new servlet entry for the counter servlet? This way you can configure separate instances of the same class with different values for the initial property.

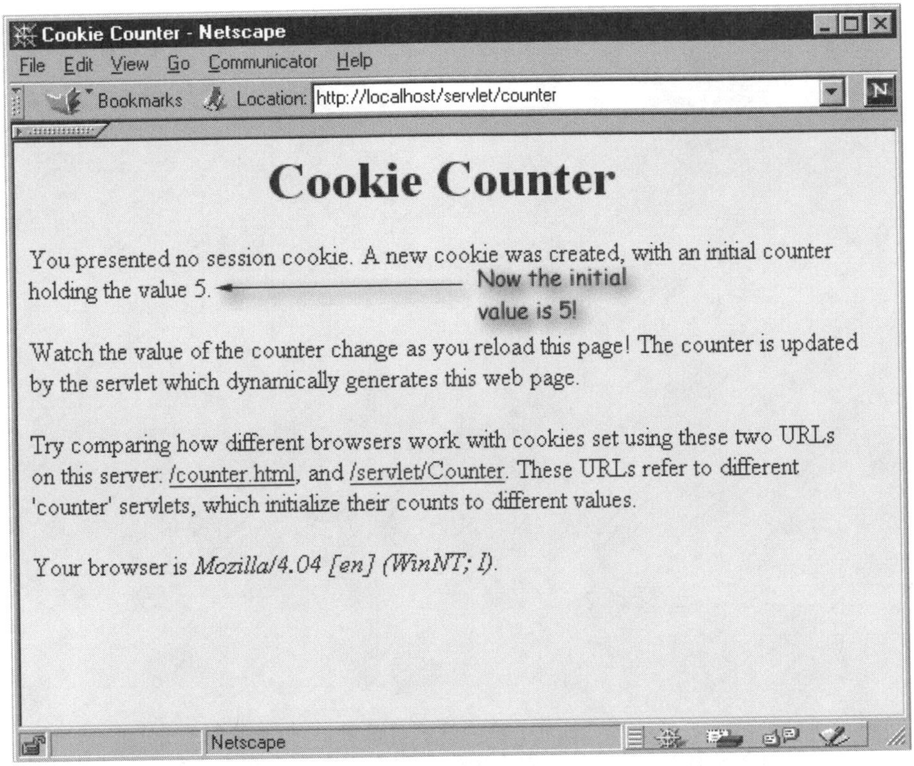

Cookie Counter - Netscape

File Edit View Go Communicator Help

Bookmarks & Location: http://localhost/servlet/counter

Cookie Counter

You presented no session cookie. A new cookie was created, with an initial counter holding the value 5. ←——————— *Now the initial value is 5!*

Watch the value of the counter change as you reload this page! The counter is updated by the servlet which dynamically generates this web page.

Try comparing how different browsers work with cookies set using these two URLs on this server: /counter.html, and /servlet/Counter. These URLs refer to different 'counter' servlets, which initialize their counts to different values.

Your browser is *Mozilla/4.04 [en] (WinNT; I)*.

Netscape

Figure 4-27 Now the initial value is "5"!

Core Note

Servlets are singleton objects, which means that there is one object shared by all incoming requests—that is, one instance per servlet entry, not one instance per class. Multiple servlet entries that use the same class will have multiple instances in memory, so data is not automatically shared between these instances (although static data is shared among all of the instances because they belong to the same class).

Name this new entry `counter2`, and use the same class name, `Counter` (Figure 4-29).

If you've accidentally clashed with a name that already exists, you'll get a response back from the Admin applet reporting the error (Figure 4-30).

After you've successfully created the new servlet entry, you should be on familiar territory as you're sent back to the `configuration` and `properties` tabs for the new servlet. Open up the properties tab and press the `add` button to create a new property for your `counter2` servlet. A new row should appear in blue beneath the

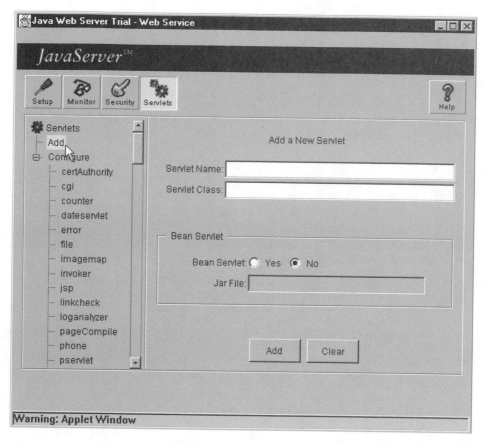

Figure 4-28   Adding a new servlet.

title bar of the table. In the property field type "initial" and start the counter off at two by putting a "2" in the value field. Press the Save button at the bottom of the configuration panel, and then send your Web browser to `http://localhost/servlet/counter2`. Figure 4-31 shows the results of contacting the `counter` servlet.

Core Tip

If you didn't receive the same view as the screen shot, close all of your browser windows, restart the browser, and reconnect to the `counter2` servlet. Owing to how the `Counter` class works internally, any remaining cookies from an old session can change your output.

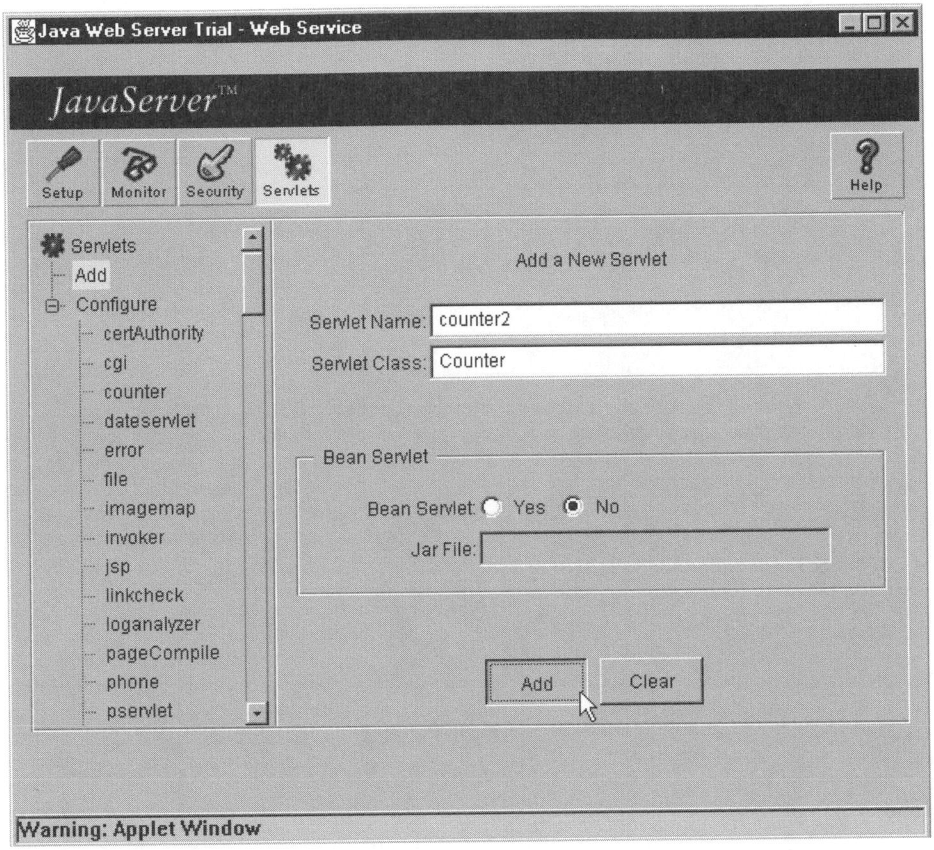

Figure 4-29   Making a new counter.

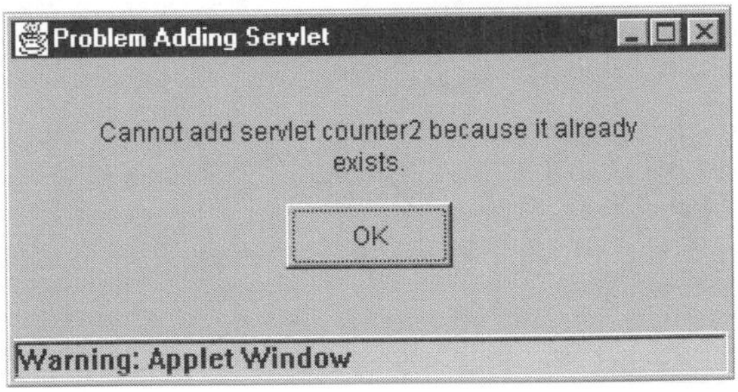

Figure 4-30   Oops! The name already exists!

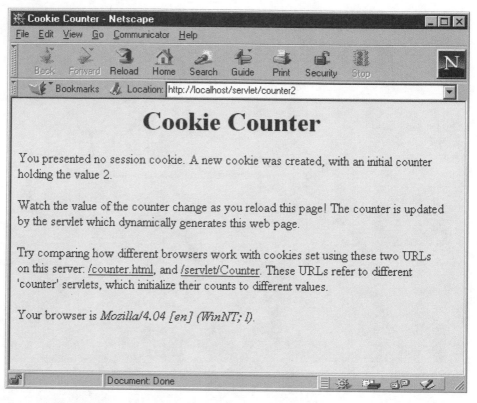

Figure 4-31   Visiting the counter2 servlet

Bravo! You've successfully added a servlet to the Java Web Server. The only task that remains for you to learn is how to remove a servlet. Fortunately, removing a servlet is the easiest of the three (installing, configuring, and removing) tasks, but if it's done carelessly it can lead to some serious consequences! Using the `counter2` servlet as your first removal victim, select its entry in the tree control. There should be a button bar beneath the configuration panel in the view area, and on that button bar should be a button labeled `Remove`. Pressing that button will create a pop-up dialog asking you to confirm the deletion. If you've agreed to remove the servlet, it should disappear from the tree control.

Core Tip

You can't remove any of the "essential" servlets from the system. The `Remove`
*button is disabled when you inspect an essential servlet's entry in the configuration
panel. You can make your own servlets nonremovable by editing the properties file*
`servlets.properties` *in the* `server_root\properties\server\`
`javawebserver\webpageservice` *directory. Find your servlet entry and
add the following line:*

`servlet.[servlet name].allow_delete=false`

*Administrators won't be able to remove your servlet from the configuration panel
any more. Conversely, you can remove these lines to make previously nonremovable servlets go away.*

"Where Have All the Servlets Gone?"

Perhaps the congratulations were a tad premature, since all you accomplished was
adding a new servlet *entry* into the system. You haven't yet added a new servlet *class*
to the Java Web Server. A good question to ask along those lines is "Where are the
servlet classes stored?"

The answer lies beneath the Java Web Server installation directory. From there,
you should see a subdirectory named `servlets`. All servlet classes should be placed
in that directory, and if the classes exist in a package structure, the entire package
hierarchy needs to be copied over as well.

Core Note

Classes stored beneath the `servlets` *directory are automatically reloaded if
they are updated.*

Installing Servlet Beans

If you're familiar with the JavaBeans component model, a servlet bean is a servlet that
complies to the JavaBean introspection conventions (in English, this means the class
uses **get** methods to access properties and **set** methods to configure properties).
If you're not familiar with the JavaBeans specifications, don't worry, because we're
going to tell you exactly what you need to know in order to use beans with the Java
Web Server. A servlet has to meet only two requirements to be considered a
ServletBean:

- It has to be serializable.
- It has to support the get/set method naming conventions.

You can make any class serializable by implementing the `java.io.Serializable` interface, *and* by making sure that all of its member variables are serializable as well.

Core Note

More information on serialization and other JavaBean-related concepts can be found at `http://www.javasoft.com/beans`

The get/set naming convention ties together the concept of accessing a bean's properties ("properties" is a fancy way of saying "member variables"). The JavaBeans specification requires that a bean be customizable, and those customized settings are saved to a serialized file (hence the serialization requirement!). You *can* have a bean without any customizable settings, but it won't be a very useful bean!

Properties are read from a bean using a `get[property name]` method call. For example, if a sample bean had a property called `copyright`, a beans-enabled system could read this property if the sample bean had a public method named `getCopyright`. Additionally, a bean can be customized using any `set[Property name]` method implemented by the object. The copyright message could be configured if the example bean had a public method named `setCopyright`.

Now, before you go and start tagging all of your servlets as serializable objects, you should know that *all servlets derived from the class* `GenericServlet` *are servlet beans!* That means all of your `HttpServlets` are serializable, too!

JavaBeans are packaged in a special structure called a JAR (Java archive) when they are distributed. Tucked away within this JAR file is the Java class file for the bean and any serialized configurations. When the bean is instantiated, it can choose to use one of these frozen configurations to place it in some known state.

This is where the administration comes in. Adding a servlet bean to the Java Web Server requires the bean to be packaged in a JAR. Serialized objects aren't required, but the Java Web Server will use them if they are available. Once you have the JAR, copy it into the *server_root*\servletbeans directory. As an example, we've copied over one of the beans written in the servlet beans programming chapter. The bean is called `SimpleBean` and its packaged in a JAR called `Simple.jar`. Next, open up the servlet configuration panel and make a new servlet entry named "Beanie", with the servlet class "SimpleBean". Since this servlet *is* a bean, you'll want to pay attention to the lower portion of the panel this time. Click on the `Yes` radio button over the question `Bean Servlet` and write the name of the JAR in the text field labeled `Jar File`. Figure 4-32 shows how you add a servlet bean.

The configuration panel looks a little different this time. Anything related to starting and stopping the servlet has been disabled. This is a key difference between regular servlets and servlet beans: servlets have values only while they are running, but servlet

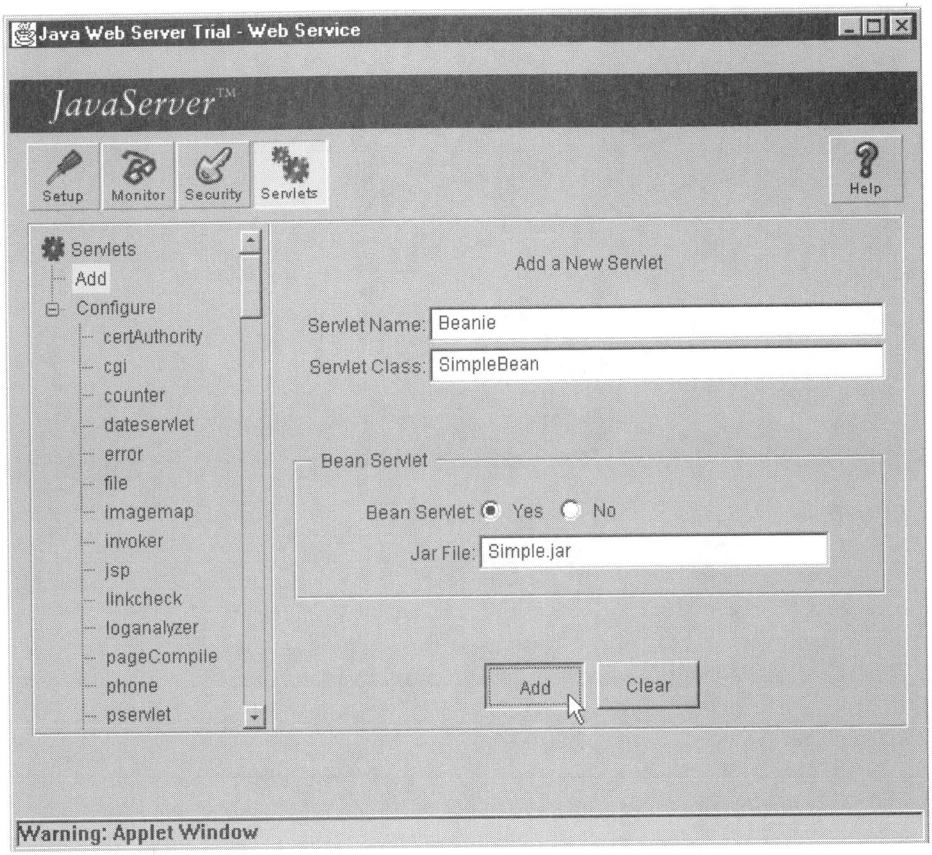

Figure 4-32   Adding a servlet bean.

beans can save their state (because they are stored within a JAR file as serializable objects), so the started/not started states don't make any sense. Consequently, as an administrator you have no control over whether servlet beans are active in memory or not.

Moving on to the `properties` tab, you should see that some properties have been defined for you (Figure 4-33). In reality, the Java Web Server has used Java's *intro-spection* facilities to find all of the accessible properties on the `SimpleBean` class.

Core Note

Any Java program can inspect a Java object's methods and properties using special methods attached to the `Class` class. Specifically, Bean containers like the Java Web Server look for public methods starting with the prefix `get` and `set`. This procedure is called introspection.

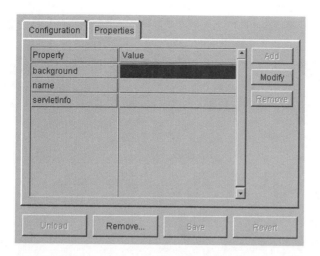

Figure 4-33   A servlet bean's premade properties.

The background property for this servlet bean is an HTML BGCOLOR attribute (a # followed by RGB values in hexadecimal) and the name property is used to greet the browser. Put your favorite background color as the background property value, your name as the name property value, and save the changes Next, fire up your browser and access the configured servlet bean at http://localhost/servlet/Beanie (Figure 4-34).

When the server is shut down, Beanie's properties will be safely stored away in the JAR as a serialized SimpleBean object. This autosaving provides an additional benefit for servlet developers and administrators alike: you can preconfigure servlets using your own Java Web Server installation, then deliver the JARs to your customers *ready to run right out of the box!*

More to Come with Servlets

Servlets, in one form or another, are the main topic of the rest of the book. So far you've only touched briefly on the administrative aspects of development and deployment. If you want to start writing your own servlets, we suggest that you read Chapter 5 ("Generic Servlets"), Chapter 6 ("Advanced Generic Servlets"), and Chapter 8 ("HTTP Servlets") for a tutorial on the core servlet API.

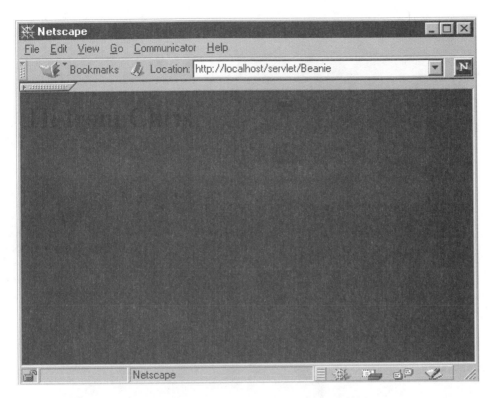

Figure 4-34   The Beanie servlet in action.

Servlet Aliases

Did you notice that there is a pattern to the URL used to access a servlet? For example, when you connected to the counter servlet in the configuration examples, you used the URL http://localhost/servlet/counter, and when you accessed the counter2 servlet, you used the URL http://localhost/servlet/counter2. The similarities between the two URLs aren't a coincidence, but merely a product of *servlet aliases* in action. Do you remember that, when we were describing servlets, we said an "essential" servlet called invoker was responsible for activating a servlet? Yet nowhere in the URL does the name invoker appear, so how does the Java Web Server know to activate it?

The answer to this question is tucked away in the setup portion of the Admin applet's service configuration panel. Navigate through the tree control into the node named Servlet Aliases, and in the view area you should see a table control mapping aliases to servlets (Figure 4-35).

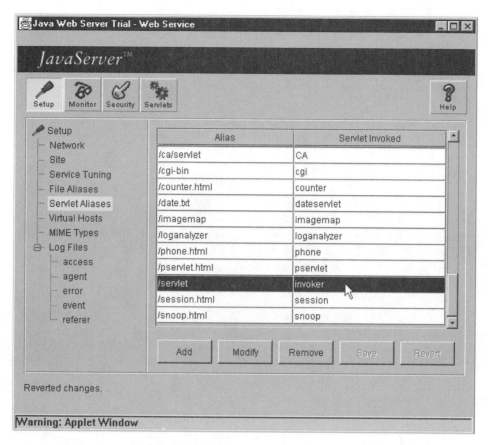

Figure 4-35 Listing the Java Web Server's servlet aliases.

There are two columns in the tree control. The Alias column tells the Java Web Server what should trigger this alias. The following three types of aliases can be triggered by Web requests:

- General directory alias
- Specific Web page alias
- General file-type alias

General Directory Alias

A general directory alias maps any request prefixed with a special string to be trapped and redirected to a servlet. The `invoker` servlet is a general directory alias, as all requests beginning with the name `/servlet` are sent to it for handling. The `cgi` servlet is another general directory alias, as it receives all requests beneath the directory `/cgi-bin`.

Specific Web Page Alias

A specific Web page alias makes a servlet appear to be a single static Web page. If you scroll down the table control in the view area, you should see one of the demonstration servlets named `phone` mapped to the alias `/phone.html`. When the URL `http://localhost/phone.html` is received by the Java Web Server, the request will be dispatched to the phone servlet.

Web page aliases are particularly cool, since they can be used during development to "stub out" pieces of functionality until the Web site is finished. You can use static Web pages while the servlets are being developed. When the servlets are ready to go, you can plug them into the site by adding a servlet alias for each of the existing "stubbed" static pages.

General File-type Alias

The `jsp` servlet is an "extra" we mentioned earlier in the chapter. Its job is processing special files containing Java code and HTML. These files are called `jsp` files because they have the file extension `.jsp`. When a request for any `jsp` file is received by the Java Web Server, it delegates the request to the `jsp` servlet because of a special kind of alias called a general file-type alias.

A general file-type alias maps a file extension to a specific servlet: the `jsp` servlet receives requests for `.jsp` files, the `pageCompile` servlet receives requests for `.jhtml` files, and the `ssinclude` servlet receives requests for `.shtml` files when the Java Web Server is installed. Figure 4-36 shows these and other file-type aliases in the Admin GUI.

File-type aliases are a great way to add scripting-language support to the Java Web Server. Although you can already script the server with JSP, which provides a lot of useful features (check out Chapter 15 on JSP for more details), you might want to provide Perl or Tcl support as well. For example, you could make an alias from `*.pl` to a servlet named perl that called a Perl interpreter.

File-type aliases also give the Java Web Server a method to "hook" requests for specific files for preprocessing. Imagine a case where you've stored documents in a compressed file, but you want to provide those documents to your clients on demand. Instead of wasting valuable disk space uncompressing all of the files, a servlet can be configured to trap these file requests, extract only the single file being requested, and return the uncompressed file to the server.

Servlet aliases are stored in the properties file `rules.properties` in the format [alias]=[servlet name]. If you make any changes to the file, you'll need to restart the Java Web Server for them to take effect.

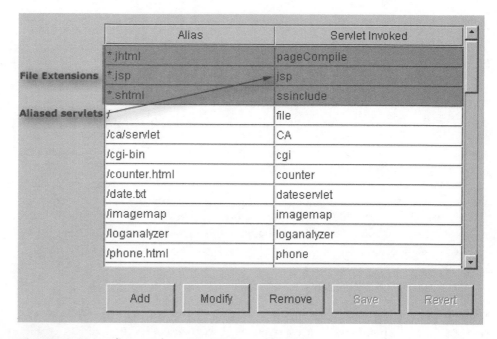

Alias	Servlet Invoked
*.jhtml	pageCompile
*.jsp	jsp
*.shtml	ssinclude
/	file
/ca/servlet	CA
/cgi-bin	cgi
/counter.html	counter
/date.txt	dateservlet
/imagemap	imagemap
/loganalyzer	loganalyzer
/phone.html	phone

File Extensions

Aliased servlets

[Add] [Modify] [Remove] [Save] [Revert]

Figure 4-36   File-type aliases mapped to servlets.

Configuring MIME Types

Data comes in many shapes and sizes. Divining the type of a data blob is one of the most important parts of any system, and the HTTP protocol is no exception. HTTP uses the MIME standard for typing the data it exchanges with clients. It's up to the Web server to specify the MIME type of the files that it serves.

The Java Web Server stores its MIME configuration information beneath the setup section of the service configuration panel. Navigate through the tree control into the node named MIME types, and you'll be presented with a table containing all of the currently configured MIME types. Figure 4-37 shows all of the configured MIME types.

The Java Web Server uses the MIME information for two of its responsibilities:

- Reporting the type of a file requested by the client.
- Creating dynamic servlet chains.

When a client requests a file from the Java Web Server, the file servlet (an "essential" servlet aliased to the '/' directory) sends the MIME type of the file along with its content. It uses the file's extension to figure out its MIME type, which defaults to text/plain if the type can't be derived from the table (signified by the "*" entry at the top of the table). If you need to support additional file types like streaming audio or video, you'll want to add these to the MIME table.

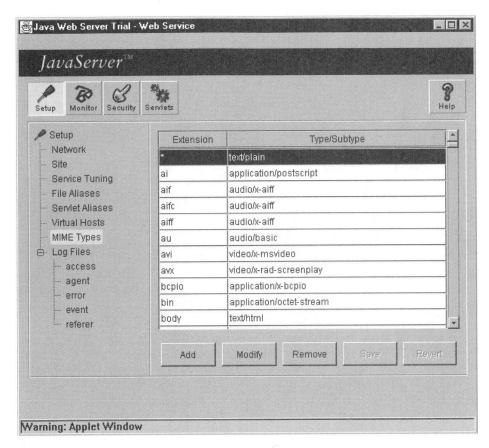

Figure 4-37   The MIME configuration table.

Servlet chaining is a feature specific to the Java Web Server. When a servlet sends data to the client, it specifies the MIME type of the data through a call to `setContentType`. If servlet chaining is enabled, the Java Web Server checks to see if any servlet is responsible for handling that type of data. If so, it *chains* the first servlet's output as input to the second servlet (hence the name "servlet chain").

Unfortunately, there aren't any GUI configuration tools for creating these servlet chains. You're reduced to hand-editing the file mimeservlets.properties. The format of the file is [MIME type]=[servlet name]. For example, if you wanted all GIF images to be processed by a servlet you've written to watermark data (for copyright protection purposes), you could make the association

```
image/gif=WatermarkServlet
```

You'll need to restart the Java Web Server for these changes to take effect.

Realms, Groups, Users, and Security

Web server security is like the goalie in a soccer game. When things go right, no one notices, but everyone is up in arms when someone sneaks in a shot. That said, securing your Web site is one of the topics least talked about, yet servers (and the Java Web Server in particular) provide excellent tools for keeping out the bad guys.

Securing the Java Web Server is a three-step process:

- Identify the users, groups, and realms.
- Create access control lists (ACLs).
- Apply ACLs to various Web resources.

Identify the Users, Groups, and Realms

Users are the smallest addressable identity unit within a security system. In English, this means that security is applied to users. Groups are used to apply security rules to a set of users at once. Groups and users aren't anything new; operating systems like UNIX have had them for over twenty years.

But what's with this "realm" thing?

To quote the Request For Comments document, RFC 2068, "Hypertext Transfer Protocol—HTTP/1.1," realms "allow the protected resources on a server to be partitioned into a set of protection spaces, each with its own authentication scheme and/or authorization database." Again, in English, a realm is like a black box that holds secrets. Realms implementers are free to use whatever secret-storing mechanism they want.

Under the Java Web Server, there are four built-in realms:

- defaultRealm
- OS-specific [NT, Solaris] realm
- servletMgrRealm
- certificateRealm

Realms can't be created from the Admin applet. Programmatically creating your own realms will be discussed in the chapter on security later on in the book. For now, be happy with using the already existing realms for your security needs.

Core Note

Since a realm is tied to a specific secret-storing database, the security of the system depends on the security of that database.

Security settings are maintained beneath the security section of the service control panel (Figure 4-38).

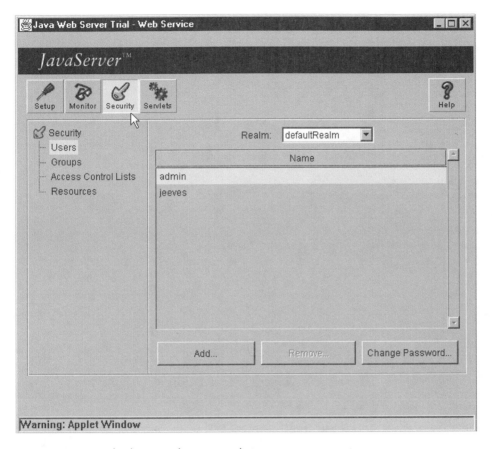

Figure 4-38   Checking out the Java Web Server's security settings.

Beneath the tree control are four leaves:

- Users
- Groups
- Access Control Lists
- Resources

Creating and removing users and groups is pretty straightforward. Begin by pressing the Add button in the user management panel of the view area (Figure 4-39).

The Admin applet should present the Add User dialog. Enter the user's name, followed by the user's initial password twice (Figure 4-40).

When you press the OK button after you've filling out the dialog, you should see the new user account appear in the user configuration panel.

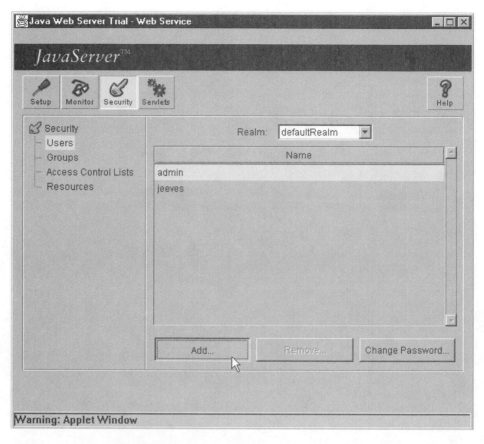

Figure 4-39   Adding a new user.

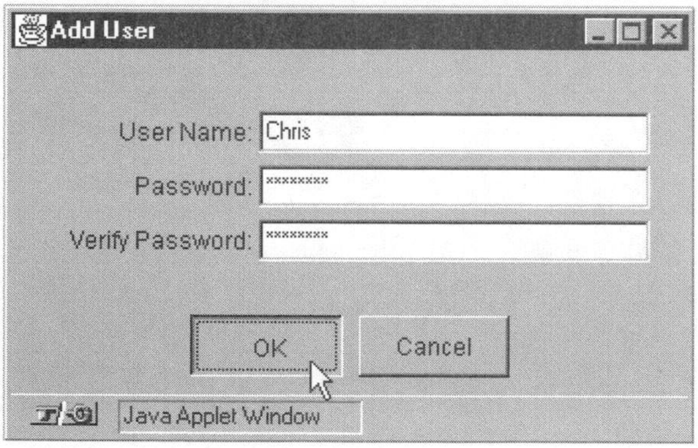

Figure 4-40   Filling out the paperwork.

Making groups is just as simple as making users. Navigate over to the group configuration panel through the tree control. When it appears, you should see that the group configuration panel is split into two parts: the group selection area and the selected group management area (Figure 4-41).

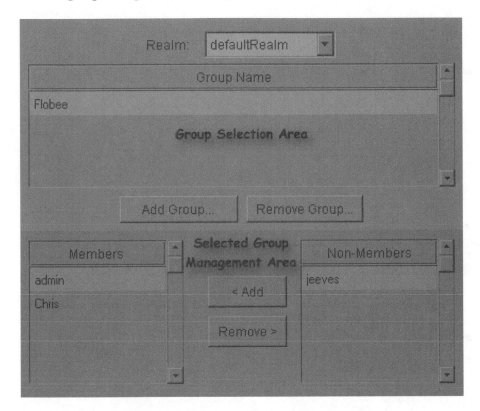

Figure 4-41   Introducing the group management panel.

Press the `Add Group` button from the group selection area to create a new group. You should be prompted for a group name; enter it and press the `Add` button. If all went according to plan, the new group name should appear in the Group Name list.

Next, add any users you want in the new group by selecting their names in the `Non-Members` field and pressing the `Add` button. In our example we've added a user named `Chris` and made him the sole member of the new group "Flobee."

Create Access Control Lists

With our sample group and user created, the time has come to create an access control list for protecting Web resources. Navigate to the `Access Control Lists` node in the tree control. You should be presented with the access control list (ACL) configuration panel, which is also split into two parts: the ACL selection area above and the selected ACL permission area below. Figure 4-42 displays the ACL configuration panel.

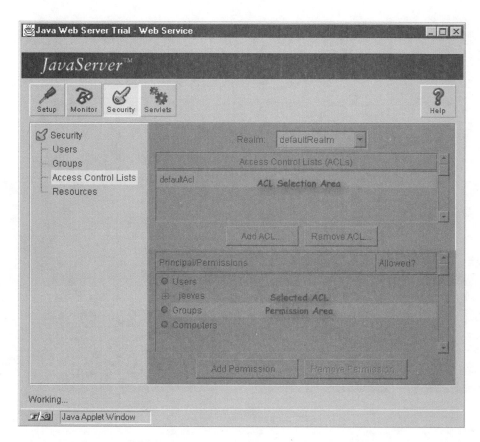

Figure 4-42   Introducing the ACL configuration panel.

Do you see the ACL named `defaultAcl` in the selection area? Click on the `defaultAcl` entry, and the selected ACL permission area should convey the security options contained with that ACL. By reading the output you can see that the `defaultAcl` allows the user Jeeves from the `defaultRealm` realm to send HTTP GET and POST requests.

To create a new ACL, press the `Add ACL` button from the selection area. You should be prompted for a name for the ACL. Enter the desired name and press the `Add` button. If nothing goes wrong, the ACL's name should appear in the selection area. We use "Core_Java_Web_Server_Test_ACL" as our ACL's name.

Next, you will want to add permissions to the ACL. An ACL acts as a container for permission settings; a single ACL can contain multiple permission entries. In an operating system such as Windows NT, these permission entries are called ACEs (Access Control Entries), but under the Java Web Server they are called permissions (same thing, different name). To add a permission, press the `Add Permission` button to enter the permission configuration dialog. Figure 4-43 shows the permissions configuration dialog.

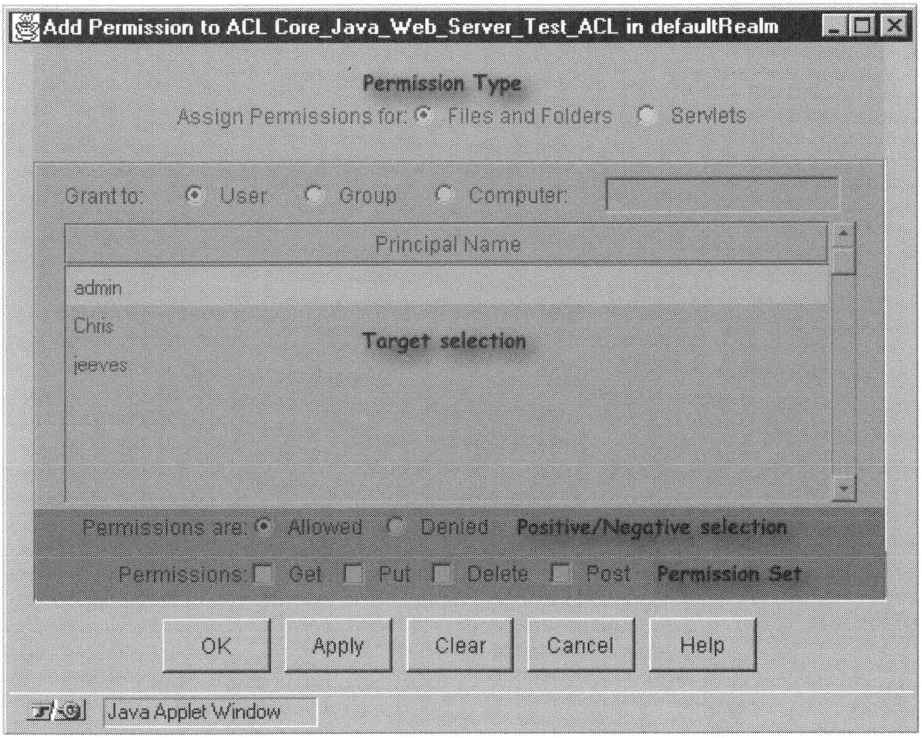

Figure 4-43   Taming the permission configuration dialog.

The permission configuration dialog is split into four areas:

- Permission type
- Target selection
- Positive/negative selection
- Permission set

Permission Type

The permission type is used to differentiate which kind of resource this permission object will protect. It changes the options that are made available in the permission set. For example, you can GET, PUT, POST, and DELETE files or directories of files on a Web server. Servlet permissions are used to control a signed servlet's sandbox (say that three times fast!).

Target Selection

The target selection is akin to the subject of an English sentence, "User [blank] can GET the default Web page." When protecting files, you can select users, groups, or machines, but servlets can be protected only against users and groups.

Positive/Negative Selection

This radio selection either grants or denies the target the specified permission, and that's it!

Permission Set

The permission set specifies what the target of the permission entry can (or can't) do to a Web resource. Currently, there are only two types of permissions: files and servlets. Each type has its own permission set. These types and their respective permission sets are listed in Table 4-2.

Table 4-2   Permission Types, Entries, and Their Descriptions

Permission Type	Permission Set Entry	Description
Files and Folders	GET	Will the HTTP GET request be allowed/denied by the Java Web Server on this resource?
	POST	Will the HTTP POST request be allowed/denied by the Java Web Server on this resource?
	PUT	Will the HTTP PUT request be allowed/denied by the Java Web Server on this resource?
	DELETE	Will the HTTP DELETE request be allowed/denied by the Java Web Server on this resource?
Servlets	Load Servlet	Can this servlet be loaded by the client's request?

Permission Type	Permission Set Entry	Description
Servlets *(cont.)*	Write Files	Can this servlet write to the file system during the client's request?
	Listen to Socket	Can this servlet create a ServerSocket (TCP) or receive from a DatagramSocket (UDP) during the client's request?
	Link Libraries	Can this servlet load native code libraries during the client's request?
	Read Files	Can this servlet read the file system during the client's request?
	Open Remote Socket	Can this servlet connect to a remote server port during the client's request?
	Execute Programs	Can this servlet call System.exec during the client's request?
	Access System Properties	Can this servlet make a call to System.getProperty during the client's request?

As an example, we'll disallow the new user "Chris" from making GET requests to a file or from loading servlets. This requires two separate permission entries in the ACL. After you've created both permissions, the ACL permission area should look like Figure 4-44.

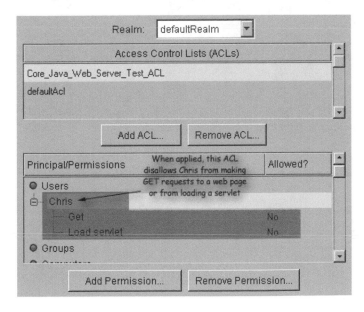

Figure 4-44   An example ACL with two permissions.

Apply ACL to Web Resources

The last remaining task is to protect your Web server with the ACLs by applying them to specific resources on the Java Web Server. You apply ACLs through the resources node in the `security` section's tree control. Navigate to this node, and you should be presented with the resource protection panel in the view area, as shown in Figure 4-45.

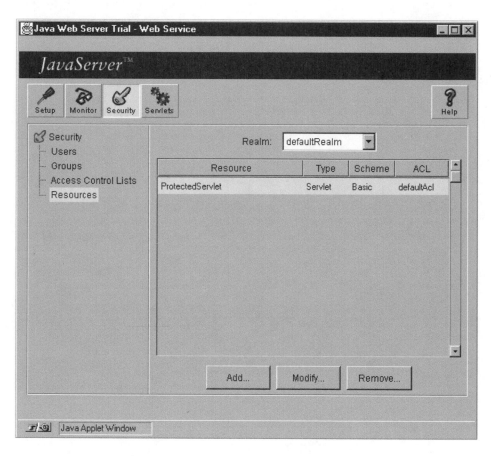

Figure 4-45   Introducing the resource protection panel.

You can add a new resource protection by pressing the `add` button. This action should trigger the resource protection dialog to appear. This dialog is where you specify the name and type of the resource to secure, as well as the ACL that is used to protect it. Furthermore, you can specify which authentication scheme should be used to protect the resource. There are three schemes to choose from: `Basic`, `Digest`, and `SSL`.

Core Note

The SSL *scheme will be grayed out unless your Web server is SSL-enabled. SSL (Secure Sockets Layer) encrypts data as it goes back and forth from the client and the server. While its encryption makes transmitted information secure, SSL also provides user identification through an X.509 certificate. The SSL scheme uses the certificate information to authenticate a user's identity.*

The `Basic` scheme sends a user's login and password in the clear to the server. If someone has the right equipment to "sniff" the network, the password can be compromised.

The `Digest` scheme doesn't transmit the password across the network. Instead, it calculates a one-way hash using the password and sends this hash value to the server. Since the server has the user's password, it can recalculate the hash and compare it against the received value. Unfortunately, most Web browsers don't support `Digest` authentication, so if you aren't sure whether your client's browsers will support it, just use `Basic` authentication to be safe.

Enabling Servlet Chains

Servlet chains allow groups of servlets to work together like a pipeline, passing processed data down to each in turn. However, servlet chains are considered a security risk because there is the potential for misuse. A malicious servlet can pipe bad information to others, or read the information that another servlet sends to it.

The Java Web Server comes with servlet chains disabled. You will need to navigate to the `site` node of the `setup` option's tree control. From there select the `options` tab to reveal a radio button to enable/disable servlet chains, as shown in Figure 4-46.

You can make this change directly by editing the `httpd.properties` file. Find the line starting with `enable.filters` and set its value to true. You'll have to restart the Java Web Server for the changes to take effect.

Enabling/Disabling Security Checks

While security is a great feature to support, using it *does* require extra processing time. If you aren't using the Java Web Server's security facilities, you can eke out some additional performance by turning off security checks.

Navigate to the site node in the setup section's tree control. Select the options tab in the view area, and you should see a radio box labeled "Security Checks." After you turn this option off and save your settings, no more security checks will be done.

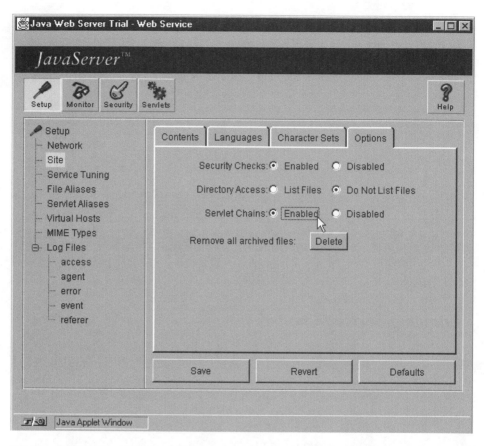

Figure 4-46   Enabling servlet chains.

Core Note

ALL *security checks will be turned off when you disable this option. Make sure
you fully understand the consequences of leaving your site completely open!*

This option can be hand-configured by editing the `httpd.properties` file.
Search for the line starting with `enable.acls` and set the value equal to false:

```
enable.acls=false
```

The change will take effect after you restart the Java Web Server.

List/Hide Directory Contents

When clients request directories on a Web server, but no default page can be found, the server has two options:

- Return a generated HTML file hyperlink reference to the directory contents.
- Send a 403 (forbidden) error code to the client.

Because returning the contents of a directory is a possible security risk, the Java Web Server will send back a 403 error to the client. The Java Web Server isn't configured to return directory information by default, but you can change this behavior by navigating to the site node in the `setup` section's tree control. Select the `option` tab and you should see a radio box labeled `directory access` in the view area. Toggle this switch. Now the Java Web Server should produce directory listings instead of errors.

You can also change this option by hand-editing the file `httpd.properties`. Search for the line that looks like:

```
enable.browseDirs=false
```

and change it to:

```
enable.browseDirs=true
```

Save your changes and restart the Java Web Server for it to take effect.

Configuring the Log Files

The Java Web Server stores its status information across the following five log files:

- access log
- agent log
- error log
- event log
- referrer log

The logs are stored beneath the directory `server_root\logs\ javawebserver\webpageservice`. These log files have different, specialized purposes, yet they all are configured in the same way using the Admin applet. To configure the logs, navigate to the `log files` node in the `setup` section's tree control. The logging configuration panel should appear in the view area across from the tree control, as shown in Figure 4-47.

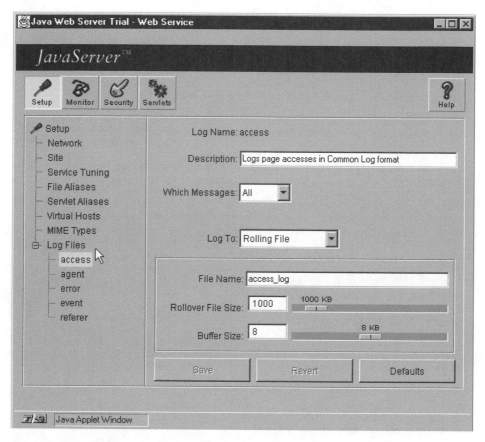

Figure 4-47   Introducing the logging configuration panel.

Each log entry has the same options available:

- Description
- Which messages
- Log to

The description is just a text string for describing the purpose of this particular log file. The which messages field is used to specify which messages should be logged; it acts like a filter. Its values range from "log nothing" to "log everything," with intermediate values between the two.

Core Note

The more you log, the slower your Java Web Server will run. The engineers at JavaSoft have done an excellent job of optimizing logging, but it's still slower than no logging at all.

The `log to` field specifies the type of the log file. Four types come with the Java Web Server (and an API is provided for adding your own logging classes):

- Rolling file
- Single file
- Standard output
- Error output

By default all of the logs are `rolling files`: they have a maximum size, and when that maximum size is reached, the Java Web Server will create a new file and begin again. Furthermore, the rolling file has a performance-enhancing cache that reduces the number of hits to the file system.

The `single file` option is a standard log file: the Java Web Server just keeps appending entries to the file forever.

`Standard output` sends its logging information to `System.out.println`, and `error output` sends its information to `System.err.println` of the Java Web Server's console.

Core Note

If you've started the Java Web Server as an NT service with *output logging options, those messages will drop straight into the bit bucket and be lost forever. The *output file options are more useful for debugging servlets from the Java Web Server's console window.

Customizing Error Messages

Try a little experiment. Open up your Web browser and request the page `http://localhost/foobar`. You should get an error response back from the Java Web Server, because there isn't any page named "foobar" (Figure 4-48).

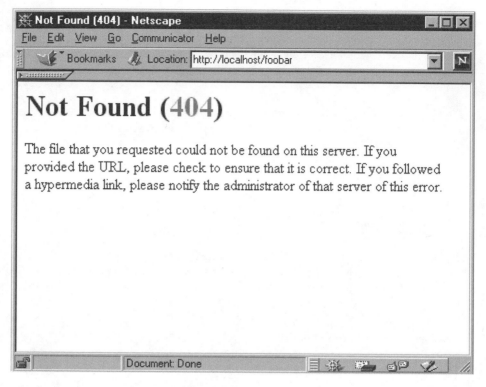

Figure 4-48   Receiving the dreaded "404 error."

Now, where did that page come from? Did the Java Web Server automatically generate the page when it couldn't find anything named "foobar"?

After a little investigation, we found a directory named *server_root*\system\errors containing a set of curiously named files:

400.html
401.html
403.html
404.html
406.html
500.html
503.html

These file names looked like HTTP status codes. We theorized that the Java Web Server sent back one of these files to the client when something went wrong. Seeking the truth, we edited the 404.html file and put the words "Core Java Web Server" in the title of the page. Again, we tried to retrieve the "foobar" file in the Web browser, with the results shown in Figure 4-49.

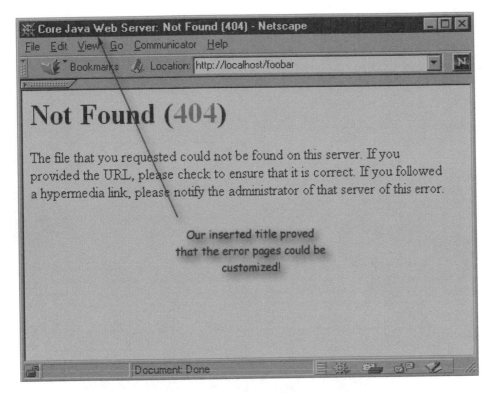

Figure 4-49   The error messages are configurable, Watson!

As you can see, our theory was correct. We leave it up to you to create your own error messages to meet your site's particular needs.

Monitoring Your Server

When something goes wrong with a server program, the first thing a good administrator does is pick through the log files. Like black boxes on downed aircraft, they seem to survive some of the nastiest crashes.

Picking through the rubble of a crash with only a log file as a guide can be a tedious task! Fortunately, the Java Web Server comes with some handy graphical tools for interpreting logging information. These tools are found beneath the `monitor` section of the service configuration panel, as shown in Figure 4-50.

Three monitoring tools are available for use:

- Log Output
- Log Statistics
- Resource Usage

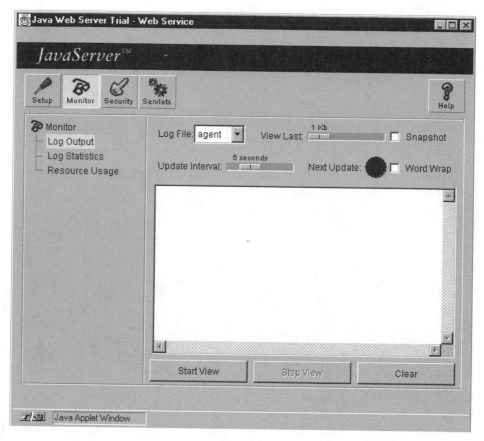

Figure 4-50   Checking out the Java Web Server's monitoring tools.

Log Output

The `log output` tool is used to look at the latest log entries. The tool has several configurable options:

- Log file
- View Last
- Snapshot
- Update interval
- Word wrap

The `log file` choice box lets you choose which log to look at. The `view last` slider bar lets you select how much of the log file to display at a time, ranging from

1 KB up to 5 KB. The `snapshot` check box toggles between a "one-shot" retrieval of the log file and a continuous poll of the logs for new information (a snapshot is considered a "one-shot" retrieval). The `update interval` lets you choose how many seconds to wait before the next transfer of logging information. `Word wrap` does what it says: if a line is longer than the display, it breaks it up across multiple lines so the viewer doesn't have to scroll to the right to read an entire message (Figure 4-51).

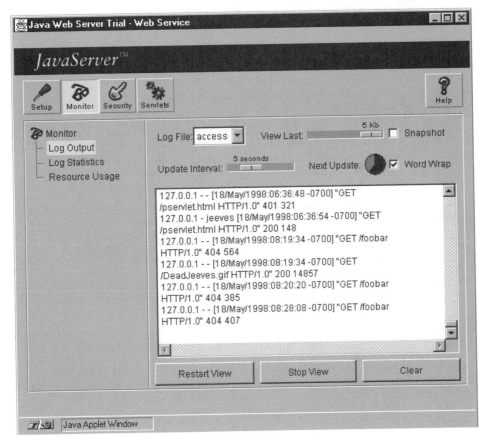

Figure 4-51   Reading the access log through the Log Output tool.

Log Statistics

The `log statistics` monitoring tool graphs log data by time (when) or domain (from where) as a pie chart, bar chart, or table. Unfortunately, someone forgot to put a choice box for the log file on this panel, so the only way to switch logs is to navigate back to the `Log Output` screen and change the selection from there.

Resource Usage

The `resource usage` monitoring tool provides access to three pieces of information from the Java Web Server:

- Memory
- Handler threads
- Requests

The `memory` column is split into two subcolumns: `Total` and `Available`. The `total` column shows all of the memory in kilobytes, while the available column shows how much memory is available for the service being monitored. If the `available` number stays consistently low, the virtual machine running the Java Web Server will be forced to garbage collect more often, incurring a performance penalty.

The handler threads column shows how many worker threads are being utilized. If you consistently see a low number in the available subcolumn, the Java Web Server doesn't have a large enough thread pool to maintain this level of load. You can increase the thread-pool size from the `site` node under the `setup` section's tree control. Conversely, if you see a large number of threads with nothing to do, you might want to consider lowering the minimum thread count (each thread uses valuable memory, so reducing the number of threads can help out).

The requests column shows the total number of HTTP requests in comparison to the number of HTTP GET requests. A large disparity between the numbers means that a good amount of the work is processing POST requests and other nonretrieval HTTP operations like PUT and DELETE (Figure 4-52).

Summary

The Java Web Server, like all other Web servers, requires a little bit of administrative TLC in order to run properly. Knowing this to be the case, the engineers at JavaSoft thoughtfully provided a cross-platform administrative tool called the *Admin applet* to act as an assistant during configuration tasks.

This chapter has covered a lot of ground from an administrator's perspective. We streamlined the chapter by organizing it as a series of tasks that an administrator needs to accomplish.

We also wanted to avoid simply reprinting the on-line documentation. By spending the extra time probing around the system, we showed you how to accomplish the same tasks that the Admin applet does by editing the Java Web Server's configuration files. Armed with this information, you could write scripting tools to automate server changes.

For more information on specific administrative topics, click on the *Help* button located in the upper-righthand corner of the Admin applet. It provides context-sensitive help for your current selection via HTML.

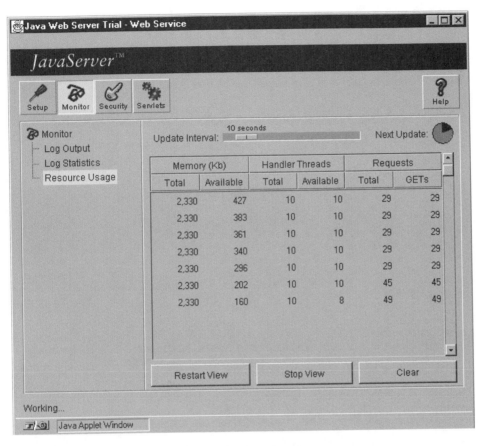

Figure 4-52 Monitoring the Java Web Server's resources.

GENERIC SERVLETS

Topics in This Chapter

- Servlets and applets
- The Brat: your first servlet
- Installing the Servlet Development Kit
- Testing your servlets
- Customizing your servlets

Chapter 5

You've probably been hearing about servlets for quite a while now, and if you're reading this chapter, you're interested in how to develop your own. Servlets are fun to write, and unlike their browser-based cousin the applet, they aren't restricted to a few boring operations. With servlets you can let your mind and ideas run wild. You can build a chat server using RMI, or tie your Web server into a relational database via JDBC, or design a three-tiered system using HTML as a user interface! The possibilities are endless!

This chapter shows you how to develop servlets, and it aims to get you excited about what you can do with them. They're exciting because they are a breed of cross-platform components written in one of the most advanced programming languages around: Java! Typical problems that plague servers, such as memory leaks, portability problems, and fragile implementations that eschew extensions don't exist when you program with servlets. We firmly believe that servlets will overshadow applets in the next few years, unlocking the power of Java on the server, so you'd better get started learning how to write them.

To put it more formally, this chapter provides an introductory approach to servlet programming. It intends to introduce moderately experienced Java programmers to the superclass of all servlets, the GenericServlet. Programmers who already are familiar with the GenericServlet class may also find this chapter informative, as it covers nonprogramming servlet topics such as lifetimes and configuration. All subsequent chapters will assume the knowledge that is presented here about GenericServlets.

Servlets: Applets on the Server?

Servlets have similarities to their client-based cousin, the applet. Servlets have well-defined lifetimes, from their initialization when they are first loaded, to execution on incoming requests, to their destruction when they are no longer needed. Like an applet, servlets have method *entry-points* that are called automatically by the Web server when required, as shown in Table 5-1.

Table 5-1	Apples and Oranges, Servlets and Applets	
Situation	*Applet*	*Servlet*
Object Created	init	Init(ServletConfig sc)
Start Working	start	Service (ServletRequest sr, ServletResponse res)
Stop Working	stop	—
Object Destroyed	destroy	Destroy

Notice how servlets don't have a `stop` method. So, how do they know when to stop working? Does this API difference change our first impression of servlets as applets on the server?

Perhaps if you understand what the applet `stop` method is used for, this difference will make more sense. An applet gets a stop message from the Web browser on a page change. Acting as "good neighbors" who don't litter, Applet programmers use the `stop` method to clean up any threads they have created. Like the rest of the AWT, applets are event-driven GUIs. Servlets, on the other hand, have no user interface, nor are they event driven.

So an applet works as long as it is visible to the user. In comparison, a servlet works on a request, and it provides the result in a response. The `ServletRequest` and `ServletResponse` parameters of the servlet's `service` call reveal the true length of work a servlet is required to perform as the length of the method: all work must be completed before the method returns.

Core Note

Work does not always end when the `service` *method returns. Consider a* `service` *method which spawns a thread to do extra work on the* `ServletResponse`. *Such threads can continue working on the* `ServletResponse` *object even after the* `service` *call returns.*

Revising the previous comparison shown in Table 5-1, you can see a closer relationship between applets and servlets here in Table 5-2.

Table 5-2	Servlets versus Applets (Take Two)	
Situation	*Applet*	*Servlet*
Object Created	init	Init(ServletConfig sc)
Lifetime	start	Service (ServletRequest sr, ServletResponse res)
	stop	
Object Destroyed	destroy	Destroy

Enough with the Theory, Let's Code!

Now that you are familiar with the lifetime of a servlet, let's write a simple program to show off our smarts. In Listing 5-1, we'll complain every time someone wants us to do something.

Listing 5-1	Brat.java (Take 1)

```java
import javax.servlet.*;
public class Brat extends GenericServlet
{
   public void init(ServletConfig sc)
   throws ServletException
   {
     System.out.println ("I don't wanna wake up!");
   }
   public void service (ServletRequest req,
   ServletResponse res) throws ServletException
   {
     System.out.println("I don't wanna do anything!");
   }
   public void destroy ()
   {
     System.out.println("I don't wanna go to bed!");
   }
}
```

Since this is the first time you've looked at servlet code, let's take this line by line. Whenever you plan to write a servlet, you'll need to import the `javax.servlet` package.

Core Note

Importing a package is not like using the C language `#include` *directive. Importing a package only includes the package's name into the current name-space (it's like the* `using [namespace]` *statement in C++). We can then refer to classes by their common name and not their full name (e.g.,* `GenericServlet` *instead of* `javax.servlet.GenericServlet`*). While making source code easier to read, using the import can cause problems (for example, using the Date class after importing both the* `java.sql` *and* `java.util` *packages would result in a compiler error that "the class X could not be found ").*

All servlets extend `GenericServlet` (either directly or from a descendant of `GenericServlet`), so we declare our Brat class to extend from `GenericServlet`.

`GenericServlet` implements two important interfaces: `Servlet` and `ServletConfig`, shown in the following API passages.

SERVLET

`public void destroy`

Performs any last-minute clean-up before the servlet is removed from service.

`public void init (ServletContext sc) throws ServletException`

Called once before any service calls are made. Used to initialize the servlet (open any database connections)

`public void service (ServletRequest res, ServletResponse res) throws ServletException, IOException`

This is where the servlet does any requested work. Most of the servlet's code will be executed here.

`public ServletConfig getServletConfig`

Gets the `ServletConfig` object for this servlet. A `ServletConfig` object has initialization and startup information that can be useful for changing the behavior of a Servlet.

`public String getServletInfo`

Returns a String representing miscellaneous information about a servlet, such as the author's name, a copyright message, or the date the servlet was created.

SERVLETCONFIG

```
public ServletContext getServletContext
```

Gets the ServletContext object for this servlet. The ServletContext class provides methods to access information about the servlet's environment.

```
public String getInitParameter (String parameterName)
```

Retrieves the initialization value associated with parameterName, or null if parameterName does not exist.

```
public Enumeration getParameterNames
```

Retrieves an Enumeration of Strings representing the names of available initialization parameters. This Enumeration is empty if no initialization parameters exist.

Each of these interfaces contains a substantial number of methods for the developer to implement. Fortunately for us, we are saved a large amount of work by extending GenericServlet: only the `service` method needs to be coded, saving us from writing seven other functions.

The Brat also overrides `GenericServlet`'s `init` method. This is where our Brat will complain about having to wake up. In a "real" servlet, it is a good practice to call `super.init` before returning from our `init` method.

Core Tip

When overriding the init method of a servlet, it is imperative to call super.init(sc), where sc is the ServletConfig *parameter passed to our* init *method, if any information about the servlet's environment is needed in either the* ser- vice *or* destroy *methods. The behavior of* GenericServlet's init *method is to cache the* ServletConfig *object in a local variable, so if this method is never called, the* ServletConfig *object is lost to the servlet after* init *completes. (The* getServletConfig *method will return null.)*

All of the servlet's work (or lack thereof in the case of our Brat!) occurs in the service method, which in our example consists of a bitter complaint over "forced" labor.

Complete the Brat by overriding the `destroy` method of `GenericServlet` on line 15. Since we didn't do any substantial work in either `init` or `service`, we'll just finish up with a verbal-last ditch effort to get out of going to bed early. Failing that, we are tucked into bed until we are wakened at some later date.

Core Alert

A servlet will have `destroy` *called once before it is removed from the system. However, there is no guarantee that all servlet requests have completed when* `destroy` *is called. It is the duty of the servlet developer to handle this case.*

Now that you've explored the code for our example servlet, let's watch it complain in action. You have a choice between two methods for testing our Brat servlet: install the Brat as a service underneath the Java Web Server, or execute him in a stand-alone servlet environment. Imagine that a servlet is like a rebuilt race-car engine—putting it in the Java Web Server is like installing the engine into the race car, while using the stand-alone environment is like putting the engine up on a test bed, exposed for the sole purpose of testing. While the race car is where the engine will ultimately be used, changing out the engine for every problem found is time consuming. So for testing our servlets, use a test bed made by JavaSoft called the Servlet Development Kit.

Core Note

As this book went to press, JavaSoft decided to make servlets a standard extension to the JDK. All future development will be done with JDK1.2 instead of the Servlet Development Kit. However, as of this writing the JDK1.2 is still in beta, and we suggest that you use the Servlet Development Kit for servlet testing.

Actually, you have a choice of test-bed environments for our engines. JavaSoft provides the Servlet Development Kit (the latest copy can be found at `http://jserv.javasoft.com`) for the Win32 and Solaris platforms, but other engines also exist:

- Live Software's JRun™ (Although included on the CD-ROM, the latest copy can be found at `http://jserv.javasoft.com`)
- New Atlanta Communications ServletExec™ (`http://www.newatlanta.com`)
- Servlet Express (`http://www.ibm.com/java/servexp/`)

If you are developing for the Macintosh, ServletExec is the only engine currently supporting the Mac (although more may available by the time this book is published).

Setting Up the Servlet Development Kit

The Java Servlet Development Kit installation is a quick two-step process: Choose where you want to install the kit, and add its `bin` directory to your path. On the Win32 platform, we installed the JSDK to the `d:\jsdk` directory. The second step is to add the JSDK's `bin` directory to your path. On Windows NT, we added `d:\jsdk\bin` to your path environment variable by using the `System Properties` control panel.

In Windows 95, you have to edit the `autoexec.bat` file, appending `d:\jsdk\bin` to the path variable. Unlike Windows NT, Windows 95 requires a shutdown and restart for the changes to take effect. On the Solaris platform, you can install the JSDK in your home directory, `/home/corejws/JSDK`. After installation, you should add the JSDK directory to your PATH variable in your `.cshrc` file.

After adding the `<servlet directory>\bin` to the PATH environment variable, you can test the JSDK installation by running `srun.exe /?` from the command line as shown in Figure 5-1.

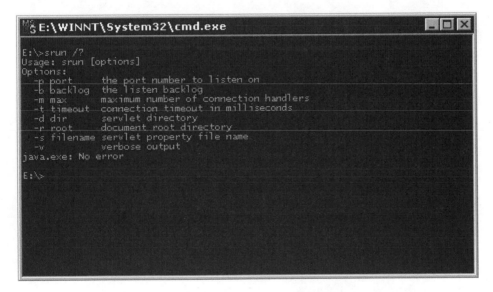

Figure 5-1 Verifying that the JSDK has been correctly installed.

If you receive output like that of Figure 5-1, you have successfully installed the Java Servlet Development Kit.

Testing the Brat

With the Servlet Development Kit properly installed, we can see our Brat in action. Compile the `Brat.java` source file into a Java class file with the `javac` program.

Core Note

If the Java compiler (`javac`) complains that it can't locate the `javax` package, that means the `classes.zip` from the JSDK hasn't been added to the classpath. Add the text `<JSDK directory>\lib\classes.zip;` to the end of the classpath variable, where `<JSDK directory>` is where you installed the Servlet Development Kit (for example, `d:\jsdk\lib\classes.zip`).

Now we'll use Servlet Runner (srun) to test out the Brat. Servlet Runner has several possible parameters that can be given at the command line, which we have summarized in Table 5-3 as a quick reference.

Table 5-3   Parameters Accepted by srun

Parameter	Description	Example
–p [port #]	The port number for Servlet Runner to listen on. This corresponds to the URL port number for a page request (e.g. `http://testmachine:1234/servlets/Brat`). The default port number is 8080.	srun –p 1234
–d [directory]	The directory from which servlets will be loaded on a request. When any URL that requests a servlet by Invocation (`http://testmachine:1234/servlet/<my servlet name>`) or File mapping (`http://testmachine:1234/mapped_to_servlet.html`) is received by the Servlet Runner, this directory will be searched for the requested servlet. The default is the local directory.	srun –d d:\test_servlets\
–v	This enables verbose output from the Servlet Runner. Useful for debugging purposes.	srun –v
-s [property file]	Specifies the name and location of a property file that describes servlets and their initialization parameters. The default is servlet.properties in the current directory. This differs from the JSDK README file. After adequate experimentation (try srun –v –d d:\somewhere and look at the output), we found that the README file was incorrect. The properties file is the only place where servlet initialization parameters can be specified.	srun –s d:\test\params
–r [directory]	The directory where the Servlet Runner will retrieve requested Web pages. This is equal to the root directory of a Web server (e.g., `c:\javawebserver1.1\public_html`). The default is the current directory.	srun –r d:\mytestpages\

Core Note

You can ignore the b, m, *and* t *parameters because you'll never need to use them. Interested readers should refer to the README file included in the JSDK.*

If you are happy with the defaults, start the Servlet Runner in the same directory as your Brat servlet. Using a Web browser (in this case Netscape, shown in Figure 5-2), connect to the Brat at `http://surfer:8080/servlet/Brat`. You should be presented with the screen shown in Figure 5-3.

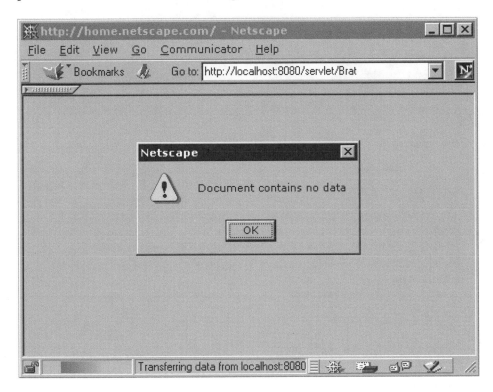

Figure 5-2   Connecting to the Brat with Netscape.

If we look at the Servlet Runner's output window, we see that our Brat has been woken up by our Web page request and then asked to do some chores (but, like most brats, refused to do anything but complain!). If we do another request, our Brat will complain again, *but won't be asked to wake up!* This behavior is to be expected after our discussion of a servlet's life cycle: `init` is called only once by the Servlet Runner when the Brat is first loaded.

Singleton is the first example of a design pattern used in the Java Web Server.

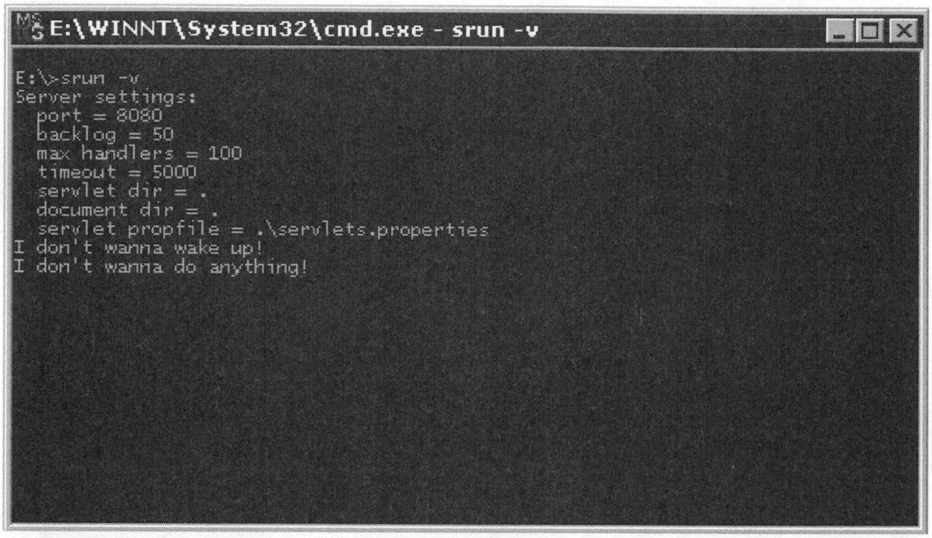

```
MS E:\WINNT\System32\cmd.exe - srun -v                    _ □ ×

E:\>srun -v
Server settings:
  port = 8080
  backlog = 50
  max handlers = 100
  timeout = 5000
  servlet dir = .
  document dir = .
  servlet propfile = .\servlets.properties
I don't wanna wake up!
I don't wanna do anything!
```

Figure 5-3   Testing the Brat servlet with the Servlet Runner.

Core Design Pattern

The Singleton pattern enforces a maximum of one instance per class per program. Servlets are treated as instance Singletons by the servlet engine, with only one active servlet object per configured servlet entry. Therefore, we could have multiple instances of the same class active, but there can be only one active instance per entry.

Communicating with the Browser

When we sent our Netscape browser to test our Brat servlet, we received the error message "Document Contains No Data." What does that mean? The Web browser is expecting some sort of response when it makes a request, but what is it expecting?

Perhaps a better question would be, "How does a servlet serve a browser when a browser comes a–callin'?" In other words, how does the Brat know when to complain?

If we go back to our original discussion on servlets as server-based applets, we compared the entry-point methods and found similarities. Besides having the same method names as applets, servlets also exist in a *framework*.

Core Design Pattern

A Framework is a behavioral pattern that follows the Hollywood principle "Don't call us, we'll call you." Servlets receive a "phone call" from the servlet engine when work becomes available. By extending GenericServlet, *we can add our own unique behavior to the system without changing the structure of the existing framework.*

So how do we get our Brat to take its case to whoever is telling it what to do, instead of just quietly mumbling to itself? If our Brat could talk, what would it talk with to get its point across?

Remember the ServletResponse object that gets passed into our service call by the framework? That object has a simple set of methods allowing us to send information back to our caller.

JAVAX.SERVLET.SERVLETRESPONSE

```
public ServletOutputStream getOutputStream throws IOException
```

Gives the caller a ServletOutputStream back to our caller. Anything we want the caller to see should be placed in this OutputStream.

```
public void setContentType (String type)
```

Sets the MIME type of the content being returned to the user. For example, if we were writing HTML back to the client, we would set the content type to be "text/html".

```
public void setContentLength (int size)
```

Tells the underlying framework how much data we are expecting to send back to the caller. This can be used as a performance-enhancement mechanism.

```
public PrintWriter getWriter throws IOException
```

Gives the caller a PrintWriter object. The PrintWriter class is new to JDK 1.1, and it was introduced to properly support international applications (which was difficult with OutputStream objects as they are *byte oriented*).

Core Note

You can substitute PrintWriter *objects for the* ServletOutputStream *objects we used in our examples.*

We need a ServletOutputStream object to send our complaints where they belong, so to get it we call getOutputStream on the ServletResponse object passed into the service method.

A ServletOutputStream is an extension of java.io.OutputStream, and it provides two sets of seven methods for placing Java's intrinsic types onto the stream. The first set prints out the type (the print methods), and the second set follows the type with a carriage-return-and-line-feed (CRLF) character (the println methods).

To illustrate the use of the ServletOutputStream, we've made some changes to our Brat servlet shown in Listing 5-2.

Listing 5-2   Brat.java (Take 2)

```java
import javax.servlet.*;
import java.io.*;
public class Brat extends GenericServlet
{
  public void init(ServletConfig sc)
  throws ServletException
  {
    System.out.println ("I don't wanna wake up!");
  }
  public void service (ServletRequest req,
  ServletResponse res) throws ServletException
  {
    try
    {
      ServletOutputStream sos = res.getOutputStream();
      sos.println("I don't wanna do anything!");
      sos.close();
    }
    catch (IOException ioe) { ioe.printStackTrace(); }
  }
  public void destroy ()
  {
    System.out.println("I don't wanna go to bed!");
  }
}
```

JAVAX.SERVLET. SERVLETOUTPUTSTREAM

NO CRLF APPENDED TO STREAM

```
public void print (boolean) throws IOException
```
converts a boolean to a string ("true" or "false") and prints it to the stream.
```
public void print (char) throws IOException
```
prints a single character to the stream.
```
public void print (double) throws IOException
```
converts a double to a string and prints it to the stream.
```
public void print (float) throws IOException
```
converts a float to a string and prints it to the stream.
```
public void print (long) throws IOException
```
converts a long into a string and prints it to the stream.
```
public void print (int) throws IOException
```
converts an integer into a string and prints it to the stream.
```
public void print (String) throws IOException
```
prints the string to the stream.

CRLF APPENDED TO STREAM

```
public void println throws IOException
```
prints a CRLF to the stream.
```
public void println (boolean) throws IOException
```
converts a boolean to a string ("true" or "false") and prints it to a stream, following it with a CRLF.
```
public void println (char) throws IOException
```
prints a single character to the stream, following it with a CRLF.
```
public void println (double) throws IOException
```
converts a double to a string and prints it to the stream, following it with a CRLF.
```
public void println (float) throws IOException
```
converts a float to a string and prints it to the stream, following it with a CRLF.
```
public void println (long) throws IOException
```
converts a long into a string and prints it to the stream, following it with a CRLF.
```
public void println (int) throws IOException
```
converts an integer into a string and prints it to the stream, following it with a CRLF.
```
public void println (String) throws IOException
```
prints the string to the stream, following it with a CRLF.

If we look at the body of the service method, we see that the old `System.out.println` has been replaced with the allocation of a `ServletOutputStream` object, printing the message "I don't wanna do anything" onto the `ServletOutputStream` and closing the `ServletOutputStream`, flushing its contents back to the browser.

We've changed the body of the `service` method, elevating our voice from a disgruntled murmur to a vocal response.

Once again we run the Servlet Runner and analyze the output, as shown in Figures 5-4 and 5-5. As if by magic, the Brat's message of disobedience has been transported away from the servlet runner to the browser window.

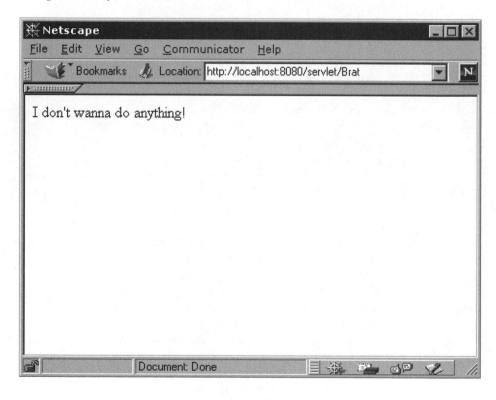

Figure 5-4   Testing the Brat servlet (take two): Netscape client.

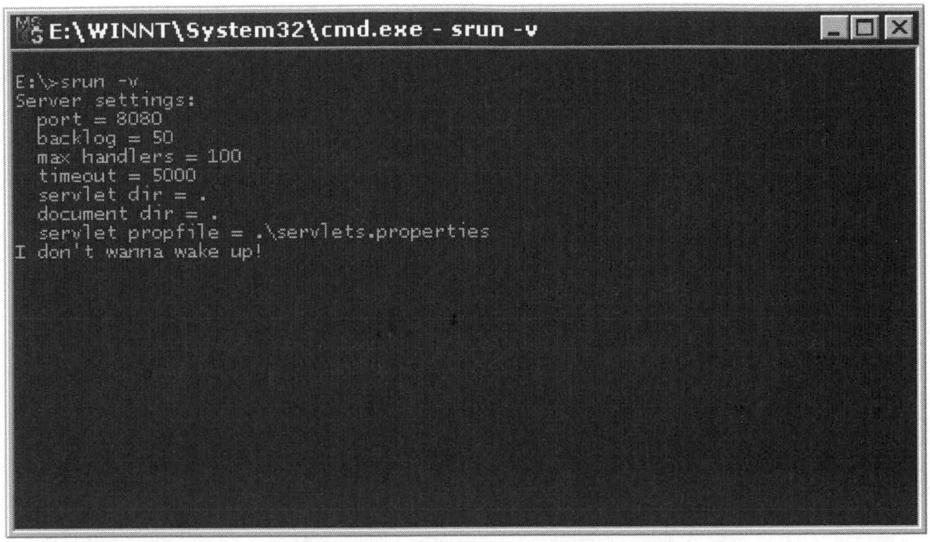

Figure 5-5   Testing the Brat servlet (take two): Servlet Runner.

It's All a Matter of Interpretation!

The browser output looks suspiciously like HTML, but our servlet never mentioned anything about HTML in its code. We can verify if the output is HTML by selecting the `Page Info` menu choice under the `View` menu, as shown in Figure 5-6.

So, how did the browser know the content of the Brat's response was HTML? We never used any HTML tags in our message, nor did we ever mention that the text should be interpreted as HTML.

It seems that the default MIME type for a response is text/html. So, how would we go about changing the browser's interpretation of our content? Fortunately for us, the `ServletResponse` object has a method that can help called `setContentType`. `setContentType` takes a String parameter that describes the MIME type of the returned data.

Let's pretend that our Brat wanted his words to look like plain text and not HTML. To accomplish this, we should specify that the returned data be interpreted as plain text by calling `setContentType("text/plain")` on the `ServletResponse` object:

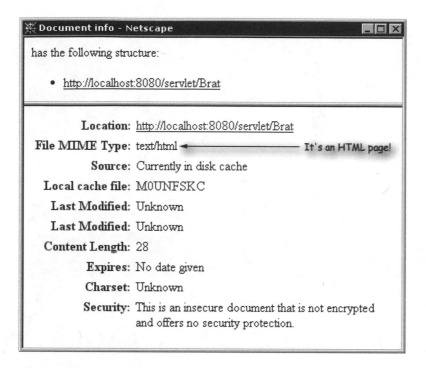

Figure 5-6   Page Info for the Brat servlet's response.

```
public void service (ServletRequest req, ServletResponse res)
throws ServletException
{
    res.setContentType("text/plain");
    try
    {
        ServletOutputStream sos = res.getOutputStream();
        sos.println ("I don't wanna do anything!");
        sos.close();
    }
    catch (IOException ioe) { ioe.printStackTrace(); }
}
```

This time our Brat's output looks different; the text isn't as snazzy as HTML. Viewing the page's information in Figures 5-7 and 5-8 shows us that the content is being interpreted as plain text instead of HTML as in the previous run.

Figure 5-7   The Brat complains in plain text!

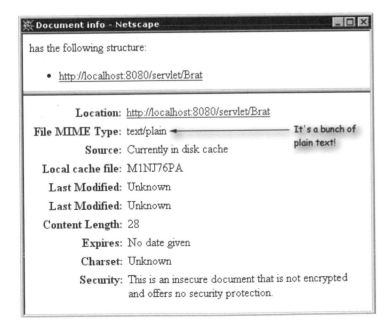

Figure 5-8   Yup! It's plain text, all right!

We aren't restricted to just returning different types of text, either. We can return any MIME type we wish, whether it be streaming audio, graphics, or custom data that we have created for our own purposes. All we need to do is to specify the proper MIME type in the response, and the browser will handle the rest!

"Java Web Server, We Have a Problem"

So far in our trivial examples we haven't run into any problems that would cause a servlet to be unable to handle requests, but we could easily think of some cases when that might be true. Consider a servlet that requires access to a file for information, perhaps a security servlet that compares names and passwords to those stored in a file. What would be the appropriate behavior if that file were missing?

We have a choice: either we can recheck the file during every service call, or we can give up the first time the file can be located by issuing a `ServletException`. `ServletExceptions` inform the framework that our servlet has had a problem.

So, what's the difference between the two? In a nutshell, it's all a matter of responsibility. When a servlet throws a `ServletException`, the framework will block any new calls to the servlet, even if the erroneous condition has been fixed. If the servlet *doesn't* throw a `ServletException`, it can gracefully reestablish itself when the file becomes available.

Let's revisit the Brat code and issue a `ServletException` when we're asked to do some work:

```
public void service (ServletRequest req, ServletResponse res)
throws ServletException
{
   throw new ServletException ("I don't wanna do anything");
}
```

We recompile our Brat and check him out through our Web browser, as shown in Figure 5-9.

Yuck! That isn't the kind of response we want the users of our servlets to see! Not only is it uninformative, but it's user unfriendly to boot! Fortunately, this is only the response from the servlet runner. The same servlet underneath the Java Web Server looks like Figure 5-10.

While the Java Web Server gives more information back to the browser than the servlet runner, it still displays a message which is inappropriate for viewers of your site. It follows, then, that a servlet shouldn't throw a `ServletException` unless an unrecoverable error has occurred; instead, it should try and recover by degrading gracefully. Instead of throwing a `ServletException` when a recoverable error occurs, we recommend that you pretty-print a proper error message:

Figure 5-9 Ugly Response from our ServletException.

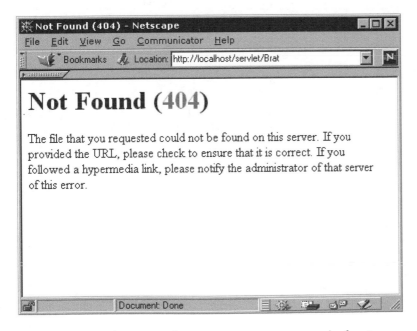

Figure 5-10 The Java Web Server's response is not much of an improvement.

```
public void service (ServletRequest req, ServletResponse res)
throws ServletException
{
  try
  {
    ServletOutputStream sos = res.getOutputStream();
    sos.println("<html><head><title>Oops!</title></head>");
    sos.println ("<body>We've hit a problem!
                 Please try again "+ "later!</body>");
    sos.println ("If it is an emergency, contact
                 <a "+ "href=mailto:cstaylor@pacbell.net");
    sos.println ("Christopher Taylor</a>
                 immediately.</body></html>");
    sos.close();
  }
  catch (IOException ioe) { ioe.printStackTrace(); }
}
```

This time we end up with a simple HTML-formatted error message that provides a user-friendly response when an error occurs (Figure 5-11).

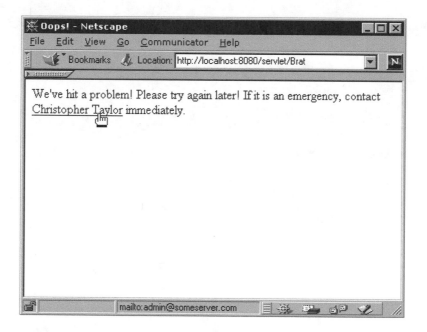

Figure 5-11   A better way to handle errors.

So what are `ServletExceptions` good for? They are great for debugging a servlet: They provide the line number and stack-frame listing of the location where our problem occurred.

Where does this important information end up? It wasn't sent to the browser, so where did it go? Once again, it depends on which servlet system is in use: in the case of the servlet runner, `ServletExceptions` are displayed in the output window as shown in Figure 5-12.

```
E:\WINNT\System32\cmd.exe - srun -v                       _ □ ×

E:\>srun -v
Warning: JIT compiler "nojit" not found. Will use interpreter.
Server settings:
    port = 8080
    backlog = 50
    max handlers = 100
    timeout = 5000
    servlet dir = .
    document dir = .
    servlet propfile = .\servlets.properties
I don't wanna wake up!
javax.servlet.ServletException: I don't wanna do anything!
        at Brat.service(Brat.java:14)
        at sun.servlet.http.HttpServerHandler.sendResponse(HttpServerHandler.jav
a:143)
        at sun.servlet.http.HttpServerHandler.handleConnection(HttpServerHandler
.java:110)
        at sun.servlet.http.HttpServerHandler.run(HttpServerHandler.java:87)
        at java.lang.Thread.run(Thread.java:474)
```

The line where our code failed

Figure 5-12   ServletException output in the servlet runner.

Core Tip

If the words `compiled code` *appear instead of a source-code filename and a line number, that means a JIT (Just In Time) compiler is installed on the system. While a JIT can vastly increase Java's runtime performance, it is difficult to work with during debugging. In the case of Sun's Java Performance Pack (JPP), the environment variable* `JAVA_COMPILER` *is set to* `symcjit`. *Setting the* `JAVA_COMPILER` *variable to nothing* (`set JAVA_COMPILER=` *on Win32 systems) can temporarily remove JIT processing.*

Now we know where to go look for our error: on line 14 of our `Brat.java` source file.

Servlets and Applets Revisited

Servlets and applets are looking more alike all the time: they have similar life cycles, they both exist in a framework, and they both require a default constructor.

Default constructor? Why do our servlets require a default constructor? Let's see what happens if we declare a nondefault constructor in our Brat servlet in Listing 5-3.

Listing 5-3   Brat4.java

```
import javax.servlet.*;
import java.io.*;
public class Brat4 extends GenericServlet
{
  public Brat4 (String s) {}
  public void service (ServletRequest req,
  ServletResponse res) throws ServletException
  { }

}
```

We've added a public constructor for our Brat4 servlet that takes a single String parameter. As this example is only for testing our hypothesis, we have an empty body for the both the constructor and the `service` method.

Fire up the Servlet Runner again, invoke the servlet, and you'll get the results shown in Figure 5-13.

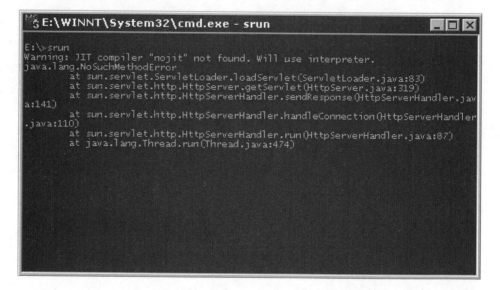

Figure 5-13   Crash and burn—no default constructor.

From the wreckage, it looks like an object of type sun.servlet.ServletLoader throws a NoSuchMethodError when our servlet is first loaded. A NoSuchMethodError is thrown when the method newInstance is called on a class object for a class that has no default constructor. If the ServletLoader uses this feature of the class Class, we must declare a default constructor, and our hypothesis was correct: servlets, like applets, require a public default constructor.

What is this ServletLoader, anyway? A ServletLoader is a type of ClassLoader, and its responsibilities are:

- Retrieving a servlet class file from the disk
- Creating a new instance of the servlet class
- Initializing the servlet instance (calling init)

Core Note

ClassLoaders *are also a key part of the Java Security Model. More information about* ClassLoaders *can be found in* Core Java, *by Cay Horstmann and Gary Cornell, 2nd Ed., Vol. 2.*

Tracing Our Steps Through the Log File

If we could convince our Brat to do some work, we should write it down for posterity's sake. But where could we put it so the information doesn't get lost? We have several choices:

- Send it to the console (System.out).
- Send it to the browser (ServletOutputStream).
- Log the information (log).

Core Note

There are more choices for storing persistent information. However, these are the only easy choices at this stage in our servlet development.

GenericServlet has a public method called log that takes a String (the message to log) as a parameter. public void log(String msg) writes the String message to the server-dependent event log. The standard format of the log is <classname>:<log message>, which can cause problems if multiple instances of the same servlet are configured as different services. In that case, the servlet developer should override this method to provide some instance information that will differentiate the log entries from each other. Using the log method will store our "He cleaned his room! " message forever (or until someone erases the log).

Listing 5-4 shows the modified Brat source code with the log entry added.

Listing 5-4   Brat5.java

```java
import javax.servlet.*;
import java.io.*;
public class Brat5 extends GenericServlet
{
  public void init(ServletConfig sc) throws ServletException
  {
    System.out.println ("I don't wanna wake up!");
  }
  public void service (ServletRequest req,
  ServletResponse res) throws ServletException
  {
    try
    {
      ServletOutputStream sos = res.getOutputStream();
      sos.println("Okay. I'll clean my room.");
      sos.close();
      log("He cleaned his room!");
    }
    catch (IOException ioe) { ioe.printStackTrace(); }
  }
  public void destroy ()
  {
    System.out.println("I don't wanna go to bed!");
  }
}
```

We compile the Brat5 servlet and test it through the Servlet Runner as shown in Figure 5-14.

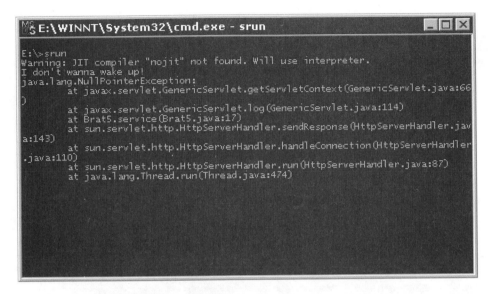

Figure 5-14   "The Log is Missing," he wrote.

Uh oh! Why did we get a NullPointerException, especially in code we didn't write? (We inherited the code for getServletContext from GenericServlet!)

After a rigorous inspection of the log-method source code (found in the src subdirectory of the JSDK), we see that GenericServlet's log method is a wrapper that forwards our call to ServletContext's log method:

```
public void log(String msg)
{
   getServletContext().log(getClass().getName() + ": "+ msg);
}
```

Okay, so how does our getServletContext() method retrieve our ServletContext? Again, we turn to the GenericServlet source code for the answer:

```
public ServletContext getServletContext()
{
   return config.getServletContext();
}
```

config is a local variable of type ServletConfig, which is initialized *during the init method* (line 148 of GenericServlet.java)! Since we overrode the default behavior of GenericServlet's init method, this variable never gets properly initialized, and consequently we receive a NullPointerException when we try to use this uninitialized variable during our log-method call.

Core Tip

All servlets should call their parent's init *method so that the* ServletContext *is properly stored for future use. Failure to do so can lead to strange behavior, such as a* NullPointerException *in code that was unchanged.*

We quickly change our init method to call our parent's (GenericServlet's) init method before returning:

```
public void init(ServletConfig sc) throws ServletException
{
  System.out.println ("I don't wanna wake up!");
  super.init(sc);
}
```

Once again, run the servlet through the Servlet Runner and get the correct results shown in Figure 5-15.

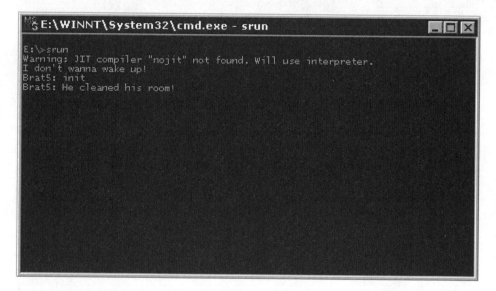

Figure 5-15   Logs...checked.

Logging is a powerful mechanism that should be used for both debugging and "checkpoint" messages. For example, if our Brat had a bag of marbles that it lent out to each visiting browser, it should log to whom it gave a marble (Listing 5-5).

Listing 5-5   Brat6.java

```java
import javax.servlet.*;
import java.io.*;
public class Brat6 extends GenericServlet
{
  public void init(ServletConfig sc)
  throws ServletException
  {
    super.init(sc);
    System.out.println ("I don't wanna wake up!");
  }
  public void service (ServletRequest req,
  ServletResponse res) throws ServletException
  {
    String host = req.getRemoteHost();
    try
    {
      ServletOutputStream sos = res.getOutputStream();
      sos.println("Have a marble, "+host);
      sos.close();
      log("Gave a marble to "+host);
    }
    catch (IOException ioe) { ioe.printStackTrace(); }
  }
  public void destroy ()
  {
    System.out.println("I don't wanna go to bed!");
  }
}
```

As you can see, we send a "checkpoint" message to the log system, recording to whom we gave the marble. Figures 5-16 and 5-17 show the results.

Core Note

Checkpointing is an excellent aid for finding out what went wrong with a servlet, and we recommend using checkpoints if you plan to distribute your servlets to other users. When checkpoints exist in a log file, it becomes a much easier task to track down what caused the problem.

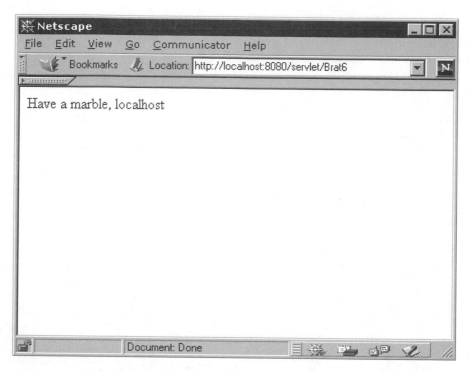

Figure 5-16   The localhost gets a marble.

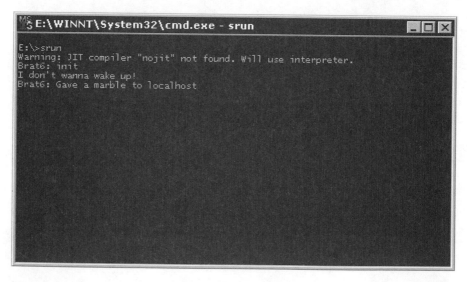

Figure 5-17   Our Brat keeps track of his marble loan.

"Who's at the Door, Honey?"

We must confess, we sneaked some unexplained code into the Brat6 example—specifically, where we make a call to a method called `getRemoteHost` on the ServletRequest object.

What `getRemoteHost` did was return a String containing the hostname of the client taking marbles from our Brat. Hostnames are easy-to-read aliases for networked machines; they provide a simpler mechanism for connecting with a machine than just plain IP addresses. As shown in Figure 5-18, hostnames are retrieved by asking a special computer called a *name server* to give us the name corresponding to a certain IP address.

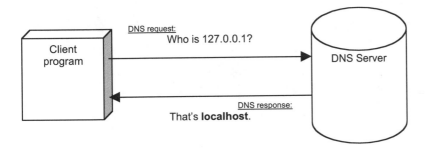

Figure 5-18   Resolving IP addresses into hostnames with DNS.

When you ran the Brat6 example, did you notice the pause between when the servlet was first accessed and when the results were sent? That pause occurred when our code needed to retrieve the hostname from the name server. A name service request can take a while to complete, depending on the current status of the network.

Core Tip

While useful for debugging purposes during testing, a working servlet should not rely on `getRemoteHost` *for retrieving hostname information. The IP address is just as informative and a lot less expensive to retrieve during execution.*

As a performance-minded servlet, our next example will replace the call to `getRemoteHost` with its more cost-effective cousin, `getRemoteAddr`. This is shown in Listing 5-6.

Listing 5-6   Brat7.java

```java
import javax.servlet.*;
import java.io.*;
public class Brat7 extends GenericServlet
{
  public void init(ServletConfig sc)
  throws ServletException
  {
    super.init(sc);
    System.out.println ("I don't wanna wake up!");
  }
  public void service (ServletRequest req,
  ServletResponse res) throws ServletException
  {
    String host = req.getRemoteAddr();
    try
    {
      ServletOutputStream sos = res.getOutputStream();
      sos.println("Have a marble, "+host);
      sos.close();
      log("Gave a marble to "+host);
    }
    catch (IOException ioe) { ioe.printStackTrace(); }
  }
  public void destroy ()
  {
    System.out.println("I don't wanna go to bed!");
  }
}
```

As we can see by the output on both Netscape (Figure 5-19) and the Servlet Runner (Figure 5-20), the hostname has been replaced by the IP address of the requesting client.

The ServletRequest object has several methods to provide various pieces of information about a client's request to a servlet.

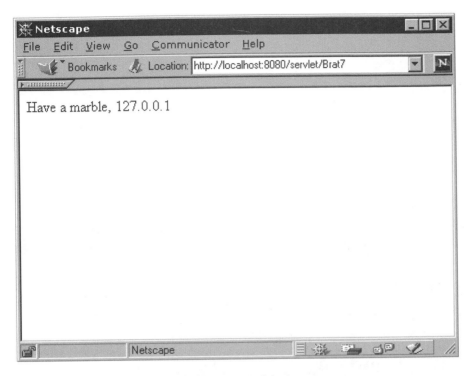

Figure 5-19 Using the IP address instead of the hostname.

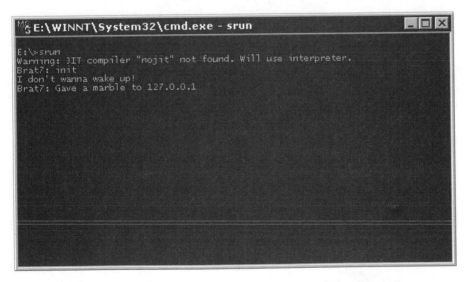

Figure 5-20 Servlet Runner using IP addresses instead of hostnames.

JAVAX.SERVLET.SERVLETREQUEST

```
public String getServerName
```

returns the hostname of the server that received the request. In our case, this would be "localhost."

```
public int getServerPort
```

returns the port number of the server that the request was received by. In our case, this would be 8080.

```
public String getRemoteHost
```

returns the hostname of the client that sent the request. This can take some time to complete and should not be used in a performance-intensive environment.

```
public String getRemoteAddr
```

returns the IP address of the client that sent the request. This operation provides information similar to that returned by `getRemoteHost`, but without the overhead of a DNS request.

While the `getRemoteHost` and `getRemoteAddr` methods make sense, why would our servlet be interested in the *server's* port and hostname? Having access to this information lets the servlet developer (that's us) customize a servlet's output in several ways:

- Conditional output (e.g., if the server is on machine localhost, display "Welcome from Localhost!")
- Security (e.g., only certain hosts can access certain servers)
- Logging

Making the GenericServlet Less Generic

When we revisited our comparison between servlets and applets, we noted that their respective frameworks ignore specialized constructors. If we can't specify any parameters to a constructor, we have to ask how a servlet can customize its behavior.

Once again we turn to the applet and inspect its customization behavior. Applets are configured through initialization parameters that typically are tucked away in the HTML between the open and close `applet` tags:

```
<applet code=TestApplet.class width=300 height=300>
<param name="message" value="Hello World!">
</applet>
```

The applet author can make calls to the get Parameter method to retrieve the value of a named parameter. Continuing our example, Listing 5-7 shows the code to retrieve the message parameter.

Listing 5-7   A simple applet

```
import java.applet.*;
import java.awt.*;
public class TestApplet extends Applet
{
  public void init ()
  {
    String messageValue = getParameter("message");
    Label l = new Label(messageValue);
    add(l);
  }
}
```

Now compile the TestApplet and run it through the appletviewer for the results shown in Figure 5-21.

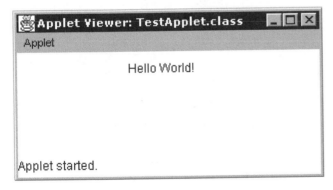

Figure 5-21   TestApplet with a "Hello World!" message.

We can reconfigure the TestApplet without recompiling our source code by making some changes to the HTML:

```
<applet code=TestApplet.class width=300 height=300>
<param name="message" value="Java is Cool!">
</applet>
```

Again we rerun our TestApplet though the appletviewer, as shown in Figure 5-22.

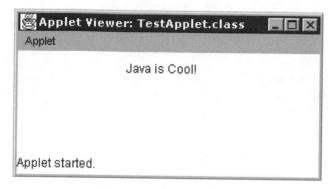

Figure 5-22   TestApplet speaks the truth.

Wouldn't it be nice if servlets had the same capabilities? Fortunately for us, they do! `GenericServlet` provides two methods, `getInitParameter` and `getInitParameterNames` for retrieving parameter values passed in through the servlet environment:

```
public String getInitParameter(String name).
```

Retrieves the value paired to the parameter name.

```
public Enumeration getInitParameterNames.
```

Retrieves an `Enumeration` of Strings corresponding to all of the parameter names.

Now, with an applet, we specify its parameters in an HTML file. Servlet parameters are passed in a servlet engine-dependent manner: with the Servlet Runner servlets receive their parameters from a special properties file. This properties file is typically called `servlets.properties`, with each servlet object requiring two entries:

```
servlet.[name].code=[class name]
servlet.[same name as above].initArgs=[comma-delimited list
of name-value pairs]
```

So, if we had a servlet named Brat8 that needed to be initialized with the parameter message="Hello Java Web Server!", the file would look like:

```
servlet.Brat.code=Brat8
servlet.Brat.initArgs=message=Hello Java Web Server!
```

Before we continue, though, we need to make a Brat8 servlet that will utilize the initialization parameters being passed to it. Listing 5-8 will cache the value for the "message" argument in a local member variable and use that information during service requests.

Listing 5-8   Brat8.java

```java
import javax.servlet.*;
import java.io.*;
public class Brat8 extends GenericServlet
{
  private String m_message;

  public void init(ServletConfig sc)
  throws ServletException
  {
    super.init(sc);
    m_message = getInitParameter("message");
  }
  public void service (ServletRequest req,
  ServletResponse res) throws ServletException
  {
    try
    {
      ServletOutputStream sos = res.getOutputStream();
      sos.println(m_message);
      sos.close();
    }
    catch (IOException ioe) { ioe.printStackTrace(); }
  }
}
```

As you can see in the Brat8 servlet, we retrieve the value of the parameter named "message" and store it in the instance variable named m_message, which will later be sent to the client on a service request. We start up the Servlet Runner and connect to our Brat8 servlet for testing with the URL http://surfer:8080/servlet/Brat.

But wasn't our servlet named Brat8, and not Brat? How did the servlet runner know which servlet to execute? This information was stored in the servlets.properties file that we created to pass parameters to our Brat8 servlet. In that file we specified that the servlet named Brat was to use Brat8.class.

Core Tip

When there is a choice between the servlets.properties *file and the servlet directory, the* servlets.properties *file takes precedence. For example, if we had a servlet called Brat in the servlet directory, and we had the Brat entry in the* servlet.properties *file mapped to the Brat8 servlet, a client using the URL* http://surfer:8080/servlet/Brat *would activate the Brat8 servlet.*

Let's change the `init` parameters in the properties file and reconnect to our Brat8 servlet to see the changed results shown in Figures 5-23 and 5-24.

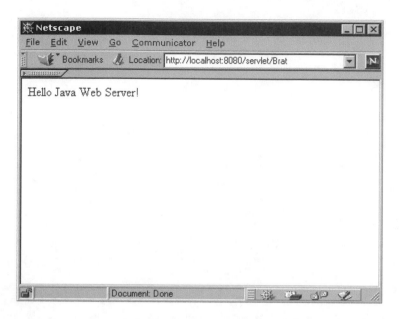

Figure 5-23   Configuring a servlet through init parameters results in this...

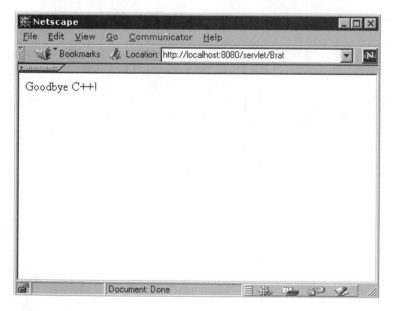

Figure 5-24   ...and this.

Summary

Wow! This chapter has been a whirlwind of APIs, object diagrams, and example programs. You just got a taste of the superclass of all servlets, the `GenericServlet`, along with some nonprogramming servlet topics such as lifetimes and configuration. Although we still have a lot of material left to cover, you should be feeling more at home with the following servlet programming concepts:

- All servlets extend the `GenericServlet` class.
- Like applets, servlets have a defined life cycle.
- Servlets can be configured through initialization parameters.
- Servlet requests are handled by the `service` method.
- It is a good practice to call `super.init` when overriding the init method.
- `ServletExceptions` should never make it out of production code.
- Host information can be obtained through the `getRemoteAddr` and `getRemoteHost` methods of `ServletRequest`.
- We can log important information using the `log` method.
- All output to the browser goes through a `ServletOutputStream` obtained from the `ServletResponse` object in the `getOutputStream` method.

ADVANCED SERVLETS

Chapter 6

In the previous chapter we introduced the `GenericServlet` class, kicked the tires a little, and drove it around the block with a few toy examples. Now we're going to get under the hood, introduce you to the engine that powers the JavaWeb Server, and, most importantly, show you the life cycle lived by every servlet. This knowledge will come in useful when you have to make some design decisions with your own servlet projects. We also show you how to protect critical sections in your servlet, how to chain servlets together, and how to write code which can help you debug your servlets more effectively. All of the scenarios in this chapter were earned through various mistakes and program *features* that we ran into in our own projects, and we firmly believe that this experience should be shared so that we can save you from those same headaches.

Framework Foibles

You have most likely seen an example of a software framework. Frameworks provide a set of tested, reusable code, encapsulating most of the necessary components required for getting a job done. In the Microsoft Windows world, the most popular programming framework is Microsoft's Microsoft Foundation Classes (MFC). MFC gives you access to common windowing facilities through objects, hiding many of the tedious housekeeping chores behind friendly member functions. Instead of mucking around with API calls and event loops, you can add new behavior to a subclass. These new classes are then plugged into the existing framework, requiring only a fraction of the development time normally required to get something up and running. Likewise, the Abstract Windowing Toolkit (AWT) classes of the Java Development Kit (JDK) serve a similar purpose for writing GUI programs with a similar look and behavior running on different operating systems.

Frameworks have been a popular tool for developing client applications, but they haven't received as much attention from programmers writing servers. Some misconceptions that surround frameworks may lead you to believe that a framework is not suited for writing a server application.

DEBUNKING THE MYTHS SURROUNDING FRAMEWORKS

Myth1: *Frameworks make me code around their view of the world.*
Answer: While some frameworks enforce policies (such as the document/view architecture of MFC) that may not be well suited for your particular needs, not all frameworks require you to accept such policies. Lightweight frameworks that provide the minimum behavior necessary may be a better solution.

Myth2: *Frameworks make my code run slow.*
Answer: Like any other kind of code, poorly optimized frameworks can produce slow execution. Frameworks sometimes escape companies as products before they're ready, because no one has tried writing a real application with them. Called *eating your own dog food*, writing an application with a framework is the best way to test the framework's quality.

Myth3: *I don't have time to learn a framework and write this server application.*
Answer: With any project, a good portion of programming time is devoted to bug fixing. Bugs are typically introduced in new, untested code. When you use a framework, the number of bugs decreases ,because the framework provides a solid base of tested software to build upon. Learning a framework may take longer than simply *gunning away* at the problem cowboy style, but, as the saying goes, *a stitch in time saves nine*—and utilizing existing code means fewer bugs to fix (and every programmer that we've run into *hates* fixing bugs).

So what frameworks are available for writing server applications? Sun Microsystems has put together a Java framework called the Java Server Toolkit (see `jserv.javasoft.com`), which is useful for writing cross-platform servers that require efficient multithreading. They've also slurped down the dog chow by offering several products written with the Java Server Toolkit, the most popular of them being the Java Web Server.

What kind of services does the Java Server Toolkit provide for programs like the Java Web Server? You've already seen one of the most important parts of the Toolkit: servlets. The Java Server Toolkit provides the base servlet engine used by the Java Web Server. The development team extended portions of this base code, creating Web-specific extensions built on the `GenericServlet`, `ServletRequest`, and `ServletResponse` classes, named `HttpServlet`, `HttpServletRequest`, and `HttpServletResponse` respectively. Since these classes are derived from their Generic ancestors, the code from the Java Server Toolkit remained unchanged as a tested framework for building server applications.

Figure 6-1 shows what this servlet engine looks like:

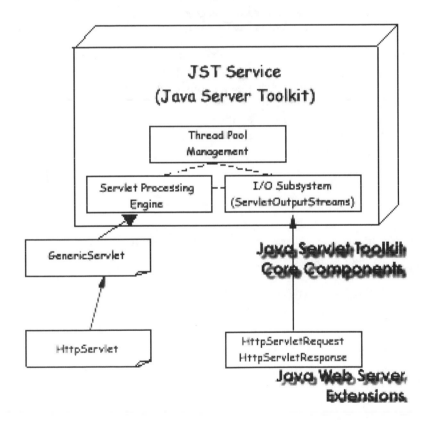

Figure 6-1   The servlet engine.

As you can see from the drawing, servlets are an instance of the Singleton pattern: Only one servlet object exists for all requests that are made. Each request is handled by a *worker thread* that receives the work request, finds the correct servlet, calls into its servlet's `service` method, releases the work request, and then goes to retrieve more work.

Core Design Pattern

Threads, even in Java, are computationally expensive to create and maintain. The worker-thread pattern solves this problem by prestarting a minimum number of threads (e.g., 5) that wait for work requests to be given to them. As work requests are made, each worker thread takes a work object from the queue and performs the operations required to do that work. If more work is available than workers to complete it, more workers are hired (thread creation), up to a maximum number (e.g., 80). If the amount of work tapers off, workers are "fired" (thread destruction), until the minimum number of threads is reached.

As in other multithreaded programs, *data collisions* can occur when multiple threads access servlets simultaneously. A data collision occurs when two or more threads enter a portion of code that should execute as an atomic unit (e.g., reading a variable, operating on that data, then writing the variable back again). Data collisions can create strange program behavior and are often difficult to debug because of the unpredictable nature of thread scheduling. Code that should be executed together needs to be wrapped in a synchronized block:

```
synchronized (this)
{
 // put code here
}
```

More information about thread-safe coding exists in *Core Java*.

The typical programmer gut reaction is to lock down the servlet with a `synchronized` call:

```
public synchronized void service (ServletRequest req,
ServletResponse res)
```

While this solves the problem of multithreaded access, it also removes any of its benefits! Marking the service method as synchronized allows only one thread at a time to be active in our servlet's `service` method. With other threads waiting in line to use our servlet, we force more threads to be created by the framework, and if the maximum number of workers is reached, clients must wait until a thread becomes available before their work can get done. We need a better way to protect our servlets.

In order to solve this performance bottleneck, we need to take a more sophisticated look at the problem of concurrent access. What does a synchronized method mean? Since every object in Java has a *monitor* attached to it, a thread making a synchronized-method call must *own* this monitor before entering the method body. As only one thread may own a monitor's lock at any time, synchronization provides controlled access to an object. Monitors act like a receptionist for an object, permitting access to only one visiting thread, keeping track of the waiting visitors, and ushering the next visitor into the object when the previous one is finished.

The entire body of the service method probably does not need to be executed as an *atomic unit*. Only certain *critical sections* need to be executed together, while the rest of the code can be unprotected. By reducing the size of these critical sections, we can minimize the amount of time that the servlet can be accessed by only one thread. However, there is a performance penalty for locking an object. Depending on the code being protected, locking and unlocking an object multiple times may take longer to execute than locking the object once for the entire body of the method.

As an example, we'll code a servlet that needs to synchronize its access to a file. The file in Listing 6-1 is used to log and timestamp service requests.

Listing 6-1 NaiveFileServlet .java

```java
import javax.servlet.*;
import java.io.*;
import java.util.Date;

public class NaiveFileServlet extends GenericServlet
{
  private PrintWriter m_pw;
  private int m_id = 0;
  private static final String DEFAULT = "out";

  public void init (ServletConfig cfg) throws ServletException
  {
    super.init(cfg);
    String filename = null;
    try
    {
      filename = cfg.getInitParameter("filename");
      if (filename == null)
      {
        filename = DEFAULT;
      }
      m_pw = new PrintWriter (new FileWriter(filename));
    }
    catch (IOException ioe)
    {
      throw new ServletException("Could Not Open Output: "+filename);
    }
  }
```

continued

```
public void service (ServletRequest req, ServletResponse res)
throws ServletException, IOException
{
  m_pw.print("Hello Request # "+m_id++);
  m_pw.print(" calling from "+req.getRemoteAddr());
  m_pw.println();
  m_pw.flush();
}

}
```

What's wrong with our `NaiveFileServlet`? When we compile it, we don't get any errors, and when we test it under the servlet runner, the log file looks correct. But when we deploy it for use on our corporate Web server, we get garbage output in the log file, as if *multiple people had been writing to the file at the same time!*

We received incorrect results because we failed to see that the PrintWriter object, m_pw, is a *shared resource* provided by the servlet for all incoming requests. A Shared Resource is an object that can be accessed by multiple threads. Accesses to these objects that change their state (mutable methods) need to be protected so that multiple (possibly conflicting) changes do not leave the object in an improper state. In our example, the log file was left in a garbled state, where records were not written intact. You need to protect access to it through some sort of locking mechanism.

This time we use synchronization to provide restricted access to the log:

```
public void service (ServletRequest req, ServletResponse res)
throws ServletException, IOException
{
  StringBuffer sb = new StringBuffer();
  sb.append("Hello Request # ");
  sb.append(m_id++);
  sb.append(" calling from ");
  sb.append(req.getRemoteAddr());
  synchronized(m_pw)
  {
    m_pw.println(sb.toString());
    m_pw.flush();
  }
}
```

The use of synchronization has been restricted to the brief moment where it is needed: accessing the log file. We should always get proper results with this new code, no matter how heavy a load the server is under. This only guarantees that records remain intact. There still is the possibility that records could be out of order (record 7 appearing in the log before record 6).

In the case of a `PrintWriter` object, this additional locking is unnecessary. A quick glance at the source code in the src subdirectory of the JDK shows that the

OutputStreamWriter (the superclass of the FileWriter) serializes access to itself with a synchronization call. Our additional locking of the PrintWriter class, while a good exercise in defensive programming, is an extra step that is not needed at this time.

The thread pool is managed by the servlet system, and parameters such as the maximum and minimum number of worker threads can be changed to improve performance. In the Java Web Server, we use the Administration Applet to configure these settings.

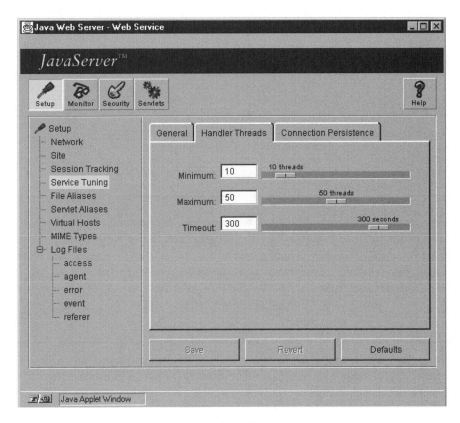

Figure 6-2   Administering the thread pool.

"Exit...Stage Left"

One method of handling exceptions in a Java program is called the *Autopsy Approach*, where the program is considered unusable when an error occurs, so it terminates after printing out the stack trace of the exception:

```
try
{
  // do some code here
}
catch (Exception e)
{
  e.printStackTrace();
  System.exit(1);
}
```

Although this method is frowned on as an amateur approach to fixing problems in a program, many successful software companies use it as a form of error handling. Servlets can also call `System.exit()` in case of an error condition, but with the additional consequence that the Java Web Server shuts down!

Core Note

Microsoft Windows often throws in the towel when a program misbehaves, lamely excusing itself by informing the user that the errant program has created a "General Protection Fault." Mac users are also familiar with the "bomb" icon that appears when an unrecoverable error occurs.

This is not the way to handle errors with servlets! We cannot stress this point enough. `System.exit()` is provided for programs to terminate themselves and return an error condition back to the operating system. Applets are restricted from calling `System.exit()` by a `SecurityManager` installed by the Web browser, but servlets are not restricted by any `SecurityManager`. Local servlets are not restricted. Servlets loaded over the network have more restrictions.

Core Note

Owing to the nature of the Java Security model, only one `SecurityManager` may be loaded in a virtual machine at a time. This will be improved in future releases of the JDK.

As most Web masters will not be Java programmers, or have access to a servlet author's source code, it is imperative that they be able to trust a servlet not to crash their Web server. If that trust isn't warranted, anyone with a copy of the JDK can search the class file of a servlet for a call to the `System.exit()` method as follows:

On Win32 Platforms:

```
javap <ServletClassName> -c | find /I "invokestatic #10
<Method void exit(int)>"
```

On UNIX:

```
javap <ServletClassName> -c | grep /I "invokestatic #10
<Method void exit(int)>"
```

For example, if we were running Windows NT and wanted to check that the Brat servlet didn't call `System.exit()`, we would type:

```
javap Brat -c | find /I "invokestatic #10 <Method void exit(int)>"
```

and receive an empty output (if the servlet didn't call `exit`) or the lines of disassembled Java bytecode (if the servlet did call `exit`). Unfortunately, this check doesn't work if the servlet makes a method call to another object that calls `System.exit`. A cautious administrator might want to *dry-run* a servlet under different test conditions before using it on a production server.

Servlets with Training Wheels

Most programmers expect a framework to provide a flexible and safe environment, where a new piece of code cannot break code already in place. For example, overriding a method without calling the superclass version should not cause other code to break. Unfortunately, the default implementation of the `GenericServlet` class doesn't provide a programmer with enough of this kind of protection. Remember the problem with forgetting to call `GenericServlet`'s `init` method covered in the last chapter? This failure can create unrelated problems to show up in code untouched by the developer, because data structures used by the `GenericServlet` are stored during the `init` method.

Why doesn't the applet class have this same problem? The applet class is protected from it by providing an init method that has no requirement to call the superclass version. This inconsistency in `GenericServlet` is like driving without a seatbelt: as long as you're careful, no one will get hurt, but as soon as something goes wrong, your passengers are in the hospital. Listing 6-2 builds a seatbelt for driving in the Java Web Server by deriving from `GenericServlet`.

Listing 6-2   TrainingServlet.java

```java
import javax.servlet.*;

abstract public class TrainingServlet extends GenericServlet
{
  public final void init (ServletConfig cfg) throws ServletException
  {
    super.init(cfg);
    init();
  }

  public void init () throws ServletException {}
}
```

The first step of protection is to isolate the code that can cause an accident. In the init scenario, the problems happen when the GenericServlet's init method doesn't get called. Since we are guaranteed that the framework will call the init method, the simplest solution is to mark the init method as final. Then no subclass can override it. This solution, however, also produces an interesting dilemma: how do we give subclasses the ability to have certain code executed before any service requests are made? If we can't put our own code into the init method, where can we put it?

The solution is obvious: provide another method that will be called by the TrainingServlet after all initialization is complete. As a mnemonic convenience, let's call this method init (without any parameters). As with an applet, classes derived from our TrainingServlet don't have to worry about forgetting the super.init call; all necessary data structures are initialized before init is called. To prove that this works, let's set up a crash test in Listing 6-3. We'll bring in the Brat code from the last chapter—the same code that failed because we had forgotten to call super.init(ServletConfig).

Listing 6-3   Brat5.java

```java
import javax.servlet.*;
import java.io.*;

public class Brat5 extends TrainingServlet
{
  public void init() throws ServletException
  {
    System.out.println ("I don't wanna wake up!");
  }

  public void service (ServletRequest req,
                               ServletResponse res)
  throws ServletException
  {
    try
    {
      PrintWriter pw = res.getWriter();
      pw.println("Okay. I'll clean my room.");
      pw.close();
      log("He cleaned his room!");
    }
    catch (IOException ioe) { ioe.printStackTrace(); }
  }
  public void destroy ()
  {
    System.out.println("I don't wanna go to bed!");
  }
}
```

Notice how the method signature for the `init` method has been changed to no longer take a `ServletConfig` object. The new `init` method will get called automatically because of its parent, the `TrainingServlet` superclass. Compile the revised `Brat5` servlet and stick him into the servlet runner. Figure 6-3 shows the Brat in action in Netscape's browser, and Figure 6-4 shows the Brat complaining to standard out.

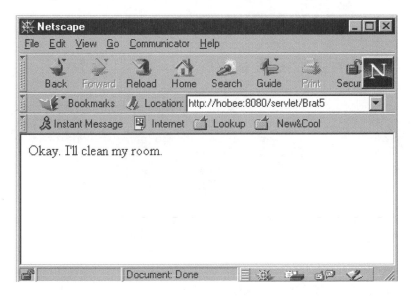

Figure 6-3   The Brat in action.

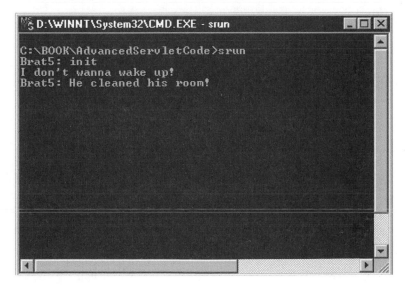

Figure 6-4   The Brat complains to standard out.

The seatbelts pass the test with flying colors! By restricting access to the sensitive code, we've removed an easy way to mess up the initialization of our servlets.

Core Note

TrainingServlet *is an excellent replacement for the* GenericServlet *class.*

Understanding the Servlet Life Cycle

When we took a comparative tour of the GenericServlet and its life cycle in the previous chapter, we left several important questions unanswered. One of them dealt with the servlet life cycle. While we are familiar with the init/service/destroy cycle that all servlets must go through, we don't know when, how, and who decides when it takes place. By taking a second look at how a servlet is brought into this world, we can make some sense out of what is happening behind the curtains of the servlet system.

Like a midwife, an object called the ServletLoader is the first person to hold the newborn servlet. As a specialized classloader, its responsibilities include:

- Locating the class of a specified servlet.
- Creating an instance of that class.
- Initializing the servlet.
- Storing the servlet for later reference.
- Retrieving a servlet by name for service() processing.
- Using timestamps to decide if a servlet's class has changed. If the timestamp has changed, destroy the old servlet instance, reload the class, and initialize the new instance.

From this lengthy list of responsibilities, it is difficult to see how you'd know what phase of the servlet life cycle a servlet is currently in: uninitialized, initialized, or destroyed. Unfortunately, you can't get that information with the current implementation, because it isn't tracked.

Why is the state of the servlet important? From the responsibility list, you see that you can retrieve servlets by name from the ServletLoader. This is a useful feature that isn't well documented by the servlet API: your requests can be handled by a collaboration of servlets. (This shouldn't be confused with *servlet chaining*, a feature in which servlets act as set of filters on a stream of data. Servlet chaining will be covered further on in the chapter.) But this flexibility comes with the price of reduced safety: any servlet can invoke methods on other servlets, no matter what state that servlet currently is in.

So how would you add this useful information to the Servlet API? You can't modify the code for the `ServletLoader`, nor replace the `ServletLoader` with a new implementation, because there isn't a way to inject a new class into the servlet system. A better approach would be to add this information into a servlet class that other servlets can subclass. Let's introduce a new class called `StateServlet` that privately tracks its own state and provides convenience methods to access this information. Listing 6-4 presents the complete source for the `StateServlet`.

Listing 6-4   StateServlet.java

```java
import javax.servlet.*;

public class StateServlet extends GenericServlet
{
  private static final int UNINITIALIZED = 0;
  private static final int INITIALIZED = 1;
  private static final int DESTROYED = 2;

  private int m_state = UNINITIALIZED;

  public void init (ServletConfig cfg)
  throws ServletException
  {
    super.init(cfg);
    m_state = INITIALIZED;
  }

  public void destroy ()
  {
    m_state = DESTROYED;
  }

  public boolean isUnitialized ()
  {
    return (m_state == UNINITIALIZED);
  }

  public boolean isInitialized ()
  {
    return (m_state == INITIALIZED);
  }

  public boolean isDestroyed ()
  {
    return (m_state == DESTROYED);
  }
}
```

Unfortunately, this class suffers the same consequences that the GenericServlet faces if a subclass overrides init or any other method listed above. Like the previous example of the TrainingServlet, we need to make these methods accessible, but unalterable by other servlet developers. The CoreServlet class in Listing 6-5 adds these extra features.

Listing 6-5   CoreServlet.java

```java
import javax.servlet.*;
import java.io.*;

abstract public class CoreServlet extends GenericServlet
{
  private static final int UNINITIALIZED = 0;
  private static final int INITIALIZED   = 1;
  private static final int DESTROYED     = 2;

  private int m_state = UNINITIALIZED;

  public final void init (ServletConfig cfg)
  throws ServletException
  {
    if (m_state == UNINTIALIZED)
    {
      super.init(cfg);
      init();
      m_state = INITIALIZED;
    }
  }

  protected void init () throws ServletException
  {
  }

  public final void destroy ()
  {
    if (m_state != DESTROYED)
    {
      m_state = DESTROYED;
      try
      {
        cleanup();
      }
      catch (ServletException se)
      {
```

```
        CharArrayWriter  cw = new CharArrayWriter();
        PrintWriter pw = new PrintWriter(cw);
        se.printStackTrace(pw);
        log(cw.toString());
      }
    }
  }

  protected void cleanup () throws ServletException
  {
  }

  public final boolean isUnitialized ()
  {
    return (m_state == UNINITIALIZED);
  }

    public final boolean isInitialized ()
    {
    return (m_state == INITIALIZED);
    }

  public final boolean isDestroyed ()
  {
    return (m_state == DESTROYED);
  }
}
```

The `CoreServlet` combines the state-tracking features of the `StateServlet` together with the finalized `init` method of the `TrainingServlet`. These two features are complementary, and when implemented together they provide a better framework than the vanilla `GenericServlet`. We've also declared the overridable `init` and `cleanup` methods as protected and wrapped calls to them with state checks. The reasoning for this paranoid coding may not be immediately obvious, but imagine that someone had a reference to a servlet and attempted to re-initialize it through a call to `init`:

```
Servlet uhoh = getServletContext().getServlet("SomeServlet");
uhoh.init(null); //disaster!!!
```

The default implementation of the `GenericServlet` allows this kind of dangerous behavior. Unfortunately, the servlet API documentation only provides a warning to developers about using the `getServlet` and `getServletNames` methods in this manner; it does not help protect servlets from this kind of misuse. By extending the `CoreServlet`, developers are protected both from accidental misuse of their own code and from possible malevolent attack from other servlet code.

The Brat Pack

Now that you can safely access other servlets directly, let's explore an example configuration that illustrates a collaboration of servlets. This collaboration will be between two servlets, one providing a Web page, the other providing fortunes (see Listings 6-6 and 6-7).

Listing 6-6   PageBrat.java

```java
import javax.servlet.*;
import java.io.*;


public class PageBrat extends CoreServlet
{
  public void service (ServletRequest req,
                            ServletResponse res)
  throws ServletException, IOException
  {
    res.setContentType("text/html");
    PrintWriter pw = res.getWriter();
    FortuneBrat fb =
(FortuneBrat)getServletContext().getServlet("FortuneBrat");
    String fortune = fb.getFortune();
    pw.println ("Your Fortune: "+fortune);
    pw.close();
  }
}
```

Listing 6-7   FortuneBrat.java

```java
import javax.servlet.*;
import java.io.*;
import java.util.*;

public class FortuneBrat extends CoreServlet
{
  private Vector fortunes;
  private int current;

  protected void init () throws ServletException
```

```
{
   fortunes = new Vector();
   fortunes.addElement("Learn Java Now!");
   current = 0;
}

public void service (ServletRequest req,
                         ServletResponse res)
throws ServletException, IOException
{
   PrintWriter pw = res.getWriter();
   pw.println (getFortune());
   pw.close();
}

public String getFortune ()
{
   if (current >= fortunes.size())
   {
     current = 0;
   }
   return (String)fortunes.elementAt(current++);
}

public void addFortune (String fortune)
{
   fortunes.addElement(fortune);
}
}
```

The output from the `PageBrat` servlet under the servlet runner looks like that shown in Figures 6-5 and 6-6.

The servlet runner output looks familiar for the PageBrat. When the request for `http://localhost:8080/servlet/PageBrat` was made, the `ServletLoader` found the class file on the disk, made a new instance, and initialized that instance. However, the servlet runner also says that it initialized the FortuneBrat servlet as well. But why did it load the `FortuneBrat` servlet? The reason for this mysterious background loading lies on the third line of PageBrat's service method, where the `ServletContext` is asked to retrieve a servlet named FortuneBrat. Since the FortuneBrat hadn't been loaded, the `ServletLoader` loaded it on demand, giving a reference to the initialized FortuneBrat instance back to the `PageBrat` in the `getServlet` call. That reference was then used to get a fortune, which was used as data for the `PageBrat`'s output stream.

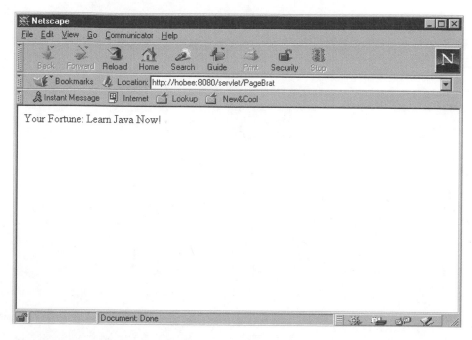

Figure 6-5   The FortuneBrat spits out a fortune.

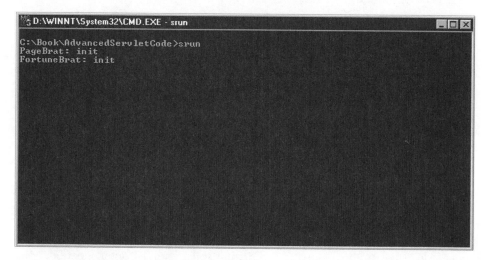

Figure 6-6   Output displayed by the PageBrat.

This is a cool way to separate functionality into multiple modules. However, this behavior isn't consistent among servlet environments, which becomes apparent when the same experiment is attempted under the Java Web Server. This time, the call to `getServlet` returns null; the `FortuneServlet` is *not* loaded automatically when referenced by name. Why not? It isn't loaded because the Java Web Server provides a secure environment where authorization is required before issuing certain actions, such as starting servlets.

So, how do we guarantee that the `FortuneServlet` is running before we try to use its services? The easiest method is to configure the Java Web Server to load the `FortuneBrat` automatically at startup, as shown in Figure 6-7.

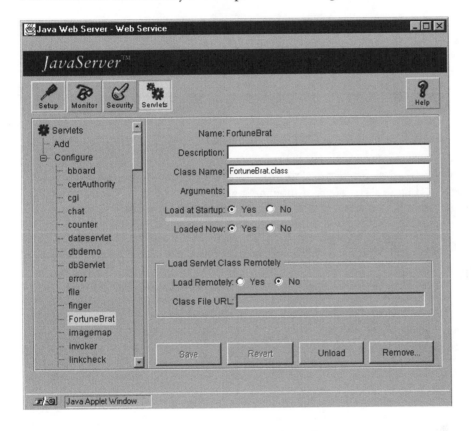

Figure 6-7 Configuring a servlet to load automatically.

SERVLETCONTEXT

```
public Servlet getServlet (String servletname) throws
ServletException
```

Gets a servlet mapped to the name servletname, or null if the servlet can't be found.

```
public Enumeration getServletNames () throws
ServletException
```

Gets an enumeration of Strings that are the names of all available servlets (some servlets may not be accessible because they are in a different namespace).

It's a Servlet Conga Line!

Anyone who is familiar with the UNIX operating system knows about its *pipe-and-filter* design (Figure 6-8), where a pipeline consists of sources and sinks connected together, flowing the output of the source into the input for the next sink.

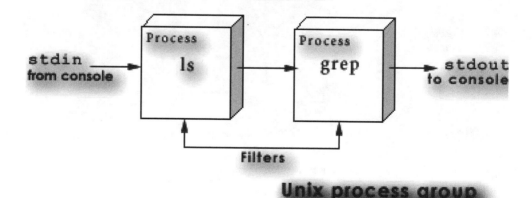

Figure 6-8   The UNIX pipe-and-filter design.

Let's take the simple example of finding a group of Web pages in a directory. In UNIX, the command to list all files is called "ls," and the command to search for sub-strings is called "grep." Those not familiar with the history of UNIX might wonder at the sanity of naming utilities in this manner. Each of these names is an abbreviation of its function: Grep stands for general regular expression parser, and ls stands for list files.

A special character called the pipe symbol is used by UNIX to connect the two commands in the following manner:

```
<source command> | <sink command>
```

Finishing the Web-page example, the command would say,

```
ls | grep html
```

and when executed, would produce a list of Web-page files in the current directory.

Servlets can act as a pipeline as well. Then they are called *servlet chains*, where the output from the first servlet becomes the input for the second servlet, continuing until the last servlet is reached, where the last servlet in the chain produces the output that is returned to the client. Figure 6-9 shows this interaction. Servlet chains are an excellent way to modularize a solution by splitting up the work responsibilities among several servlets, and this is the supported protocol for servlet collaboration.

A typical servlet chain will consist of roughly three stages:

1. Reading the input, issuing commands to some processing stage.

2. Processing the commands, issuing abstract formatting commands.

3. Producing concrete output from the abstract formatting commands.

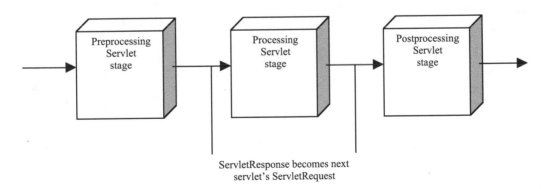

Figure 6-9   Servlet chain in action.

We may well ask, "Why all the extra work? Can't I just call to other servlets by getting a reference to them through a `getServlet` invocation?" If a similar approach had been taken with the UNIX commands, ls would have needed an option for every program that wanted to receive its output in a pipeline! By uncoupling the commands from each other and hooking them together *dynamically* through the use of the pipe symbol, any group of commands can be used together to provide the desired output.

For example, if you wanted to replace the use of grep with perl, ls would never know the difference. This modularity is a common approach taken by network stacks, where different protocols can be stacked on top of hardware drivers to be called on for services. depending on what data is entering or exiting the system. Likewise, the Java Web Server provides a similar capability with its servlet chains, where the output of a "lower" servlet is fed into the appropriate servlet waiting above it.

Let's put together a group of three servlets that process a remote database request. The servlet in Listing 6-8 reads incoming information from an HTML form submitted from a Netscape client and formulates that data into a data request to be passed on for processing.

Listing 6-8   FormBrat.java

```java
import javax.servlet.*;
import java.io.*;
import java.util.*;

public class FormBrat extends CoreServlet
{
   private static final String PARAM = "NAME";

   public void service (ServletRequest req,
                              ServletResponse res)
   throws ServletException, IOException
   {
     String[] vals = req.getParameterValues(PARAM);

     if (vals != null)
     {
       String data = vals[0];
       if (data.length() > 0)
       {
         PrintWriter pw = res.getWriter();
         pw.println (data);
         pw.close();
       }
       else
       {
         throw new ServletException("Invalid Form");
       }
     }
     else
     {
       throw new ServletException("Invalid Form");
     }
   }
}
```

```
<html>
<head>
<title>Search our Directory!</title>
</head>
<body>
<form action="http://hobee:8080/servlet/FormBrat" method=post>
Enter a name here <input type=text name=NAME size=20>
<input type=submit value="Search">
</form>
</body>
</html>
```

This HTML is a very simple form that asks for a name to be entered. Our FormBrat receives that information from the client using the getParameterValues() method of the ServletRequest object.

JAVAX.SERVLET.SERVLETREQUEST

```
public abstract String[] getParameterValues(String name)
```

Returns an array of values that correspond to the named parameter. If there is no parameter by this name, the returned value is null.

The retrieved value is immediately written out to the ServletOutputStream and onto the Netscape client, as shown in Figures 6-10 and 6-11.

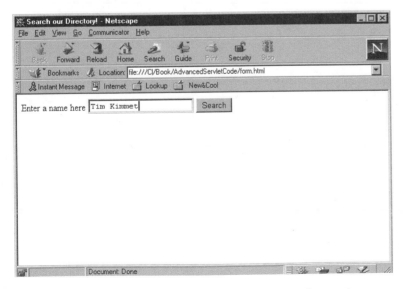

Figure 6-10   A form used to POST search criteria to the DatabaseBrat servlet.

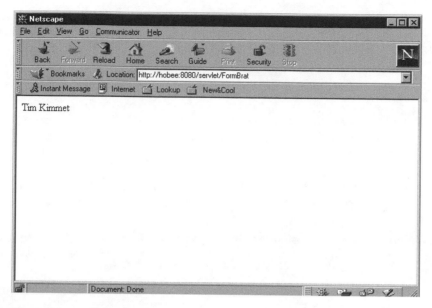

Figure 6-11   DatabaseBrat in action.

A hashtable will be used as a simple database in the second stage, managed by the DatabaseBrat servlet. This servlet reads a name from the incoming data stream and produces either the record corresponding to that name, or an empty response if no records exist for that name (Listing 6-9).

Listing 6-9   DatabaseBrat.java

```java
import javax.servlet.*;
import java.util.*;
import java.io.*;

public class DatabaseBrat extends CoreServlet
{
  private Hashtable m_records;

  protected void init () throws ServletException
  {
    m_records = new Hashtable();
    DatabaseRecord tim =
      new DatabaseRecord("Tim","Kimmet","123 Main Street",
                         "San Jose","CA","95124");
    m_records.put("TIM",tim);
    DatabaseRecord chris = new DatabaseRecord("Christopher",
                         "Taylor","555 1st Street",
                         "Sunnyvale","CA","94086");
    m_records.put("CHRIS",chris);
```

```
  }

  public void service (ServletRequest req,
                              ServletResponse res)
  throws ServletException, IOException
  {
    ServletInputStream sis = req.getInputStream();
    byte[] buf = new byte[4096];
    sis.read(buf);
    String name = new String(buf).trim().toUpperCase();
    PrintWriter pw = res.getWriter();

    if (m_records.containsKey(name))
    {
      DatabaseRecord db = (DatabaseRecord)m_records.get(name);
      if (db != null)
      {
        pw.print (db.getFirstName()+":"+db.getLastName()+":");
        pw.print (db.getAddress()+":"+db.getCity()+
                      ":"+db.getState()+":");
        pw.println (db.getZip());
      }
    }
    pw.close();
  }
}

class DatabaseRecord
{
  private String m_firstName, m_lastName, m_address;
  private String m_city, m_state, m_zip;

  public DatabaseRecord (String first, String last,
                            String addr, String city,
                            String state, String zip)
  {
    m_firstName = first; m_lastName = last; m_address = addr;
    m_city = city; m_state = state; m_zip = zip;
  }

  public final String getFirstName() { return m_firstName; }

  public final String getLastName() { return m_lastName;   }

  public final String getAddress() { return m_address; }

  public final String getCity() { return m_city; }

  public final String getState() { return m_state; }

  public final String getZip()   { return m_zip; }
}
```

Since the DatabaseBrat expects to receive input in the form of single string (the name to use as the search key in the database), the best way to watch it operate is to use a telnet client. (Telnet is a remote-terminal utility that comes with most UNIX operating systems, Windows NT, and Windows 95.) The version that comes free with Windows 95 and Windows NT isn't a good implementation. We've included a share-ware terminal program called CRT on the CD-ROM that comes with the book. All of the telnet screen shots used in the book were taken with CRT.

The DatabaseBrat can be activated manually by connecting to port 8080 (the default port for the servlet runner) with a telnet program and impersonating a Web browser by making some HTTP requests by hand.

Core Alert

The following HTTP example uses a pretty arcane syntax that won't be described here. The next chapter covers HTTP in detail, and interested readers should skip ahead to understand the meaning of the example HTTP dialog shown here.

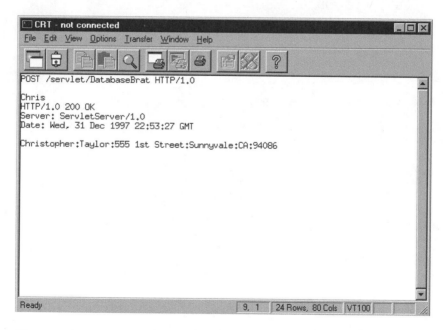

Figure 6-12   Running the DatabaseBrat manually via telnet.

The final servlet needed for this example is the FormatterBrat, a formatter that takes the database results presented by the DatabaseBrat and prints them out into an HTML table. A `StringTokenizer` object handles the job of parsing the colon-separated results, with the parsed tokens placed into separate column elements in the table. The complete source is presented in Listing 6-10.

Listing 6-10 FormatterBrat.java

```java
import javax.servlet.*;
import java.util.*;
import java.io.*;

public class FormatterBrat extends CoreServlet
{
  public void service (ServletRequest req,
                                ServletResponse res)
  throws ServletException, IOException
  {
    ServletInputStream sis = req.getInputStream();
    PrintWriter = res.getWriter();
    byte[] b = new byte[4096];
    String results = new String(b,0,sis.read(b)).trim();
    StringTokenizer st = new StringTokenizer(results,":");
    sis.close();
    pw.println ("<html>\n<body>\n<table border>\n<tr>");
    pw.print ("<th>First Name</th><th>Last Name</th>");
    pw.print ("<th>Address</th><th>City</th><th>State</th>");
    pw.println ("<th>Zip Code</th></tr><tr>");
    while (st.hasMoreTokens())
    {
      String token = st.nextToken();
      pw.print("<td>"+token+"</td>");
    }
    pw.println ("</tr>\n</table>\n</body>\n</html>");
    pw.close();
  }
}
```

Like the DatabaseBrat, the best way to test the FormatterBrat is to use a telnet client. As the database has only two entries (one for Tim and one for Chris), this test will ask for the Tim record. Figure 6-13 shows output created by the FormatterBrat.

The work of handling a data request has been split into three separate components:

1. FormBrat (receiving the request)
2. DatabaseBrat (processing the request)
3. FormatterBrat (formatting the output)

Like building blocks, these components provide useful services when connected together. There are two choices: *statically* connected or *dynamically* connected. Constructing a chain using the static approach is like a laying an underground pipe,

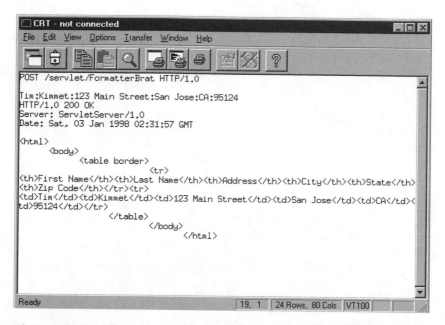

Figure 6-13   Using Telnet to see output created by the FormatterBrat servlet.

where the servlets act as service points that flow information through the plumbing. The static approach is easier, but you pay the cost of runtime flexibility, because the chain is always established. (Imagine having to dig up your plumbing every time you need water in a different room.) Statically chaining servlets together is a three-step process:

1. Create the appropriate servlet entries in the servlet configuration panel.

2. Create an alias for the chain in the servlet alias section of the setup configuration panel.

3. Enable servlet chaining in the setup configuration panel.

Create the Appropriate Servlet Entries

Use the configuration panel to create the servlet entries for the example servlets: FormBrat, DatabaseBrat, and FormatterBrat. The configuration panel is accessed via the Java Web Server administrative server (usually on default port 9090) as an applet (http://localhost:9090/). See Figure 6-14.

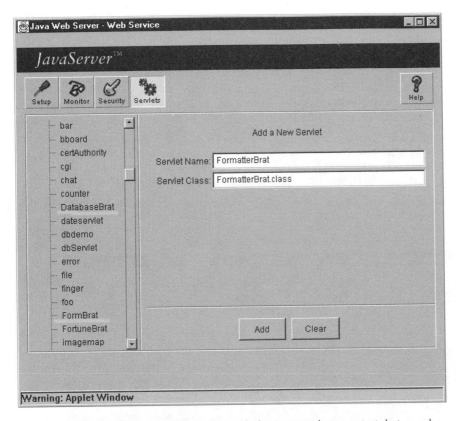

Figure 6-14   Configuring the servlets with the Java Web Server's Admin applet.

Make an Alias for the Servlet Chain

With the configuration applet still open, switch to the general panel and add a new servlet alias. Like most servlet aliases, a pseudo Web-page URL is mapped to a servlet that gets invoked when the Web page is requested. The panel has two field entries: `Alias` and `Servlet Invoked`. The URL /SimpleDatabase.html should be entered as the `Alias`, while the `Servlet Invoked` should be a comma-separated list of servlets participating in the chain. The `InvokerServlet` (one of the built-in servlets covered in Chapter 4, "Administrating the Java Web Server") uses this list to call each servlet in turn when a request is made. This list acts as the piping described above, connecting the servlets together as a chain.

Enable Servlet Chaining in the Setup Configuration Panel

Although servlet-chaining is a great feature, it's considered a security risk by the Java Web Server. This is like the telephone game, where one kid tells another kid who tells another kid, and eventually the message gets garbled by the time it reaches the last kid in the chain. Plus, there is always the wise guy who purposely changes the message to mess up the next kid, usually with hilarious results. But since Web services are usually no laughing manner, giving a servlet access to information may put that information at risk. The Java Web Server developers recognized this potential problem and disabled servlet chaining by default, so it needs to be enabled in order to use it. This option is found in the `site` option of the general page in the configuration applet shown in Figure 6-15.

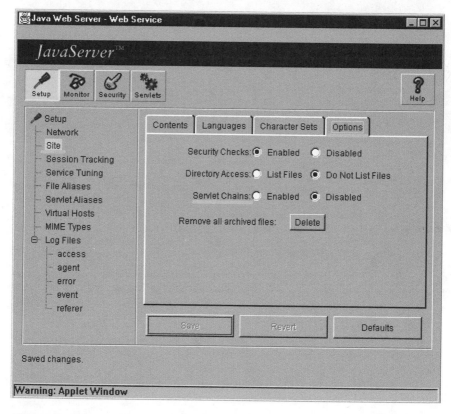

Figure 6-15   Enabling servlet chaining in the Java Web Server.

Core Note

Unfortunately, this option doesn't take immediate effect. In order for chaining to be enabled, the server needs to be shut down and restarted.

Now that the chain has been established, let's test it out! Copy the three classes (`FormBrat.class`, `DatabaseBrat.class`, and `FormatterBrat.class`) into the `servlets` subdirectory of the Java Web Server home directory (e.g., `d:\javawebserver1.1\servlets`), then open up a Web browser and connect to `http://localhost/SimpleDatabase.html`.

Figure 6-16 InstantiationException due to improperly installing DatabaseRecord class.

Oops, by the looks of Figure 6-16, we have a problem! We forgot to copy a support class called `DatabaseRecord`, a class that `DatabaseBrat` uses to store information. According to the Java Web Server documentation, there are three possible choices for where this class should go:

- `servlets` subdirectory
- local classpath
- `classes` subdirectory

While putting the class in the `servlets` directory works, it doesn't make sense, since `DatabaseRecord` isn't a servlet. The local machine's `classpath` variable would work as well, but any changes to that variable that forgot to include our classes would break our servlet as a side effect. The best solution is to place support classes into the directory named `classes`.

Dynamic Servlet Chaining

Static chains work, and for simple scenarios like the three-section pipeline (form ->database->formatter), they are sufficient for getting the job done. Yet in a sense locking these servlets together isn't an object-oriented solution. A truly object-oriented design requires chain construction to be delayed until the moment it is needed, giving the system freedom to route requests between an arbitrary set of servlets. In terms of the plumbing analogy, you would lay the pipe between rooms as the data is flowing through it, and each room could have several pipes leading to other rooms.

Links between servlets are created by the content type of the data flowing through them. Specifically, a servlet is registered to receive data for a specific MIME type. These mappings are made in the `mimeservlets.properties` file.

Core Note

Servlet chaining is one of the few features in the Java Web Server that cannot be configured via the Admin applet.

As an example, create a servlet receiving all requests for `text/html` by adding an entry into the `mimeservlets.properties` file (Listing 6-11).

Listing 6-11   DynamicServletTest.java

```java
import javax.servlet.*;
import javax.servlet.http.*;
import java.io.*;

public class DynamicServletTest extends CoreServlet
{
  public void service (ServletRequest req,
              ServletResponse res)
  throws IOException, ServletException
  {
    PrintWriter pw = res.getWriter();
    pw.println ("Overriding HTML output");
    pw.close();
  }
}
```

The `mimeservlets.properties` file consists of [mime type]=[servlet name] entries. Open the file in your favorite text editor and add the entry:

```
text/html=DynamicServletTest
```

You'll need to restart the Java Web Server after making this change. After the server has been restarted, open up your Web browser and connect to `http://local-host/`. Instead of the typical "Welcome to the Java Web Server" initial screen, you'll see the DynamicServletTest's "Overriding HTML output" message.

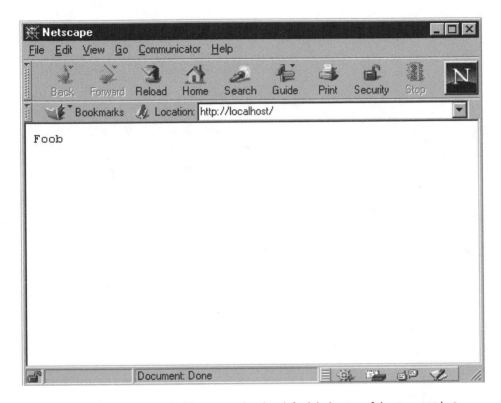

Figure 6-17   Our example filter overrides the default behavior of the Java Web Server.

What happened? Well, even though you didn't see it, the `File` servlet (one of the built-in servlets that comes with the Java Web Server) retrieved the root Web page at our request. When it sent the Web page out, the outbound content was intercepted by the DynamicServletTest servlet, because it was registered to receive all `text/html` output in the `mimeservlets.properties` file. The content wasn't lost; if the DynamicServletTest had opened its `ServletRequest`'s `InputStream` (via a call to `req.getInputStream`), it had access to all of the HTML data.

Let's try that. By adding a few lines to the DynamicServletTest servlet, we can output the raw HTML to the browser, as shown in Listing 6-12.

Listing 6-12   Presenting the raw HTML data to the browser

```
import javax.servlet.*;
import javax.servlet.http.*;
import java.io.*;

public class DynamicServletTest extends CoreServlet
{
  public void service (HttpServletRequest req,
                       HttpServletResponse res)
  throws IOException, ServletException
  {
    InputStream is = req.getInputStream();
    byte[] buffer = new byte[is.available()];
    is.read(buffer);
    is.close();
    PrintWriter pw = res.getWriter();
    pw.write(new String(buffer));
    pw.close();
  }
}
```

Compile the servlet and move it over to the Java Web Server's servlets subdirectory. Now, reload the root Web page again to see what happens.

How come the Web browser didn't interpret the HTML as a Web page? This depends on the version of the Java Web Server that you are using. In Chapter 5 we commented that the MIME content type of returned data was text/html, but here the browser is interpreting the content as text/plain. The Java Web Server development team made this change between versions 1.1 and 1.1.1. If you had tried to run the example on versions 1.1 and earlier, you would have received an ugly "OutOfMemory" exception from the Java Web Server's console.

The Java Web Server runs out of memory because it entered a recursive state. Since the DynamicServletTest receives all data of content type text/html, and our servlet doesn't specify the content type of its output, the Java Web Server chains its output back to itself endlessly (until the server runs out of memory and kills the thread).

This brings up an important rule about servlet chaining.

Core Note

Whenever you construct a servlet chain, make absolutely sure that you haven't introduced any infinite loops into the system. We suggest designing the chain on paper and working out all of the content-type-created pipes before you try to put the system together.

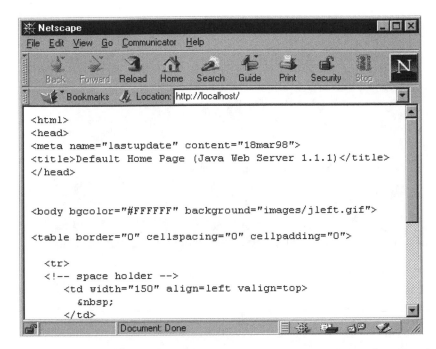

Figure 6-18 Receiving the raw HTML data from the DynamicServletTest servlet.

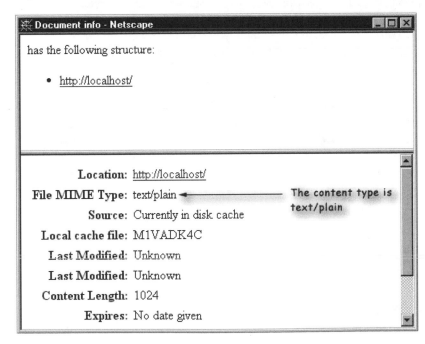

Figure 6-19 The output is text/plain.

```
D:\WINNT\system32\CMD.EXE - httpd                              _ □ ✕

javawebserver: This version of Java Web Server 1.1 Expires on Wed Jun 03 22:25:5
2 PDT 1998. Please visit Java Web Server homepage at http://java.sun.com/product
s/java-server/webserver/ to purchase a licensed copy.
javawebserver:
javawebserver: This version of Java Web Server 1.1 Expires on Wed Jun 03 22:25:5
2 PDT 1998. Please visit Java Web Server homepage at http://java.sun.com/product
s/java-server/webserver/ to purchase a licensed copy.
javawebserver:
javawebserver: java.lang.OutOfMemoryError:
javawebserver:    at java.io.OutputStreamWriter.<init>(OutputStreamWriter.java:106
)
javawebserver:    at java.io.OutputStreamWriter.<init>(OutputStreamWriter.java:83)
javawebserver:    at sun.servlet.http.HttpResponse.getWriter(HttpResponse.java:634
)
javawebserver:    at ServletTest.service(ServletTest.java:11)
javawebserver:    at javax.servlet.http.HttpServlet.service(HttpServlet.java:588)
javawebserver:    at com.sun.server.ServletState.callService(ServletState.java:204
)
javawebserver:    at com.sun.server.ServletManager.callServletService(ServletManag
er.java:940)
javawebserver:    at com.sun.server.webserver.FilterThread.run(FilterManager.java:
241)
```

Figure 6-20   Oops! Out of memory!

This recursive property of servlet chains creates an interesting dilemma: how does a servlet alter information of a specific content type without creating an infinite loop? Well, it can't. Although filtering content would have been an interesting responsibility for servlet chains, there isn't an easy way to accomplish it without creating a loop.

Instead of filtering data, you can use dynamic servlet chains to create communication channels between servlets. Like the `Form->Database->Formatter` example in the static servlet-chaining section, you could provide the same interaction by registering the `Database` and `Formatter` servlets for specific content types. This brings us to the second rule about servlet chaining:

Core Note

When creating communication channels between servlets using the content-type method, it would be a good idea to see a MIME type that isn't already used for something else (for example, `text/html`*). The Java Web Server development team recommends using the major MIME type of "java-internal."*

You could apply this second rule of servlet chaining and register the two servlets as:

```
java-internal/database=DatabaseBrat
java-internal/format=FormatterBrat
```

in the `mimeservlets.properties` file. Next, you'll need to make some changes to the source code for `FormBrat` and `DatabaseBrat`, as shown in Listing 6-13 and Listing 6-14.

Listing 6-13   DynamicFormBrat.java

```java
import javax.servlet.*;
import java.io.*;
import java.util.*;

public class DynamicFormBrat extends CoreServlet
{
  private static final String PARAM = "NAME";

  public void service (ServletRequest req, ServletResponse res)
  throws ServletException, IOException
  {
    String[] vals = req.getParameterValues(PARAM);
    res.setContentType("java-internal/database");
    if (vals != null)
    {
      String data = vals[0];
      if (data.length() > 0)
      {
        PrintWriter pw = res.getWriter();
        pw.println (data);
        pw.close();
      }
      else
      {
        throw new ServletException("Invalid Form");
      }
    }
    else
    {
      throw new ServletException("Invalid Form");
    }
  }
}
```

Listing 6-14   DynamicDatabaseBrat.java

```java
import javax.servlet.*;
import java.util.*;
import java.io.*;

public class DynamicDatabaseBrat extends CoreServlet
{
  private Hashtable m_records;
```

continued

```
protected void init () throws ServletException
{
  m_records = new Hashtable();
  DatabaseRecord tim =
    new DatabaseRecord("Tim","Kimmet","123 Main Street",
                                "San Jose","CA","95124");
  m_records.put("TIM",tim);
  DatabaseRecord chris = new DatabaseRecord("Christopher",
                                "Taylor","555 1st Street",
                                "Sunnyvale","CA","94086");
  m_records.put("CHRIS",chris);
}

public void service (ServletRequest req,
                              ServletResponse res)
throws ServletException, IOException
{
  res.setContentType("java-internal/format");
  ServletInputStream sis = req.getInputStream();
  byte[] buf = new byte[4096];
  sis.read(buf);
  String name = new String(buf).trim().toUpperCase();
  PrintWriter pw = res.getWriter();

  if (m_records.containsKey(name))
  {
    DatabaseRecord db = (DatabaseRecord)m_records.get(name);
    if (db != null)
    {
      pw.print (db.getFirstName()+":"+db.getLastName()+":");
      pw.print (db.getAddress()+":"+db.getCity()+
                        ":"+db.getState()+":");
      pw.println (db.getZip());
    }
  }
  pw.close();
}
}
```

Update the servlet entries with the Admin applet to use the classes
DynamicDatabaseBrat.class and DynamicFormBrat.class instead of
DatabaseBrat.class and FormBrat.class. Once those change are completed,
edit the servlet alias entry for database.html, mapping a request only to FormBrat
instead of FormBrat,DatabaseBrat,FormatterBrat chain (Figure 6-21).

With the Java Web Server configured to dynamically route messages by content type,
reconnect to http://localhost/form.html and test the chain (Figure 6-22).

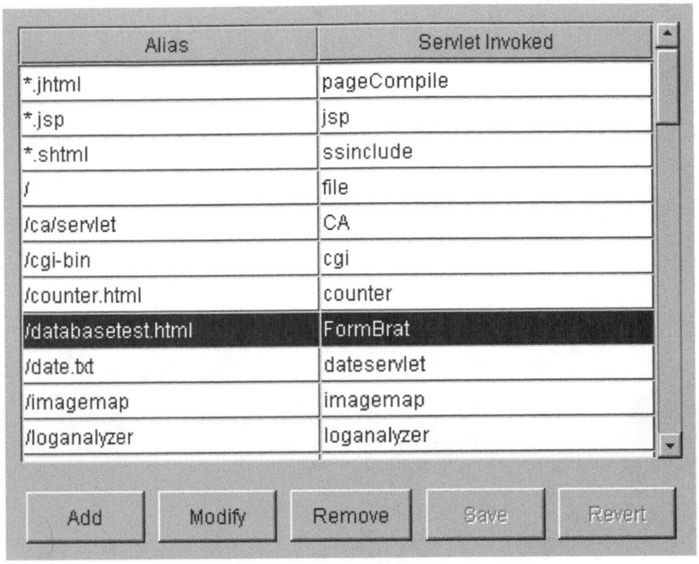

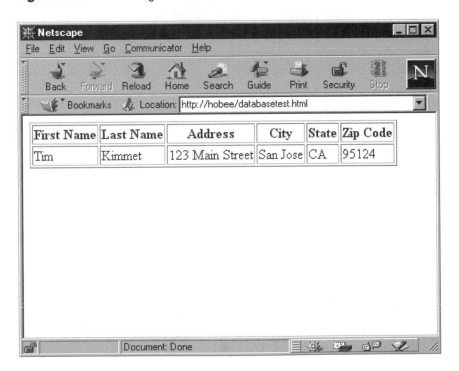

Figure 6-21 Removing the static servlet chain.

Figure 6-22 Testing the dynamic servlet chain... Success!

Servlet Debugging

Servlet development, like Java development in general, is much easier when a good debugger is available. For example, it would be a nice feature to see the incoming requests as they enter a servlet, displaying status information such as the host name of the client, the time the request was made, and what data was sent to the server. This information can be made available by using the old quick-and-dirty debugging approach of printing to the console, as shown in Listing 6-15.

Listing 6-15   DebugBrat.java

```java
import java.servlet.*;
import java.io.*;
import java.util.*;

public class DebugBrat extends CoreServlet
{
  protected void doDebug (ServletRequest req)
  {
    String hostname = req.getRemoteHost();
    Date d = new Date();
    System.out.println (hostname+" "+d+" ");
    for (Enumeration e = req.getParameterNames();
                         e.hasMoreElements();)
    {
      StringBuffer sb = new StringBuffer();
      String name = (String)e.nextElement();
      String[] vals = req.getParameterValues(name);
      sb.append(name+"=");
      for (int loop = 0; loop < vals.length; loop++)
      {
        sb.append(vals[loop]+" ");
      }
      System.out.print (sb.toString());
    }
  }

  public void service (ServletRequest req,
                       ServletResponse res)
  throws ServletException, IOException
  {
    doDebug(req);
    // Insert Servlet Code Here
  }
}
```

Once again the getParameterNames() and getParameterValues() methods are used to provide the necessary input information, and all of the debugging code is wrapped by the protected doDebug() method, which is called by service() before any other code is executed. This implementation has the same problem for subclasses as the GenericServlet did for initialization, where forgetting to call super.service causes no debugging information to be shown. This problem can be alleviated by finalizing the service method and providing a similar replacement (i.e., doService).

While that solves the subclass problem, there still remains the performance issue of printing out debugging information for every service request, whether it is wanted or not. This feature should be enabled on demand, not built into the class as overhead for every request. This limitation is avoided by checking a variable for some sentinel value before calling doDebug, where the only overhead would be the check itself (if debugging had been disabled).

But the worst of the three limitations with this design is the lack of modularity inherent in placing debugging code directly into the program, in effect enforcing a debugging policy of console operations, which may not be the optimum debugging solution. While a subclass could override the doDebug method to add their own debugging operations, a better solution is to provide an interface to attach a debugger object. Listing 6-17 implements the CoreDebugger interface presented in Listing 6-16 to provide a mechanism for debugging servlets extending CoreServlet.

Listing 6-16   CoreDebugger.java

```java
import javax.servlet.*;

public interface CoreDebugger
{
   public void doDebug (ServletRequest req);
   public void stopDebugging(CoreServlet servlet);
}
```

Listing 6-17   CoreServlet.java

```java
import javax.servlet.*;
import java.io.*;

abstract public class CoreServlet extends GenericServlet
{
   private static final int UNINITIALIZED = 0;
   private static final int INITIALIZED   = 1;
   private static final int DESTROYED     = 2;
```

continued

```java
private CoreDebugger m_debugger = null;
private int m_state = UNINITIALIZED;

public final void init (ServletConfig cfg)
throws ServletException
{
  super.init(cfg);
  String className = getInitParameter("debug");
  if (className != null)
  {
    try
    {
      Object obj = Class.forName(className).newInstance();
      if ( !(obj instanceof CoreDebugger) )
      {
        log("Class "+className+" is not a debugger");
      }
      else
      {
        m_debugger = (CoreDebugger)obj;
      }

    }
    catch (Exception e)
    {
      log("Could not locate debugging class: "+className);
    }
  }
  init();
  m_state = INITIALIZED;
}

protected void init () throws ServletException
{
}

public final void service (ServletRequest req,
                           ServletResponse res)
throws ServletException, IOException
{
  if (isInitialized())
  {
    if (m_debugger != null)
    {
      m_debugger.doDebug(req);
    }
    doService(req,res);
  }
}

abstract protected void doService (ServletRequest req,
                                   ServletResponse res)
```

```
    throws ServletException, IOException;

    public final void setDebugger (CoreDebugger cd)
    {
      if (m_debugger != null)
      {
        m_debugger.stopDebugging(this);
      }
      m_debugger = cd;
    }

    public final void destroy ()
    {
      if (m_debugger != null)
      {
        m_debugger.stopDebugging(this);
      }
      m_state = DESTROYED;
      try
      {
        cleanup();
      }
      catch (ServletException se)
      {
        CharArrayWriter  cw = new CharArrayWriter();
        PrintWriter pw = new PrintWriter(cw);
        se.printStackTrace(pw);
        log(cw.toString());
      }
    }

    protected void cleanup () throws ServletException
    {
    }

    public final boolean isUnitialized ()
    {
      return (m_state == UNINITIALIZED);
    }

    public final boolean isInitialized ()
      {
      return (m_state == INITIALIZED);
    }

    public final boolean isDestroyed ()
    {
      return (m_state == DESTROYED);
    }
}
```

This CoreDebugger interface provides two responsibilities:

- Debugging a request (doDebug()).
- Closing the debugging session (stopDebugging()).

While the doDebug method may be obvious, why would a stopDebugging call be needed? A debugger may want to know when a servlet is no longer sending messages to it (if a new debugger has been attached, or if the servlet is shutting down), so this information is conveyed in the stopDebugging message (a function similar to the servlet destroy method).

The service method has been made final (just like the init and destroy methods), where all requests are first wrapped in a state check for safety purposes, then forwarded on to a user-defined doService method. The init method has been rewritten to check for a initialization parameter named "debug" (which is explained below). The service method now checks for an attached debugger, and makes a call to that debugger's doDebug method.

Debugging objects (instances that implement the CoreDebugger interface) can attach to a CoreServlet in two ways:

- By having their classname specified in an initialization parameter named debug.
- By connecting to the CoreServlet through a setDebugger method call.

The only limitation to using the initialization parameter is that the debugging object must have a public default constructor, owing to the use of Class.newInstance(). All that is left to complete the console-mode debugger is an implementation class. Listing 6-18 provides a simple implementation of the CoreDebugger interface.

Listing 6-18   ConsoleCoreDebugger.java

```java
import javax.servlet.*;
import java.io.*;
import java.util.*;

public class ConsoleCoreDebugger implements CoreDebugger
{
  public void doDebug (ServletRequest req)
  {
    String hostname = req.getRemoteHost();
    Date d = new Date();
            System.out.print(hostname+" "+d+" ");
```

```
    for (Enumeration e = req.getParameterNames();
    e.hasMoreElements();)
    {
      StringBuffer sb = new StringBuffer();
      String name = (String)e.nextElement();
      String[] vals = req.getParameterValues(name);
      sb.append(name+"=");
      for (int loop = 0; loop < vals.length; loop++)
      {
        sb.append(vals[loop]+" ");
      }
      System.out.print (sb.toString());
    }
    System.out.println();
  }

  public void stopDebugging (CoreServlet servlet)
  {
    //do nothing for now
  }
}
```

A quick change to the servlet runner's properties file for the FormBrat, an example explained in the previous section on servlet chaining:

```
servlet.FormBrat.class=FormBrat
servlet.FormBrat.initArgs=debug=ConsoleCoreDebugger
```

produces the output shown in Figure 6-23 when activated from a form.

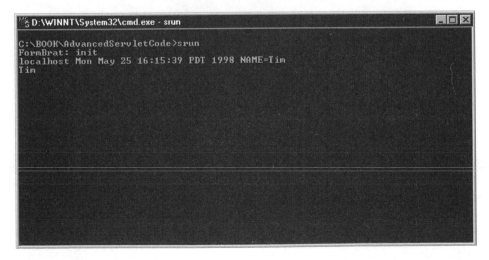

Figure 6-23   Checking out the console debugger.

While console-mode debuggers are a useful tool, we like using GUI tools for our own work, so we've implemented a similar debugger using the Swing JFC components that you can use as well. Since you already have an idea of how the debugging works, we won't be explaining this code, but we present it instead as a useful tool. The code in Listing 6-19 shows a Swing version of our console debugging tool, and the image in Figure 6-24 shows you what the GUI tool looks like

Listing 6-19   SwingCoreDebugger.java

```java
import javax.servlet.*;
import java.io.*;
import java.util.*;
import java.awt.*;
import java.awt.event.*;
import java.text.*;
import com.sun.java.swing.*;
import com.sun.java.swing.table.*;
import com.sun.java.swing.event.*;

public class SwingCoreDebugger implements CoreDebugger
{
  private SwingCoreDebuggerDataModel m_model =
          new SwingCoreDebuggerDataModel();

  private JTable m_table = new JTable(m_model);
  private JFrame m_frame = null;

  public SwingCoreDebugger ()
  {
    m_table.setColumnSelectionAllowed(false);
    m_table.setRowSelectionAllowed(false);
  }

  public void doDebug (ServletRequest req)
  {
    if (m_frame == null)
    {
      m_frame = new JFrame("SwingCoreDebugger");
      m_frame.getContentPane().add(
            JTable.createScrollPaneForTable(m_table));
      m_frame.setSize(400,300);
      m_frame.setVisible(true);
    }
```

```
      m_model.doDebug(req);
      if (!m_frame.isVisible())
      {
        m_frame.setVisible(true);
      }
    }

    public void stopDebugging (CoreServlet servlet)
    {
      if (m_frame != null)
      {
        m_frame.dispose();
      }
    }
}

class SwingCoreDebuggerDataModel extends AbstractTableModel
{
    private static final String[] COLUMNS =
          { "Host","Time","Parameters" };

    private Vector m_data = new Vector();
    private DateFormat m_formatter =
          DateFormat.getDateTimeInstance(
          DateFormat.MEDIUM,DateFormat.MEDIUM);

    public Object getValueAt (int row, int col)
    {
      return ((Vector)m_data.elementAt(row)).elementAt(col);
    }

    public void doDebug (ServletRequest req)
    {
      int row = 0;
      synchronized (this)
      {
        row = m_data.size();
        Vector v = new Vector(3);
        v.addElement(req.getRemoteHost());
        v.addElement(m_formatter.format(new Date()));

        StringBuffer sb = new StringBuffer();
        for (Enumeration e = req.getParameterNames();
            e.hasMoreElements();)
        {
```

continued

```
        String name = (String)e.nextElement();
        sb.append(name+"=");
        String[] vals = req.getParameterValues(name);
        for (int index=0;
            vals!= null && index < vals.length;index++)
        {
          sb.append(vals[index]+" ");
        }
      }
      v.addElement(sb);
      m_data.addElement(v);
    }
    fireTableChanged (new TableModelEvent(this,row));

  }

  public int getColumnCount ()
  {
    return COLUMNS.length;
  }

  public int getRowCount ()
  {
    return m_data.size();
  }

  public void setValueAt (Object val, int row, int column)
  {
    System.out.println ("setValueAt() called");
  }

  public String getColumnName (int columnIndex)
  {
    return COLUMNS[columnIndex];
  }
}
```

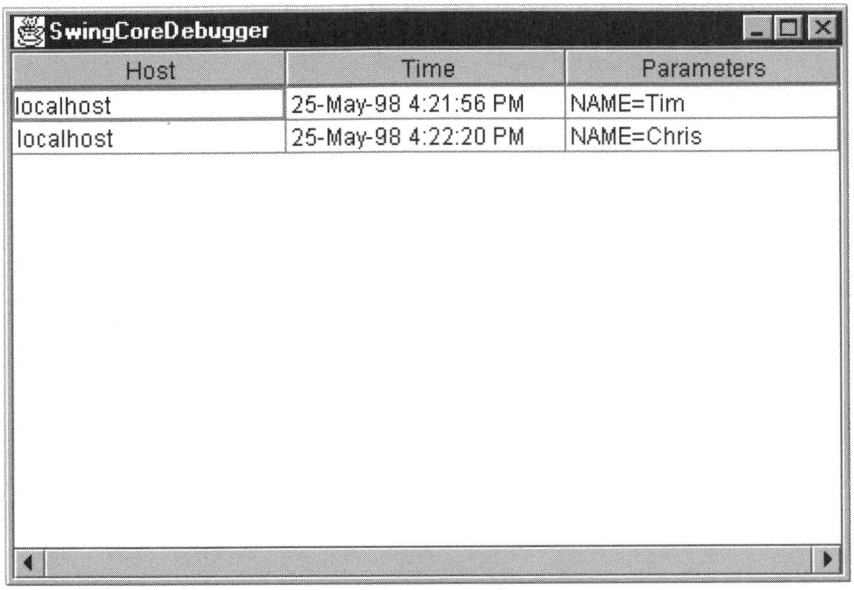

Figure 6-24   Using a GUI to debug servlets.

Summary

Whew! This ends our extensive and exhaustive coverage of the `GenericServlet` class. This chapter lightly covered the underlying engine under the hood of the Java Web Server—the Java Server Toolkit (JST). We discussed the problems encountered by not protecting critical sections in your servlets and showed you how synchronizing in blocks (not complete methods) can maximize thread performance. We showed you how servlet chaining can employ multiple servlets to solve a problem in a more meaningful, component-oriented fashion. Finally, throughout this chapter we evolved a servlet called CoreServlet which can be used as a base class to all your servlets, giving them a debugging tool and forcing a call to `super.init`.

In these last two chapters, we mainly coded servlets by extending from the `GenericServlet` class. There are other classes which extend `GenericServlet` and offer the developer a much richer set of tools, with `HttpServlet` being the most popular. Most of your servlets will extend functionality of these higher-level classes instead of directly extending from `GenericServlet` alone. But before we jump into some of these higher-level classes, you will need to brush up on the underlying theory, so you understand what problems we are attempting to solve. The next chapter will give you a crash course on the fundamentals of the HTTP protocol.

INTRODUCTION
TO HTTP

Topics in This Chapter

- The insides of an HTTP message
- HTTP methods
- HTTP request messages
- HTTP response messages

Chapter 7

In the previous chapter you covered the `GenericServlet` and its supporting classes. While `GenericServlets` are an important part of the Java Web Server, in your own projects you will most likely use a class derived from `GenericServlet`, called `HttpServlet`. The `HttpServlet` speaks the HTTP (HyperText Transfer Protocol) language. To fully understand what an `HttpServlet` can do, then, you need an *essentials* introduction to HTTP. If you are already familiar with HTTP, you may want to quickly skim through this chapter before heading on to Chapter 8, "HTTP Servlets."

In the Beginning There Were RFCs...

The Internet has become the de facto standard for communication among the computing generation. Its infrastructure consists of a set of computers talking to each other based on some standard set of protocols. The implementations of many protocols that our browsers use are based on a collection of *Request For Comments* documents, commonly known as RFCs.

The purpose of an RFC is to define an experimental protocol that can be used to perform a specific task. A good example is RFC 2068, which describes HTTP. In this case the document explains the rules which govern the HTTP protocol, including how to correctly encode an HTTP message, all of HTTP's methods, HTTP requests, and HTTP responses, etc. You can find a complete listing of all of the Web-related RFCs at www.w3.org. Each RFC is freely available, giving the Internet community the chance to brainstorm new ideas and validate implementation details before (and while) a protocol is put into use.

241

HTTP: An RFC or a Standard?

Anyone who has been surfing the Web and hasn't heard of the Hypertext Transfer Protocol is either asleep at the wheel or blissfully ignorant of what `http://` means in a URL. The backbone of the Web consists of protocols which are used to transfer data from one computer to another. In the early days of the Web, Gopher and FTP were used as the primary protocol to carry hyperlinked data across the wire. Introduced in 1990, the HTTP protocol became well accepted and since the mid 1990s has been used as the primary protocol to carry hypermedia information across the World Wide Web.

HTTP uses text-based formatted messages that allow communication and data transfer between a client and a server, much as mail servers handle our e-mail messages (a protocol which is explained in another RFC!). Visiting a Web page is a lot like sending a letter. A letter consists of a delivery address, a return address, and its content. With regard to these elements the post office has defined a set of rules that everyone must follow in order to insure successful delivery. The Post Office relies on these rules in order to provide an efficient way to deliver mail; without them, mail delivery would be sporadic at best, chaos at worst. In the same way, a Web request requires (1) an address for some desired resource and (2) a returning body holding the content of the resource that was requested. This exchange is called an *HTTP transaction*.

HTTP Transactions

You can simulate an HTTP transaction by using the telnet program on your computer. For example, you can initiate a telnet session between your computer and a remote host by doing the following:

1. Initiate a telnet session. (We used CRT 1.1.4 for our telnet program, Copyright 1995, 1996 Van Dyke Technologies; `www.vandyke.com`.)

   `telnet TIMBO:``(in this example` *TIMBO* `is the name of the machine containing the Web server)`

2. Request information from the remote host using the `HTTP GET` method.

   `GET /form.html HTTP / 1.0`

3. Press **ENTER** twice.

The remote host should respond by sending back a bunch of text similar to that shown in Figure 7-1.

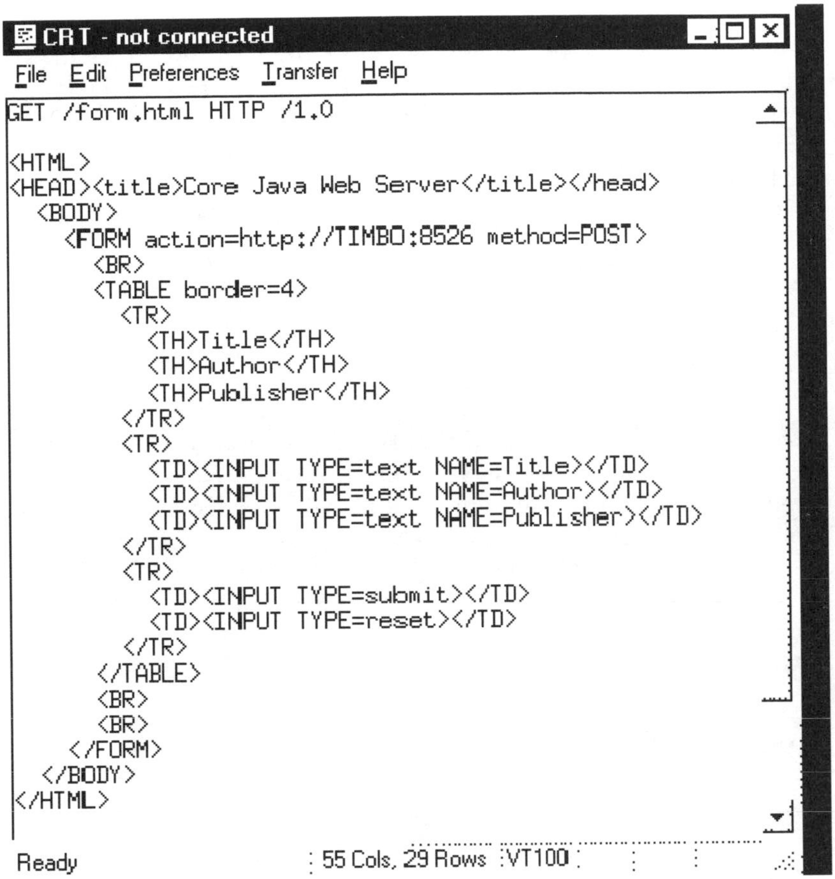

```
CRT - not connected                              _ □ ×

File  Edit  Preferences  Transfer  Help

GET /form.html HTTP /1.0

<HTML>
<HEAD><title>Core Java Web Server</title></head>
  <BODY>
    <FORM action=http://TIMBO:8526 method=POST>
      <BR>
      <TABLE border=4>
        <TR>
          <TH>Title</TH>
          <TH>Author</TH>
          <TH>Publisher</TH>
        </TR>
        <TR>
          <TD><INPUT TYPE=text NAME=Title></TD>
          <TD><INPUT TYPE=text NAME=Author></TD>
          <TD><INPUT TYPE=text NAME=Publisher></TD>
        </TR>
        <TR>
          <TD><INPUT TYPE=submit></TD>
          <TD><INPUT TYPE=reset></TD>
        </TR>
      </TABLE>
      <BR>
      <BR>
    </FORM>
  </BODY>
</HTML>

Ready                    : 55 Cols, 29 Rows :VT100:
```

Figure 7-1   Simulation of an HTTP transaction.

Congratulations! You just successfully executed your first manual Web transaction. Now let's look at what you did.

When you initiated a telnet session to the machine called TIMBO, the telnet program created a socket connection to port 80, the well-known port number for the HTTP Web server (well-known ports are defined in yet another RFC!) located on the machine called TIMBO. (In this case, TIMBO is a machine on the local network, however, it could have been any machine, such as `http://developer.javasoft.com`). Once the connection to TIMBO is made, you submitted the HTTP request by entering:

```
GET /form.html HTTP/ 1.0
```

where GET is the HTTP GET method. A GET request informs the server that the client wants the file with the name `/form.html`. Omitting the filename is like asking for the daily special; the Web server will return the default page (more commonly known as the *home page*). Following the filename is the version identifier (i.e., HTTP/ 1.0)—a number that reports the version of HTTP spoken by the client. (The version numbers and their meaning are covered in more detail in the HTTP RFCs.) Concluding the request line are a pair of carriage return/line feeds, which tell the server that the client's request is complete. With the request in hand the server retrieves the file and writes it back to the telnet window.

While the nitty-gritty details of the HTTP protocol might be new to you, the results are not. The output shown by the telnet program is an HTML file, which typically would be rendered visually by a browser such as Netscape Navigator.

HTTP Messages

An HTTP message consists of two parts: (1) the HTTP message headers, followed by (2) an optional message body. The headers contain information about the data that is being transmitted, such as what kind of files the browser can understand (graphics formats, application types, etc.). For example, a Web browser may want to tell a server that, along with HTML, it can render gifs, jpgs, etc. If data is being sent via HTTP, a message header called Content-Length gives the number of bytes that are in the message body. The HTTP specification lists over forty message headers used to transfer information about a request from a client or a response from a server.

Message Headers

The HTTP RFC (RFC 2068) lists three levels of header fields, including general headers, request headers (or response-header fields for HTTP responses), and entity-header fields. These next four sections will explain how these header fields differ.

General Header

The general-header field contains headers that don't have any relation to the message that is being sent. Two common general-header fields are:

- Date
- Transfer encoding

Request Header

The request headers are used by the client (i.e., a Web browser) to send information to a server (i.e., a Web server). The Web server will use this information to respond to the user appropriately. For example, the Web server can look at values assigned to the User-Agent message header to determine the browser name (i.e., Netscape) as well as finding out what browser and version that sent this request. Some common request-header fields are as follows:

- Accept
- Accept-Charset
- Accept-Language
- Host
- If-Modified-Since
- If-Unmodified-Since
- Referrer
- User-Agent

Response Headers

The response-specific-header fields are used by the Web server to send data back to the client. These are fields that give specific information about the Web server. See the HTTP RFC (RFC 2068) for more information on response-specific headers.

Entity Headers

Perhaps some of the most important header fields in the HTTP message are the entity-header fields, which give you information about the actual message that is being sent (whether the message is a request from a browser, or a response from a web server). In Chapter 8 we write a guest-book servlet which allows users to sign a personalized guest book. We look at the Content-Length entity-header field to determine the length of the HTTP message that is POSTed by the client. We may want to allow messages of a certain length to be downloaded to the server, so if the Content-Length is too large, we may choose to refuse the POSTed message. Some common entity-header fields are:

- Content-Base
- Content-Encoding
- Content-Language
- Content-Length
- Content-Location
- Content-MD5
- Content-Range
- Content-Type
- Expires
- Last-Modified

The message headers shown in the last four sections are not a complete list. You can find the complete list in the HTTP RFC at http://www.w3.org/ Protocols/rfc2068/rfc2068.

A Sample HTTP Message

Figure 7-2 presents a sample HTTP message sent by a Netscape browser, a conversation recorded with a piece of code presented later in this chapter.

Message head

```
POST / HTTP/1.0
Referer: file:///d:/book/sockets/form.html
Connection: Keep-Alive
User-Agent: Mozilla/4.03 [en] <WinNT; I>
Host: TIMBO:8526
Accept: image/gif, image/x-xbitmap, image/jpeg, image/pjpeg, */*
Accept-Language: en
Accept-Charset: iso-8859-1,*,utf-8
Content-type: application/x-www-form-urlencoded
Content-length: 78
```

Message body

```
Title=Core+Java+WebServer&Author=T+Kinmet+and+C+Taylor&Publisher=Prentice+Hall
```

Figure 7-2   This request was generated by the HTML form returned in Figure 7-1.

This HTTP request also has a message body containing data entered by the user. For example, notice the part of the body that contains

```
&Publisher=Prentice+Hall
```

Now flip back to the telnet example. Do you notice the <input type=text name=publisher> HTML tag? This is the same publisher that shows up in the returning message body. *Publisher* is an input type field that is on the form; *Prentice Hall* is the value that the user entered in the Publisher input field. The + is used to encode white spaces.

Core Note

Not all messages contain a message body. For example, a HEAD message does not.

Two Categories of HTTP Messages

HTTP messages fall into two main categories: the HTTP Request and the HTTP Response. The HTTP Request is sent by the client when it wants something from the server, such as retrieving a file. The HTTP Response message is sent by the HTTP Server in response to a client's request. It is important that you understand this difference in order to effectively write HTTP-specific servlets (the topic of the next chapter). The servlet API contains two objects called `HTTPServletReqest` and `HTTPServletResponse`, which are tightly coupled with the HTTP request messages and HTTP response messages, respectively.

HTTP Request

Every time you point your browser to a different URL, you are generating an HTTP Request. By doing so, you are asking the remote HTTP server to perform some task. What is this task? Well, the writers of the HTTP protocol have defined a set of capabilities, or methods, that can be used between a client and an HTTP server. The methods supported by the HTTP 1.1 specification include OPTIONS, GET, HEAD, POST, PUT, DELETE, and TRACE. The rest of this section will help you get acquainted with these methods.

OPTIONS

The HTTP OPTIONS method is used to find out the capabilities of the specified resource. These capabilities include whatever methods (i.e., GET, HEAD, POST, PUT, etc.) can be called on this resource. For example, to find out what specific HTTP methods a CGI program will support, a browser can ask:

```
OPTIONS /some-CGI-program-url HTTP/1.1
```

You can also find out what the server can do as a whole by sending the following request:

```
OPTIONS * HTTP/1.1
host:timbo
```

Figure 7-3 shows the output that Java Web Server gives in response to this request. Notice that the response is a message header called accept and that no body is returned in this response.

GET

The HTTP GET method is used to retrieve a document from a Web server. Each time you visit a Web site, your browser sends an HTTP GET method to port 80 (unless you specify a different port) asking for the default Web document, usually referred to as `index.html`. See Figure 7-4.

HEAD

The HTTP HEAD method is very similar to the GET method; in fact, the message header is the same as with a GET method. The key difference is that the HEAD method does not contain any data, therefore there is no message body. So what value does the HEAD method have?

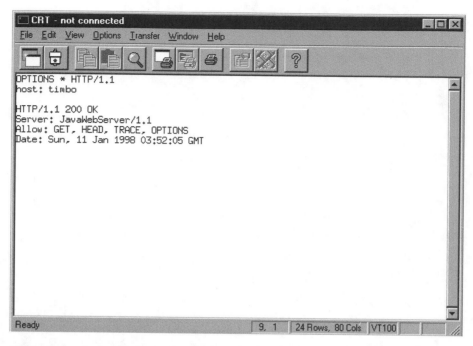

Figure 7-3   Example of an HTTP OPTIONS request.

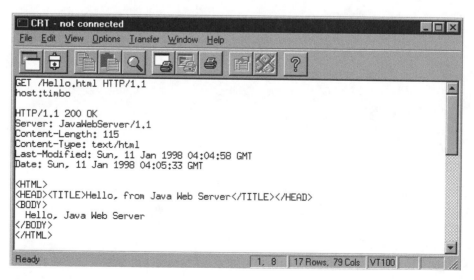

Figure 7-4   Example of an HTTP GET request.

The HEAD method provides information about a resource. The most frequent use of the HEAD method is for caching, which is employed by your browser to save time. Your browser will use information given in the HTTP HEAD message header to determine the modified date of a document and will use this information to justify downloading a fresh copy of the document. (The if-modified-since and if-unmodified-since HTTP message-header fields are used to support caching.)

This caching mechanism saves you time, especially if the document contains a large amount of data. It also reduces network traffic on the server machine. Figure 7-5 shows the output from a HEAD request.

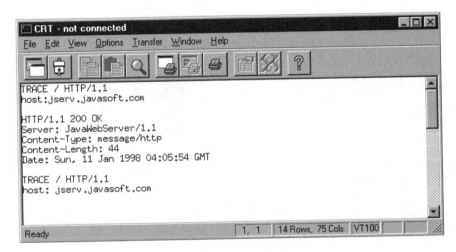

Figure 7-5   Example of an HTTP HEAD request.

POST

The HTTP POST method is used to send data to the server. Perhaps its most familiar use is the processing of form data. Most forms have a submit button. When it is pressed, the browser will collect the user-entered data from the form and send it in the body of the POST request message. The SimpleServer program presented in the last section of this chapter shows the HTTP POST method in action. Another useful example of a POST-based application is a form-driven file upload system which allows a client to upload files from his computer to the remote Web server.

PUT

The HTTP PUT method is used for document publishing. It operates in a similar manner to FTP and is the opposite of the HTTP DELETE method. Netcom provides an interesting example of PUT usage with its "Free Form Web Page Builder," which is used by customers to publish personal Web pages on Netcom's server. Just like DELETE, its usage isn't a light matter; improper configuration of a server that accepts PUT requests may provide an easy foothold for computer hackers.

DELETE

The HTTP DELETE method is used to delete resources on the Web server. DELETE can be disastrous if not managed properly, so it should be used with caution. Since most Web servers don't support the HTTP DELETE method, and situations when delete can be used *safely* are rare, we aren't providing a visual example of a DELETE operation.

TRACE

The HTTP TRACE method is perhaps the one least frequently employed. It can be used to view a message as it passes from one server to another. A good example is the *tracert*—an advanced version of *ping* that allows you to see which servers handle your message as it is being sent from start to destination. Figure 7-6 shows sample output from the tracert program in the Windows NT operating system. In this case we sent an HTTP TRACE request to javasoft.com.

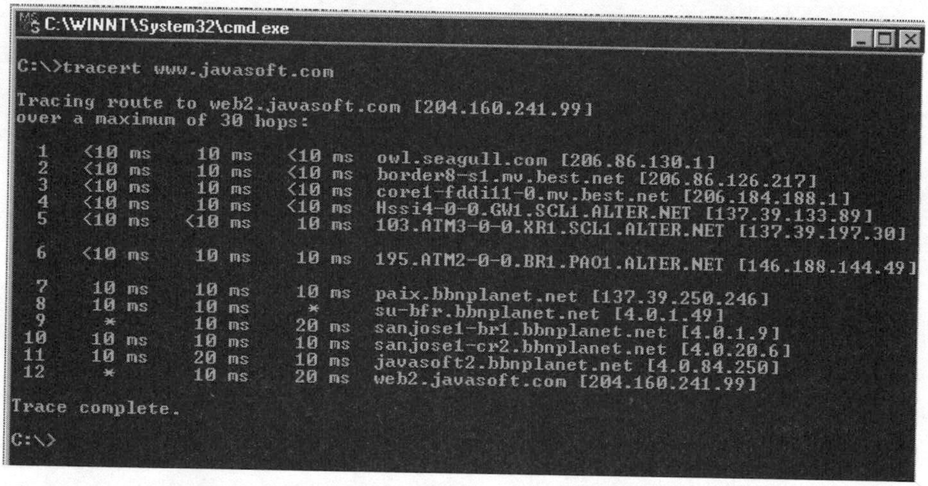

```
C:\WINNT\System32\cmd.exe                                                    _ □ ×

C:\>tracert www.javasoft.com

Tracing route to web2.javasoft.com [204.160.241.99]
over a maximum of 30 hops:

  1    <10 ms     10 ms    <10 ms   owl.seagull.com [206.86.130.1]
  2    <10 ms     10 ms    <10 ms   border8-s1.mv.best.net [206.86.126.217]
  3    <10 ms     10 ms    <10 ms   core1-fddi1-0.mv.best.net [206.184.188.1]
  4    <10 ms     10 ms    <10 ms   Hssi4-0-0.GW1.SCL1.ALTER.NET [137.39.133.89]
  5    <10 ms    <10 ms     10 ms   103.ATM3-0-0.XR1.SCL1.ALTER.NET [137.39.197.30]

  6    <10 ms     10 ms     10 ms   195.ATM2-0-0.BR1.PAO1.ALTER.NET [146.188.144.49]

  7     10 ms     10 ms     10 ms   paix.bbnplanet.net [137.39.250.246]
  8     10 ms     10 ms      *      su-bfr.bbnplanet.net [4.0.1.49]
  9      *        10 ms     20 ms   sanjose1-br1.bbnplanet.net [4.0.1.9]
 10     10 ms     10 ms     10 ms   sanjose1-cr2.bbnplanet.net [4.0.20.6]
 11     10 ms     20 ms     10 ms   javasoft2.bbnplanet.net [4.0.84.250]
 12      *        10 ms     20 ms   web2.javasoft.com [204.160.241.99]

Trace complete.

C:\>
```

Figure 7-6   Output from tracert.

We can also send a TRACE request to the Java Web Server by using the telnet program. Figure 7-7 shows a response from the Java Web Server after receiving a TRACE request. In this case, we sent the TRACE request to jserv.javasoft.com.

Notice that the response to this request does not have a lot of information. The TRACE method is meant as a debugging aid for requests that pass through several layers of *proxy* servers. Proxy servers act as gateways between a client and a destination server. Proxies can provide performance enhancements such as site caching, and security services such as site blocking. The Java Web Server has a built in proxy server *service*.

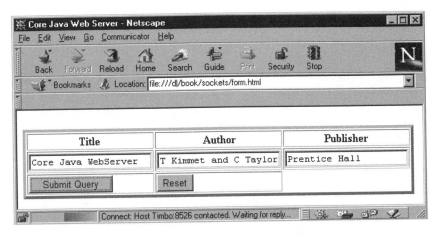

Figure 7-7   Output from TRACE to jserv.javasoft.com.

HTTP Response

The HTTP Response sings the opposing part of the HTTP transaction duet. It is the way that a server tells the client what it thought about its request, which can range from a simple thumbs-down error message to a megabytes-long file transfer. The browser uses the header fields in the response message to effectively display the contents of the HTML file. One of the most popular header fields in the HTTP Response is the *mime-type* header field. This tells the browser what type of data is being sent, with the most common mime type being *text/html*.

The HTTP response line is always the first line in the HTTP response message. It gives the client a quick status for the request. An example HTTP response looks like:

```
HTTP/1.1 200 OK
```

The 200 is an HTTP status code. Included with each status code is an optional *reason-phrase* that gives a small informative description of the status code. The HTTP RFC describes five levels of status codes, where each level is distinguished by the first digit. You should familiarize yourself with each level to help in the debugging of your servlets. Table 7-1 shows each level along with its meaning.

Table 7-1   Five Levels of HTTP Status Codes

Status-Code Level	Meaning
100s	The request has been received and is being processed
200s	The client request was communicated successfully
300s	The client's request was redirected
400s	The client is at fault
500s	The server is at fault

A Simple Scenario

Earlier we promised that we would tell you how to retrieve the complete HTTP message from the Netscape browser. This next section will walk you through a simple scenario to aid in your understanding of an HTTP conversation between client and server. As we said before, a conversation gets started by pointing your browser at a Web site. That Web site is handled by a remote server that must have software to handle incoming requests. This software is commonly known as a *Web server.* Java Web Server, Netscape Enterprise Server, and Apache Web Server are some well-known examples of Web server software programs.

For testing purposes, we wrote a simplified Web server called *SimpleServer* that records HTTP conversations. The SimpleServer will listen for incoming connections on port 8526, an arbitrary port that we chose.

When a request is made by a client—in this case the Web browser—our SimpleServer spits out the conversation like a cheap wiretap. Figure 7-8 displays the Netscape browser with an HTML form along with some data that has been entered by a user.

```
D:\WINNT\System32\cmd.exe - java HTTPServer
POST / HTTP/1.0
Referer: file:///d!/book/sockets/form.html
Connection: Keep-Alive
User-Agent: Mozilla/4.03 [en] (WinNT; I)
Host: Timbo:8526
Accept: image/gif, image/x-xbitmap, image/jpeg, image/pjpeg, */*
Accept-Language: en
Accept-Charset: iso-8859-1,*,utf-8
Content-type: application/x-www-form-urlencoded
Content-length: 78

Title=Core+Java+WebServer&Author=T+Kimmet+and+C+Taylor&Publisher=Prentice+Hall
```

Figure 7-8   An HTML form with input fields.

When you click on the *submit* button, your browser will package the form data into an HTTP message and send it to port 8526 on the remote host TIMBO. How does the browser know where to send this form? The HTML that generated this form contains the following HTML tag:

```
<FORM action=http://TIMBO:8526 method=POST>
```

(You can view the HTML file that created this form by looking at the output of our telnet example presented earlier in this chapter.)

This tag tells your browser where to send the results of this form. Notice that port 8526 was specified in this example. If you don't specify this port, your browser will attempt to submit the form to port 80, which is not what you want because the server program listens on port 8526. The request uses the HTTP POST method to submit this request, shown by the use of the *method=post* form attribute. The server program receives the HTTP message and prints it out. An example of this transaction is shown in Figure 7-9.

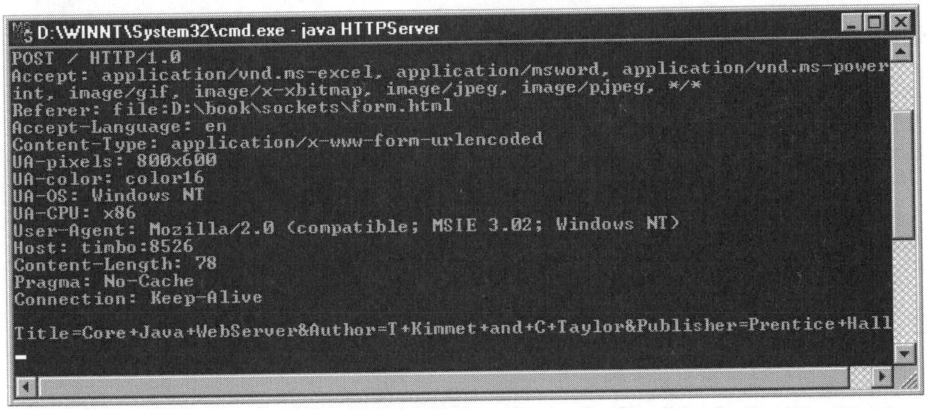

Figure 7-9 HTTP message sent by Netscape Navigator.

This is the full-blown HTTP message that was sent by Netscape Navigator. Notice that it consists of a message header and a blank line that separates the message header from the message body. This HTTP request message contains a request line and several other HTTP header fields that give some information about the message and about the browser itself. This is different from an HTTP Response, which contains a response line. If you look closely at the message body, you can see that this HTTP message is transferring data that the user has entered in the form.

Figure 7-10 displays an HTTP message that was sent by Microsoft's Internet Explorer. Notice how this HTTP message differs from the one that was sent by Netscape. In fact, most browsers will not send the same message headers in an HTTP message, so you cannot rely on every browser's returning the same message headers.

Listing 7-1 displays the code for the SimpleServer program used to retrieve the HTTP messages that were just presented. This program consists of two classes—`SimpleServer` and `RequestHandler`. The SimpleServer sits in an endless loop listening on port 8526 for incoming requests made by the client. When a connection is created, the SimpleServer will create an object of type `RequestHandler` and pass it a socket connection bound to the client. The `RequestHandler` will use the socket connection to retrieve the HTTP message and echo it to standard out.

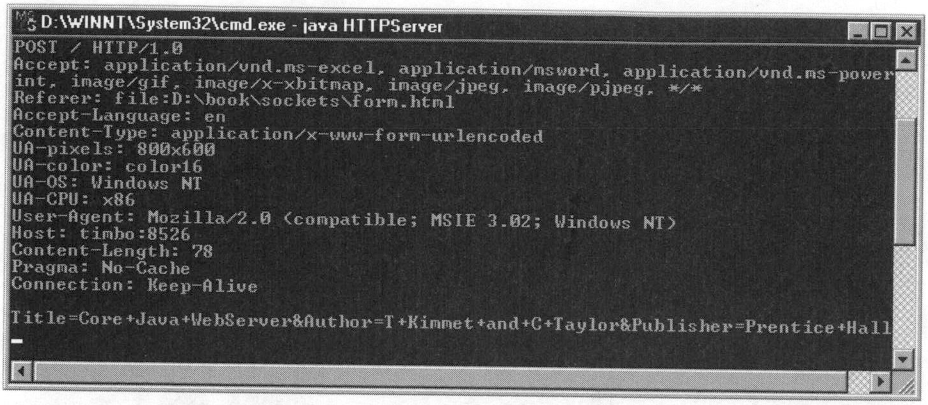

```
D:\WINNT\System32\cmd.exe - java HTTPServer                          _ □ ×
POST / HTTP/1.0
Accept: application/vnd.ms-excel, application/msword, application/vnd.ms-power
int, image/gif, image/x-xbitmap, image/jpeg, image/pjpeg, */*
Referer: file:D:\book\sockets\form.html
Accept-Language: en
Content-Type: application/x-www-form-urlencoded
UA-pixels: 800x600
UA-color: color16
UA-OS: Windows NT
UA-CPU: x86
User-Agent: Mozilla/2.0 (compatible; MSIE 3.02; Windows NT)
Host: timbo:8526
Content-Length: 78
Pragma: No-Cache
Connection: Keep-Alive

Title=Core+Java+WebServer&Author=T+Kimmet+and+C+Taylor&Publisher=Prentice+Hall
_
```

Figure 7-10   HTTP message sent by Internet Explorer.

Listing 7-1   SimpleServer

```java
import java.net.Socket;
import java.net.ServerSocket;

public class SimpleServer
{

   public static void main(String args[])
   {
     SimpleServer server = new SimpleServer();
     server.runServer();
   }

   public void runServer()
   {
     try
     {
        ServerSocket ss = new ServerSocket(8526);

        while(true)
        {
          Socket incoming = ss.accept();
          new Thread(new RequestHandler(incoming)).start();
        }
     }
     catch(Exception e)
     {
       e.printStackTrace();
     }
   }
}
```

Core Note

The Runnable interface is in the `java.lang` *package. The Java compiler automatically imports all classes in the* `java.lang` *package into your source files, so you do not need to import* `java.lang`.

The entry point into this program is the main method. It creates an instance of SimpleServer and calls its `runServer()` method. Once the `runServer()` method is called, SimpleServer sits in an endless loop waiting for a client to make a request. The heart of SimpleServer lies in the following code snippet:

```java
ServerSocket ss = new ServerSocket(8526);
while(true)
{
    Socket incoming = ss.accept();
    new Thread(new RequestHandler(incoming)).start();
}
```

First, an instance of `ServerSocket` is created, which listens for client requests on port 8526 (specified in its constructor). Once this object is created, the server signals that it's ready for business by calling `accept`, then sits in an endless loop waiting for a request. When a request is made by the client, the call to `accept` returns the client's socket. At this point the `ServerSocket` acts as a foreman—it passes work off to its worker, the `RequestHandler`. The `RequestHandler` is able to take advantage of Java's powerful threading facilities by implementing the Runnable interface and defining the `run()` method. The `RequestHandler` is presented in Listing 7-2.

Core Note

You may be wondering why we didn't extend from `Thread` *instead of implementing the Runnable interface. Remember that classes should not be subclassed unless the programmer plans on extending functionality or modifying the behavior of the base class. Here, we don't want to have our* `RequestHandler` *be a thread; we only plan to have our* `RequestHandler` *run in a thread, so implementing the* `java.lang.Runnable` *interface is what we want.*

Listing 7-2   RequestHandler

```java
import java.net.Socket;
import java.io.*;

public class RequestHandler implements Runnable
{
    private Socket theRequest;
```

continued

```
public RequestHandler(Socket theRequest)
{
  this.theRequest = theRequest;
}

public void run()
{

  try
  {
    BufferedReader br = new BufferedReader(new
            InputStreamReader(theRequest.getInputStream()));

    boolean more = true;

    String line = br.readLine();

    while(more)
    {

      System.out.println(line);
      if((line = br.readLine()) == null)
      {
        more = false;
      }
    }

    theRequest.close();
  }
  catch(IOException ioe)
  {
    ioe.printStackTrace();
  }
}
}
```

The RequestHandler begins its day when its foreman—the SimpleServer—makes the following call:

```
new Thread(new RequestHandler(incoming)).start();
```

The call to the RequestHandler constructor takes the incoming socket connection and stores it for later use. Then, the RequestHandler is bound to a thread when the server makes a new object of type Thread and passes the RequestHandler (a Runnable object) to it.

The fun begins when start is invoked on the new thread instance. [`Thread.start()` calls `run()` on our Runnable `RequestHandler`.] The `RequestHandler`'s job is to handle the dirty work of the HTTP transaction. It uses the `getInputStream()` method to open an input stream on the socket connection. We use Java's `Reader` classes to read lines from the socket and write these lines to standard out until we reach the end of the input stream.

An industrial HTTP server program, although much more robust, provides a similar structure to the SimpleServer. Instead of printing the contents of a request to the output stream as we do here, a Web server would read the HTTP message and handle it appropriately—usually sending back a response message to the client. This topic is the focus of this next chapter, where we introduce you to HttpServlets.

Summary

Our purpose in this chapter has been to help you understand the HTTP protocol before you go on to the next chapter, "HttpServlets". Many of the concepts introduced in this chapter will be used in the chapters that follow. We did not give you a complete explanation of the entire HTTP protocol. Nor did we provide a complete list of all request/response header fields. Interested readers can visit `www.w3.org` for a more complete HTTP specification. We have given you a quick tour of parts of the HTTP protocol which you will use often as you code servlets to extend Java Web Server. Hopefully by now you have mastered the following concepts behind the HTTP protocol:

- HTTP is a text-based protocol that contains a message header and a message body.
- The HTTP message header contains information about the data being sent.
- The HTTP message body contains data being transmitted by the client, or HTTP server.
- Not all messages have a message body (HEAD is one such example).
- There are two categories of HTTP messages—the HTTP Request and the HTTP Response.
- The HTTP Request is sent by the client to an HTTP server requesting for a service.
- The HTTP Response is a response sent by the HTTP Server to the client.
- HTTP 1.1 defines the following seven methods: OPTIONS, GET, HEAD, POST, PUT, DELETE, TRACE.
- HTTP defines a set of status codes that can be useful in debugging transactions.

HTTP SERVLETS

Topics in This Chapter

- The Core HTTP classes
- Dispatching HTTP requests, the service method
- Default handlers and status codes
- Using servlets to create dynamic Web content
- Passing data to your servlets

Chapter 8

In the last chapter you learned some of the key ideas behind the HTTP protocol. You gained a bird's-eye view of the HTTP methods, including OPTIONS, GET, HEAD, POST, PUT, DELETE, and TRACE. In this chapter we will show you how to use these methods to put the HTTP protocol to work by extending from a subclass of `GenericServlet`, the `HttpServlet` class. We start with a quick overview of the core HTTP classes, then jump into examples for some hands-on experience writing Web servlets.

Why HttpServlets?

Bob: When you change to the following: "HTTP server—an existing HTML document which exists on the server…" It makes it sound like we are talking about the HTTP server, not the HTML document being static. Static can mean several things in the programming world. So, here I want the reader to know the following:

- A significant amount of the web documents today are static.
- By static I mean they are not created by the HTTP server.
- They simply exist on the hard drive (as a file) and are fetched by the HTTP daemon and sent to the client.

Most Web documents today contain static data. *Static* refers to a Web document that is not generated by the HTTP server—an existing HTML document which exists on the server and is fetched by the HTTP daemon when the client requests it.

For example, when you visit a Web page on the Internet, you are usually looking at their default page called *index.html*. In most cases, index.html is just a file that resides on the remote HTTP server and gets updated only when a Web master decides to do so. This can cause problems, since some links within the Web page might expire, and thus data becomes outdated. Wouldn't it be great if you could generate dynamic HTML content on the fly and keep viewers of your Web site updated with the latest information? The servlet API provides the Java savvy Web developer with a set of tools to do just that and more!

With the HttpServlet class you can produce HTML that is dynamic (i.e., generated on the fly), keeping your customers updated with the most recent information. You can use JDBC to provide access to useful data stored in a company database, which is particularly necessary in electronic commerce applications (like an on-line shopping system). The Java cryptography classes can be used to provide secure transactions between two entities. Advanced applications can also take advantage of caching and session management to improve performance and personalize the customers experience.

The Essential HttpServlet Classes

The core of the HttpServlet API consists of two classes called HttpServlet and HttpUtils along with two interfaces called HttpServletRequest and HttpServletResponse. These core classes and interfaces provide the necessary methods that are needed to write effective HTTP specific servlets.

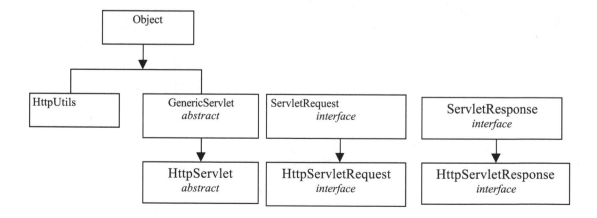

Figure 8-1   The core HttpServlet classes.

You will soon become familiar with `HttpServlet`, `HttpServletRequest`, and `HttpServletResponse`, since they will serve as the backbone to all of your HTTP specific servlets.

What Happened to GenericServlet?

By now you should be comfortable with the mother of all servlets, the `GenericServlet`. It was created to make developing servlets easier by implementing the `Servlet` and `ServletConfig` interfaces, only requiring you to override a single abstract method—the `service` method. However, `GenericServlet` is inadequate for processing the HTTP protocol. The `HttpServlet` class derives from `GenericServlet` and extends its functionality by providing methods to handle requests defined by the HTTP 1.1 protocol. In addition, `HttpServlet` implements the `service` method for you, allowing you to focus on your dynamic Web content, rather than worrying about the gory details introduced by the HTTP protocol.

Requests and Responses

In earlier chapters we used the `ServletRequest` interface to gather information from the client and the `ServletResponse` interface to send data back to the client. These two interfaces are great for the general request/response life cycle, however, they do not provide the necessary methods needed to fully support HTTP specific protocol. `HttpServlet` uses two new interfaces—`HttpServletRequest` and `HttpServletResponse` which extend the `ServletRequest` and `ServletResponse` interfaces, respectively, adding functionality to support Web requests and responses.

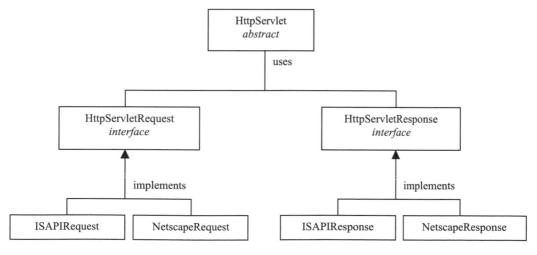

Figure 8-2   Server vendors implement the interfaces.

Core Note

If you are not using the Java Web Server, you will need to get an implementation of the servlet API that is supported by your specific Web server.

The `HttpServletRequest` and `HttpServletResponse` are interfaces that are used to hide an application from the details of individual server vendors. It is up to the server vendor (or some third party) to implement the `HttpServletRequest` and `HttpServletResponse` interfaces. For example, the `NetscapeRequest` and `NetscapeResponse` objects implement the `HttpServletRequest` and `HttpServletResponse` interfaces, respectively, to provide support for servlets running in Netscape's Enterprise or FastTrack servers. See Figure 8-2.

HttpServletRequest

The `HttpServletRequest` is used to get data from the client. The `HttpServlet`'s `service` method uses this interface to parse header fields contained in the HTTP message sent by the client. For example, the `service` method uses the following line to get the HTTP method that was requested by the client:

```
String method = req.getMethod();
```

where `req` is an Object of type `HttpServletRequest`. The `getMethod` member function returns a String that could be any one of "OPTIONS," "GET," "HEAD," "POST," "PUT," "DELETE," or "TRACE." You can also use the `HttpServletRequest` to access the header fields contained in an HTTP message. The following code snippet can be used to print out all of the HTTP headers in the HTTP request message:

```
for(java.util.Enumeration enum = req.getHeaderNames();
enum.hasMoreElements();)
{
        String header = (String)enum.nextElement();
        System.out.println(header + ": " + req.getHeader(header));
}
```

`req.getHeaderNames()` returns an object of type Enumeration. During each pass in the `for` loop, `nextElement` [Enumeration.nextElement() returns an Object, so you must cast it back to a String] is used to get the next header name in the HTTP request message and `getHeader` is used to get the value (a String) for that header. Each header/value pair is printed to `stdout`. The `HttpServletRequest` also has methods for more advanced applications that support session management and security.

JAVAX.SERVLET. HTTP.HTTPSERVLETREQUEST

```
public abstract String getMethod()
```

Returns the HTTP request method (i.e., OPTIONS, GET, HEAD, POST, PUT, DELETE, and TRACE) sent in this HTTP request.

```
public abstract Enumeration getHeaderNames()
```

Returns a java.util.Enumeration of header names found in this HTTP request. It is up to the server implementer to provide functionality for getting HTTP header fields; therefore, this method will return null if the HTTP server does not support this functionality.

```
public abstract String getHeader(String name)
```

Returns the HTTP header value corresponding to this header name in the HTTP request. For example, calling `req.getHeader("ContentType")` might return "text/html".

parameters:
name   The HTTP header name.

HttpServletResponses

The `HttpServletResponse` is used to manipulate the HTTP protocol's response message that is returned to the client. The `HttpServlet`'s `service` method uses this interface to set header fields in the HTTP message before it is sent off to the client. In the last chapter we introduced you to the HTTP status codes that are used to return useful debugging information to the client.

For example, a successful HTTP response will contain a response line (the first line in the HTTP response message) that will contain status code 200, which indicates that the request was successfully processed. This is represented in the `HttpServletResponse` as a class constant:

```
public static final int SC_OK
```

The HttpServlet Framework

So, how are the `HttpServletRequest` and `HttpServletResponse` objects sent to your `HttpServlet`? Implementers create their own servers called *servlet servers* to handle incoming HTTP requests. Their sole purpose is to accept incoming socket connections made by a client and to read, plus dispatch, these requests accordingly. These servlet servers are multithreaded and can handle multiple incoming requests simultaneously.

The servlet server stores each request in a queue of requests to be processed by handler threads; these threads then grab work requests from the connection queue, initialize the request and response objects, and call the `service` method in the `HttpServlet` class, passing it the initialized request and response objects. This process is represented in Figure 8-3.

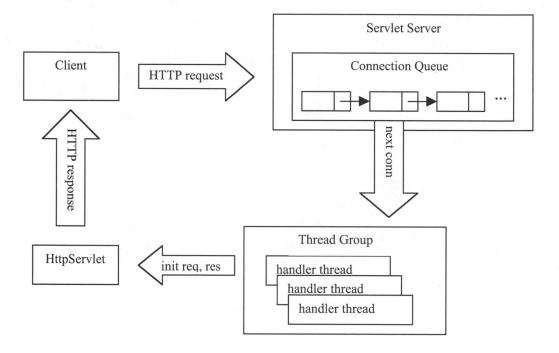

Figure 8-3   The HttpServlet framework.

Core Alert

Remember that your `HttpServlet` acts as a Singleton object (it has only a single instance) that is called on by multiple threads to handle incoming requests, so you must synchronize access to critical sections of your servlet.

Dispatching Requests:
The Brat Goes Data Surfing

Do you remember the Brat, the Java example that refuses to do what he's told? In this chapter our brat reappears and gains knowledge of the Web by adopting the `HttpServlet` class as his new parent. As you will soon see, he is a true WebBrat!

Our first brat had only a few chores, including waking up during initialization (the `init` method), processing service calls (the service method), and going to bed when asked (the destroy method). In this chapter our brat's service method gains much more responsibility, as he is asked to handle methods in the HTTP protocol. The WebBrat can be asked to respond to any of the HTTP methods. As our first brat did, he will complain every time you ask him to do something. If you compile the WebBrat and use the servlet runner (introduced in Chapter 5, "Generic Servlets"), you can use your Web browser to see the WebBrat in action. For example, a URL of form

```
http://localhost:8080/servlet/WebBrat
```

will ask the WebBrat to handle the HTTP GET method. The WebBrat will continue to complain when asked to do his chores, this time he'll respond by saying "I don't wanna handle a GET," as illustrated in Figure 8-4.

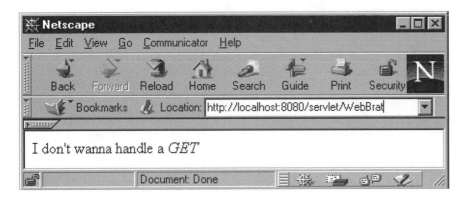

Figure 8-4   This Brat is certainly not behaving.

You can also submit an HTTP POST request and the WebBrat will respond by saying

```
"I don't wanna handle a POST!"
```

Listing 8-1 takes a look inside the WebBrat class to see what makes him such a brat when he is asked to handle methods in the HTTP protocol.

Listing 8-1   The WebBrat Speaks HTTP

```java
import javax.servlet.*;
import javax.servlet.http.*;
import java.io.*;

public class WebBrat extends HttpServlet
{
    public void init(ServletConfig sc)
            throws ServletException
    {
      super.init(sc);
      System.out.println ("I don't wanna wake up!");
    }

    public void service (HttpServletRequest req,
                         HttpServletResponse res)
                         throws ServletException, IOException
    {

      res.setContentType("Text/HTML");
      PrintWriter pw  = res.getWriter();

      String httpMethod = req.getMethod();

      if(httpMethod.equals("GET"))
      {
          pw.println("I don't wanna handle a <i>GET</i>");
      }
      else if(httpMethod.equals("HEAD"))
      {
          pw.println("I don't wanna handle a <i>HEAD</i>");
      }
      else if(httpMethod.equals("POST"))
      {
          pw.println("I don't wanna handle a <i>POST</i>");
      }

    }

    public void destroy ()
    {
      System.out.println("I don't wanna go to bed!");
    }
}
```

You probably have noticed by now that the WebBrat is significantly different from the first brat. The WebBrat is a subclass of `HttpServlet`, the base class for all servlets wanting to support the HTTP protocol. The following three lines of code allow the WebBrat to make himself noticed:

```
res.setContentType("text/html");
PrintWriter pw = res.getWriter();

String httpMethod = req.getMethod();
```

First, he'll let the client know what language he speaks by setting the content type to the `"text/html"` mime type. Then he obtains writer Object (`PrintWriter`) by calling `getWriter` on the response. The WebBrat finds out what HTTP method is being requested by calling `getMethod` on the request. The `getMethod` returns a String that contains the HTTP method that is being requested by the client; this can be any one of the HTTP protocol supported methods.

If you have any experience with the `HttpServlet` class, you may be cringing and calling us unprintable names about now, and with good reason! That is because the WebBrat didn't need to override the service method to process the HTTP `GET` and `POST` methods.

Recall that when you were introduced to the mother of all servlets, the `GenericServlet`, you needed to override the service method to make it work. That's because it is an abstract method in the `GenericServlet` class, so classes that derive from `GenericServlet` must implement its service method. That is not the case with the `HttpServlet`—the `HttpServlet` class derives from `GenericServlet` and overrides the `service` method for you. In fact, you will hardly ever need to override the `service` method to support most of your HTTP needs.

The HttpServlet Service Method

When a request is made to your `HttpServlet`, its service method is called. `HttpServlet` overrides the service method in the `GenericServlet` class and acts as a dispatcher to all incoming requests; it calls on methods in `HttpServlet` that correspond to HTTP methods sent by the client. This interaction is summarized in Figure 8-5.

Different methods will be called by the service method, depending on the type of request issued by the client. Table 8-1 summarizes methods in the `HttpServlet` class that correspond to HTTP request methods.

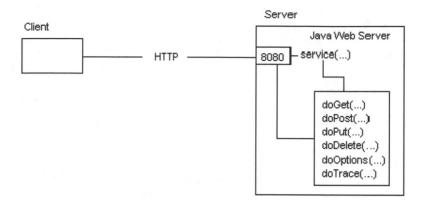

Figure 8-5   The HttpServlet service method.

Core Note

It is important that you understand this table before you attempt to write `HttpServlets`*, because overriding the wrong methods can cause unexpected results.*

Table 8-1   HttpServlet Methods

HttpServletMethod	*HTTP Request Handled*
doGet	GET, conditional GET, HEAD
doPost	POST
doPut	PUT
doDelete	DELETE
doOptions	OPTIONS
doTrace	TRACE

A Closer Look at doGet

Notice that by overriding the `doGet` method you automatically handle the HTTP GET, conditional GET, and HEAD requests. Taking a closer look at the conditional GET and HEAD methods, you can see why `doGet` is able to support all three. Remember in Chapter 7, "Introduction to HTTP," that the HTTP head is the equivalent to a GET, minus the message body. So, all the Web server has to do for a HEAD request is to return the appropriate HTTP message headers. The conditional GET gives the Web server more information to work with, by allowing it to decide when to return a complete response to the client. Most Web browsers these days cache copies of previously visited Web pages locally, so the next time you ask the remote server to GET the page you will only GET the page if it is newer than the one you currently have. This important topic is more commonly known as *message caching* and will be covered in Chapter 10, "Caching."

The Improved WebBrat

Now that you know how the service method in the HttpServlet really works, why not recode the WebBrat to show off this knowledge? To be consistent with the previous example, Listing 8-2 is called WebBrat2.

Listing 8-2   WebBrat2

```
import javax.servlet.*;
import javax.servlet.http.*;
import java.io.*;

public class WebBrat2 extends HttpServlet
{
    public void init(ServletConfig sc)
            throws ServletException
    {
      super.init(sc);
      System.out.println ("I don't wanna wake up!");
    }

    public void doGet(HttpServletRequest req,
                      HttpServletResponse res)
                throws ServletException, IOException
    {
      res.setContentType("Text/HTML");
      PrintWriter pw = res.getWriter();
      pw.println("I don't wanna handle a <i>GET</i>");
    }

    public void doPost(HttpServletRequest req,
                       HttpServletResponse res)
                throws ServletException, IOException
    {
```

continued

```
    res.setContentType("Text/HTML");
    PrintWriter pw = res.getWriter();
    pw.println("I don't wanna handle a <i>POST</i>");
  }

  public void destroy ()
  {
    System.out.println("I don't wanna go to bed!");
  }

}
```

WebBrat2 acts like the WebBrat, but without overriding the service method, because the existing service method provides logic to call the appropriate *do* method handler, depending on the type of HTTP request. These handlers are called the *default handlers*, because they provide implementations for HTTP methods that you don't support; this idea is similar to the adapter classes in the new AWT event-delegation model.

Core Note

The AWT 1.1 Event model uses Adapter classes to make life easier for the developer. As an example, consider registering a GUI component as a WindowListener. The WindowListener interface has seven methods you must somehow implement in order to satisfy your contract agreement with it. The `WindowAdapter` *class provides a default implementation for all seven methods in the WindowListener interface for you, saving you the grief of implementing all seven methods yourself. Likewise, the HttpServlet class provides default implementations for all of the HTTP 1.1 methods, saving you the grief of implementing all of them in your servlet.*

Default Handlers

Have you ever called someone, only to get an annoying computer voice that asks you to leave a message? The `HttpServlet`'s default handlers provide a similar service to developers: you can be as lazy as you want and messages will still get through. Likewise, if you do not override a specific do handler method (i.e., `doGet`, `doPost`, etc.), `HttpServlet`'s service method will handle the request for you by calling the default implementation for `doGet`, `doPost`, etc.

So, what would happen if the WebBrat received a request that it didn't handle? Say, for example that our WebBrat didn't implement the `doGet` method, and a client sent a HTTP GET request to the brat. What would happen? Since we didn't implement the doGet method, the default doGet method in the `HttpServlet` class would handle the request. The default doGet would simply do the following:

```
resp.sendError(HttpServletResponse.SC_BAD_REQUEST,
            "GET is note supported by this URL");
```

In this case the browser would display a message indicating that your server does not provide support for the HTTP GET method, as shown in Figure 8-6.

Figure 8-6   Default-handler error message.

JAVAX.SERVLET.HTTP. HTTPSERVLETRESPONSE

```
public abstract void sendError(int sc) throws IOException
```

Used in special cases to send an HTTP status code back to the client. An IOException is thrown if there is a problem with the InputStream associated with this request.

parameters:

sc   The status code for this message. For a complete list of status codes, see the static member fields contained in the `HttpServletResponse` interface.

continued

```
public abstract void sendError(int sc,
                        String msg) throws IOException
```

Used in special cases to send an HTTP status code back to the client. An IOException is thrown if there is a problem with the InputStream associated with this request.

parameters:

sc   The status code for this message. For a complete list of status codes, see the static member fields contained in the `HttpServletResponse` interface.

msg   Used by servlet implementers to provide a useful message along with the status code. This is commonly known as a *reason phrase*.

JAVAX.SERVLET.HTTP.HTTPSERVLET

```
protected void doOptions(HttpServletRequest req,
    HttpServletResponse resp) throws ServletException,
    IOException
```

Provides support for the HTTP OPTIONS method. `HttpServlet` provides a default implementation for this method. There rarely is a need to override the default implementation.

Parameters:

req   The HTTP specific request containing HTTP header fields that are accessed by servlet developers and the `HttpServlet` service method.

resp   The HTTP specific response that is manipulated by servlet developers and the `HttpServlet` service method to return data to the client that made the request.

```
protected void doGet(HttpServletRequest req,
    HttpServletResponse resp) throws ServletException,
    IOException
```

Overridden by the servlet developer to provide support for the HTTP GET method. The `HttpServlet` class provides a default method in case you choose not to support the GET method. This method can be used for a wide variety of applications, including message caching, a topic which is covered in a later chapter. By overriding the doGet method, you are providing support for the HTTP GET, conditional GET, and HEAD methods.

Parameters:

req
The HTTP specific request containing HTTP header fields that are accessed by servlet developers and the `HttpServlet` service method.

resp
The HTTP specific response that is manipulated by servlet developers and the `HttpServlet` service method to return data to the client that made the request.

```
protected void doPost(HttpServletRequest req,
HttpServletResponse resp) throws ServletException,
IOException
```

Overridden by the servlet developer to provide support for the HTTP POST method. The `HttpServlet` class provides a default method in case you do not choose to support the POST method. The POST method is most commonly used to handle the POSTing of HTML FORM data. The HTTP POST method also supports file uploads from an HTML FORM.

Parameters:

req
The HTTP specific request containing HTTP header fields that are accessed by servlet developers and the `HttpServlet` service method.

resp
The HTTP specific response that is manipulated by servlet developers and the `HttpServlet` service method to return data to the client that made the request.

```
protected void doPut(HttpServletRequest req,
HttpServletResponse resp) throws ServletException,
IOException
```

Overridden by the servlet developer to provide support for the HTTP PUT method. The `HttpServlet` class provides a default method in case you do not choose to support the PUT method.

Parameters:

req
The HTTP specific request containing HTTP header fields that are accessed by servlet developers and the `HttpServlet` service method.

resp
The HTTP specific response that is manipulated by servlet developers and the `HttpServlet` service method to return data to the client that made the request.

continued

```
protected void doDelete(HttpServletRequest req,
HttpServletResponse resp) throws ServletException,
                                        IOException
```

Overridden by the servlet developer to provide support for the HTTP DELETE method. The `HttpServlet` class provides a default method in case you do not choose to support the DELETE method.

Parameters:

req   The HTTP specific request containing HTTP header fields that are accessed by servlet developers and the `HttpServlet` service method.

resp   The HTTP specific response that is manipulated by servlet developers and the `HttpServlet` service method to return data to the client that made the request.

```
protected void doTrace(HttpServletRequest req,
        HttpServletResponse resp) throws ServletException,
        IOException
```

Provides support for the HTTP TRACE method. `HttpServlet` provides an implementation for this method, therefore you will rarely override it.

Parameters:

req   The HTTP specific request containing HTTP header fields that are accessed by servlet developers and the `HttpServlet` service method.

resp   The HTTP specific response that is manipulated by servlet developers and the `HttpServlet` service method to return data to the client that made the request.

```
protected void service(HttpServletRequest req,
        HttpServletResponse resp) throws ServletException,
        IOException
```

This is the HTTP specific service method; it acts as the dispatcher of all incoming HTTP requests. It will call the proper `HttpServlet` method, depending on the type of HTTP request that is being made (i.e., GET, POST, etc.).

Parameters:

req   The HTTP specific request containing HTTP header fields that are accessed by servlet developers and the `HttpServlet` service method.

resp   The HTTP specific response that is manipulated by servlet developers and the `HttpServlet` service method to return data to the client that made the request.

```
public void service(ServletRequest req,
         ServletResponse res) throws ServletException,
         IOException
```

This service method acts as a dispatcher to the HTTP specific service method. It attempts to cast the req/res to the `HttpServletRequest`/`HttpServletResponse`, respectively, and calls the HTTP specific service method with the new `HttpServletRequest`/`HttpServletResponse`.

Parameters:

req   This parameter is assumed to be the HTTP specific request containing HTTP header fields that are accessed by servlet developers and the `HttpServlet` service method.

resp   This parameter is assumed to be the HTTP specific response that can be manipulated by servlet developers and the HttpServlet service method to return data to the client that made the request.

Deploying Dynamic Content: The GuestBookServlet

Most of a servlet's power lies in its ability to quickly deploy dynamically-generated Web pages. The idea behind a guest book is to allow visitors of your site to provide feedback on the look and design of your Web site. This will help you improve your site based on comments from viewers all over the world. To keep it simple, our guest book example will only record the visitor's name and e-mail address. Figure 8-7 shows the HTML form which is used to POST data to the `GuestBookServlet` servlet.

This form is very short, asking the user to fill out only two text areas. You should take the same approach; having the visitor of your site fill out a two-page form is great for you, but the average Web surfer is much more likely to fill out a small form than a very long one. After completing the form by pressing the Submit Query button, the `GuestBookServlet` will generate HTML, displaying the most recent list of signees, and then send it to the client. Figure 8-8 displays a simple class diagram of `GuestBookServlet`.

`GuestBookServlet` extends from `HttpServlet` and has a Java Vector that stores from zero to n `Signee` objects. We define a `Signee` to be any visitor that enters data into the guest-book form and presses the Submit Query button.

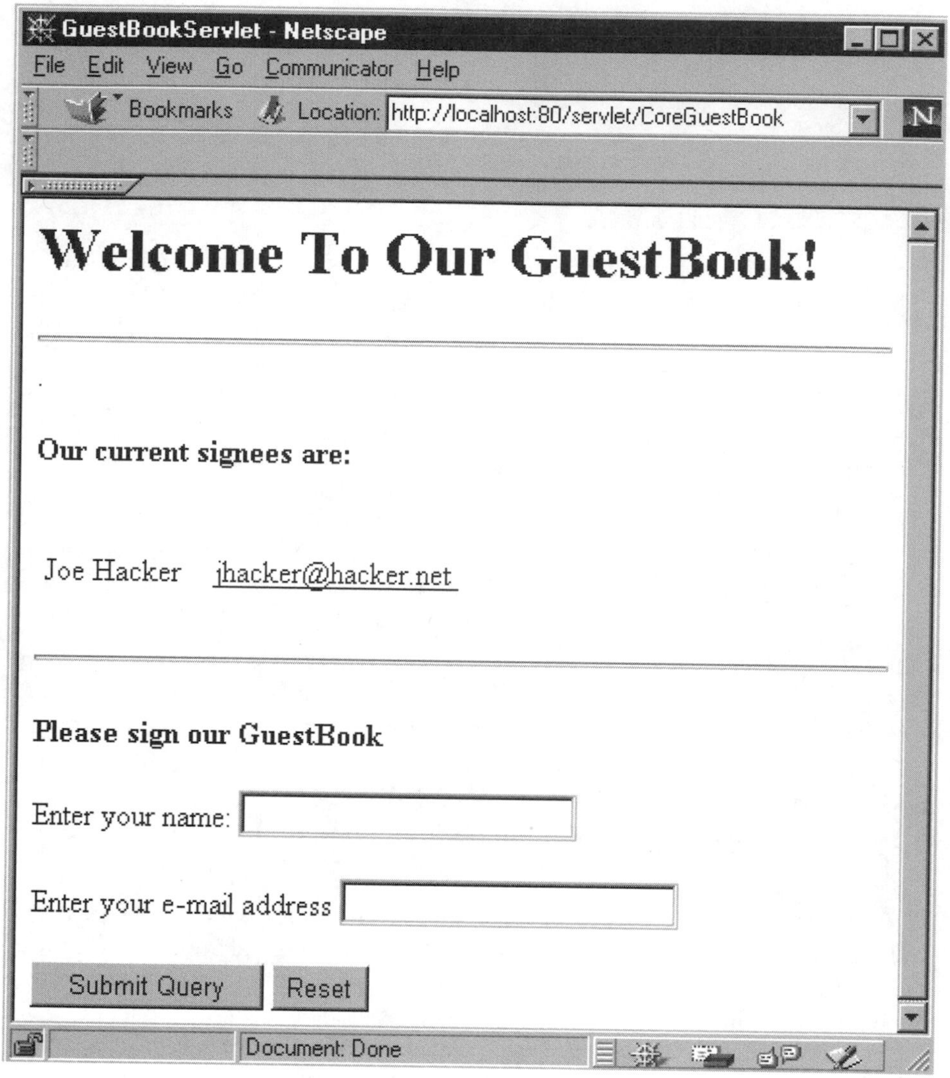

Figure 8-7   The guest-book HTML form.

The Signee class in Listing 8-3 is a simple container for storing the guest's name and e-mail address.

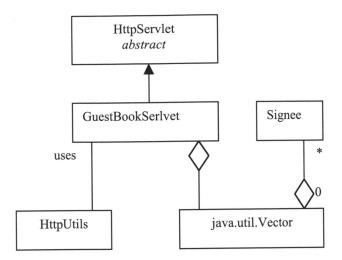

Figure 8-8   *guest-book OO diagram.*

Listing 8-3   The Signee Class

```java
public class Signee
{
  private String name;
  private String email;

  public Signee(String name, String email)
  {
    this.name = name;
    this.email = email;
  }

  public String getName()
  {
    return this.name;
  }

  public String getEmail()
  {
    return this.email;
  }
}
```

GuestBookServlet's doPost method is used to handle the POSTing of new signees. By taking advantage of the parsePostData method in the HttpUtils class, you can easily parse the InputType/value data that was submitted from the form. All methods in the HttpUtils class are static; therefore, you don't need to instantiate the HttpUtils class to use them.

This static method takes as input the size of the InputStream (here, the content length of the request) and a ServletInputStream and returns a Hashtable that contains the parsed form data with key/value pairs, where keys map to the names of INPUT TYPE tags in the HTML form; and values map to the text typed by the user:

```
java.util.Hashtable formData =
    HttpUtils.parsePostData(req.getContentLength(),
                            req.getInputStream());
String[] name = (String[])formData.get("name");
String[] email = (String[])formData.get("email");
addSignee(name[0], email[0]);

doGet(req,res);
```

Notice that Hashtable's get method returns a string array, not a string. An HttpServletRequest object may contain multiple values for a single NAME attribute. The get method returns string array with all the NAMEd values. The GuestBookServlet gets the values for two input types (name and e-mail) and uses the addSignee method to add a new Signee object to the vector.

There is no need to generate HTML and send it back to the user in the doPost method. The doGet method already does that for us, so you need only call the doGet method to send a response back to the client.

GuestBookServlet overrides the doGet method to dynamically generate HTML to be sent back and rendered by the client. It uses the getSigneeInfo method to generate the dynamic portion of the HTML. The getSigneeInfo method traverses through the vector of Signee objects and creates an HTML table that stores the current list of Signees and returns the table as a string. Listing 8-4 shows the complete source for GuestBookServlet.

Core Tip

The getSigneeInfo method uses a StringBuffer as an optimization technique. Remember that Java Strings are immutable, therefore, simply appending to an existing String is expensive, as the compiler must create a new String to hold the existing string plus the new string appended to it. The StringBuffer efficiently concatenates strings and allows you to convert to a String at any time by calling the toString method. Furthermore, sb.append(String1); sb.append(String2); is much more efficient than sb.append(String1 + String2).

Listing 8-4   GuestBookServlet

```java
import java.io.*;
import javax.servlet.*;
import javax.servlet.http.*;

public class GuestBookServlet extends HttpServlet
{
  private java.util.Vector guests = new java.util.Vector();


    public void doGet(HttpServletRequest req,
                      HttpServletResponse res)
                      throws ServletException,
                      IOException
    {
        PrintWriter pw = res.getWriter();

        res.setContentType("text/html");

        pw.print("<HEAD><TITLE>GuestBookServlet");
        pw.println("</TITLE></HEAD>");
        pw.println("<BODY>");
        pw.print("<H1> Welcome To Our GuestBook!");
        pw.println("</H1>");
        pw.println("<HR>");
        pw.println("<H4>Our current signees are:");
        pw.println("</H4><P><BR>");

        String signees = getSigneeInfo();

        pw.println(signees);
        pw.println("<P><HR>");
        pw.print("<H4>Please sign our ");
        pw.println("GuestBook</H4>");

        String serverName = req.getServerName();
        String serverPort = "" + req.getServerPort();

        pw.print("<FORM action=http://");
        pw.print (serverName + ":" + serverPort + req.getServletPath());
        pw.println(" method=POST>");
        pw.println("Enter your name:");
        pw.println("<INPUT TYPE=text NAME=name><P>");
        pw.println("Enter your e-mail address");
        pw.println("<INPUT TYPE=text NAME=email><P>");
        pw.println("<INPUT TYPE=submit>");
```

continued

```java
        pw.println("<INPUT TYPE=reset>");
        pw.println("</BODY>");
        pw.println("</HTML>");

        pw.close();
    }


    public void doPost(HttpServletRequest req,
                       HttpServletResponse res)
    throws ServletException, IOException
    {
        java.util.Hashtable formData =
            HttpUtils.parsePostData(req.getContentLength(),
                                    req.getInputStream());
        String[] name = (String[])formData.get("name");
        String[] email = (String[])formData.get("email");
        addSignee(name[0], email[0]);

        doGet(req,res);
    }

    public String getSigneeInfo()
    {
        StringBuffer sb = new StringBuffer(150);
        sb.append("<Table>\n");

        for(int i = 0; i < guests.size(); i++)
        {
            Signee signee = (Signee)guests.elementAt(i);
            sb.append("<TR>\n");
            sb.append("  <TD>");
            sb.append(signee.getName());
            sb.append("</TD>\n");
            sb.append("  <TD><A HREF=mailto:");
            sb.append(signee.getEmail());
            sb.append("> ");
            sb.append(signee.getEmail());
            sb.append(" </A></TD>");
            sb.append("\n");
            sb.append("</TR>\n");
        }

        sb.append("</TABLE>\n");
        return sb.toString();
    }
```

```java
    public void addSignee(String name, String emailAddress)
    {
       guests.addElement(new Signee(name, emailAddress));
    }

    public String getServletInfo()
    {
        return "A GuestBook servlet.";
    }

}
```

The Improved GuestBook

The GuestBookServlet is missing some very important functionality. If you reload the GuestBookServlet, you will see that all of our guests that signed the guest book are lost. So what should we do—ask them all to sign the guest book again? You could claim that this version of the guest book is in beta (as one very well-known company would do) and maybe you would only lose a couple of customers as a result of this inconvenience. With a little extra work, you can make the GuestBookServlet remember all signees, even if it were reloaded.

GuestBookServlet2 replaces the GuestBookServlet, adding functionality to persistently store the vector of Signee objects. Here are the steps required to do this:

1. Make the Signee class implement the java.io.Serializable interface.
2. Add functionality to store the vector of Signee objects incrementally.
3. Force the servlet to save the vector of Signee objects before it is shut down.
4. Reload the vector of Signee objects when the GuestBookServlet is reloaded.

Figure 8-9 shows the OO class diagram for GuestBookServlet2.

The flush method is used to serialize the current state of the vector. It obtains a new ObjectOutputStream and calls writeObject to serialize the guest's vector to a file.

```java
            ObjectOutputStream oos = new ObjectOutputStream(new
                    FileOutputStream(FILENAME));
            oos.writeObject(guests);
            oos.close();
            dirty = false;
```

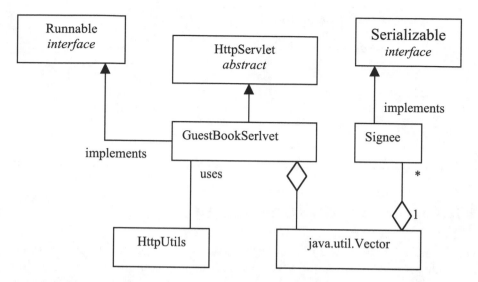

Figure 8-9   Class diagram for an improved GuestBookServlet.

In order to serialize the Vector, you must make sure that objects contained in the Vector implement the Serializable (or Externalizable) interface. GuestBookServlet uses a vector to store `Signee` objects, so we must make the `Signee` class serializable. The `Signee` class can be made serializable by redefining the class definition to implement the `java.io.Serializable` interface as follows:

```
public class Signee implements java.io.Serializable
{
    ...
}
```

You could save the state of the vector just before GuestBookServlet shuts down. This can be accomplished by making a call to flush in the `destroy` method, since the `destroy` method will be called just before the servlet dies:

```
public void destroy ()
{
    if (dirty) _flush();
    shouldStop = true;
}
```

Notice that we have a member field called `dirty` that is set to true when a new `Signee` object is added to the vector. This follows a very important policy that should be implemented in all servlets: *only do work if there is work to be done* (i.e., only save the state of the vector if the vector has changed).

Now the vector of `Signees` will be saved to disk when the servlet gracefully stops, but we still haven't completely solved the problem of a possible system crash. What we need is a way to incrementally save the state of the vector. By implementing the `Runnable` interface, we can create a background thread to incrementally save the state of the vector. The thread is started toward the end of `GuestBookServlet2`'s `init` method by calling `start` on a new instance of the `Thread` class:

```
new Thread(this).start();
```

Core Note

Make sure that you call `start`*, not* `run` *on the new instance of a* `Thread`*. By calling start on the thread you are allowing the compiler to allocate the necessary resources to run the thread. Calling the* `run` *method would bypass this and could cause unexpected results.*

Eventually the `run` method in the `GuestBookServlet` will be called, and it will continue to execute in a background thread. This thread will serialize the state of the vector every thirty seconds. This is accomplished by calling `flush` (again, we only call `flush` if the vector is "dirty") and making a call to `Thread.sleep(30000)`, which will cause the thread to temporarily cease execution for thirty seconds. When the servlet is stopped, the `destroy` method will be called, and the following line will cause the `run` method to return, causing the background thread to fall into a dead state.

```
shouldStop = true;
```

This call is made in the `destroy` method. The complete source for `GuestBookServlet2` can be found in Listing 8-5.

Listing 8-5   GuestBookServlet2

```
import java.io.*;
import javax.servlet.*;
import javax.servlet.http.*;
import javax.servlet.http.HttpUtils;

public class GuestBookServlet2 extends HttpServlet
                               implements Runnable
{
  private java.util.Vector guests = null;
  private boolean dirty = true;
  private static final String FILENAME = "GUEST.DAT";
  private boolean shouldStop = false;

    public void init (ServletConfig config)
               throws ServletException
    {
```

continued

```java
      File f = new File(FILENAME);
      if (f.canRead())
      {
        try
        {
          ObjectInputStream ois =
              new ObjectInputStream(new FileInputStream(f));
          try
          {
            guests = (java.util.Vector)ois.readObject();
          }
          catch (ClassNotFoundException cnfe)
          {
            cnfe.printStackTrace();
          }

          ois.close();
        }
        catch (IOException ioe)
        {
          guests = new java.util.Vector(0,10);
          ioe.printStackTrace();
        }
      }
      else
      {
        guests = new java.util.Vector(0,10);
      }
        new Thread(this).start();


  }


  public void doGet(HttpServletRequest req,
                    HttpServletResponse res)
                    throws ServletException,
                    IOException
  {
      PrintWriter pw = res.getWriter();
      res.setContentType("text/html");

      pw.print("<HEAD><TITLE>GuestBookServlet2");
      pw.println("</TITLE></HEAD>");
      pw.println("<BODY>");
      pw.print("<H1> Welcome To Our GuestBook!");
      pw.println("</H1>");
      pw.println("<HR>");
      pw.println("<H4>Our current signees are:");
```

```
    pw.println("</H4><P><BR>");

    String signees = getSigneeInfo();

    pw.println(signees);
    pw.println("<P><HR>");
    pw.print("<H4>Please sign our ");
    pw.println("GuestBook</H4>");

    String serverName = req.getServerName();
    String serverPort = "" + req.getServerPort();

    pw.print("<FORM action=http://");
    pw.print (serverName + ":" + serverPort + req.getServletPath());
    pw.println(" method=POST>");
    pw.println("Enter your name:");
    pw.println("<INPUT TYPE=text NAME=name><P>");
    pw.println("Enter your e-mail address");
    pw.println("<INPUT TYPE=text NAME=email><P>");
    pw.println("<INPUT TYPE=submit>");
    pw.println("<INPUT TYPE=reset>");
    pw.println("</BODY>");
    pw.println("</HTML>");

    pw.close();
}


private final void _flush ()
{
  try
  {
    ObjectOutputStream oos = new ObjectOutputStream(new
              FileOutputStream(FILENAME));
    oos.writeObject(guests);
    oos.close();
    dirty = false;
  }
  catch (IOException ioe)
  {
    ioe.printStackTrace();
  }
}

public void run ()
{
  while (!shouldStop)
  {
    if (dirty)
```

continued

```
      {
        _flush();
      }

      try
      {
        Thread.sleep(30000);
      }
      catch (InterruptedException ie)
      {
        ie.printStackTrace();
      }
    }
  }

  public void destroy ()
  {
    if (dirty) _flush();
    shouldStop = true;
  }

  public void doPost(HttpServletRequest req,
                     HttpServletResponse res)
throws ServletException, IOException
  {
      java.util.Hashtable formData =
          HttpUtils.parsePostData(req.getContentLength(),
                                  req.getInputStream());
      String[] name = (String[])formData.get("name");
      String[] email = (String[])formData.get("email");
      addSignee(name[0], email[0]);

      doGet(req,res);
  }

  public String getSigneeInfo()
  {
    StringBuffer sb = new StringBuffer(150);
    sb.append("<Table>\n");

    for(int i = 0; i < guests.size(); i++)
    {
      Signee signee = (Signee)guests.elementAt(i);
      sb.append("<TR>\n");
      sb.append("   <TD>");
      sb.append(signee.getName());
      sb.append("</TD>\n");
      sb.append("   <TD><A HREF=mailto:");
```

```
      sb.append(signee.getEmail());
      sb.append("> ");
      sb.append(signee.getEmail());
      sb.append(" </A></TD>");
      sb.append("\n");
      sb.append("</TR>\n");
   }

   sb.append("</TABLE>\n");
   return sb.toString();
}

public void addSignee(String name, String emailAddress)
{
   guests.addElement(new Signee(name, emailAddress));
   dirty = true;
}

public String getServletInfo()
{
    return "A GuestBook servlet.";
}

public java.util.Vector getGuests()
{
   synchronized(guests)
   {
     return (java.util.Vector)this.guests.clone();
   }
}
}
```

Now What?

GuestBookServlet2 still has some problems! We need to guard against the possibility of large amounts of data being POSTed to the servlet. For example, Joe Hacker may copy the contents of a large file and paste that information into both of the INPUT TYPEs on the guest-book form and submit the request. GuestBookServlet will do its usual chores: accept the request, add the new Signee to the vector, and at some time the large amount of data that Mr. Hacker submitted will be written to disk by our background thread. Mr. Hacker could continue to submit these large requests, and sooner or later the server would run out of disk space. Guarding against these attacks is easily accomplished by adding the following code in the doPost method:

```
int reqLength = req.getContentLength();
    if(reqLength <= MAX_REQUEST_LENGTH)
    {
        //handle the POST in the usual way
    }
    else
    {
      res.sendError(
        HttpServletResponse.SC_REQUEST_ENTITY_TOO_LARGE,
        "<P>The length of your request was " +
        reqLength + "<BR>This servlet only" +
        " accepts requests that are of" +
        " length <= " + MAX_REQUEST_LENGTH);
    }
```

The MAX_REQUEST_LENGTH is the maximum content length that CoreGuestBook will accept. Any requests with content length greater than or equal to the MAX_REQUEST_LENGTH will not be processed, and we notify the client by sending him the SC_REQUEST_ENTITY_TOO_LARGE status code, along with a brief description of the problem. Figure 8-10 shows this in action.

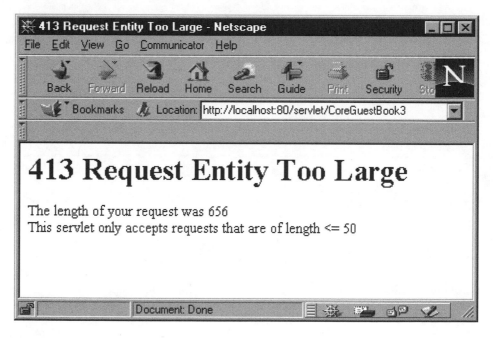

Figure 8-10   Uh oh, the request is too big.

Here, the content length of the request (656) was much too large than the MAX_REQUEST_LENGTH (50); therefore GuestBookServlet rejected the request and notified the client.

Passing Data to Your Servlet

As you can see, your servlet is the expressway that gets data into and out of your server. The GuestBookServlet retrieved its data via the POST method. As you will soon see, there are other ways to get data to your servlet. Two common ways can be demonstrated by the following HTML FORM tags:

```
<FORM ACTION=http://localhost:port/servlet/MyServlet METHOD=GET>
<FORM ACTION=http://localhost:port/servlet/MyServlet METHOD=POST>
```

The first uses the GET method to submit FORM data and the second uses the POST method to submit FORM data. Say, for example, you are using the GET method to send data to MyServlet. The HTML that generates this request may look like:

```
<HTML>
<BODY>
<FORM ACTION=http://localhost:port/servlet/MyServlet METHOD=GET>
<TABLE>
  <TR>
    <TD>FirstName, Middle Initial
    <TD><INPUT TYPE=text NAME=first_name>
  </TR>
  <TR>
    <TD>Last Name
    <TD><INPUT TYPE=text NAME=last_name>
  </TR>
</TABLE>
<P><INPUT TYPE=submit>
</FORM>
</BODY>
</HTML>
```

If Joe D. Hacker wanted to submit a request, he would do so by entering data into the form as shown in Figure 8-11.

In this case the following HTTP request line would be generated:

```
GET /servlet/MyServlet?first_name=Joe+D&last_name=Hacker HTTP/1.0
```

You can view the complete HTTP message generated by this request by using SimpleServer.java and the form presented in Figure 8-11.

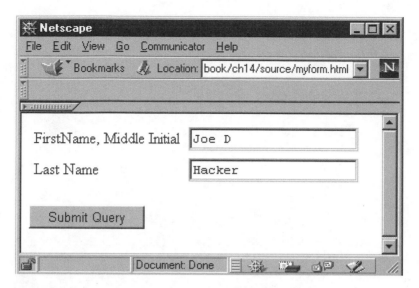

Figure 8-11   POSTing data using the GET method.

Notice that the form parameters appear after the question mark ("?") in this request. This is known as the *query string*. The GET method uses the query string to send data with the HTTP request. The POST method works quite differently. If we were to change METHOD=GET to METHOD=POST in the HTML and resubmit the same form data as represented in Figure 8-11, the following request line would be present in the HTTP header for this request:

```
POST /servlet/MyServlet HTTP/1.0
```

Notice that no query string is present in this request line. That is because the HTTP POST method sends its data in the message body. The message body for this request would look like:

```
first_name=Joe+D&last_name=Hacker
```

Both the GET and the POST methods encode the form parameters in the same way by following some simple rules:

- An equals sign "=" separates the INPUT TYPE from its value.
- The plus "+" sign denotes white spaces.
- An ampersand "&" separates INPUT TYPE/value pairs.

Using GET to Parse Form Data

In our last example of this chapter, the GuestSearchServlet (Listing 8-5) shows how the GET method can be used to send form data to a servlet. The following HTML is used to get search criteria that is used to search for clients that have signed the guest book:

```
<HTML>
<HEAD><TITLE>Search for guests on this site.</TITLE></HEAD>
<BODY>
<FORM action=http://localhost/servlet/CoreGuestSearch method=GET>
Enter the person to search for:
<INPUT TYPE=text NAME=search_name><P>
<INPUT TYPE=submit>
<INPUT TYPE=reset>
</FORM>

</BODY>
</HTML>
```

The following code snippet shows how GuestSearchServlet gets the form data and uses the search criteria to search for guests that have signed the guest book:

```
java.util.Hashtable ht =
        HttpUtils.parseQueryString(req.getQueryString());
String searchName[] =
        (String[])ht.get("search_name");
String results = doSearch(searchName);
```

Notice that the HttpUtils saves us work again by providing a method to parse the query string. The parseQueryString method parses the form data that is contained in the query string of this GET request. This method performs the same task as the parsePostData method that was used by the GuestBookServlet to parse form data send by the HTTP POST request.

The doSearch method performs the search. It uses the ServletContext interface to find the GuestBookServlet. Notice that we passed "CoreGuestBook2" into the getServlet(String) method. When we registered GuestBookServlet2 in Java Web Server we aliased it to the name CoreGuestBook2, so that is the name we must use in the getServlet method. GuestSearchServlet asks the GuestBookServlet for the current list of signees by calling the getGuests method:

```
ServletContext sc = getServletContext();

Servlet s = sc.getServlet("CoreGuestBook2");
GuestBookServlet2 guestBook = (GuestBookServlet2)s;
java.util.Vector guests = guestBook.getGuests();
```

and searches each `Signee` object by name, comparing it with the search criteria. Listing 8-6 shows the complete source for `GuestSearchServlet`.

Listing 8-6   GuestSearchServlet

```
import java.io.*;
import javax.servlet.*;
import javax.servlet.http.*;
import javax.servlet.http.HttpUtils;

public class GuestSearchServlet extends HttpServlet
{
  public void doGet(HttpServletRequest req,
                    HttpServletResponse res)
                    throws ServletException, IOException
  {
    res.setContentType("text/html");

    PrintWriter pw = res.getWriter();

    pw.print("<HEAD><TITLE> GuestSearchServlet");
    pw.println(" search results </TITLE></HEAD>");
    pw.println("<BODY>");
    pw.println("<H1> Guest Search Results! </H1>");

    java.util.Hashtable ht =
      HttpUtils.parseQueryString(req.getQueryString());

    String searchName[] = (String[])ht.get("search_name");

    String results = doSearch(searchName);

    pw.println(results);

    pw.println("</BODY>");
    pw.println("</HTML>");
    pw.close();
  }

  public String doSearch(String[] searchName)
                              throws ServletException
  {
      ServletContext sc = getServletContext();
      Servlet s = sc.getServlet("GuestBookServlet2");

      GuestBookServlet2 guestBook = (GuestBookServlet2)s;
```

```java
    java.util.Vector guests = guestBook.getGuests();

    if(guests.size() == 0)
    {
      return "No Guests have signed up yet!";
    }

    StringBuffer sb = new StringBuffer();
    sb.append("<Table>\n");

    int numFound = 0;

    for(int i = 0; i < guests.size(); i++)
    {
      Signee signee = (Signee)guests.elementAt(i);
      String name = signee.getName().toLowerCase();

      if(name.indexOf(searchName[0].toLowerCase()) != -1)
      {
        numFound++;
        sb.append("<TR>\n");
        sb.append("<TD>");
        sb.append(signee.getName());
        sb.append("</TD>");
        sb.append("\n<TD><A HREF=mailto:");
        sb.append(signee.getEmail());
        sb.append(" > ");
        sb.append(signee.getEmail());
        sb.append(" </A></TD>\n");
        sb.append("</TR>\n");
      }
    }
    sb.append("</TABLE>\n");

    if(numFound > 0)
      return sb.toString();
    else
     return "No matches found with search string <i>" +
            searchName[0] + "</i>";
  }

public String getServletInfo()
{
    return "Searches for guests in the guestbook.";
}

}
```

In order to support the GuestSearchServlet, you need to add a new method in the GuestBookServlet to return the vector of Signee objects. The getGuests method returns the current list of signees:

```
public java.util.Vector getGuests()
{
    synchronized(guests)
    {
        return (java.util.Vector)this.guests.clone();
    }
}
```

The getGuests method returns a copy of the *current* list of signees. We synchronize the guests vector during the clone to assure that only the current list of signees is returned. Therefore, the result of a search returns only those who have signed the GuestBook at the time the search was made.

Core Tip

This code follows a similar approach commonly used by the Java AWT 1.1 delegation model. When an event source fires an Event, access to the list of EventListeners for that Event is blocked (i.e., synchronized), while a copy is made (using clone). This cloned copy is used, along with the EventListener interface, to call back on all registered listeners. As a result, only those who are registered at the time the event was fired are called back to handle the event.

JAVAX.SERVLET.HTTPSERVLETREQUEST

```
public abstract String getPathInfo()
```

Returns the rest of the path information that follows the script name, not including the query string.

For example, if the request were GET `http://host:port/MyServlet/core/jws?abcde HTTP/1.1`, then `getPathInfo` would return `/core/jws`.

```
public abstract String getPathTranslated()
```

Returns the same thing as getPathInfo, translated to a real path.

```
public abstract String getQueryString()
```

Returns the query string in the request, if there is one. For example, if the request is GET `http://host:port/MyServlet/core/jws?abcde HTTP/1.1` then `getQueryString` returns abcde.

```
public abstract String getRequestURI()
```

Returns the complete request URI, not including the query string. For example, For example, if the request is GET `http://host:port/MyServlet/core/jws?abcde HTTP/1.1`, then `getRequestURI` returns `http://host:port/servlet/MyServlet/core/jws`.

```
public abstract String getServletPath()
```

Returns the virtual path to the servlet that is currently running. For example, if the request is GET `http://host:port/MyServlet/core/jws?abcde HTTP/1.1`, then `getServletPath` returns `/servlet/MyServlet`.

Who Wins, GET or POST?

Now you have seen the two different ways that data can be passed into your servlet. Both methods are commonly used, so which method you use is entirely up to you. There is one determining factor that will persuade you to use the POST method over GET when transferring large amounts of data. The query string in an HTTP GET method is limited in size. This size can be different depending on your platform, but typically is limited to 4K. Nevertheless, sending data to your servlet via the GET method will create a problem if you are sending large amounts of data. In this case you must use the POST method to send data to your servlet.

JAVAX.SERVLET.HTTPUTILS

```
public static Hashtable parseQueryString(String s)
```

Parses the query string found in the HTTP request. This method is usually paired with the getQueryString method, which returns the query string in the request. A Hashtable is used to hold the key/value pairs. Remember that one key can have several values, so the Hashtable's get method returns a string array that can possibly contain several values for a single key.

parameters:

s   The query string in this request, which can be obtained from the getQueryString method.

```
public static Hashtable parsePostData(int len,
                                      ServletInputStream in)
```

Parses the form data that is sent in the HTTP message body of this request. Remember that one key can have several values, so the Hashtable's get method returns a string array that can possibly contain several values for a single key.

parameters:

len   The length of the form data (can be obtained by using the getContentLength method) in the ServletInputStream for this request (can be obtained by using the getInputStream method).

Summary

You now have the core knowledge needed to put the HTTP protocol to work in your servlets. In this chapter, we introduced you to the core classes which are used to write effective HTTP servlets. We walked you through the `HttpServlet` class, introduced you to its default handlers (i.e., `doGet`, `doPost`, etc.), and briefly explained how the `service` method is used to call handler methods. The HttpServletRequest and HttpServletResponse interfaces were examined to give you a better understanding of how HTTP request and response messages are handled within the Java Web Server.

We gave you a quick tour of the `HttpServlet` framework to help you understand how the Java Web Server handles requests and creates responses. The GuestBookServlet example was provided to show how servlets can be used to create dynamic Web content and incrementally, persistently store the state of objects. The GuestSearchServlet example was provided to show how servlets can communicate with each other to get work done.

Finally, we ended the chapter by showing off two ways to send data to your servlet (i.e., GET and POST). The GuestBookServlet presented in this chapter is not the most efficient servlet, because it regenerates HTML for each request. This next chapter will show how you can squeeze more speed out of the GuestBookServlet as we compare it with a CGI implementation of the on-line guest book.

ADVANCED HTTP SERVLETS

Topics in This Chapter

- From CGI to servlets
- Configuring Java Web Server to run CGI scripts
- A CGI version of the GuestBookServlet
- The CGI/Servlet benchmark framework
- Getting better performance out of the GuestBookServlet

Chapter

9

In the early days of the Web, interaction between a client and the Web server was very simple—a static Web page was downloaded from a HTTP server and displayed on the client's machine. Then came the Common Gateway Interface (CGI), a specification used to invoke a server-side executable program. This was a large improvement, quickly accepted by the Internet community as a basis for providing dynamic Web content. In this chapter we focus on the differences between the Java Servlet technology and CGI. First we show you how to use CGI with the Java Web Server. Then we compare Servlets and CGI head-to-head to help you see why Servlets offer superior performance over CGI.

What Is CGI?

CGI is not a programming language, it is a specification. It is not confined to any one language, which makes it a very attractive solution to server-side programming for a wide variety of applications. CGI acts as a gateway—the mediator between your server-side extension and the outside world. The most common CGI scripting language is the Practical Extraction and Reporting Language, commonly known as Perl. However, CGI has been written using various programming languages and shell scripts including Java, C, C++, Fortran, TCL, REXX, Python, Icon, VB, AppleScript, UNIX shell script, and even the good old DOS batch file. Each time your CGI script is called, the server computer (the computer running the HttpServer) creates a process for your script to run, initializes some variables for your script to use, and invokes your script.

CGI Environment Variables

During execution, your script can access a set of environment variables which can be used to gather data about the HTTP request. They are defined by the CGI specification and are initialized before your CGI script begins execution.

These environment variables are highly coupled to the HTTP protocol, and the HTTP server and underlying operating system jointly initialize them. These initialized environment variables are visible in each language used for CGI; for example, Perl exposes them as the %ENV associative array. In Perl you can find which HTTP request method (i.e., GET, POST, etc.) was sent to your script by accessing the REQUEST_METHOD environmental variable:

```
$http_request_method = $ENV{'REQUEST_METHOD'};
```

HttpServlets use a similar technique. When your servlet is invoked, it gets a object, which is initialized with information parsed from the HTTP request message. Where Perl uses an associative array as a container for these environment variables, servlets receive HTTP request information through an object of type `HttpServletRequest`. The `HttpServletRequest` class has a set of methods that can be used to get information about the request. Table 9-1, although not a complete list of CGI environment variables, shows those that relate to methods in the `HttpServletRequest` class.

Table 9-1   CGI Environmental Variables Corresponding to HttpServletRequest Methods.

CGI Environment Variable	Corresponding HttpServletRequest Method
AUTH_TYPE	getAuthType
CONTENT_LENGTH	getContentLength
CONTENT_TYPE	getContentType
HTTP_ACCEPT	getHeader
HTTP_USER_AGENT	getHeader
PATH_INFO	getPathInfo
PATH_TRANSLATED	getPathTranslated
QUERY_STRING	getQueryString
REMOTE_ADDR	getRemoteAddr
REMOTE_HOST	getRemoteHost
REMOTE_USER	getRemoteUser
REQUEST_METHOD	getMethod
SCRIPT_NAME	getServletName
SERVER_NAME	getServerName
SERVER_PORT	getServerPort
SERVER_PROTOCOL	getProtocol

Notice that getHeader is listed as the corresponding method for the HTTP_ACCEPT and HTTP_USER_AGENT environment variables. The getHeader method takes as input a String corresponding to the HTTP header to retrieve. For example, you can request information on the MIME types the client accepts by passing the "Accept" literal to the getHeader method:

```
getHeader("Accept");
```

which is equivalent to the HTTP_ACCEPT environment variable. So, what literals are supported under HttpServletRequest's getHeader method? It supports all standard HTTP 1.0 and 1.1 headers. These standard headers are presented in Table 9-2.

Table 9-2   HTTP Headers Supported by the `getHeader` Method

Accept	*Accept-Charset*	*Accept-Encoding*	*Accept-Language*
Accept-Ranges	Age	Allow	Authorization
Cache-Control	Connection	Content-Base	Content-Encoding
Content-Language	Content-Length	Content-Location	Content-MD5
Content-Range	Content-Type	Date	Etag
Expires	From	Host	If-Modified-Since
If-Match	If-None-Match	If-Range	If-Unmodified-Since
Last-Modified	Location	Max-Forwards	Pragma
Proxy-Authenticate	Proxy-Authorization	Public	Range
Referrer	Retry-After	Server	Transfer-Encoding
Upgrade	User-Agent	Vary	Via
Warning	WWW-Authenticate		

The Java Web Server also supports the extension headers presented in Table 9-3.

Table 9-3   Extension Headers Supported by the `getHeader` Method

Alternates	*Content-Version*	*Cookie*	*Derived-From*
Keep-Alive	Link	MIME-Version	URI
URI			

Three CGI environment variables have no corresponding methods in the HttpServletRequest. These are GATEWAY_INTERFACE, REMOTE_INDENT, and `SERVER_SOFTWARE`. Not all of the methods listed in Table 9-1 actually reside in the `HttpServletRequest` class. Remember that `HttpServletRequest` extends from `ServletRequest`, which contains the following methods inherited by `HttpServletRequest`:

```
getContentLength
getContentType
getRemoteAddress
getHost
getServletName
getServerPort
getProtocol
```

Transitioning from CGI to Servlets

Most companies that do a significant amount of Web hosting have a lot of money tied up in CGI scripts. Transitioning from the CGI world to the new servlet technology is very simple, because the Java Web Server supports CGI. You can run your current CGI scripts, and, as time permits, you can begin porting old scripts to more efficient servlets.

Running CGI within Java Web Server

You can use the CgiServlet servlet provided with the Java Web Server to run all of your current CGI scripts. The CgiServlet servlet looks in the `cgi-bin` directory (specified by the bindir property) to locate incoming requests with a CGI extension to respective CGI scripts. In order for this to work properly, you must have the appropriate initialization parameters set. This section will show you how to properly configure the CgiServlet to run your CGI scripts.

Configuring CgiServlet

In order to configure the CgiServlet you must be logged into the JavaServer Administration applet. You can do so by entering

```
http://host:port/
```

where `host` is your machine name and `port` is the port that the JavaServer Admin tool is currently running on. If you have just installed the Java Web Server, then you should be able to access the Admin tool by entering

```
http://localhost:9090/
```

in Netscape. From a DOS or UNIX command prompt you can access the JavaServer Admin tool by using Appletviewer:

```
appletviewer http://localhost:9090/
```

After you have logged in, you are only a couple of mouse clicks away from the CGI Servlet configuration panel, as listed below. (If you just installed the Java Web Server, the user name and password is *admin*.)

1. Double click on Web Service to bring up the Web Service frame.

2. Click on the Servlets button.

3. Click on Servlets -> Configure -> cgi. This will allow you to configure CgiServlet.

4. Click on the Properties tab.

At this point your screen should look similar to Figure 9-1.

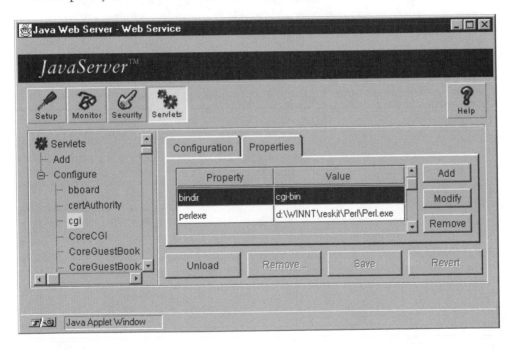

Figure 9-1   Configuring CgiServlet.

CgiServlet has five initialization parameters that are key to its operation. These are listed in Table 9-4.

Table 9-4 CgiServlet Initialization Parameters		
bindir	Location of your CGI scripts	cgi-bin
cgiexe	Location to the native cgi launch program	bin/cgilaunch.exe
dns	If true a dns reverse lookup is performed	false
path	Overrides your current path settings	current PATH settings
perlexe	Full path to the Perl executable (Perl.exe)	not set

The two most important variables listed in Table 9-4 are `bindir` and `perlexe`. The term *location* refers to the Java Web Server root directory, which is:

```
c:\javawebserver1.1\
```

on the authors' machine. The `cgi-bin` directory is where you should place all your CGI scripts. This directory exists in the Java Web Server root directory by default. CgiServlet will search this directory looking for your CGI scripts.

The *perlexe* property tells CgiServlet where the Perl executable (`Perl.exe`) can be located. This is the fully qualified path to the `Perl.exe`; on our machine `Perl.exe` resides in `D:\WINNT\reskit\Perl`, so the value entered in for the perlexe property would be

```
D:\WINNT\reskit\Perl\Perl.exe
```

This parameter is absolutely necessary to Windows95 and WinNT machines. Probably you won't need to set any of these parameters if you are running on a UNIX machine. To validate your configuration, you can invoke your favorite CGI script by visiting

```
http://localhost:8080/cgi-bin/your_cgi.pl
```

where `your_cgi.pl` is the name of the PERL script that you want to run. This script must reside in the directory that you specified for the *bindir* property when you configured CgiServlet.

So, how is CgiServlet notified when you make a request by visiting `http://localhost:8080/cgi-bin/your_cgi.pl`? The CgiServlet is aliased to the bindir that you supplied when you set up CgiServlet. You can verify this by visiting the Servlet aliases in the admin tool in Figure 9-2. Notice that cgi is the name assigned to the CgiServlet and cgi is aliased to the `cgi-bin` directory. This is the same directory that we specified for the bindir property (see Figure 9-1).

Core Alert

Pay special attention to any changes you make in the admin tool. Tinkering with its parameters can cause you grief if you are not careful. The cgi-bin directory is specified in two places, once for the bindir property (see Figure 9-1) and also as Servlet alias to the CgiServlet, so if you decide to move your CGI scripts to another directory, you must revisit the admin tool and change the Servlet alias in addition to changing the bindir property for the CgiServlet.

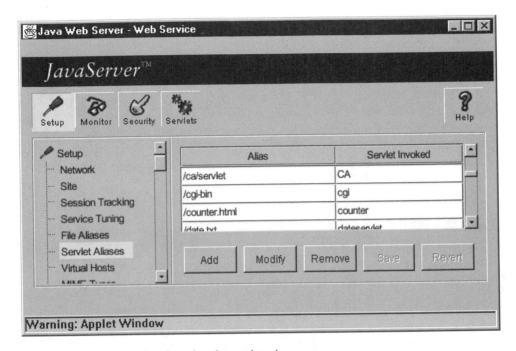

Figure 9-2 CgiServlet aliased to the cgi-bin directory.

In the last chapter we introduced you to the GuestBookServlet, which implemented a simple guest book. In this chapter we introduce you to a CGI equivalent, GuestBookCGI.pl. The common Web surfer would not see any difference between the Servlet and CGI versions of the guest book, because they both produce the same results.

Our intent is not to show you how to code CGI scripts, but to provide a CGI script that will serve as a test bed for our CGI/Servlet benchmark. We must admit that much of the work for this CGI script is done behind the scenes, using a well-known library called cgi-lib.pl. This extensive library of Perl routines was made available by Steven E. Brenner (visit `http://cgi-lib.stanford.edu/cgi-lib/` for more information).

GuestBookCGI

GuestBookCGI is a CGI version of the GuestBookServlet2 presented in the last chapter. It provides similar functionality to GuestBookServlet2 by:

- Implementing the HTTP GET method which returns the current list of signees and displaying a FORM that is used to POST new signee information

- Handling incoming form data via the HTTP POST method
- Dynamically generating and displaying a current list of signees
- Providing a mechanism for persistent storage

We coded this version of the guest book in Perl and sprinkled the code with useful comments, so even the unseasoned Perl hacker should have an easy time reading the script. We should mention a couple of things which make this version of the guest book very different from the servlet version presented in the last chapter. Two key differences lie in the way this CGI version handles persistence and FORM processing.

Persistence

The most important difference is the way that GuestBookCGI implements persistence storage. In a nutshell, GuestBookCGI uses the Perl open, print, and flock functions to store data in a file:

```
open(GUESTBOOK,">>GuestBook.dat") || &CgiDie
        ("Problem occurred while opening file.");
flock (GUESTBOOK, $EXCLUSIVE_LOCK);
//write to GuestBook.dat data file
flock(GUESTBOOK, $UNLOCK);
```

First, we open the file (GuestBook.dat) by using the open routine. We prepend ">>" in front of GuestBook.dat because we want to append signees to the GuestBook.dat data file. If opening the file was successful, GUESTBOOK acts as a file handle to the GuestBook.dat data file.

The call to flock is perhaps the most important piece of code in the GuestBookCGI script. We call flock, passing it the handle to the opened file, and attempt to lock the file exclusively by passing it the $EXCLUSIVE_LOCK, which is defined as

```
$EXCLUSIVE_LOCK = 2;
```

Note that flock(filehandle, 2) locks the file exclusively and flock(filehandle, 8) unlocks the file, thus allowing other processes to gain exclusive access. It is important that we lock the file each time that we write to it, because several processes may be running the GuestBookCGI.pl script simultaneously, thus increasing the chances of the GuestBook.dat file's becoming corrupt.

Getting and Parsing Form Data

Another key difference lies in the gathering of form data. The Servlet programmer takes advantage of the parsePostData method in the HttpUtils class to parse data that was POSTed to the Servlet. The parsePostData hides the gory details from the Servlet programmer. With CGI, you can hide the ugly details by taking advantage of the ReadParse routine found in the cgi-lib.pl library written by Stephen E. Brenner. Form processing can be summarized in the following lines of code:

```
require "cgi-lib.pl";
&ReadParse(*form_data);
$signeeName = $form_data{'name'};
$signeeEmail = $form_data{'email'};
```

The require function causes the Perl code found in "cgi-lib.pl" file to be loaded into memory so that we can take advantage of its functions—in particular, the ReadParse function. We pass the ReadParse function a reference to a hash called form_data. When ReadParse returns, form_data will contain the INPUT TYPE/value pairs corresponding to the form data contained in the message body of the HTTP request. Then, $form_data{'<INPUT TYPE name>'} accesses data entered into the INPUT TYPE on the form, where <INPUT TYPE name> is the name of the INPUT TYPE on the HTML form. Listing 9-1 displays the code for GuestBookCGI.pl.

Listing 9-1   GuestBookCGI.pl

```
#!/usr/bin/perl

print "Content-type: text/html", "\n\n";

#—require the cgi-lib.pl library
require "cgi-lib.pl";

#—get the request method, this can be GET, POST, ...
$http_request_method = $ENV{'REQUEST_METHOD'};

if($http_request_method eq "GET")
{
   &doGET;
}
if($http_request_method eq "POST")
{
   &doPOST;
}

#—if not a GET or a POST then send error, since this
#—script only handles those two methods
&sendError;

#————————————————
#— handle the HTTP GET operation
#————————————————
```

continued

```perl
sub doGET
{
  print "<HTML>\n";
  print "<HEAD><TITLE>GuestBookServlet</TITLE></HEAD>\n";
  print "<BODY>\n";
  print "<h1> Welcome To Our GuestBook! </h1>\n";
  print "<HR>\n";
  print "<H4>Our current signees are:</H4><P><BR>\n";
  print "<Table>\n";


  #—Open the GuestBook.dat and
  #—read the current list of signees
  open(GUESTBOOK,"GuestBook.dat") || &CgiDie
        ("Problem occurred while opening file.");

  while(<GUESTBOOK>)
  {
    print $_;
  }

  close(GUESTBOOK);

  print "</TABLE>\n";
  print "<P><HR>\n";
  print "<H4>Please sign our GuestBook</H4>\n";
  print "<FORM action=http://localhost:80/",
        "cgi-bin/GuestBookCGI.pl method=POST>\n";
  print " Enter your name:\n";
  print "<INPUT TYPE=text NAME=name><P>\n";
  print " Enter your e-mail address\n";
  print " <INPUT TYPE=text NAME=email><P>\n";
  print " <INPUT TYPE=submit>\n";
  print " <INPUT TYPE=reset>\n";
  print "</BODY>\n";
  exit(0);
}


#—————————————————-
#— handle the posting of data from the form
#—————————————————-
sub doPOST
{
  #—needed for flock
  $EXCLUSIVE_LOCK = 2;
  $UNLOCK = 8;
```

```
#—use the cgi-lib.pl library to read form data
&ReadParse(*form_data);

#— Open the GuestBook.dat and read the current list of signees
open(GUESTBOOK,">>GuestBook.dat") || &CgiDie
    ("Problem occurred while opening file.");

#— lock the file so no one else can get to it
#— you do not want to overwrite any data!
flock (GUESTBOOK, $EXCLUSIVE_LOCK);

$signeeName = $form_data{'name'};
$signeeEmail = $form_data{'email'};

print GUESTBOOK "\n<TR><TD>", $signeeName,
                "<TD><TD><A HREF=mailto:",
                $signeeEmail, ">", $signeeEmail,
                "</A></TR>";

#— unlock the file for someone else to use
flock(GUESTBOOK, $UNLOCK);

close(GUESTBOOK);

#—finish off the request; call the doGET method
&doGET;

exit(0);
}


#——————————————————--
#—send a message to the client
#——————————————————--

sub sendError
{
    print "<HTML>\n";
    print "<HEAD><TITLE>Method not supported.</TITLE></HEAD>\n";
    print "  <BODY>\n";
    print "      <H3>The HTTP ", $ENV{'REQUEST_METHOD'},
          " method is not supported.</H3>\n";
    print " </BODY>\n";
    print "</HTML>\n";
    exit(0);
}
```

Servlets Make the GuestBook Look Good!

Three fundamental differences between CGI and servlets make the servlet version of GuestBook look really good:

> `GuestBookServlet` acts as a Singleton.
>
> `GuestBookServlet` is always alive.
>
> `GuestBookServlet` can incrementally store signees persistently.

Servlets follow a design pattern that is well known in the Object Oriented community called *Singleton*. A Singleton class has only a single instance, and Java Servlets follow this pattern, allowing Servlets to take advantage of state information gathered from earlier requests.

GuestBookServlet is always *alive*, ready to handle the next incoming request. Each time a request is made to GuestBookCGI, a new process is created and is alive for the life of a single request. When GuestBookCGI is finished doing its chores, it dies and is not restarted until the next request comes in. Creating a new process for each transaction can be a very expensive operation.

By taking advantage of Java's powerful multithreading facilities, GuestBookServlet is able to use a background thread to its current list of signees incrementally (every 30 seconds). In contrast, GuestBookCGI must write to disk after each POST in order to record the next incoming signee. It cannot take advantage of an incremental save because it is alive only for the lifetime of a single request.

These three key differences make servlets a very attractive alternative to traditional CGI.

The CGI/Servlet Benchmark

The rest of this chapter will be dedicated to our CGI/servlet benchmark. This benchmark will run GuestBookServlet2 head-to-head with GuestBookCGI and compare the time differences between them.

First, we must code up a framework that can be used to shoot a blob of requests at both versions of the guest book and record the time taken to handle them. Three players make up the benchmark (TimedThread, WorkerThread, and Controller); these are included in the diagram provided in Figure 9-3.

Controller is a Java Applet that is used to start the benchmark (see Figure 9-4). It will spawn a specified number of worker threads and keep track of time. Each worker thread will create a connection to the specified host and send it an HTTP POST message. To keep track of time, we derive WorkerThread from TimedThread.

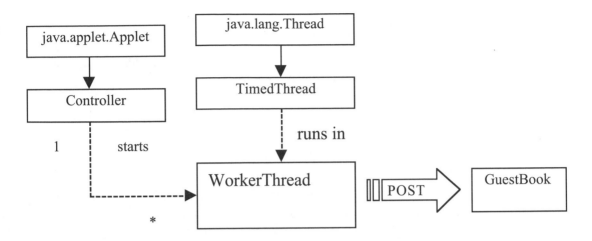

Figure 9-3 Simple class diagram of Java Servlet/CGI benchmark.

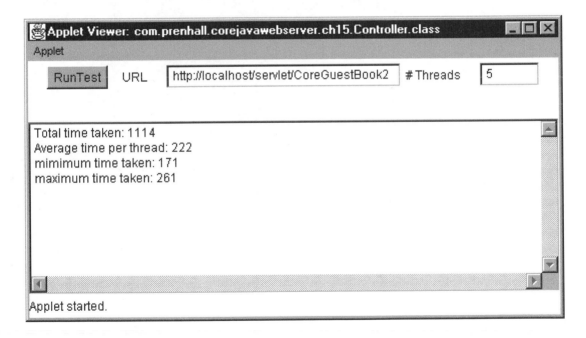

Figure 9-4 Controller in action.

TimedThread

TimedThread extends the functionality of java.lang.Thread by adding a timing mechanism to it. A data field is used to keep the time:

```
private long delta = 0L;
```

and the time is kept in the run() method:

```
long start = System.currentTimeMillis();
super.run();
long stop  = System.currentTimeMillis();
delta = stop - start;
```

The code for TimedThread.java can be found in Listing 9-2.

Listing 9-2   TimedThread.java

```java
public class TimedThread extends Thread
{
  private long delta = 0L;

  public TimedThread(Runnable r, String name)
  {
    super(r, name);
  }

  public void run ()
  {
    long start = System.currentTimeMillis();
    super.run();
    long stop  = System.currentTimeMillis();
    delta = stop - start;
  }

  public long getDelta ()
  {
    return delta;
  }
}
```

WorkerThread

The WorkerThread does all the work in the benchmark framework. WorkerThread
implements the java.lang.Runnable interface and runs in a TimedThread.

The `run` method shows the meat of the algorithm. First, INPUT TYPE/value
pairs are encoded which will be included in the message body of the HTTP request:

```
String postData = "name=" +
        Thread.currentThread().getName() +
        "&email=" +
        Thread.currentThread().getName()
        + "@javasoft.com";
```

It is a good idea to assign a different name to each TimedThread so you can see
which thread POSTed each HTTP message. `Thread.currentThread().`
`getName()` returns the name of the current TimedThread in which this
WorkerThread is running. The TimedThread is assigned a name upon creation:

```
threadList[i] = new TimedThread(new
                        WorkerThread(theURL),
                        "TimedThread_" + i);
```

where threadList is an array used as a container to hold from one to *n* TimedThread
objects in the Controller. The code for WorkerThread can be found in Listing 9-3.

Listing 9-3   WorkerThread.java

```java
import java.awt.*;
import java.net.*;
import java.io.*;

class WorkerThread implements Runnable
{


  private URL theURL;
  private String postData;

  public WorkerThread(URL theURL)
  {
    this.theURL = theURL;
  }

  public void run ()
  {
    String postData = "name=" +
```

continued

```
                          Thread.currentThread().getName() +
                          "&email=" +
                          Thread.currentThread().getName()
                          + "@javasoft.com";
    int contentLength = doPOST(theURL, postData);
  }

  public int doPOST(URL theURL, String postData)
  {
      try
    {
      URLConnection conn = theURL.openConnection();
      conn.setDoOutput(true);
      conn.setUseCaches(false);
      PrintWriter pw = new
        PrintWriter(conn.getOutputStream());
      pw.println(postData);
      pw.flush();
      pw.close();

      conn.getContent();
      return 0;
    }
    catch(Exception e)
    {
       e.printStackTrace();
    }
    return 0;
  }

}
```

Controller

Controller acts as the foreman in the benchmark; it starts the simulation, runs the specified number of threads, and prints the results to a TextArea on the applet window. Figure 9-4 (presented earlier in this chapter) shows the controller after a sample run.

Here we ran five threads, each creating a connection to http://localhost/servlet/CoreGuestBook (the CoreGuestBookServlet2 presented in the last chapter and aliased as CoreGuestBook in the Java Web Server) and posting the following data:

```
name=TimedThread_i&email=TimedThread_i
```

where i is the *i*th TimedThread running in the benchmark. Then, the results were printed in the TextArea. A visit to GuestBookServlet2 will prove that the controller successfully posted data to the guest book. Figure 9-5 displays the results.

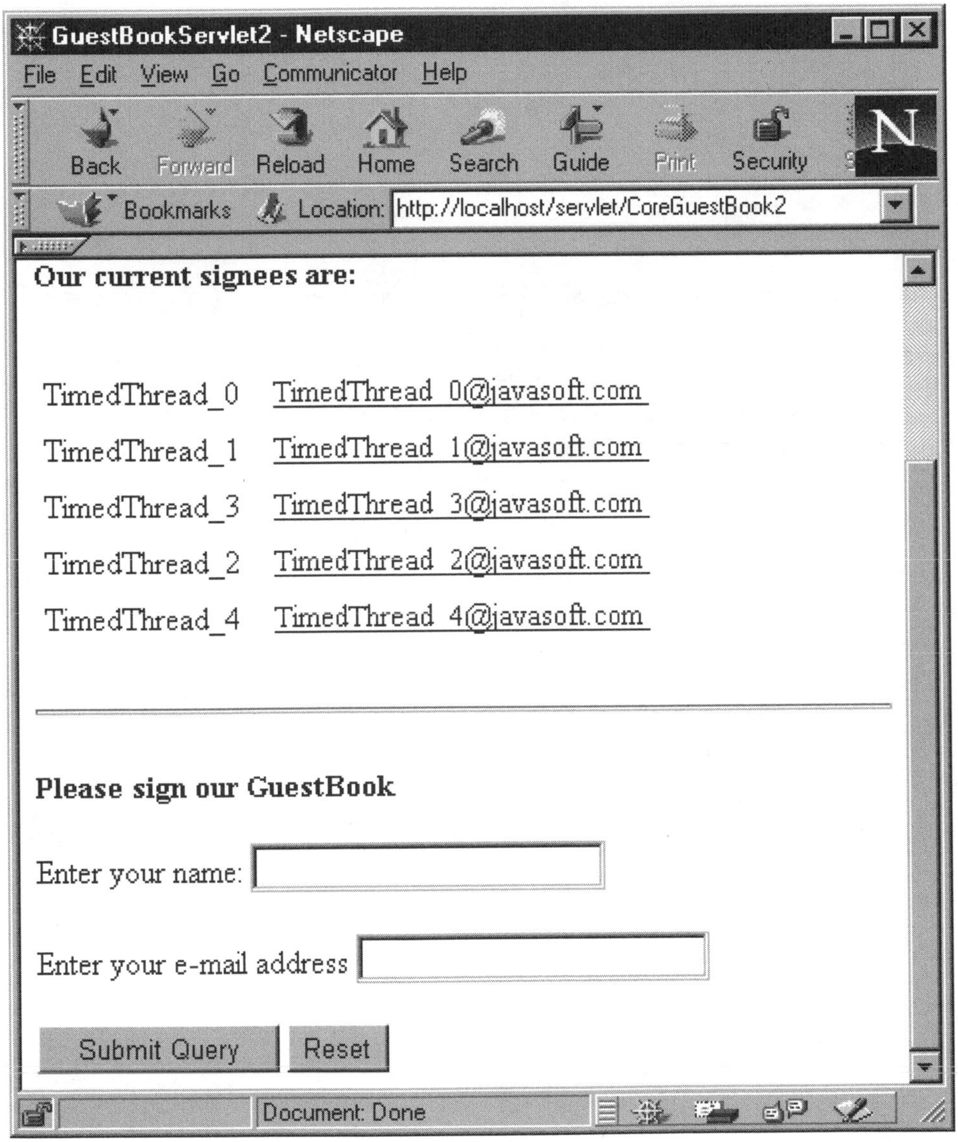

Figure 9-5   Results from POSTing to the GuestBookServlet2.

You can see by looking at Figure 9-5 that this framework represents true multi-threading. Notice the order in which each thread POSTed to CoreGuestBook2. We started the threads in order (from zero to *n* (1), and you can see in Figure 9-5 that TimedThread_3 POSTed before TimedThread_2. Listing 9-4 shows the code for Controller.

Listing 9-4 Controller.java

```java
import java.io.*;
import java.awt.*;
import java.awt.event.*;
import java.net.*;

public class Controller extends java.applet.Applet
{

  protected Button btnRunTest;
  protected TextField txtfURL;
  protected TextField txtfNumThreads;
  protected TextArea txtaOutput;

  public void init()
  {

    //use Border Layout for this applet
    setLayout(new BorderLayout());

    //Panel to hold input
    Panel pInput = new Panel();
    pInput.setLayout(new FlowLayout());

    btnRunTest = new Button("RunTest");

    //implement the ActionListener interface
    //using an anonymous class
    btnRunTest.addActionListener(
      new ActionListener()
      {
        public void actionPerformed(ActionEvent ae)
        {
          txtaOutput.setText(txtfURL.getText());
          try
          {
```

```
          URL theURL = new
                  URL(txtfURL.getText().trim());
          int numThreads =
              Integer.parseInt(txtfNumThreads.getText());
          if(numThreads < 1)
            txtaOutput.setText("You cannot run " +
                                  numThreads + " threads!");
          else
            runTest(numThreads, theURL);
        }
        catch(MalformedURLException murle)
        {
          txtaOutput.setText("The URL you entered " +
                                "is invalid. " +
                                murle.getMessage());
        }
        catch(NumberFormatException nfe)
        {
          txtaOutput.setText("Enter the number " +
            "of threads you want to run.");
        }

    }
  }
);

pInput.add(btnRunTest);

//make a new TextField to get the URL
pInput.add(new Label("    URL"));
txtfURL = new TextField(30);
//add this URL input field to the Input Panel
pInput.add(txtfURL);

//make a new TextField to get the
//number of threads to use in the test
pInput.add(new Label("# Threads"));
txtfNumThreads = new TextField(5);
pInput.add(txtfNumThreads);

//add the Input Panel to this applet's panel
add(pInput, "North");

//Create a Panel to hold output
Panel pOutput = new Panel();
pOutput.setLayout(new BorderLayout());
txtaOutput = new TextArea();
```

continued

```
      pOutput.add(txtaOutput, "Center");
      add(pOutput, "South");



  }


  //run the test with this many threads, at the URL
  public void runTest(int numThreads, URL theURL)
  {

    TimedThread threadList[] = new TimedThread[numThreads];


    for(int i = 0; i < numThreads; i++)
    {
      threadList[i] = new TimedThread(new
                          WorkerThread(theURL),
                                    "TimedThread_" + i);
      threadList[i].start();
    }

      long min = Long.MAX_VALUE;
      long max = Long.MIN_VALUE;
      long total = 0;


      for(int i=0; i < numThreads; i++)
      {
        try
        {
          threadList[i].join();
          long thisTime = threadList[i].getDelta();
          if(min > thisTime)
            min = thisTime;
          if(max < thisTime)
            max = thisTime;
          total += thisTime;
        }
        catch (InterruptedException ie)
        {
          ie.printStackTrace();
        }
      }

    txtaOutput.setText("Total time taken: " +
                      total + "\n");
    txtaOutput.append("Average time per thread: "+
```

```
                              total/numThreads + "\n");
    txtaOutput.append("minimum time taken: " +
                      min + "\n");
    txtaOutput.append("maximum time taken: " +
                      max + "\n");


  }
}
```

The CGI/Servlet Benchmark

Our CGI/Servlet benchmark uses two computers, both running Windows NT 4.0. One computer hosts the Java Web Server, the other acts as a client running the benchmark program over a 10Base-T network. The configuration of each machine is summarized in Table 9-5.

Table 9-5 Server/Client Configurations			
Component	*Ram*	*MHz*	*Chip*
Client	80	200	Intel Pentium
Server	64	75	Intel Pentium

The benchmark consists of a series of tests, each running the specified number of threads and keeping track of the time taken to complete n HTTP POST operations. Table 9-6 shows the results recorded from the average time taken to run each thread.

Table 9-6 CGI/Servlet Thread Benchmark Raw Data		
No. of Threads	*CGI*	*Servlet*
1	731	390
5	2151	259
10	9352	778
20	8,000	3,284
30	28,379	12,852
40	45,377	17,017
50	86,885	44,349

Looking at the data in Table 9-6, you can see that the Servlet version of the guest book is much faster than the CGI version. Figure 9-6 shows a plot of the data in Table 9-6.

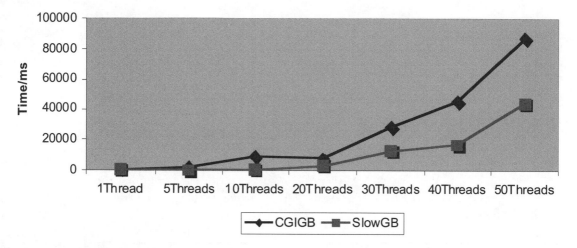

Figure 9-6   Graph of CGI/Servlet benchmark; average time.

You can see from the plot that as the number of POSTs increases, the Servlet version becomes much more efficient than the CGI version of the GuestBook.

Where's the Bottleneck?

So, why are servlets faster? As we noted above, servlets are always alive, *waiting for a new request to come a-knocking*. Traditional CGI implementations are exactly the opposite. Each time a new request comes in, a new process is created and is alive for the life of a single transaction. When your CGI script is finished doing its chores, it dies, ending the process that it is running in. Creating a new process for each transaction becomes a very expensive operation. This may not be important to you if you don't have many transactions on your server, but consider a Web server that gets many requests per second—one slow request handler could bring your Web server to a screaming halt!

Each time the GuestBookCGI is invoked, it must reopen, lock, write data, close, and unlock the `GuestBook.dat` data file. This expensive operation is responsible for most of the performance loss in GuestBookCGI. When multiple requests are made simultaneously, many GuestBookCGI processes are created, each attempting to open and lock the data file. These processes end up competing against each other, trying to gain access to the data file, thus reducing performance even more. In contrast, GuestBookServlet maintains a *once-alive, always-alive* life cycle, enabling it to store its list of signees in virtual memory and allowing it to bypass the opening and closing of files, which greatly enhances its performance.

Just How Fast Are Servlets?

Sun Microsystems claims that Java Servlets are "10 to 15 times faster than CGI on Java Web Server." If you look at the results in Table 9-6, you can clearly see that this is not the case in this particular scenario. (For more information visit `http://java.sun.com/pr/1997/dec/pr971203.html`.)

Perhaps we should revisit the code for the Servlet implementation of the guest book and see if we can squeeze some better performance out of it. GuestBookServlet uses a Java Vector to hold Signee objects. Each time a request is made, we regenerate HTML by walking through the Vector and creating an HTML table of signees. The Vector became very useful when we wrote the GuestSearchServlet, because we were able to search easily through the list of Signee objects, but using the Vector to regenerate the HTML for every request in the GuestBookServlet was not the optimal approach—in fact, as you will soon see, it is a performance nightmare in comparison with our new version.

Squeezing for Performance

It is obvious that GuestBookServlet wasted a significant amount of time regenerating HTML for each HTTP request. Instead of holding the list of signees in a Vector, you can use a StringBuffer to hold the list of signees:

```
private StringBuffer guests = null;
```

Each time a POST request comes in, you can create another table row that holds the new signee and append it to the StringBuffer. This can be done by recoding the `addSignee` method:

```
public void addSignee(String name, String emailAddress)
    {
      synchronized(guests)
      {
        guests.append("<TR><TD>");
        guests.append(name);
        guests.append("</TD><TD><A HREF=mailto:");
        guests.append(emailAddress);
        guests.append("> ");
        guests.append(emailAddress);
        guests.append(" </A></TD></TR>");
      }
      dirty = true;
    }
```

Then, when it comes time to return the current list of signees, generating the HTML table is simple:

```
String table = "<TABLE>" + signees.toString() + "</TABLE>";
```

Generating HTML in this manner is much more efficient than using a Vector, because the HTML is already made, stored in the StringBuffer. There is no need to walk through the Vector to regenerate the HTML each time a request is made. Table 9-7 displays the same information presented in Table 9-6, with an additional benchmark added. The new benchmark incorporates the new StringBuffer approach.

Table 9-7   CGI, Slow/Fast Servlet benchmark raw data.

Type	1Thread	5Threads	10Threads	20Threads	30Threads	40Threads	50Threads
CGIGB	731	2,151	9,352	8,000	28,379	45,377	86,885
(the CGI version of the GuestBook)							
SlowGB	390	259	778	3,284	12,852	17,017	44,349
(GuestBookServlet using a Vector to hold the list of signees)							
FastGB	741	312	553	1492	2,567	2,851	5,403
(GuestBookServlet using a StringBuffer to hold the list of signees)							

Figure 9-7 shows a plot of the raw data presented in Table 9-6. The performance of the GuestBookServlet was greatly enhanced by using a StringBuffer to hold pre-generated HTML.

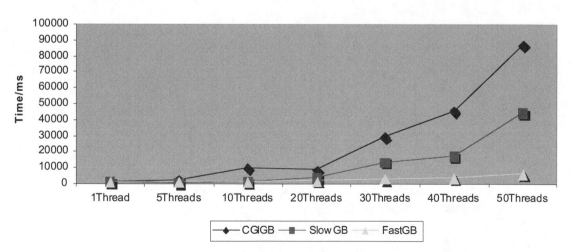

Figure 9-7   Graph of CGI/Servlet benchmark; average time.

So, in short, you can make servlets about as fast as you want them to be by programming intelligently.

A Word on Synchronization

The careful reader may be wondering why we synchronized while appending a new signee to the StringBuffer in the add method:

```
synchronized(guests)
{
  guests.append("<TR><TD>");
  guests.append(name);
  guests.append("</TD><TD><A HREF=mailto:");
  guests.append(emailAddress);
  guests.append("> ");
  guests.append(emailAddress);
  guests.append(" </A></TD></TR>");
}
```

The guests StringBuffer is a member field in the new implementation of the GuestBookServlet class. Each Servlet acts as a Singleton, and so multiple threads must share its member fields (i.e., the guests StringBuffer is a *shared resource*). Imagine what would happen if we commented out the synchronized access in the addSignee method and ran the controller with 50 threads—what would happen? Figure 9-8 shows a sample outcome.

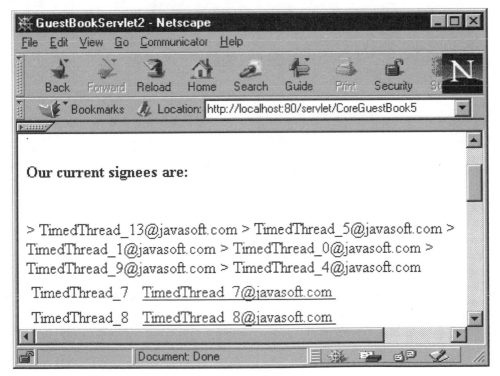

Figure 9-8   Outcome of a nonsynchronized addSignee method.

It looks as though the server has mangled the POST data, and the output is a complete mess. The `append` method in the StringBuffer is synchronized, so how did the data get so mangled? Notice that the `addSignee` method makes seven calls to the `StringBuffer.append` method:

```
guests.append("<TR><TD>");
guests.append(name);
guests.append("</TD><TD><A HREF=mailto:");
guests.append(emailAddress);
guests.append("> ");
guests.append(emailAddress);
guests.append(" </A></TD></TR>");
```

Therefore, if you don't synchronize access to guests, a competing thread could call `append` on guests, even though the current thread is not finished appending all of its data to guests. Notice that if we appended only once, synchronizing access to guests would not be needed.

Summary

This concludes our benchmark of the CGI/servlet guest book. This benchmark mainly covers traditional CGI. Other products can be used to provide a more efficient alternative to traditional CGI scripting, such as FastCGI, Microsoft's ISAPI, and Netscape's NSAPI. Covering these topics in great detail is beyond the scope of this book.

The goal in this chapter was to provide you with a CGI version of our GuestBookServlet to help pinpoint key differences between servlets and their CGI cousins. We described the "once-alive, always-alive" mentality shared by servlets and the way in which CGI scripts suffer from having to fork a new process to handle each HTTP request. In addition, we showed how to code smarter to gain performance in your servlets and how to synchronize critical sections in your servlets to maintain consistent data.

This chapter also sought to help current CGI developers transition quickly from the CGI to the servlet model of Web programming. We provided a mapping from CGI environment variables to servlet equivalent methods and showed you how to configure the Java Web Server to run your existing CGI scripts.

You now have the necessary knowledge to develop sophisticated servlets. But don't stack this book on the shelf just yet—the chapters that follow will extend your knowledge and expertise even further, showing you classes which can be used with the `HttpServlet` and `GenericServlet` base classes covered thus far. This added knowledge will help you become more productive in your current projects.

We continue our tour by showing you how to minimize traffic flow into the Java Web Server through caching, the topic of the next chapter.

IMPROVING PERFORMANCE THROUGH CACHING

Topics in This Chapter

- HTTP caching mechanisms
- Client-side caching
- The role of proxy servers
- Caching within servlets

Chapter 10

S ervlets act like a pipeline: data is read in, the servlet processes the data, and results are sent back to the user. This three-stage pipeline is the form in which servlets are typically written. The time spent in each stage, though, isn't evenly proportioned. The servlet spends most of its processing time crunching on the data, and much less time reading in the input and writing out the output. If some of this processing time could be distributed across several requests for the same information, the server's capacity would be dramatically increased.

This is where caching comes in. Clients can cache results from their requests so that they aren't required to retrieve the same information again (unless it has been updated on the server). Similarly, servlets can utilize caching mechanisms to reduce the amount of required work (but at a cost to memory usage). As a servlet developer, you can improve performance by simply adding a few lines of code to your existing servlets.

This chapter will introduce you to how caching works over HTTP. You'll be introduced to the HTTP cache-specific headers and shown how Netscape Communicator and the Java Web Server use them in practice. Next, you'll get acquainted with the specific servlet API methods that will cache-enable your servlets. Finally, you'll put this knowledge to work by writing an example program that utilizes caching.

What Is Caching, and Why Should I Care?

When it was first introduced, the Internet was used for exchanging simple text-based e-mail and other useful messages. Today, multimedia-enhanced Web sites offer snazzy graphics, applets, and other eye-catching presentations. Such displays entail a bandwidth cost to the client, because feature-rich pages can take a significant amount of time to download. Face it—the average Web surfer isn't going to wait five minutes for your site to pop up on the screen. The only way to hold the client's increasingly restless attention is to take advantage of caching mechanisms in the HTTP protocol.

Different Cache Types

The two types of caches commonly used in practice today are *client-side caching* (which is typically implemented inside the Web browser) and *server-side caching* via proxy servers. On the client side, browsers like Netscape Communicator cache documents in memory and on disk. Caching is a configurable setting in most browsers. For example, you could clear all memory in cache, manage the amount of memory used for memory/disk cache, and, more importantly, control how often a document is compared to the original document on a Web server, as you will see later in this chapter.

Local caching is good for users on a single phone line at home, but several users sharing the same phone line on a network can gain a significant performance increase by using a proxy server. A proxy server acts as a middle tier between several users on a network, caching documents accessed by users on the network. Figure 10-1 shows the interaction of a proxy server being used by three clients.

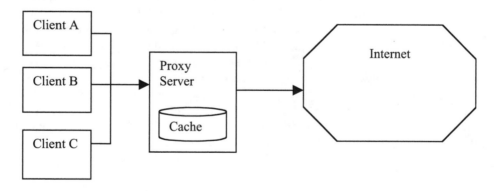

Figure 10-1   Proxy server interaction.

If Client A requests a document that has already been requested by Client B (or Client C), the proxy server will most likely have the document stored in its local cache and return it immediately, instead of asking the originating server for the document. This saves a significant amount of time, since the document is retrieved on a local server, not a server out on the Internet.

Cache-Specific HTTP Headers

The HTTP specification lists several caching request and response headers, but only a handful of them are frequently used. Each of the headers represents an agreement between the client and Web server. The most commonly used HTTP cache-specific headers are listed in Table 10-1.

Table 10-1 Frequently Used HTTP Cache-Specific Headers	
HTTP Cache Header	*Description*
Expires	Notifies clients when a document will expire
Cache-Control	Controls a client or proxy cache
Last-Modified	Set by the Web server in the HTTP Response; the date a document was last modified
If-Modified-Since	Set by the client in the HTTP request to mark an HTTP GET method as conditional ("only retrieve this document if it's been modified after ...")

The Expires Header

In the case of the Expires header, the Web server might send an HTTP response to your browser that contains an Expires header set to some GMT date (see RFC 1123 for a complete definition on GMT dates):

```
Expires: Friday, 22-May-98 04:28:43 GMT
```

A browser might store (or cache) the document represented by this message on the associated computer's hard drive until the date specified by the Expires header. Therefore, the next time a request is made to this same document, the browser will grab a new copy from the Web server only if the current one has expired.

Core Note

The interpretation of the Expires *header depends on the implementation of the cache. Some caches may be configured to expire documents sooner than the recommended date provided from the* Expires *header. Refer to the documentation of your browser or proxy server for details on document caching.*

The `Cache-Control` Header

While proxy servers save time by caching documents, problems can occur if these servers are misconfigured. For example, a proxy server can be set to cache aggressively, where it refuses to ask the originating server about the status of a document unless it has expired by settings specific to the proxy server. When a client makes a request for a document, the document may come from the proxy cache even though there might be a newer version sitting on the originating Web server. The HTTP 1.1 specification solves this problem by allowing clients to supply the `Cache-Control` header with an accompanying directive in the HTTP request message. The `no-cache` option is the most frequently used `Cache-Control` directive:

```
Cache-Control: no-cache
```

which directs all proxy servers to bypass their local caches and obtain a fresh copy of the requested document from the originating Web server. You'll get to see this in action in the next section using Netscape Communicator.

Other directives can be used with the `Cache-Control` header, but we do not list them here. If you're interested, check out RFC 2068 for a complete listing of `Cache-Control`'s directives.

Core Note

The `Cache-Control` *header didn't exist in HTTP 1.0. In HTTP 1.0, clients used the* `Pragma: no-cache` *header, which is synonymous with the* `Cache-Control: no-cache` *directive in HTTP 1.1.*

The `Last-Modified` and `If-Modified-Since` Headers

The `Last-Modified` and `If-Modified-Since` headers are used together in a "conditional GET" request. The `Last-Modified` header comes into play when a browser makes an initial request for a document. When the Web server sends the document data back to the client, the `Last-Modified` header contains the latest date for when the document was altered. When the browser caches the document data, it stores the `Last-Modified` date along with it.

Later, when the client makes a request for the same document, it sends the `If-Modified-Since` request header to the server. This is the "conditional" part of the "conditional GET," because the server uses the value of the `If-Modified-Since` header to decided whether to send the data or not. If the date sent by the client is older than the date of the content on the server, the new content is returned in the response. However, if the date is the same, then the server returns a `304 Not Modified` response back to the client. When the browser receives the `304` status code from the server, it can safely use its cached copy of the document.

Figure 10-2 illustrates this interaction between the browser and the Web server over the document `Foo.html`.

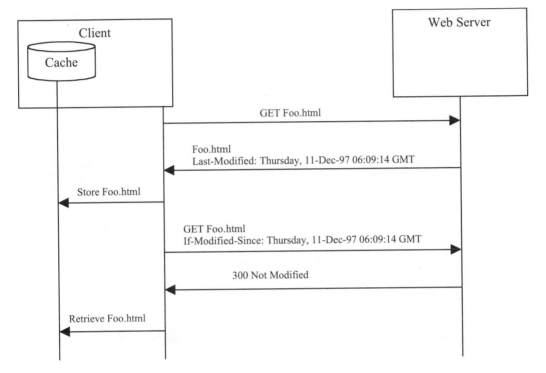

Figure 10-2   Last-Modified and If-Modified-Since sequence diagram.

Caching in Action on the Client

You can watch HTTP caching in action using Netscape Communicator and the Java Web Server. Start the experiment by opening up your browser and connecting to your Java Web Server, which will send the default page (`index.html`) to the browser. Figure 10-3 shows this transaction.

Next, select Page Info from the View menu; you can get information about the current page being displayed by the browser. This information is shown in Figure 10-4. As you can see, Netscape has stored `index.html` in the local cache file named M121CP5P, with the `Last Modified` date set to Thursday, December 11, 1997 6:09:14 GMT (the date at which `index.html` was last modified).

Now, if you were to retrieve the `index.html` file again, it would be pulled out of the cache and displayed. But what if you want to go and retrieve that page, regardless of the modification dates or the local cache? You can get Communicator to do what you want by specifying how it should treat the document request during the next GET.

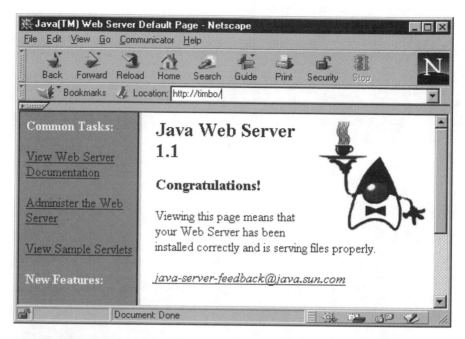

Figure 10-3   Index.html.

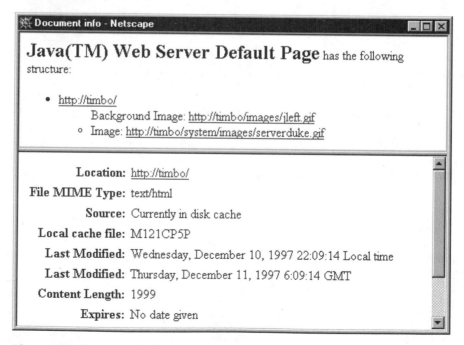

Figure 10-4   Page Info from Netscape Communicator.

If you enter `http://timbo/` in the Location field and press ENTER, the browser will send a GET message with a group of message headers like those shown in Figure 10-5. (The output in Figure 10-5 was generated by the SimpleServer program introduced in Chapter 7.)

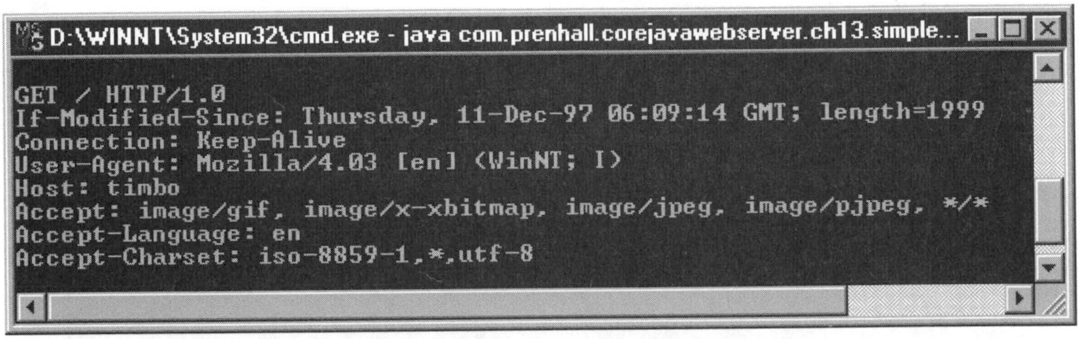

```
GET / HTTP/1.0
If-Modified-Since: Thursday, 11-Dec-97 06:09:14 GMT; length=1999
Connection: Keep-Alive
User-Agent: Mozilla/4.03 [en] (WinNT; I)
Host: timbo
Accept: image/gif, image/x-xbitmap, image/jpeg, image/pjpeg, */*
Accept-Language: en
Accept-Charset: iso-8859-1,*,utf-8
```

Figure 10-5 GET Message resulting from entering a URL in the location field.

Did you notice the `If-Modified-Since` header in Figure 10-5? The `If-Modified-Since` date in this request is the same as the `Last-Modified` GMT date shown in Figure 10-4. Communicator is using a conditional GET to ask the Web server to send a copy of `index.html` if it has changed since the last request.

So what is that Reload button used for? Again, you can use the SimpleServer example to find out! Figure 10-6 displays the browser's HTTP GET message after we pressed the Reload button to retrieve the `index.html` page.

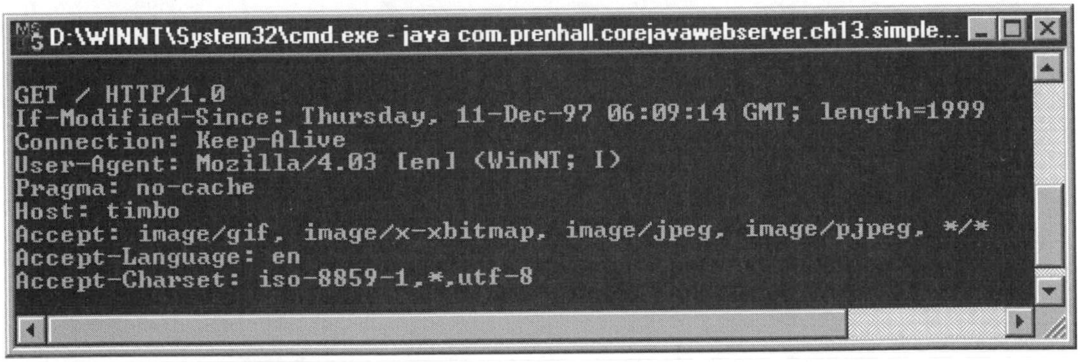

```
GET / HTTP/1.0
If-Modified-Since: Thursday, 11-Dec-97 06:09:14 GMT; length=1999
Connection: Keep-Alive
User-Agent: Mozilla/4.03 [en] (WinNT; I)
Pragma: no-cache
Host: timbo
Accept: image/gif, image/x-xbitmap, image/jpeg, image/pjpeg, */*
Accept-Language: en
Accept-Charset: iso-8859-1,*,utf-8
```

Figure 10-6 GET Message resulting from pressing the Reload button.

This GET message is identical to the GET message presented in Figure 10-6, but with the `Pragma: no-cache` header added. So what's the difference between this message and the one presented in Figure 10-6? By sending an `If-Modified-`

Since and the Pragma: no-cache directive, Communicator is bypassing caching by all proxy servers between Netscape and the destination Web server. The result is to grab a new copy of index.html, but only if it has been modified since the If-Modified-Since date. This feature is provided to make sure that intermediate caches don't return stale copies of the content.

Figure 10-7 shows the HTTP GET request sent after holding down the SHIFT key and pressing the Reload button. Notice that this message *does not* contain an If-Modified-Since header; therefore, the document will be retrieved unconditionally.

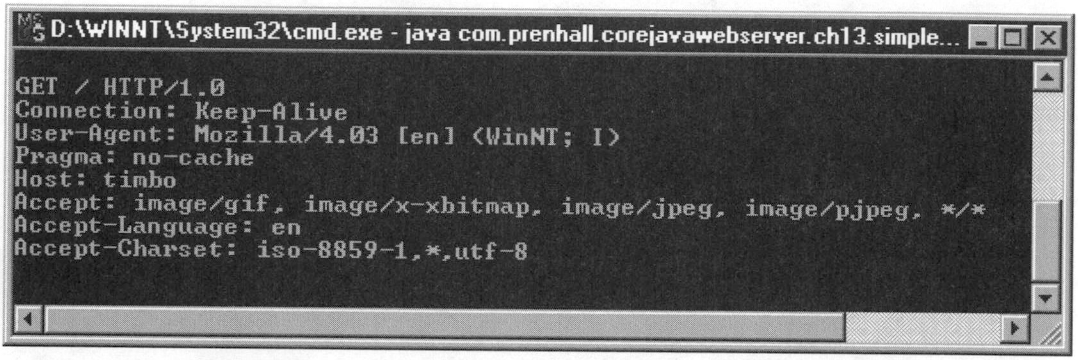

```
D:\WINNT\System32\cmd.exe - java com.prenhall.corejavawebserver.ch13.simple...  _ □ ×
GET / HTTP/1.0
Connection: Keep-Alive
User-Agent: Mozilla/4.03 [en] (WinNT; I)
Pragma: no-cache
Host: timbo
Accept: image/gif, image/x-xbitmap, image/jpeg, image/pjpeg, */*
Accept-Language: en
Accept-Charset: iso-8859-1,*,utf-8
```

Figure 10-7   GET resulting from holding down Shift and pressing Reload.

This GET message also carries the Pragma: no-cache directive, which bypasses all intermediary caches between the browser and the destination Web server.

Finally, if you want to be absolutely sure that nothing is being retrieved from the local cache, you can "flush" the cache and erase its contents. Open up the Preferences dialog from the Edit menu. Look down the tree control until you find the node labeled Advanced. Expand the node, and three child items should appear: Cache, Proxies, and Disk Space. Click on the Cache item, and the configuration information for Communicator's caching system should appear across from the tree control, as shown in Figure 10-8.

From this panel you have complete control over Communicator's cache. You can clear the memory and disk caches, change the amount of resources dedicated to caching, and configure how often the cache is compared to data on the originating Web site.

Now lets take a look at how the Java Web Server handles caching.

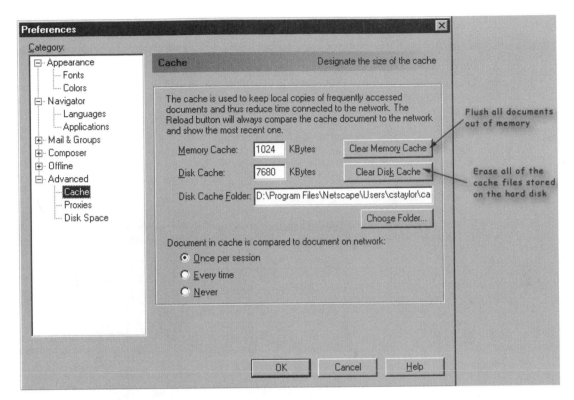

Figure 10-8   Communicator's cache panel.

Caching with the Java Web Server

After reading the previous section, you know how browsers such as Netscape Communicator use the HTTP protocol to implement caching on the client side, but how does the Java Web Server support it from the server? In this section, you'll develop a simple tool for experimenting with server caching. This time the tool acts as a client by sending an HTTP GET message to a Web server. When the server returns the response, the tool will display the server's message headers. Buried within the server response are cache-specific HTTP headers. Finally, you'll learn how servlets can be designed to take advantage of HTTP caching.

Looking at HTTP Response-Message Headers

You'll need some help to inspect the HTTP response generated by the Java Web Server. You could use a terminal program like telnet to test the server, but hand-entering HTTP requests gets tedious after two or three tries. What you need is an automated tool. This tool can be used to show which HTTP response headers are returned by the Java Web Server, and it can be used to view the message headers generated by your servlets, which can save you time when trying to debug your servlets.

The tool we wrote is an applet called SnoopHeaders. It sends an HTTP GET request to the server specified in the URL TextField and prints the returned message headers out into the text area. Figure 10-9 shows a screen shot of SnoopHeaders.

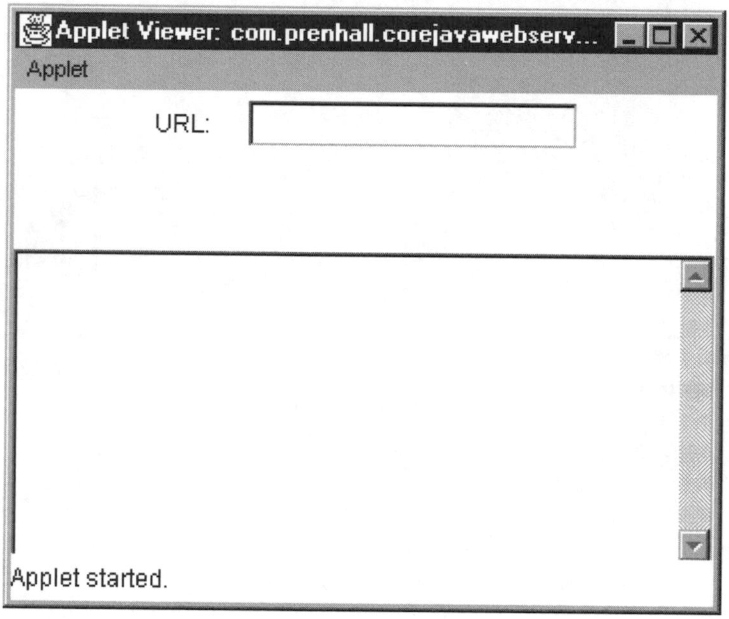

Figure 10-9   The SnoopHeaders applet.

Making the Connection

Making a connection to the server is programmatically simple, thanks to the URL and URLConnection classes provided by the JDK. First, create a new URLConnection by making a call to openConnection on the URL. Then, we make a call to the readIncoming method to read the message headers in the HTTP response.

```
URLConnection conn = theURL.openConnection();
readIncoming(conn);
```

Grabbing the HTTP Response Headers

During construction, the SnoopHeaders class allocates a String array called HTTP_RESPONSE_HEADERS to hold all the HTTP response message headers. The readIncoming method traverses the HTTP_RESPONSE_HEADERS array, using the getHeaderField method to grab message headers found in the response. Finally, we use the setText method to display each message header and its value in the TextArea.

```java
for(int i = 0; i < HTTP_RESPONSE_HEADERS.length; i++)
{
   String header_name  = HTTP_RESPONSE_HEADERS[i];
   String header_value =
       conn.getHeaderField(header_name.toLowerCase());
   if (header_value != null)
   {
     txtaOutput.append(header_name);
     txtaOutput.append(" ");
     txtaOutput.append(header_value);
     txtaOutput.append("\n");
   }
}
```

Listing 10-1 presents the complete source for SnoopHeaders.

Listing 10-1   SnoopHeaders.java

```java
import java.io.*;
import java.awt.*;
import java.awt.event.*;
import java.net.*;
import java.util.*;

public class SnoopHeaders extends java.applet.Applet
{


   protected TextField txtfURL;
   protected TextArea txtaOutput;


   /**
    *   According to RFC 2068, the HTTP/1.1
    *   response headers live in three groups:
    *   1) general-headers (general to
    *       requests/responses)
```

continued

```
 *  2) response-headers
 *  3) entity-headers
 */

private static String[] HTTP_RESPONSE_HEADERS =
{
     /**
      * general-headers
      */

  "Cache-Control",          "Connection",
  "Date",                   "Pragma",
  "Transfer-Encoding",      "Upgrade",
  "Via",

    /**
     *  response-headers
     */

  "Age",                     "Location",
  "Proxy-Authenticate",     "Public",
  "Retry-After",            "Server",
  "Vary",                    "Warning",
  "WWW-Authenticate",

    /**
     *  entity-headers
     */

  "Allow",                   "Content-Base",
  "Content-Encoding",       "Content-Language",
  "Content-Length",         "Content-Location",
  "Content-MD5",            "Content-Range",
  "Content-Type",           "ETag",
  "Expires",                 "Last-Modified",
  "extension-header"
};


public void init()
{


  //use Border Layout for this applet
  setLayout(new BorderLayout());

  //Panel to hold input
```

```
Panel pInput = new Panel();
pInput.setLayout(new FlowLayout());

//make a new TextField to get the URL
pInput.add(new Label("URL:"));
txtfURL = new TextField(20);

//implement the ActionListener interface
txtfURL.addActionListener(
  new ActionListener()
  {
      public void actionPerformed(ActionEvent ae)
      {
        txtaOutput.setText(txtfURL.getText());
        try
        {
          URL theURL = new URL(txtfURL.getText());
          doGET(theURL);
        }
        catch(MalformedURLException murle)
        {
          txtaOutput.setText("Invalid url. " +
                             murle.getMessage());
        }
      }
  }
);

//add this URL input field to the Input Panel
pInput.add(txtfURL);

//Create a Panel to hold output
Panel pOutput = new Panel();
pOutput.setLayout(new BorderLayout());
txtaOutput = new TextArea();
pOutput.add(txtaOutput, "Center");

add(pInput, "North");
add(pOutput, "South");
}


  /**
   *   send a HTTP GET request to a
   *   server at the specified URL
   */

public void doGET(URL theURL)
```

continued

```
  {
    try
    {
      URLConnection conn = theURL.openConnection();
      readImcoming(conn);
    }
    catch(Exception e)
    {
      e.printStackTrace();
    }
  }

  public void readImcoming(URLConnection conn)
                          throws IOException
  {
    txtaOutput.setText("");

    for(int i = 0; i < HTTP_RESPONSE_HEADERS.length; i++)
    {
      String header_name  = HTTP_RESPONSE_HEADERS[i];
      String header_value =
          conn.getHeaderField(header_name.toLowerCase());
      if (header_value != null)
      {
        txtaOutput.append(header_name);
        txtaOutput.append(" ");
        txtaOutput.append(header_value);
        txtaOutput.append("\n");
      }
    }
  }
}
```

How Does the Java Web Server Cache Documents?

Armed with a tool to view HTTP message headers returned by a Web server, you could use it to see what cache-specific message headers are sent. Figure 10-10 shows SnoopHeaders in action.

As you can see, the Java Web Server automatically sets the Last-Modified date for HTML documents. Does it automatically set the Last-Modified header for servlets as well? Figure 10-11 shows the message headers returned after a GET request is sent to SimpleServlet (a demonstration servlet packaged with the Java Web Server).

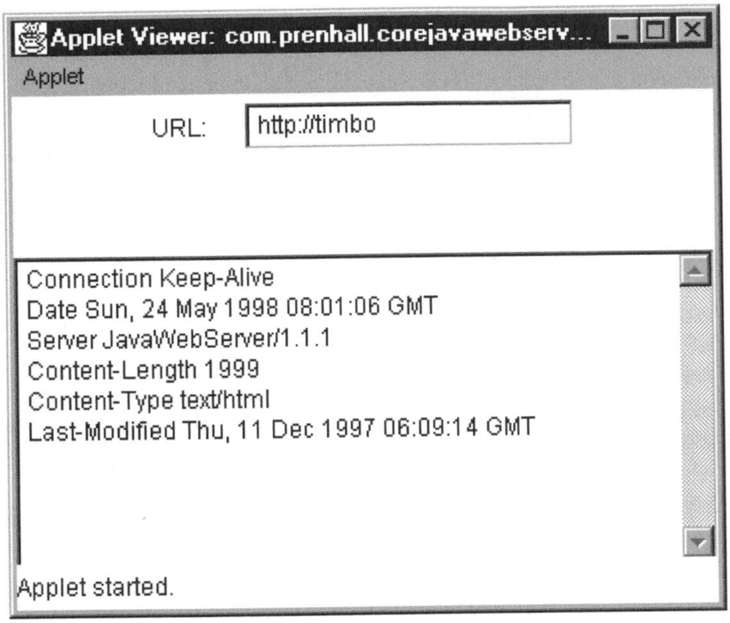

Figure 10-10   SnoopHeaders in action.

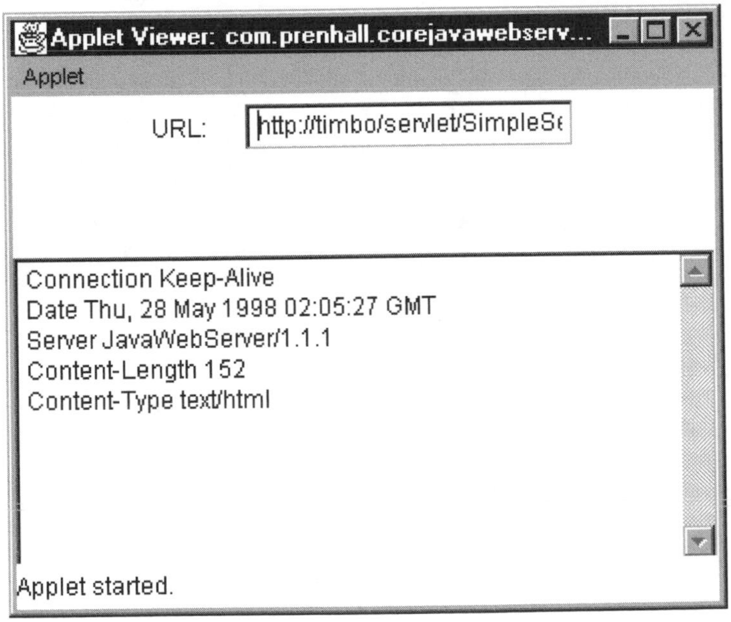

Figure 10-11   HTTP headers sent by SimpleServlet.

Take a look at the output in Figure 10-11. Did you notice that the Java Web Server did not set the `Last-Modified` header for SimpleServlet? In fact, the Java Web Server will not set the `Last-Modified` header for any of your servlets. Each servlet you write will most likely create dynamic content, so how could the Java Web Server possibly know when your servlets plan to generate new data? Instead, it's left up to you, as a servlet developer, to enable caching with your servlets.

Cache-Enable Your Servlets

As you saw in the last section, the Java Web Server does not set the `Last-Modified` header (or any other cache-specific headers) for HTTP responses generated by your servlets. The HTTP specification recommends that you use cache-specific headers (i.e., `Expires`, `Last-Modified`, etc.) wherever applicable to decrease network traffic and let clients cache retrieved documents. Cache-enabling your servlets is completely dependent on the kind of data you are returning. In the next two sections you'll see how to cache enable your servlets using the `Expires` and `Last-Modified` headers. Finally, you see how to implement these ideas in practice.

Using the `Expires` Header

In order to use the `Expires` header effectively, you'll need to know approximately when your servlet plans to change its content and set the `Expires` header to that date. Of course, this is easier said than done, since servlets were designed for automating content generation, making the `Expires` header useable only in certain situations.

One situation in which the `Expires` header could be useful would be that of a computer company that publishes its computer prices on a company Web site. This is the classical servlet example: a servlet grabs the latest prices from a database via JDBC and returns the results to the client's Web browser. If the database is updated weekly, the servlet can refresh the corresponding Web page and set the `Expires` header in the `HttpServletResponse`,

```
res.setDateHeader("Expires", expires_time);
```

where *expires_time* is dated one week after the content was last generated. Now, clients will update their cached copies only after the current one becomes *stale*. This will reduce the load on the Web server (JDBC accesses aren't free!), and customers of the site will be happy as well, since they will save time by downloading a new copy only once per week.

Using the `Last-Modified` Header

Unfortunately, there's a problem with the previous example: what if the database is updated before the old content has expired? Your customers will be forced (unless they use a `Reload` from Communicator) to use old information instead of the latest material.

Instead of using a fixed time to expire a document, you want a way to tell your customers that the document has been updated, so they can refresh their cached copies. This is what the `Last-Modified` header was designed for. The Java Web Server development team understood this need to support `Last-Modified` information to clients, and they provided a convenience API for sending it. To support the `Last-Modified`/`If-Modified-Since` conditional retrieval model, your servlet needs to override the default implementation of the `getLastModified` method in the `HttpServlet` class.

How does this work? When a client makes a GET request of your servlet, and the request contains the `If-Modified-Since` header, the Java Web Server performs a check to see if your servlet has new data to send to the client. It accomplishes this "smart update" by comparing the `If-Modified-Since` date to the number returned by the `getLastModified` method.

```
ifModifiedSince = req.getDateHeader ("If-Modified-Since");
lastModified = servlet.getLastModified (req);
```

If the `If-Modified-Since` header in the request is less than the `Last-Modified` date returned by the `getLastModified` method, then the `doGet` method is called on your servlet to return the updated data. Otherwise, a `304 Not Modified` status code is returned, notifying the client that there is no new data:

```
resp.sendError (HttpServletResponse.SC_NOT_MODIFIED);
```

The default implementation of the `getLastModified` method in the `HttpServlet` class returns a –1:

```
protected long getLastModified (HttpServletRequest req)
{
    return -1;
}
```

This default implementation tells the Java Web Server that the last-modified time is unknown and, as such, should not be used in conditional GET operations. It is up to you to override the `getLastModified` method to provide support for conditional GET operations. The getLastModified comparison occurs within `HttpServlet`'s service method. If you override the `service` method in your servlet, make sure to call `super.service` if you still want to support conditional GET requests.

Core Alert

When you override the `getLastModified` *method, make sure that you round to the nearest second. The HTTP specification says the HTTP/1.1 specification requires the transmission of Date headers on every response, and the Date values (the* `Last-Modified` *header is itself a date value) are ordered to a granularity of one second.*

JAVAX.SERVLET.HTTP.HTTPSERVLET

`getLastModified(HttpServletRequest)`

Developers override the `getLastModified` method to support the caching of documents. If a client request contains the `If-Modified-Since` HTTP header, the GET method becomes *conditional*. Therefore, if a `getLastModified` method returns a date that is later than the `If-Modified-Since` date sent by the client, the `doGet` method is called to fetch new data from your servlet. Otherwise, the Java Web Server sends the client a response that contains a 304 `Not-Modified` status code, notifying the client that there is no new data. The client will then use a cached copy of the data generated by this servlet.

Parameters:

`HttpServletRequest`	An object of type `HttpServletRequest` containing the HTTP request sent by the client.

Let's Code!

Now that you know the theory behind some of HTTP's cache-specific headers and how they are used on both the client and the server side, you can put these ideas into practice. In this next example, you'll code a chat applet that can be used by users to send simple text-based messages. Figure 10-12 shows a screen shot of the CoreChat applet.

CoreChat is a simple example of a chat applet—it was designed to show how the `Last-Modified` and `If-Modified-Since` HTTP headers could be used to provide a decent framework for caching chat messages. The CoreChat applet interacts with a servlet called ChatServlet, and this interaction can be visualized through the sequence diagram presented in Figure 10-13.

CoreChat intermittently polls ChatServlet, asking it for new chat messages submitted by other CoreChat clients. In the first request, CoreChat retrieves the current messages held by ChatServlet. ChatServlet responds by returning the current list of messages along with a `Last-Modified` header. The `Last-Modified` header signals the addition of new chat messages; each time a message is sent by a CoreChat client to the ChatServlet, the `Last-Modified` time is updated. Consequentially, ChatServlet will not have to return the entire list of messages for each GET request. Most GET requests submitted by a CoreChat applet will result in a 304 `Not-Modified` response, which will be ignored.

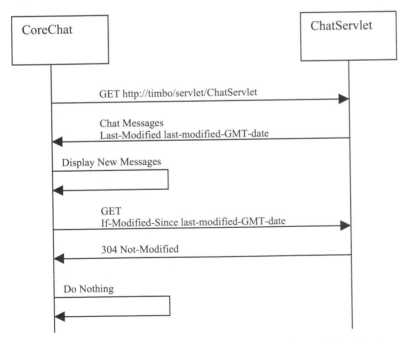

Figure 10-12 The CoreChat chat applet in action.

Figure 10-13 Sequence diagram between CoreChat and ChatServlet.

Meanwhile … on the Server Side

ChatServlet provides the server side of the chat system. Messages are sent and received through POST and GET messages from CoreChat clients. On startup, ChatServlet's `init` method is called and the lastModified time is initialized to the current system clock by making a call to the `updateLastModified` method:

```
super.init(cfg);
messages = new java.util.Vector();
updateLastModified();
```

The `updateLastModified` method makes a call to `System.currentTimeMillis` to get the local system time and then makes the necessary calculations to round the millisecond time to the nearest second (per instructions from the HTTP 1.1 specification):

```
lastModified = (long)(System.currentTimeMillis()*.001)*1000;
```

In order to support the caching model presented earlier in this chapter, you need to override the `getLastModified` method in HttpServlet. ChatServlet overrides the `getLastModified` method, returning the current value of the `lastModified` member variable:

```
public long getLastModified(HttpServletRequest req)
{
    return lastModified;
}
```

Now, each time ChatServlet receives a GET request that contains the `HTTP If-Modified-Since` header, it will return the list of chat messages only if its `lastModified` date is greater than the `If-Modified-Since` date sent by the client. Otherwise ChatServlet will send the CoreChat applet a `304 status code`, which tells the client that there are no new messages.

ChatServlet overrides the `doPost` method in HttpServlet to allow CoreChat clients to insert new messages into the chat session. First, the new message is fetched from the request by making a call to the `parsePostData` method in the `HttpUtils` class. Then the new message is added to the current list of messages by making a call to `addMessage`. Finally, access to the servlet is synchronized while a new message is added and a call to `updateLastModified` is made to update the last modified date.

```
synchronized(this)
{
    addMessage(name[0], message[0]);
    updateLastModified();
}
```

The complete source for ChatServlet is presented in Listing 10-2.

Listing 10-2   ChatServlet.java

```java
import java.io.*;
import javax.servlet.*;
import javax.servlet.http.*;
import javax.servlet.http.HttpUtils;

public class ChatServlet extends HttpServlet
{
  private java.util.Vector messages;
  private int  MAX_MESSAGES =  5;
  private long lastModified = -1;

  public void init(ServletConfig cfg)
                   throws ServletException
  {
    super.init(cfg);
    messages = new java.util.Vector();
    updateLastModified();
  }

  public void doGet(HttpServletRequest req,
                    HttpServletResponse res)
                    throws ServletException,
                    IOException
  {
    res.setContentType("text/plain");
    PrintWriter pw = res.getWriter();
    pw.println(getMessages());
    pw.close();
  }


  public void doPost(HttpServletRequest req,
                     HttpServletResponse res)
                     throws ServletException, IOException
  {
    java.util.Hashtable formData =
        HttpUtils.parsePostData(req.getContentLength(),
                                req.getInputStream());
    String[] name = (String[])formData.get("name");
    String[] message = (String[])formData.get("message");

    synchronized(this)
    {
      addMessage(name[0], message[0]);
      updateLastModified();
```

continued

```
            }

            PrintWriter pw = res.getWriter();
            res.setContentType("text/plain");
            pw.close();
        }


    public void addMessage(String name, String message)
    {
        int numMessages = messages.size();

        //Remove a message to maintain the
        //specified number of messages
        if(numMessages >= MAX_MESSAGES && MAX_MESSAGES > 0)
        {
            messages.removeElementAt(0);
        }

        StringBuffer sb = new StringBuffer();
        sb.append(name);
        sb.append(": ");
        sb.append(message);
        sb.append("\n");
        messages.addElement(sb.toString());

    }

    public String getMessages()
    {
        java.util.Vector copy;

        synchronized(messages)
        {
            //only get messages present at this time.
            copy = (java.util.Vector)messages.clone();
        }

        int numMessages = copy.size();
        StringBuffer sb = new StringBuffer();

        for(int i = 0; i < numMessages; i++)
        {
            sb.append((String)copy.elementAt(i));
        }
```

```
    return sb.toString();
  }

  public void updateLastModified()
  {
    lastModified =
          (long)(System.currentTimeMillis()*.001)*1000;
  }

  public long getLastModified(HttpServletRequest req)
  {
    return lastModified;
  }

  public String getServletInfo()
  {
    return "A simple chat servlet.";
  }
}
```

The Client Side

CoreChat is an applet that can be used by users to send simple text-based messages to other CoreChat users. CoreChat will grab existing messages from ChatServlet via the HTTP GET message and POST new chat messages to ChatServlet using the HTTP POST method. The most unique feature introduced by CoreChat lies in its caching of messages. CoreChat sends a conditional GET (by specifying the If-Modified-Since header), asking the ChatServlet servlet to send chat messages only if new messages have been posted.

The next two sections will discuss how CoreChat GETs and POSTs chat messages. We have sprinkled comments in the code to help you through areas that we do not discuss.

Grabbing New Messages

In order to understand how the GETting of new messages works you will want to brush up on the life-cycle methods (i.e., init, start, stop, and destroy) of the applet class if they are not fresh in your mind. CoreChat uses the MessageGrabber class to fetch new messages from the ChatServlet servlet. When the CoreChat applet first starts, its init method is called, and the user interface is set up. The start method in the applet class is called after the init method finishes; CoreChat overrides the start method in the applet class to start the MessageGrabber in a new thread:

```
if(messageGrabber == null)
{
  new Thread(new MessageGrabber(servlet_URL,
                                txtaOutput,
                                UPDATE_RATE)).start();
}
```

If a user leaves the Web page that contains the CoreChat applet, the stop method will be called and CoreChat will call suspend on the MessageGrabber:

```
public void stop()
{
  if(messageGrabber != null && messageGrabber.isAlive())
  {
    messageGrabber.suspend();
  }
}
```

When the user returns to the Web page containing CoreChat, the start method is called again, and we call resume to wake the MessageGrabber :

```
messageGrabber.resume();
```

When the browser shuts down (or appletviewer is shut down), the destroy method is called and we call stop on the MessageGrabber thread:

```
public void destroy()
{
  if(messageGrabber != null)
  {
    messageGrabber.stop();
  }
}
```

The MessageGrabber implements the Runnable interface and defines a run method which executes in a continuous loop, polling for new messages managed by the ChatServlet servlet.

```
while(true)
{ ...
  grabMessages(theURL);
  Thread.sleep(updateRate);
}
```

In order to reduce traffic on the Web server, the MessageGrabber will only ask for new messages every delta-t (specified by the updateRate parameter). The call to Thread.sleep puts the MessageGrabber to bed for the amount of time specified by the updateRate parameter.

The grabMessages method in the MessageGrabber class is used to fetch new messages. Given a URL to the ChatServlet, the grabMessages method will make a

`HttpURLConnection` to ChatServlet and use the `setRequestProperty` to specify an `"If-Modified-Since"` date header in the request:

```
http = (HttpURLConnection)theURL.openConnection();
    http.setRequestProperty("If-Modified-Since",
                            If_Modified_Since);
```

By setting the `If-Modified-Since` header, this GET request becomes conditional, and so the ChatServlet servlet will return new messages to the CoreChat applet only when new messages have been POSTed—otherwise ChatServlet will return a 304 status code. This will save a significant amount of time on the Web server, since ChatServlet will have to package messages only when new messages have been posted.

The `grabMessages` method makes a call to `getResponseCode` to inspect the status code returned by the ChatServer. If the status code is not 304, we display the new chat messages and set the `If_Modified_Since` variable to contain the Last-Modified date set by ChatServlet:

```
displayNewMessages(http);
    If_Modified_Since =
                http.getHeaderField("last-modified");
```

The `displayNewMessages` method is used to print the updated messages to the TextArea on the CoreChat applet:

```
public void displayNewMessages(URLConnection conn)
                            throws IOException
{
    InputStream is = conn.getInputStream();
    int num_read = is.read(buffer);
    String s = new String(buffer, 0, num_read);
    txtaOutput.setText(s);
}
```

By using a byte array, you can use the read method to grab the messages in one shot. The `setText` method is used to display the new chat messages to the screen. Listing 10-3 presents the complete source for the `MessageGrabber` class.

Listing 10-3   MessageGrabber.java

```
import java.awt.*;
import java.io.*;
import java.net.*;

public class MessageGrabber implements Runnable
{

    private TextArea txtaOutput;
```

continued

```
private long      updateRate;
private URL       theURL;
private String    If_Modified_Since =
                     "Mon, 11 May 1998 16:43:24 GMT";
private static final int BUFFER_SIZE = 2000;
byte buffer[] = null;

public MessageGrabber(URL theURL,
                         TextArea output,
                         long updateRate)
{
  this.txtaOutput = output;
  this.updateRate = updateRate;
  this.theURL     =      theURL;
  this.buffer     = new byte[BUFFER_SIZE];
}


  /**
   *   Poll ChatServlet for new messages every
   *   delta t, where t is specified by the
   *   updateRate parameter
   */

public void run()
{
  while(true)
  {

    try
    {
      grabMessages(theURL);
      Thread.sleep(updateRate);
    }
    catch(InterruptedException ie)
    {
      ie.printStackTrace();
    }
    catch(IOException ioe)
    {
      ioe.printStackTrace();
    }
  }
}


  /**
   *   Method to grab new messages from ChatServlet
```

```
    */

public void grabMessages(URL theURL) throws IOException
{
    HttpURLConnection http;
    http = (HttpURLConnection)theURL.openConnection();
    http.setRequestProperty("If-Modified-Since",
                              If_Modified_Since);

    if(http.getResponseCode() != 304)
    {
        displayNewMessages(http);
        If_Modified_Since =
                http.getHeaderField("last-modified");
    }

}


    /**
     *   method to display fetched messages
     *   to the display on CoreChat
     */

public void displayNewMessages(URLConnection conn)
                              throws IOException
{
    InputStream is = conn.getInputStream();
    int num_read = is.read(buffer);
    String s = new String(buffer, 0, num_read);
    txtaOutput.setText(s);
}
}
```

POSTing Messages

As you saw in the last section, the MessageGrabber runs in a thread, polling the ChatServlet for new messages. The CoreChat applet uses a thread to POST new messages to the ChatServlet servlet as well. When a CoreChat user enters a new message into the TextField and presses ENTER, an ActionEvent is fired and the ActionPerformed method is called in the CoreChat class:

```
public void actionPerformed(ActionEvent ae)
{
    new Thread(this).start();
}
```

The `actionPerformed` method constructs a new thread, passing it a reference to the CoreChat object, and calls start on the new thread. After it has finished initialization, start will call run in the CoreChat class. The CoreChat class implements the Runnable interface and defines a run method to POST new data to the ChatServlet:

```java
public void run()
{
  //send the message now!
  doPOST(txtMessage.getText());
  txtMessage.setText("");
}
```

The `doPOST` method is used to POST the new chat message to the ChatServlet. The complete source for the `CoreChat` class is displayed in Listing 10-4.

Listing 10-4   CoreChat.java

```java
import java.io.*;
import java.awt.*;
import java.awt.event.*;
import java.net.*;
import java.util.*;

public class CoreChat extends java.applet.Applet
            implements Runnable, ActionListener
{
  //URL to the ChatServlet
  private URL servlet_URL = null;

  //a Thread that is used
  //to fetch new messages
  Thread messageGrabber = null;

  //some components for user
  //input and message display
  private   TextField        txtUserName;
  protected TextField        txtMessage;
  protected TextArea         txtaOutput;

  //The MessageGrabber will grab new
  //messages every delta t, specified
  //by the update rate.
  private int    UPDATE_RATE  = 1000;

  //CoreChat will look for this parameter in
  //the CoreChat.html HTML file to find
  //the update rate.
```

```
private static final String UPDATE_RATE_PARAM =
                                      "update_rate";

//CoreChat will look for this parameter in the
//CoreChat.html HTML file to find the path to
//ChatServlet
private static final String SERVLET_PATH_PARAM =
                                   "chat_servlet_path";

//This is the default servlet path
private String DEFAULT_SERVLET_PATH =
                              "/servlet/ChatServlet";

//This is the default user name
private String DEFAULT_USER_NAME    = "Tim";

//This is the name of the default JPG
//file that displays the banner
private String DEFAULT_IMG = "CoreChat.JPG";

//CoreChat will look for this parameter in the
//CoreChat.html HTML file to find the name of
//a user specified banner.
private static final String CHAT_BANNER = "chat_banner";

public void init()
{

  //get the path to ChatServlet
  servlet_URL = getServletURL();

  //get the update rate, the rate at which the
  //MessageGrabber polls ChatServlet for new
  //messages
  String update_rate = getParameter(UPDATE_RATE_PARAM);

  if(update_rate != null)
  {
    UPDATE_RATE = Integer.parseInt(update_rate);
  }


  //use Border Layout for this applet
  setLayout(new BorderLayout());

  //pInput, Panel for user input
  Panel pInput = new Panel();
  pInput.setLayout(new FlowLayout());
```

continued

```
pInput.add(new Label("chat name"));
txtUserName = new TextField(10);
pInput.add(txtUserName);
pInput.add(new Label("chat message"));
txtMessage = new TextField(20);
pInput.add(txtMessage, "Center");
txtMessage.addActionListener(this);
pInput.setBackground(Color.cyan);

//pOutput, Panel for user output
Panel pOutput = new Panel();
pOutput.setLayout(new BorderLayout());
txtaOutput = new TextArea();
pOutput.add(txtaOutput, "Center");
pOutput.setBackground(Color.cyan);

setBackground(Color.blue);

//Get the image file that will be used to
//display the Core Chat banner at the top
//of the applet.
String banner_img = getParameter(CHAT_BANNER);
Image img = null;

if(banner_img != null)
{
   img = getImage(getDocumentBase(), banner_img);
}
else //use the default image filename
{
   img = getImage(getDocumentBase(), DEFAULT_IMG);
}

//Create the Banner canvas to hold the banner
Banner banner = new Banner(img);


//add panels to this Component
add(banner, "North");
add(pOutput, "Center");
add(pInput, "South");
}


/**
 *   Method to get the URL to the server side handler
 *   In our case, ChatServlet
 */
```

```
public URL getServletURL()
{

  String servlet_path = getParameter(SERVLET_PATH_PARAM);

  URL servletURL;

  try
  {
      URL db = getDocumentBase();
      servletURL = new URL(db.getProtocol(),
                           db.getHost(),
                           db.getPort(),
                           servlet_path);
    return servletURL;
  }
  catch(MalformedURLException murle)
  {
    murle.printStackTrace();
    return null;
  }
}


  /**
   *   Start a new Thread to POST a new
   *   chat message
   */

public void actionPerformed(ActionEvent ae)
{
    new Thread(this).start();
}


  /**
   *   Starts, or resumes the MessageGrabber
   */

public void start()
{
  if(messageGrabber == null)
  {
    new Thread(new MessageGrabber(servlet_URL,
                                  txtaOutput,
                                  UPDATE_RATE)).start();
  }
```

continued

```
  else
  {
    messageGrabber.resume();
  }
}


  /**
   *   stops the MessageGrabber from getting messages
   *   when a user has left the underlying Web page
   *   containing this applet.
   */

public void stop()
{
  if(messageGrabber != null && messageGrabber.isAlive())
  {
    messageGrabber.suspend();
  }
}


  /**
   *   Stop the MessageGrabber Thread when
   *   the Web browser quits.
   */

public void destroy()
{
  if(messageGrabber != null)
  {
    messageGrabber.stop();
  }
}


  /**
   *   send a message when I am alive
   */

public void run()
{
  //send the message now!
  doPOST(txtMessage.getText());
  txtMessage.setText("");
}


  /**
```

```
 *    send a HTTP POST request containing a chat
 *    message to a server at the specified URL
 */

public void doPOST(String theMessage)
{
     try
   {
     StringBuffer postData = new StringBuffer(100);
     postData.append("name=");

     if(txtUserName.getText().equals(""))
     {
        postData.append(DEFAULT_USER_NAME);
     }
     else
     {
        postData.append(txtUserName.getText());
     }

     postData.append("&");
     postData.append("message=");
     postData.append(theMessage);


     HttpURLConnection conn =
           (HttpURLConnection)servlet_URL.openConnection();
     conn.setDoOutput(true);
     conn.setUseCaches(false);
     conn.setRequestProperty("content-type",
                             "application/octet-stream");
     conn.setRequestProperty("Content-length", "" +
                             postData.length());

     PrintWriter pw =
                 new PrintWriter(conn.getOutputStream());
     pw.println(postData.toString());
     pw.close();

      conn.getContent();
     }
     catch(Exception e)
     {
       e.printStackTrace();
     }
 }


}
```

The Banner class is used to display the CoreChat.JPG image file on the CoreChat applet. It provides the necessary functionality to allow the CoreChat.JPG file to resize when the applet window is stretched. The complete source is presented in Listing 10-5.

Listing 10-5   Banner.java

```java
import java.awt.*;

public class Banner extends Canvas
{
  private Image img;

  public Banner(Image img)
  {
    this.img = img;
    MediaTracker mt = new MediaTracker(this);
    mt.addImage(img,1);
    try
    {
      mt.waitForAll();
    }
    catch (InterruptedException ie)
    {
      ie.printStackTrace();
      this.img = null;
    }
  }

  public Dimension getMinimumSize ()
  {
    if (img == null)
      return new Dimension (0,0);
    return new Dimension(img.getWidth(null),
    img.getHeight(null));
  }

  public Dimension getPreferredSize ()
  {
    return getMinimumSize();
  }

  public void paint(Graphics g)
  {
    if (img != null)
```

```
  {
    Dimension d = getSize();
    g.drawImage(img, 0, 0, d.width, d.height, this);
  }


 }

}
```

The CoreChat applet presented in this last section implements a simple caching mechanism, which still has room for improvements that would be beyond the scope of this chapter to implement. For example, session management could be used to track messages received by each user so the ChatServlet servlet would only have to send chat clients unread messages.

CoreChat runs fine with the appletviewer program. In order to use the CoreChat applet in a browser, though, you will need to do away with using the `HttpURLConnection` class and use its superclass, `URLConnection`, since Netscape Navigator and Microsoft Internet Explorer implement the `HttpURLConnection` differently from Sun's version. The `HttpURLConnection` in Sun's JDK1.1.6 has the hierarchy shown in Figure 10-14.

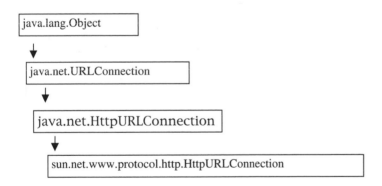

Figure 10-14 Sun's HttpURLConnection hierarchy.

So the following code snippet will work:

```
URL a_url = new URL(http://java.sun.com);

java.net.HttpURLConnection conn =
                (HttpURLConnection)a_url.openConnection();
```

since the `sun.net.www.protocol.http.HttpURLConnection` extends from `java.net.HttpURLConnection`.

Now let's take a look at Internet Explorer's 4.0 `HttpURLConnection` hierarchy in Figure 10-15.

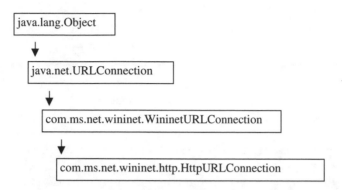

Figure 10-15   Internet Explorer's HttpURLConnection Hierarchy.

What is missing in this hierarchy? The `java.net.HttpURLConnection` is not here. Therefore, the following cast:

```
java.net.HttpURLConnection conn =
                  (HttpURLConnection)a_url.openConnection();
```

will cause a `java.lang.ClassCastException`.

Hopefully, future developments of the Java language will become standardized, so these problems will not continue to haunt developers. The Java Activator could be used as an alternative as well.

Summary

You now have the necessary knowledge to enable your servlets to support caching in HTTP. Starting with an introduction to HTTP's cache-specific headers, this chapter walked you through client caching, using Netscape's Navigator browser as an example. Then we developed the SnoopHeaders program and used it to look at cache-specific headers returned by the Java Web Server. We concluded that, in order to support caching within your servlets, you must override the `getLastModified` method in HttpServlet. Finally, we developed the ChatServlet servlet and the CoreChat chat applet to show you how caching is implemented in practice.

SESSION
MANAGEMENT

Chapter

11

So far your exposure to the Java servlet has been tied to some very simple scenarios. Data can be sent to your servlet in the HTTP request, and your servlet can return dynamic Web content to the client's browser after it has been prepackaged into an HTTP response. What if you want to hold some information that is particular to a client across multiple requests? An example may be an on-line shopping system, where each request could add to a client's ongoing order. The order must maintain its state, and we must have a mechanism for associating an order with a customer. The HTTP protocol is a stateless protocol; that is, maintaining state across multiple requests is not supported within the protocol itself. The Java Web Server solves this problem by providing support for session management—a mechanism used to turn the HTTP stateless protocol into a stateful protocol.

In this chapter we show you how servlets can be coded to take advantage of session management. We start by giving you an overview of the core classes which are used in session management. We show you how the Java Web Server uses cookies to carry data to and from a client's browser and how URL rewriting can be used as an alternative approach. In addition, we describe how the `HttpSession` class uses an event-driven architecture to manage session-specific events. Some simple coding examples are given to show how these concepts are implemented in code. Finally, we present an advanced servlet, which shows you how session management can be paired with the Java Naming and Directory Interface (JNDI) to manage a Web-based directory server.

Core Session-Management Classes

Figure 11-1 shows a simple class diagram of the core classes involved in session management.

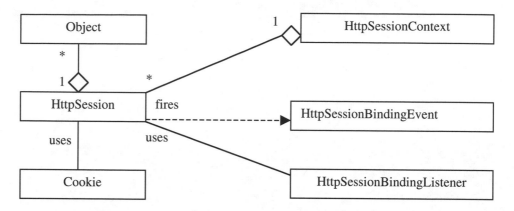

Figure 11-1   The core session-management classes.

The `HttpSession` class is responsible for managing data to be stored during a session, including the unique session Id and other Java objects. The `Cookie` class is used to manage information specific to a cookie, such as its name, Id, and expiration data. The `HttpSession` class also acts as an event source; it fires the `HttpSessionBindingEvent` and uses methods in the `HttpSessionBindingListener` interface to call back on all listeners who are registered for the `HttpSessionBindingEvent`. The `HttpSessionContext` maintains a pool of `HttpSessions` and provides an API which allows `HttpSessions` to interoperate. The sections that follow will explain these classes in much more detail.

HttpSession Class

The `HttpSession` class is used to maintain a session for a single user. Consider what happens when you log onto your UNIX or NT account. Each time you log on can be thought of as a new session. During your session, the server computer manages what you can and cannot do (delete files, access directories, etc.). Similarly, an `HttpSession` may begin after a user logs onto your Web site. It is generated by calling the `getSession` method on an `HttpServletRequest` object:

```
HttpSession = req.getSession(true);
```

Each HttpSession maps to a single user, allowing you to maintain state-specific data for that particular user. Once an HttpSession has been generated for a user, subsequent calls to req.getSession(true) will return the same HttpSession up until the session expires. Any session which is not used for a specified amount of time (thirty minutes by default) will be automatically invalidated. The duration of a session can be changed by changing the session.invalidationtime property in the server.properties file. For more information see the "Session Tracker" section later in this chapter.

You can think of the HttpSession as having two layers: (1) an application layer that manages application-specific data and (2) a session layer that manages session-specific data. The next two sections explain the application and session layers in detail.

JAVAX.SERVLET.HTTP. HTTPSERVLETREQUEST

HttpSession getSession(boolean create)

Gets the HttpSession bound to this HttpServletRequest.

Parameters

create   If create is true and there is no current session, a new HttpSession will be created and returned. Otherwise it will return the session bound to this request. If create is false, the session bound to this request is returned, or null if there is no session bound to this request.

The Application Layer

The HttpSession has a storage facility called the application layer that can be used to store any Java object. This application layer functions as a live repository, which allows you to put objects in and take objects out. Objects stored in the application layer of the HttpSession are called application-layer data.

When it is first constructed, the `HttpSession` contains an empty application layer. It is entirely up to you to store your own objects in the application layer. Choosing what to store is easily determined during the design of your application. As an example, consider an on-line shopping system. Customers can buy products that are listed on your Web site. An `HttpSession` could be created at the beginning of each new order. A ShoppingCart interface could be used to manage order items.

```
public interface ShoppingCart
{
  public void addItem(String itemId, Item the_new_item);
  public void remItem(String itemId);
  public java.util.Enumeration getItems();
}
```

Using an interface allows a design that is very much *plug and play.* For example, you can have a PersistentShoppingCart or a JDBCShoppingCart. After creating an HttpSession, you can use the `putValue` method to put an instance of the ShoppingCart into the session's application layer:

```
ShoppingCart sc = new JDBCShoppingCart();
session. putValue("shopping.theCart", sc);
```

During each subsequent request, a client can POST new items to be added to the shopping cart, which is contained in the session's application layer. The live repository which stores the application-layer data is shared by all servlets in the system. This can cause potential problems for the careless developer, since a call to `putValue` with the same name (`shopping.theCart` in our case) will overwrite the value that is currently stored.

Core Tip

You should enforce a good naming convention for all objects that you plan to store in the application layer of the HttpSession. In the ShoppingCart example above we named the ShoppingCart object shopping.theCart. Enforcing a strong naming convention will guard your servlets from overwriting each other's application-layer data, since they all share the same live repository.

You can retrieve the ShoppingCart by calling the `getValue` method, passing it the name given to the cart at the time the cart was added to the session:

```
HttpSession session = req.getSession();
ShoppingCart cart =
        (ShoppingCart)session.getValue("shopping.theCart");
cart.addItem(…, …);
```

The `putValue` and `getValue` methods give you an interface for putting and getting application-layer data into the `HttpSession`, but what if you want to find out what is already contained in the application layer without knowing the name in which the object was originally stored? The `getValueNames` method returns an array which contains all the names of the objects currently stored in the application layer. For example, the following code snippet removes all objects currently stored in the application layer:

```
HttpSession sess = req.getSession(true);
String appLayerNames[] = sess.getValueNames();
for(int i = 0; i < appLayerNames.length; i++)
{
   sess.removeValue(appLayerNames[i]);
}
```

JAVAX.SERVLET.HTTP.HTTPSESSION

`void putValue(String name, Object value)`

Puts an Object into the application layer of the `HttpSession`.

Parameters
name   A descriptive name for the object to be added
value   Any Java object.

`Object getValue(String name)`

Puts an object into the application layer of the `HttpSession`.

Parameters
name   The name of the object to retrieve from the application layer of the `HttpSession`.

`String[] getValueNames()`

Gets an array of all the names corresponding to objects in the application layer of the `HttpSession`.

`removeValue(String name)`

Removes the object in the application layer of the `HttpSession` bound to this name.

Parameters
name   The name bound to the object which is to be removed.

The Session Layer

In addition to having an application layer to handle application-specific data for a given `HttpSession`, the `HttpSession` also has a session layer that is used to handle session-specific-information. Some examples of session-specific data are the creation time of the session, the unique identifier for that session, and the time in which the session was last accessed.

Keeping the shopping-cart application in mind, consider what happens when a user completes his order. After the order information gathered from his order has been stored, there is no need to keep his session any longer. It is best to throw it away as soon as possible so that it will be garbage collected. To end a session you simply invalidate it by calling the invalidate method on the `HttpSession` object:

```
session.invalidate();
```

The Java Web Server manages the life cycle of the `HttpSession` automatically. Therefore, you will not find most of the session-layer-specific methods in the `HttpSession` class very interesting. Most of your time will be spent manipulating the application layer, not the session layer, of the `HttpSession`.

JAVAX.SERVLET.HTTP.HTTPSESSION

void invalidate()

Invalidates this session and removes it from the `SessionContext`.

The Cookie Class

So far we have told you how to create a session and how to store information in a session, but we have not told you how the Java Web Server is able to map a session to a specific user.

In the early days, Web developers used hidden input tags in an HTML form to maintain state information across multiple requests. This technique is limited, because every Web page must have a form containing hidden input types to hold the current state. Another technique, known as *URL rewriting*, stores session state in the request URL. URL rewriting works well but is still limited, because sophisticated applications require lots of data, making the URL very long and unreadable.

Recognizing the limitations of these approaches, Netscape came up with a much cleaner one: store the state information in the client's Web browser. They called this state information a *cookie*. A cookie is generated by an HTTP server (in our case, the Java Web Server) and is encoded in the message header of the HTTP response before it is sent to the client's Web browser. When the HTTP response is received, the client's Web browser will grab the cookie from the response and store it in a file. Netscape stores its cookies in a text file called *cookies.txt*. The next time a request is made to that same HTTP server, the browser will send the stored cookies in the HTTP request.

By default, the Java Web Server uses a cookie to match incoming requests to sessions stored in the Server. Figure 11-2 shows the cookie class along with its two member fields, name and value.

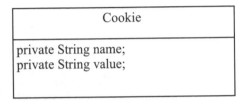

Cookie
private String name; private String value;

Figure 11-2   The cookie class.

Figure 11-3 displays an HTTP request message sent by Netscape Navigator to the `SessionServlet1` servlet presented later in this chapter.

```
D:\WINNT\System32\cmd.exe                                    _ □ ×
GET /servlet/SessionServlet HTTP/1.0
Connection: Keep-Alive
User-Agent: Mozilla/4.03 [en] (WinNT; I)
Host: localhost
Accept: image/gif, image/x-xbitmap, image/jpeg, image/pjpeg, */*
Accept-Language: en
Accept-Charset: iso-8859-1,*,utf-8
Cookie: jwssessionid=QBNZUKIAAAAALTSWQLWQAAA
```

Figure 11-3   Netscape Navigator HTTP request message.

The HTTP request message presented in Figure 11-3 contains a Cookie message header which corresponds to a Cookie object in the Java Web Server. Notice that the name/value pair for this cookie is jwssessionid/QBNZUKIAAAAALTSWQLWQAAA. The Java Web Server will use this name/value pair to identify this request with a corresponding `HttpSession`. Using the `getCookies` method, you can get all the cookies in the HTTP request that were returned by the client's browser:

```
Cookie cookie[] = request.getCookies();
```

where request is an object of `HttpServletRequest`. The `getCookies` method returns an array of `Cookie` objects, or null if there are no cookies in the request. Once you have obtained the cookies from the request, you can get the name and value associated with the cookie by using corresponding get methods:

```
String theName = cookie[i].getName();
String theValue = cookie[i].getValue();
```

A cookie also has an expiration date as well. You can get it by making a call to the getMaxAge method:

```
int expire = cookie[i].getMaxAge(int)
```

Core Note

The getMaxAge *method returns the maximum age of the cookie represented in seconds, not milliseconds.*

Unlike the HttpSession class, the cookie class gives you the power to set the maximum age of the cookie. To do so, use the setMaxAge method:

```
cookie.setMaxAge(100000);   //100, 000 seconds, not milliseconds!
```

All this talk about cookies means that the cookies class is very important and you should be intimately familiar with it—right? Wrong! Actually you will seldom need to use the cookies class, because the Java Web Server manages cookies for you automatically—so you will not have a need to manipulate them.

JAVAX.SERVLET.HTTP. HTTPSERVLETREQUEST

```
Cookie[] getCookies()
```

Gets an array containing the cookies found in this HttpServletRequest.

```
getName()
```

Gets the name of the cookie. The default value (jwssessionid) is specified by the session.cookie.name property in the session.properties property file.

```
String getValue()
```

Returns the value stored in the cookie. Java Web Server uses the value data field to store the unique session Id.

```
int getMaxAge()
```

Returns the maximum age for this cookie. Time is in seconds.

```
void setMaxAge(int expiry)
```

Sets the maximum age to the cookie. Time is in seconds.

Listeners and Events

The Java Web Server uses the JavaBeans Delegation model to pass events to objects contained in the application layer of the `HttpSession`. This model defines a design pattern based on a callback model. Consider, for example, the AWT 1.1 event model. You can create a Button and add an `ActionListener` to it through the `addActionListener` method:

```
Button myButton = new Button("click me!");
myButton.addActionListener(myComponent);
```

where `myComponent` may be a Panel or some other Component. In order for this to work, `myComponent` must implement the methods listed in the `ActionListener` interface. Then, when myButton is depressed by a mouse, the event source (the Button) will use the methods defined in the `ActionListener` interface to notify registered `ActionListeners`. Since `myComponent` registered itself (through `addActionListener`) as a listener to the `ActionEvent`, it will be called back when an `ActionEvent` occurs.

This design pattern involves three objects:

```
Event Data Source
Event Listener
Event Object
```

Objects that are interested in hearing about particular events must implement the `EventListener` interface and register themselves with the Event Data Source. The Event Data Source maintains a list of Event Listeners. When an event occurs, the Event Data Source uses methods defined in the Event Listener interface to call back on all of its registered listeners, passing each of them the Event Object. The Event Object encapsulates information about the particular event.

Using this event-driven architecture, objects can be notified when they are being bound or unbound to the application layer of the `HttpSession`. Three classes are involved:

```
HttpSession (Event Source)
HttpSessionBindingListener (Event Interface)
HttpSessionBindingEvent (Event Object)
```

The next two sections will describe these classes in greater detail.

HttpSessionBindingListener

Objects which are interested in knowing about the HttpSessionBindingEvent must implement the HttpSessionBindingListener interface. This interface contains two methods (see Listing 11-1).

Listing 11-1   The HttpSessionBindingListener interface

```
package javax.servlet.http;

public interface HttpSessionBindingListener
                    extends java.util.EventListener
{
  public abstract void
        valueBound(HttpSessionBindingEvent event);

  public abstract void
        valueUnbound(HttpSessionBindingEvent event);
}
```

Objects implementing the HttpSessionBindingListener interface are automatically registered as listeners to the HttpSessionBindingEvent. There is no need to call a corresponding addHttpSessionBindingListener method (such a method does not exist). Binding or unbinding values to the HttpSession will cause the HttpSession to fire an HttpSessionBindingEvent. There are two cases to consider:

- Binding, which occurs when putValue is invoked on an HttpSession object
- Unbinding, which occurs when removeValue is invoked on an HttpSession object

Binding values to the HttpSession will invoke the valueBound method on an HttpSessionBindingListener object. Unbinding values to the HttpSession will invoke the valueUnbound method on an HttpSessionBindingListener object.

JAVAX.SERVLET.HTTP. HTTPSESSIONBINDINGLISTENER

abstract void valueBound(HttpSessionBindingEvent event)

Method called when an object is bound to the application layer of the HttpSession.

Parameters

event   An event object which contains data for this particular event, such as the HttpSession object associated to the event and the name assigned to the object which caused the event.

abstract void valueUnbound (HttpSessionBindingEvent event)

Method called when an object is unbound to the application layer of the HttpSession.

Parameters

event   An event object which contains data for this particular event, such as the HttpSession object associated to this event and the name assigned to the object which caused this event.

HttpSessionBindingEvent

The HttpSessionBindingEvent class is an event data class, which is used to encapsulate information pertaining to an HttpSessionBindingEvent. Objects contained in the application-layer data of the HttpSession that implement the HttpSessionBindingListener interface are passed an HttpSessionBindingEvent object when new objects are bound to or unbound from the HttpSession.

An object implementing the HttpSessionBindingListener interface can find out which object was added to the application layer by calling the getName method:

```
String objectName = hbse.getName();
```

where hbse is an object of type HttpSessionBindingEvent. In addition, once you have the name of the object which caused the HttpSessionBindingEvent, and once you have obtained the session, you can retrieve it by making a call to getValue:

```
HttpSession session = hbse.getSession();
Object obj = session.getValue(objectName);
```

SessionServlet

Let's turn some of this theory into code! In order to see the frame that is displayed in this example, you will need to run the Java Web Server using the `httpdnojre.exe` program to allow `SessionServlet` to interfere with your desktop. (For more information on `httpdnojre.exe`, refer to Chapter 4, "Administrating the Java Web Server.")

The invalidation time for a session in the Java Web Server is set to thirty minutes by default. Therefore, if you create a new `HttpSession` and you do not make a request within thirty minutes (the invalidation time) the session will expire. Keeping that in mind, you may want to try changing the default invalidation time to ten seconds, so that you can see sessions being invalidated more frequently during this example. To change the invalidation time you will need to locate the `server.properties` properties file and change the `session.invalidationtime` parameter. The `server.properties` file can be found in the

```
server_root\properties\server\javawebserver
```

directory, where `server_root` is the root directory in which you installed the Java Web Server. The invalidation-time property is specified in milliseconds; hence changing the value to 10000 will cause sessions to be invalidated every ten seconds.

The SessionServlet servlet in this next example will show off the following new material introduced in this chapter:

- Create new sessions.
- Add data to the application layer.
- Implement the `SessionBindingListener` interface.

SessionServlet creates a new session only if a session does not already exist. If SessionServlet gets a request which does not have a session ID associated with an `HttpSession` stored in the Java Web Server, then the call to

```
req.getSession(false)
```

will return null, and SessionServlet will create a new one by calling

```
HttpSession session = req.getSession(true)
```

If a new session is created, SessionServlet will invoke `putValue` to put a new `SessionListenerFrame` into the application layer of the session:

```
session.putValue("session.sessionListener",
                        new SessionListenerFrame());
```

The complete source code for the SessionServlet is presented in Listing 11-2.

Listing 11-2   SessionServlet.java

```
import java.io.*;
import javax.servlet.*;
import javax.servlet.http.*;
import java.util.Date;

public class SessionServlet extends HttpServlet
{

  public void doGet(HttpServletRequest req,
                    HttpServletResponse res)
                    throws ServletException, IOException

  {
    res.setContentType("text/html");
    PrintWriter pw = res.getWriter();
    pw.println("<html><body>");

    HttpSession session = req.getSession(false);

    if(session == null)
    {
      session = req.getSession(true);
      session.putValue("session.sessionListener",
                       new SessionListenerFrame());
      pw.println("<h3>A new session was " +
                 "just created!</h3><P>");
    }
    String theUrl = req.getServletPath();

    pw.println("<form method=POST action=\""
               + theUrl + "\">");
    pw.println("<table><tr><td>Enter an item");
    pw.println("<td><input type=\"text\" name=\"item\">");
    pw.println("</tr></table>");
    pw.println("<INPUT TYPE=\"submit\" value=\"Add item "
               + "to session layer\"></form>");
    pw.println("</body></html>");
  }


  public void doPost(HttpServletRequest req,
                     HttpServletResponse res)
                     throws ServletException, IOException

  {
    HttpSession session = req.getSession(false);
```

continued

```
   if(session != null)
   {
      ServletInputStream sis = req.getInputStream();
      java.util.Hashtable formData =
            HttpUtils.parsePostData(sis.available(), sis);
      String[] items = (String[])formData.get("item");
      SessionListenerFrame slf =
          (SessionListenerFrame)session.getValue(
          "session.sessionListener");
      slf.addItem(items[0]);
   }

   doGet(req,res);
 }

}
```

Figure 11-4 shows the output produced by `SessionServlet`.

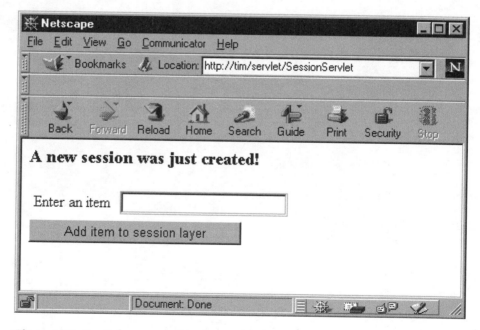

Figure 11-4   A form created by SessionServlet.

The HTML form in Figure 11-4 allows you to enter values into a text box and POST them to SessionServlet. In turn, SessionServlet will grab these values from the message body of the HTTP request and add them into the application-layer data of the HttpSession. If you are running this example using the httpdnojre.exe program, you should also see a frame (the SessionListenerFrame) similar to the one shown in Figure 11-5.

Figure 11-5   The SessionListenerFrame.

The SessionListenerFrame is stored in the application-layer data of the HttpSession. It implements the HttpSessionBindingListener interface and provides the following methods required by the HttpSessionBindingListener interface:

```
valueBound()
valueUnbound()
```

The SessionListenerFrame is created in the following call:

```
new SessionListenerFrame()
```

which calls the default constructor in the SessionListenerFrame class.

The default constructor of the SessionListenerFrame creates a new Choice which will be used as a container hold the values POSTed by the form in Figure 11-4 to SessionServlet. Since the SessionListenerFrame implements the HttpSessionBindingListener, it is a listener for the HttpSessionBindingEvent, and therefore its valueBound method is invoked after the call to putValue. The valueBound method in the SessionListenerFrame does the following:

- Calls the getSession method to get the HttpSession that corresponds to this request.
- Calls the getId method to return the unique session Id for this session.
- Calls addItem method to add this unique session Id to the chcItems choice in the SessionListenerFrame.
- Calls show to display a frame similar to the one in Figure 11-5.

During each subsequent request, SessionServlet will get the SessionListenerFrame by making a call to getValue:

```
SessionListenerFrame slf =
        (SessionListenerFrame)session.getValue(
        "session.sessionListener");
        slf.addItem(items[0]);
```

The call to addItem adds the item POSTed by the form (see Figure 11-4) to the chcItems Choice in the SessionListenerFrame. Figure 11-6 shows the result of adding a couple of items, using the form presented in Figure 11-4.

Figure 11-6   SessionListenerFrame after a few items have been POSTed to SessionServlet.

When the session expires, the Java Web Server will invoke the removeValue method on the session to remove all values stored in the application layer of that session. Since the SessionListenerFrame implements the HttpSessionBindingListener interface, its valueUnbound method will be invoked. The valueUnbound method in the SessionListenerFrame causes itself to be destroyed by calling the dispose method. Listing 11-3 shows the complete source code for SessionListenerFrame.java.

Listing 11-3   SessionListenerFrame.java

```java
import java.awt.event.*;
import java.awt.*;
import javax.servlet.http.*;

public class SessionListenerFrame extends Frame
          implements HttpSessionBindingListener
{
  private String message;
  private String session_id;
  private Choice chcItems;

  public SessionListenerFrame()
  {

    chcItems = new Choice();
```

```java
    Panel p = new Panel();
    p.add(chcItems);
    add(p);

    this.setSize(300, 60);

    addWindowListener( new WindowAdapter()
    {
      public void windowClosing(WindowEvent we)
      {
        we.getWindow().dispose();
      }
    });
  }

  public void addItem(String theItem)
  {
    chcItems.addItem(theItem);
    show();
  }

  public void valueBound(HttpSessionBindingEvent hsbe)
  {
    chcItems.addItem(hsbe.getSession().getId());
    show();
  }

  public void valueUnbound(HttpSessionBindingEvent hsbe)
  {
    dispose();
  }
}
```

But Ma, I Don't Have Any Cookies!

In the perfect world, every browser would have the needed functionality to support cookies. Unfortunately, that is not always the case. Not every Web surfer has a browser with cookie support, and some paranoid surfers turn off cookie support. Some Web sites require the Web surfer to have cookies in order to perform session-related functions. Table 11-1 lists some popular Web browsers, giving version numbers that provide support for cookies.

Table 11-1 Browser Support for Cookies	
Browser Name	*Version Number*
Netscape	1.0
Internet Explorer	2.01
WebSurfer	5
OmniWeb	2.0
GNNworks	1.2

So how do we handle a Web surfer that does not have support for cookies? The Java Web Server addresses this problem by providing support for URL rewriting. It requires that you change the way in which you encode URLs in your servlet. The `HttpServletRequest` provides two methods that you can use:

```
encodeRedirectUrl(String)
encodeUrl(String)
```

You can use the `encodeRedirectURL` method to encode a URL to be used in the `sendRedirect` method of the `HttpServletResponse`. The Java Web Server will encode the URL only if the client's browser does not support cookies.

Besides encoding URLs differently in your servlet, you will need to configure the Java Web Server to support URL rewriting. By default, URL rewriting is not enabled. To enable it, you can set the `enable.urlrewriting` property to `true` in the `session.properties` file:

```
enable.urlrewriting=true
```

For more information on `session.properties` see Chapter 4.

The SessionServlet can be recoded to support URL rewriting. The only change that needs to be made to SessionServlet to support URL rewriting is the following:

```
pw.println("<form method=POST action=\""
            + res.encodeUrl(theUrl) + "\">");
```

To see this in action, try turning off cookie support in your browser and recode SessionServlet to provide support for URL rewriting. The result should be similar to Figure 11-7.

Notice the difference between Figures 11-4 and 11-7. In Figure 11-4 the URL looks like any ordinary URL:

```
http://tim/servlet/SessionServlet
```

The URL in Figure 11-7 is quite different. It contains the same URL as Figure 11-4, with the encoded session Id appended to the end:

```
http://tim/servlet/SessionServlet;$sessionid$4BQFA4YAAAAAZTSWQLBAAAA
```

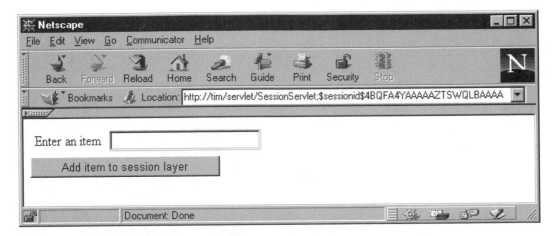

Figure 11-7 SessionServlet with URL rewriting enabled.

JAVAX.SERVLET.HTTP.HTTPSESSION

abstract HttpSessionContext getSessionContext()

Gets the `HttpSessionContext` associated with this `HttpSession`.

JAVAX.SERVLET.HTTP. HTTPSESSIONCONTEXT

abstract Enumeration getIds()

Returns a Java `Enumeration` containing the Ids to all `HttpSession` Objects contained in this `HttpSessionContext`.

abstract HttpSession getSession(String sessionId)

Returns the `HttpSession` Object, given its unique session Id.

HttpSessionContext

The `HttpSessionContext` interface is used to manage the pool of `HttpSession` objects in the current context. It is similar to the `ServletContext` interface, but with less functionality. You can get an instance of the `HttpSessionContext` by making a call to `getSessionContext` on an `HttpSession` object:

```
HttpSession session = request.getSession(true);
HttpSessionContext hsc = session.getSessionContext();
```

Once you have an instance of an `HttpSessionContext` you can walk through all sessions contained in the `HttpSessionContext`:

```
for(java.util.Enumeration enum = hsc.getIds(); enum.hasMoreElements();)
{
  HttpSession thisSession =
  hsc.getSession((String)enum.nextElement());
  //more code here
}
```

Session Swapping

Holding an `HttpSession` object for each client can be very expensive, especially if you plan to store a large amount of data in the application layer of the session. Storing more `HttpSession` objects than you can handle can result in memory exhaustion, bringing your computer to a screaming halt. The Java Web Server guards against this possibility by placing a limit on the amount of sessions which can reside in memory.

By default, the Java Web Server allows 1024 `HttpSessions` to reside in memory at any given time. It performs this magic by replicating an efficient page-replacement algorithm used by many popular operating systems—the LRU (Least Recently Used) algorithm. This algorithm follows a simple policy—once the maximum number of pages have been loaded into memory, simply replace the page which has least recently been used. Likewise, once the limit on the number of `HttpSessions` has been reached, the Java Web Server writes the least recently used sessions to disk, allowing the most frequently used `HttpSessions` to reside in memory. HttpRequests which have been written to disk will be reloaded on an as-needed basis.

Well, it's *almost* that easy! Actually, only objects that are *Serializable* are written to disk during session swapping. An object is Serializable if it implements the `java.io.Serializable` or the `java.io.Externalizable` interface.

So what happens to those objects that are not Serializable? The Java Web Server allows them to remain in memory, writing only those objects that are Serializable to disk during session swapping. It's important to ensure that you place only serializable objects into the application layer of the `HttpSession`. Otherwise, you are not allowing the Java Web Server to do its job, since objects that are not serializable will not be written to disk.

Session Persistence

So, what happens when the Java Web Server is shut down? Are all of your `HttpSessions` lost?

When shut down, the Java Web Server will walk through the list of `HttpSessions`, serializing each one of them. As with session swapping, only objects that are Serializable will be serialized to disk when the Java Web Server is shut down. Objects that are not Serializable will not be serialized to disk and will be lost forever!

The Session Tracker

The Java Web Server uses a Session Tracker to manage the pool of `HttpSessions`. The Session Tracker is responsible for high-level tasks, such as mapping session Ids to sessions, expiring invalid sessions, and creating new sessions. Most of the tasks it performs can be summarized by viewing the session tracker properties in the `server.properties` file, found in the `server_root\properties\ server\javawebserver` directory. The `server_root` is the directory in which you installed the Java Web Server. If you chose the default installation, the server root should be `\javawebserver1.1`.

Each property follows the standard `java.util.Properties` notation, where each property is represented as a key/value pair with an equals "=" sign separating them. The rest of this section will review these properties in detail. Each property is listed with its default value, just as you would see it in the `server.properties` properties file.

```
session.inavalidationinterval=10000
```

The amount of time (in milliseconds) the session tracker waits to walk the list of `HttpSessions`, expiring sessions which are invalid.

```
session.invalidationtime=1800000
```

The amount of time (in milliseconds) an `HttpSession` can be unused before it is invalidated.

```
session.swapinterval=10000
```

The amount of time (in milliseconds) the session tracker waits to count the number of `HttpSessions` which reside in memory. If the number of `HttpSessions` exceeds the number specified by the `session.maxresidents` property, session swapping will be performed.

```
enable.sessions=true
```

Used to activate the session tracker. If false, the session tracker will not perform its session tracking duties as described above. It is not recommended that you set this value to false!

```
session.maxresidents=1024
```

The maximum number of `HttpSessions` which can reside in memory at any given time.

```
session.swapdirectory=sessionSwap
```

The directory in which `HttpSessions` are written to during session swapping.

```
session.persistence=true
```

Allows sessions to be written to disk when the Java Web Server shuts down. Setting this value to false will cause you to lose every session in memory. It is not recommended that you set this value to false.

```
enable.cookies=true
```

Signals the Java Web Server to use cookies as the mechanism for storing the unique session Id.

```
session.cookie.name=jwssessionid
```

The name assigned to the session Id at the time a session is created.

```
session.cookie.comment=Java Web Server Session Tracking
Cookie
```

A comment which describes what the value of this cookie is used for.

```
enable.urlrewriting=false
```

Enables the Java Web Server to use URL rewriting as a backup mechanism for storing the unique session Id when there is no support for cookies.

At the time of this writing there is no support for setting the invalidation time for single `HttpSessions` or groups of `HttpSessions`. You must change these properties directly in the `server.properties` property file. In the near future the Java Web Server group may very well provide support for manipulating these properties in the Admin applet. Support for programmatically setting invalidation times has yet to be determined.

Putting Session Management to Work

The session-management architecture provided by the Java Web Server gives you the power to develop sophisticated applications on the Web. Traditionally the on-line shopping cart application has been among its most popular uses. Session management is used to hold the current state of a user's shopping cart, and the user's session ends when the order is complete. This chapter will not bore you with yet another implementation of a shopping-cart application! Readers who are interested in learning more are encouraged to browse the hundreds of implementations which can be found on the Web. Instead, we are going to show you how to use servlets and session management to provide Web access to a LDAP directory server.

We start this section with a short introduction to directory services. Then we introduce two technologies which are used by a servlet presented later in this chapter:

- The Netscape Directory Server (which supports the LDAP protocol)
- The Java Naming and Directory Interface (JNDI)

Finally, we end this chapter by presenting a servlet which integrates all these technologies together to provide a Web-enabled directory server.

Directory Services

Corporations use directory services to provide an easy human interface to information and services located on the network. One such example is provided by the Domain Name System (DNS). A DNS server provides you with a mechanism for locating other computers on the network. It performs this magic by resolving a human-readable name to a machine-readable IP address. The end result is a very large set of networked computers which can be easily identified through a hierarchical namespace.

The Lightweight Directory Access Protocol (LDAP) provides a mechanism for sharing information which may be scattered across multiple databases. It operates based on a client-server model, allowing multiple clients to make requests and retrieve responses from an LDAP-speaking server. LDAP is called "lightweight" because it is based on the much more extensive X.500 Directory Access Protocol (DAP). Although its functionality is not as extensive as that of its "heavyweight" DAP predecessor, LDAP can operate over TCP/IP and therefore can be used in areas where the non-TCP/IP-enabled DAP cannot.

LDAP promotes a human interface, allowing you to search for people and resources and in most cases giving a simple attribute/value pair. As an example, consider trying to find your friend Bob's e-mail address. You know that Bob's company has a directory service on its Web site, so you visit the site, log on as an anonymous user, and quickly locate Bob's e-mail address by typing in the name Bob. The directory server provides an easy interface which allows you to find Bob given the name Bob, or a possible nickname for Bob (e.g., Bobby, Bobster, etc.) Internally, all of the *common name*s for Bob would be stored as:

```
cn:  Bob
cn:  Bobby
cn:  Bobster
```

where cn is the *common name attribute* for the *attribute value* Bob.

An LDAP server can do much more than just locate your friend Bob. Consider a hotel that wants to provide printing services to all of its executive guests. It could use a directory server to provide a searchable interface for all of the printers located in the hotel. An executive with a laptop could visit the directory server to locate an available printer. He could print and then retrieve his document. using directions found in the directory server.

The LDAP is a very large topic in itself, and covering it in much more detail is beyond the scope of this book. For an excellent presentation refer to Tim Howes and Mark Smith, *LDAP Programming Directory-Enabled Applications with Lightweight Directory Access Protocol*, Macmillan Technical Publishing Company, 1997.

The capability to operate over TCP/IP makes the LDAP a very powerful component which can complement the Java Web Server. Teaming the Java Web Server with an LDAP-enabled server allows you to develop a Web-enabled directory server. But before we consider an example which uses LDAP, we need an LDAP-enabled directory server and a mechanism which allows the Java Web Server to speak to the LDAP directory server. The section that follow will explain how this is done using an LDAP server provided by Netscape and the JNDI API provided by Javasoft.

The Netscape Directory Server

The servlet presented in this chapter will use the Netscape Directory Server as an LDAP directory server. The Netscape Directory Server contains Netscape Corporation's implementation of a LDAP-enabled directory server. It provides support for versions 2 and 3 of the LDAP. You can download a free trial version of the Netscape Directory Server at `www.netscape.com`.

The Netscape Directory Server uses the LDAP Data Interchange Format (LDIF), to define a directory structure based on an easy-to-read ASCII file. It gives you the power to completely define your own directory structure based on LDIF, or you can use the one provided on the CD-ROM incorporated with this book. The LDIF file is useless to the directory server alone. You must use the `ldif2db` utility provided with the Netscape Directory Server to convert the LDIF ASCII file into a database. For more information on this process, refer to the documentation provided with the Netscape Directory Server.

JNDI

Now that we have introduced you to the LDAP protocol and a directory server which supports LDAP, we will introduce you to the API which allows Java to interface with directory servers. The Java Naming and Directory Interface (JNDI) is an API provided by Javasoft which allows you to access many directory services (DNS, LDAP, NDS, NIS, etc.) with a single API. JNDI is divided into two parts:

- The Application Programming Interface (API)
- The Service Provider Interface (SPI)

. As a developer, you will likely spend no time messing with the Service Provider Interface. The SPI is implemented by directory service providers to provide an interface to their specific directory server. Your Java applications will use the API to interface with any SPI vendor implementation in a *plug-and-play* fashion. At the time of this writing, the JNDI consists of three core packages:

```
javax.naming
javax.naming.directory
javax.naming.spi
```

The servlet presented in this chapter will use classes located in these packages to create a connection to and query a database managed by the Netscape Directory Server. For more information about JNDI refer to `www.java.sun.com/jndi`.

JndiSessionServlet

Whew! Now that all of the gory details are out of the way, we can present the featured servlet of this chapter. `JndiSessionServlet` uses the following key technologies introduced in this chapter:

- Session Management
- The Netscape Directory Server
- The Java Naming and Directory Interface

First we'll show you how to configure the `JndiSessionServlet`. Then we'll give you a quick tour of the directory services provided by `JndiSessionServlet`. Finally, we'll present the code and walk you through it.

Configuring JndiSessionServlet

In order to configure `JndiSessionServlet`, you will need to add it to the list of servlets in the Java Web Server using the Admin applet. In addition, you will need to set four properties used by `JndiSessionServlet`. To add `JndiSessionServlet` to the current list of servlets in the Java Web Server, refer to the Chapter 4. `JndiSessionServlet` uses four properties, which are summarized in Table 11-2.

Table 11-2 JndiSessionServlet Properties	
COMMAND_HANDLER	The name of the parameter used to specify command classes
JNDI_FACTORY	The factory class (e.g., javax.naming.Context) used to load the initial directory context
JNDI_SEARCHBASE	The name of the context to start searching from. Usually the root (or subroot) of a directory tree (e.g., o=foobar.com)
JNDI_URL	The URL to a Directory Server

These properties can be configured once you have added the JndiSessionServlet with the Admin Applet. To configure the properties in the Admin Applet double click on JndiSessionServlet and click on the properties tab. Click on the add button to add new properties. Figure 11-8 shows the configuration of JndiSessionServlet on the author's computer.

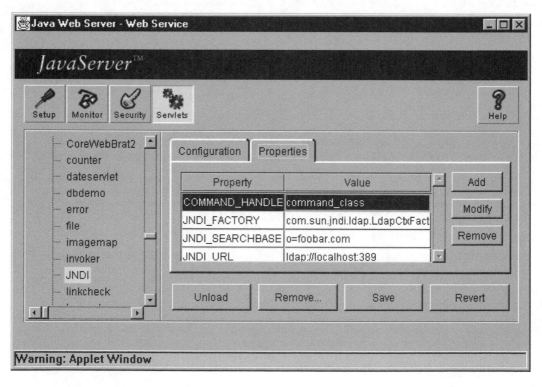

Figure 11-8   Configuring JndiSession properties.

Introduction

Let's say that you own a company called Foobar which has around a hundred employees. Currently, your admin group passes out phone lists once every two weeks to keep you (and other employees) up to date with the latest phone numbers, etc. Being the computer guru you are, you decide there must be a better approach than this paper-wasting madness! It would be really neat if your information were stored in a centralized place and organized in a manageable fashion. A directory server provides the perfect architecture, which can easily solve this problem.

The directory structure used in this example has a form similar to that shown in Figure 11-9.

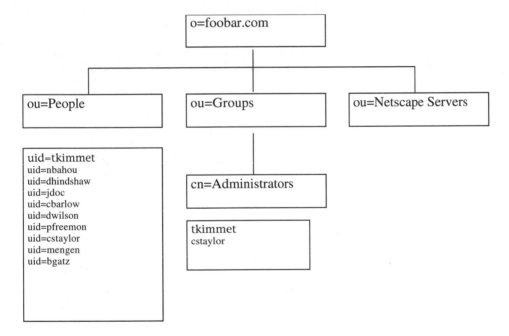

Figure 11-9   The directory tree.

This directory structure is rooted at the organization (o=foobar.com) and has three Organizational Units (OU):

- People
- Groups
- Netscape Servers

In addition, there is a group of administrators who have additional privileges; their job is to add and modify accounts within the directory server.

Core Note

The administrators group is not an organizational unit (ou). Put simply, it is a common name (cn) assigned to a group of unique members (tkimmet and cstaylor) that have special privileges defined by an ACI. To see how this is organized, see the `Foobar.ldif` *file located on the CD incorporated with this book.*

Foobar's employees are on a separate branch of the tree, rooted at ou=People. This tree structure is representative of the LDIF tree structure used in the Netscape Directory Server. Data is stored in attribute/value pairs. For example,

```
uid: tkimmet
```

is an attribute/value pair where uid (user Id) is the Attribute and tkimmet is the value for that attribute. Table 11-3 summarizes some key attributes used often in LDAP:

Table 11-3   Some Common Attribute/Value Pairs Used in LDAP

Attribute	*Value*
dn	distinguished name
uid	user Id
cn	common name
sn	sir name (last name)
o	organization
ou	organizational unit
mail	email address
telephonenumber	telephone number
userpassword	user's password

Now that we have introduced you to the directory structure, we can show you how `JndiSessionServlet` is used to search the structure starting at the directory root (o=foobar.com). Figure 11-10 shows the form that is used to log a user in:

As the owner of Foobar, you have decided to allow two kinds of users access to your employee information:

- Users, who have user Ids and passwords.
- Anonymous users, for whom no password is required.

Users of both kinds can view your directory structure. So how do they differ? For one thing, anonymous users get less extensive results when performing a search. For another, anonymous users cannot perform a search on all attributes associated with a user. This policy is implemented at the database level through the use of access control lists (ACLs). After a client who has a user Id and password has logged in by submitting the form in Figure 11-10, `JndiSessionServlet` will create a connection to the Netscape Directory Server and store a handle to the connection in the application-layer data of the `HttpSession`. Then `JndiSessionServlet` will redirect the client to a form similar to the one displayed in Figure 11-11.

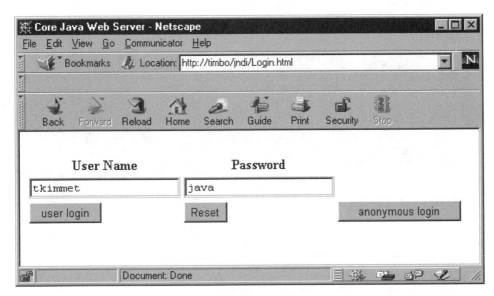

Figure 11-10   The form resulting from Login.html.

Figure 11-11   search_jndi.html.

A user can search by name, e-mail, or department. The LDAP protocol is a robust one which offers a very extensible searching mechanism. For example, to find all employees whose first name starts with C you could enter the following search criteria:

   C*

The asterisk is used as a wild-card character. This search would produce a result like one shown in Figure 11-12.

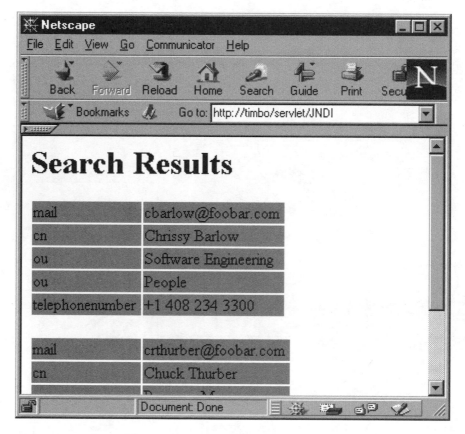

Figure 11-12   Results from a user search.

If you were logged in as an anonymous user and performed the same search, you would get results like those shown in Figure 11-13. Notice that the anonymous user does not see nearly as much information.

Figure 11-13 Results from an anonymous search.

How Does It All Work?

As you can see, an LDAP server paired with the Java Web Server can produce some exciting opportunities. Remote users can log in from anywhere in the world and use this easy interface to get information about people in the organization. You can program applications to use the LDAP server to look up e-mail addresses and other information stored in the directory server. Administrators can administer the LDAP directory from anywhere. In addition, LDAP is well accepted as a standard mechanism for centralizing a collection of resources into a single directory structure.

The sections that follow will break down `JndiSessionServlet` and explain how it all works. Figure 11-14 presents a simple class diagram which shows the classes involved in writing `JndiSessionServlet`. `JndiSessionServlet` can be divided into two parts:

- A command structure
- JndiSessionServelet

JndiSessionServlet handles the incoming requests and delegates work to its command structure. IjndiSession is an interface used by the command structure to communicate with JndiSessionServlet. The command structure is an architecture which allows you to plug in new commands to the existing structure (without recompiling it) to support new commands. The sections that follow will describe JndiSessionServlet and its command structure in great detail.

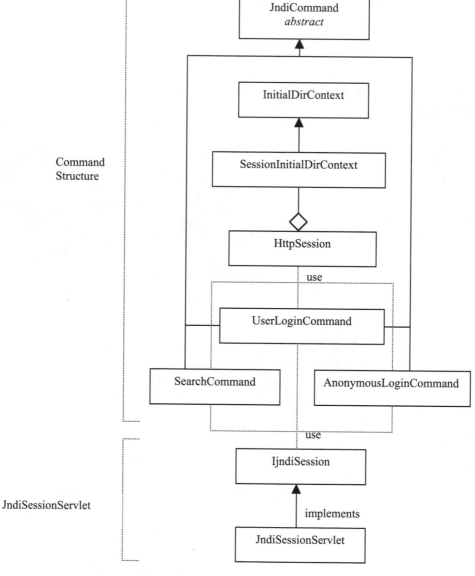

Figure 11-14   Class diagram for JndiSessionServlet.

JndiSessionServlet

JndiSessionServlet performs the following tasks:

- Initializes the servlet.
- Overrides the doPost method to handle incoming requests.
- Dynamically loads command classes to handle incoming requests.
- Implements the IjndiSession interface to provide a generic interface to the command structure.

The init method expects the four parameters summarized in Table 11-2. These four parameters are critical to the operation of JndiSessionServlet; if they are not supplied, an UnavailableException will be thrown. So why not put all of the needed functionality directly inside JndiSessionServlet?

Having all of the functionality to interface with a JNDI server in the JndiSessionServlet class would make the JndiSessionServlet class very complicated and even harder to maintain. In addition, because it is not coupled to the servlet architecture, this command structure can be used for any application (not just servlets). With that in mind, we created a separate command structure to decouple the JndiSessionServlet from JNDI specific commands. Given a request, JndiSessionServlet will dynamically load a JndiCommand for that request. For each HTTP POST, the JndiSessionServlet will use the theCommandHandler (initialized in the init method at startup) variable POSTed in the HTTP message body to get the name of the JndiCommand command to load:

```
String theClassName[] =
        (String[])formData.get(theCommandHandler);
```

Then, the loadHandler method is called to dynamically load a JndiCommand to handle the request:

```
Class theClass = Class.forName(theClassName);
cmd = (JndiCommand)theClass.newInstance();
```

Once the class has been loaded, JndiSessionServlet calls the processCommand method on the loaded JndiCommand object to handle the request. The complete source for JndiSessionServlet is presented in Listing 11-4.

Listing 11-4   JndiSessionServlet.java

```java
import java.io.*;
import javax.servlet.*;
import javax.servlet.http.*;
import javax.naming.*;

public class JndiSessionServlet extends HttpServlet
                                  implements IjndiSession
{

  public static
    final String JNDI_CONTEXT_FACTORY = "JNDI_FACTORY";
  public static
    final String JNDI_URL = "JNDI_URL";
  public static
    final String JNDI_SEARCHBASE = "JNDI_SEARCHBASE";
  public static
    final String COMMAND_HANDLER = "COMMAND_HANDLER";

  private String contextFactory;
  private String theURL;
  private String theSearchbase;
  private String theCommandHandler;

  public void init(ServletConfig config)
                 throws ServletException
  {
    super.init(config);

    contextFactory      =
          config.getInitParameter(JNDI_CONTEXT_FACTORY);
    theURL              =
          config.getInitParameter(JNDI_URL);

    theSearchbase       =
          config.getInitParameter(JNDI_SEARCHBASE);

    theCommandHandler   =
          config.getInitParameter(COMMAND_HANDLER);


    if(contextFactory      ==  null ||
       theURL              ==  null ||
       theSearchbase       ==  null ||
       theCommandHandler   ==  null)
    {
```

```
            throw new UnavailableException(this,
                    "Init parameters not set" +
                    "contextFactory= "           + contextFactory +
                    " theURL= "                 + theURL +
                    " theSearchbase= "          + theSearchbase +
                    " theCommandHandler= "      + theCommandHandler);
        }
    }

public void doPost(HttpServletRequest req,
                        HttpServletResponse res)
                        throws ServletException, IOException
{
    java.util.Hashtable formData =
        HttpUtils.parsePostData(req.getContentLength(),
                                req.getInputStream());

    String theClassName[] =
        (String[])formData.get(theCommandHandler);

    if(theClassName == null)
    {
        res.sendError(res.SC_BAD_REQUEST,
            "no hidden " + theCommandHandler + " parameter" +
            " found in FORM data.");
    }
    else
    {
        try
        {
            JndiCommand cmd =
                        loadHandler(theClassName[0], res);
            cmd.processCommand(this, req, res, formData);
        }
        catch(NamingException ne)
        {
            throw new ServletException(ne.getMessage());
        }
    }
}


public JndiCommand loadHandler(String theClassName,
                                HttpServletResponse res)
                                throws IOException
{
    JndiCommand cmd = null;
```

continued

```
       try
       {
         Class theClass = Class.forName(theClassName);
         cmd = (JndiCommand)theClass.newInstance();
       }
       catch(Exception e)
       {
         res.sendError(res.SC_NOT_IMPLEMENTED,
                          e.getMessage());
       }

       return cmd;
     }

  public String getContextFactory()
  {
    return contextFactory;
  }

  public String getURL()
  {
    return theURL;
  }

  public String getSearchbase()
  {
    return theSearchbase;
  }
}
```

The command structure for JndiSessionServlet needs a general mechanism for getting JNDI-specific initialization parameters from JndiSessionServlet. These initial JNDI parameters include:

- The context initial factory (contextFactory).
- The URL to the LDAP server (theURL).
- The search base (theSearchbase).

In order to solve this problem, we created an interface called IjndiSession to provide an easy interface between JndiSessionServlet and its command structure. JndiCommands will use methods in the IjndiSession interface to get JNDI-specific parameters. The IjndiSession interface is presented in Listing 11-5.

Listing 11-5   IjndiSession.java

```
public interface IjndiSession
{
  public String getContextFactory();
  public String getURL();
  public String getSearchbase();

}
```

The Command Structure

Perhaps the most interesting aspect of JndiSessionServlet lies in its command structure. The classes that make up the current command structure are shown in Figure 11-15.

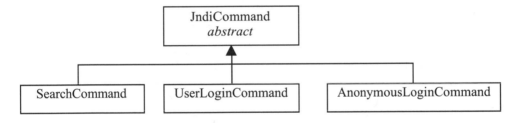

Figure 11-15   Command-structure classes

So far, only three commands have been implemented, however, others can be easily added to extend the JndiSessionServlet servlet. The JndiCommand class is an abstract class that provides the general framework that all JndiCommands must implement to support our architecture. The JndiCommand class factors out two methods which can be used by all of its derived classes:

```
isValidSession
getHostURL
```

The isValidSession method performs a test to check the validity of a session. If the current request does not have an associated session, then req.getSession(false) will return null and the isValidSession method will return false:

```
return (req.getSession(false) != null);
```

The `getHostURL` method returns the URL to the server computer by using the `getServerName` method on an `HttpServletRequest` object:

```
String serverName = req.getServerName();
return "http://" + serverName + "/";
```

The complete source for `JndiCommand` is presented in Listing 11-6.

Listing 11-6   JndiCommand

```java
import java.io.*;
import javax.servlet.*;
import javax.servlet.http.*;
import javax.naming.*;

public abstract class JndiCommand
{

    //used by some JNDI commands
  public static final String RESTRICTION =    "simple";

    //this specifies the name of the directory context
    //which is stored in the HttpSession's application
    //layer data. Every command will use this parameter
    //to either get, or put the directory context in
    //the application-layer data.
  public static final String DIR_CONTEXT =
                                    "session.dirContext";


  public boolean isValidSession(HttpServletRequest req)
  {
    return (req.getSession(false) != null);
  }

  public String getHostURL(HttpServletRequest req)
  {
    String serverName = req.getServerName();
    return "http://" + serverName + "/";
  }


  /**
   *  This is the processCommand method that is to be
   *  implemented by each command class that extends
```

```
 *    JndiCommand. So far there are three such classes:
 *    1) UserLoginCommand
 *    2) AnonymousLoginCommand
 *    3) SearchCommand
 *
 *    You may want to add your own commands. The three
 *    command classes listed above can be used as an
 *    example. Possible commands may be:
 *    1) AddNewUserCommand
 *    2) RemoveCurrentUserCommand
 *    3) EditCurrentUserCommand
 */

public abstract void   processCommand(IjndiSession jss,
                                HttpServletRequest req,
                                HttpServletResponse res,
                                java.util.Hashtable formData)
                                throws ServletException,
                                NamingException,
                                IOException;



}
```

The `processCommand` is the abstract method which must be implemented by each command class. It gets as input an instance of a class which implements the `IjndiSession` interface (in our case `JndiSessionServlet`), the `HttpServletRequest` and `HttpServletResponse` objects, and a `Hashtable` containing the form data that was POSTed to `JndiSessionServlet`. This command architecture follows a popular design pattern known as *state*.

Core Design Pattern

The state design pattern allows an object to dynamically change its behavior, depending on its current state. It is often used to get rid of unwanted switch statements and other conditional statements by representing each possible state with a new class. New states are easily added without having to recode (or recompile) the current architecture.

We use the state design pattern to get away from conditional statements. For example, we could have a bunch of if statements in `JndiSessionServlet` to determine which command to load for each request:

```
String theClassName[] = (String[])formData.get(theCommandHandler);
String command_handler = theClassName[0];
if(command_handler.equals("LoginCommand");
{
    JndiCommand cmd = loadHandler("LoginCommand");
}
else if(command_handler.equals("SearchCommand");
{
    JndiCommand cmd = loadHandler("SearchCommand");
}
...
```

This kind of command processor is frowned upon in the OO world and as such is not the recommended approach. It tightly couples the command structure to the JndiSessionServlet servlet. Adding new functionality to the servlet requires the developer to also add more conditional statements to JndiSessionServlet. By dynamically loading a command, which extends JndiCommand, JndiSessionServlet is able to get away from the unwanted conditional statements. Adding a new command can be summarized in the following steps:

1. Make a new class and derive it from JndiCommand.
2. Define the processCommand method with an identical signature to the processCommand in the abstract JndiCommand class.
3. Compile your new command class.

We have provided an implementation for three JndiCommand classes:

UserLoginCommand

AnonymousLoginCommand

SearchCommand

The LoginCommand classes provide a mechanism for logging into an LDAP-speaking directory server. The SearchCommand provides functionality that allows you to search a directory server. These command classes are dynamically loaded by JndiSessionServlet. The next section will describe how JndiSessionServlet loads commands when given a request. Then, we describe the UserLoginCommand, AnonymousLoginCommand, and SearchCommand classes in detail.

Determining Commands

JndiSessionServlet depends on data in the request to determine which command to load to handle the next request. It looks for a command_class/classname pair in the form data to determine the name of the class to load. For example, the `Login.html` file contains a hidden input type defined as

```
<INPUT TYPE=hidden NAME=command_class value="UserLoginCommand">
```

to tell `JndiSessionServlet` which class should be loaded to handle this request (in this case `UserLoginCommand`). If a client requests a command class which does not exist, then `JndiSessionServlet` will complain, saying that this command is not yet supported. For example, if the hidden input type in `Login.html` contained

```
value="Foo"
```

instead of

```
value="UserLoginCommand" //an existing login command
```

then `JndiSessionServlet` would send a response notifying you that this functionality is not implemented (see Figure 11-16).

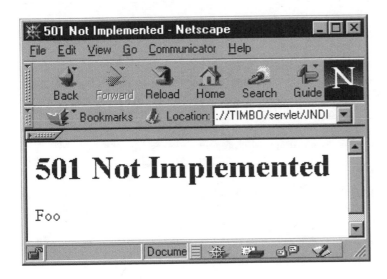

Figure 11-16   Requesting for a command which does not have an associated command class.

UserLoginCommand and AnonymousLoginCommand

The `UserLoginCommand` and `AnonymousLoginCommand` classes derive from `JndiCommand` and provide a mechanism to log into the directory server. To see how this command structure works, take a look at the associated HTML file (`Login.html`). Figure 11-10 showed the FORM used to POST data for a login request.

The *user login* and *anonymous login* buttons are used to submit login requests to JndiSessionServlet. Filling out the user_name and password fields and pressing the *user login* button would create an interaction similar to the one shown in Figure 11-17.

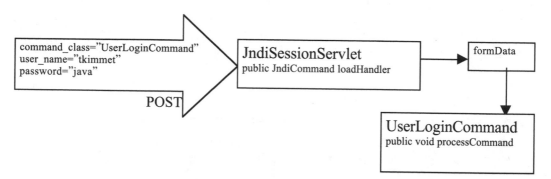

Figure 11-17   The result of a user login request.

JndiSessionServlet gets the request and determines which class to load (UserLoginCommand.class) by looking for the value assigned to the command_class input type. Once the UserLoginCommand is loaded, its processCommand method is invoked.

First the username and password are fetched from the form data. Then we check to make sure that this user does not already have a valid session:

```
If(!isValidSession(req))
```

If this user does not have a valid session, we attempt to log the user in and create a new session. In order to log a user into the LDAP server, we must do the following:

1. Create an environment.
2. Call the InitialDirContext constructor, passing it the environment.

The environment is represented as a Hashtable or, alternatively, as an instance of the Properties class. It contains the name of the JNDI context factory to use and a String representing the URL to the LDAP server. The SECURITY_AUTHENTICATION property is used to set the level of the security to use for this authentication.

```
env.put(DirContext.INITIAL_CONTEXT_FACTORY,
              ijs.getContextFactory());
env.put(DirContext.PROVIDER_URL, ijs.getURL());
env.put(DirContext.SECURITY_AUTHENTICATION,
         RESTRICTION);
```

In order to log in an nonanonymous user (a user that has a user Id and password) we must also set the SECURITY_PRINCIPAL and SECURITY_CREDENTIALS parameters in the environment.

```
env.put(DirContext.SECURITY_PRINCIPAL,
        "uid=" + usr + ", ou=People, " +
        ijs.getSearchbase());
env.put(DirContext.SECURITY_CREDENTIALS, pwd);
```

Finally, a new instance of InitialDirContext is created by calling the InitialDirContext constructor, passing it the environment:

```
return new InitialDirContext(env);
```

The complete source for the UserLoginCommand command class is presented in Listing 11-6.

Listing 11-6   UserLoginCommand.java

```java
import javax.servlet.*;
import javax.naming.directory.*;
import javax.naming.*;
import javax.servlet.http.*;
import java.util.*;
import java.io.*;

public class UserLoginCommand extends JndiCommand
{

    //this user name will be used to authenticate this
    //user and attempt to log him into the LDAP server
    //This is retrieved from the form data that is
    //passed into processCommand
  public static final String USER_NAME   = "user_name";


    //this password will be used to authenticate this
    //user and attempt to log him into the LDAP server
    //This is retrieved from the form data that is
    //passed into processCommand
  public static final String PASSWORD    =  "password";

      //redirect the user to this URL
      // if he successfully logs in
  public static final String REDIRECT_TO =
                            "jndi/search_jndi.html";
```

continued

```java
public void processCommand(IjndiSession ijs,
                           HttpServletRequest req,
                           HttpServletResponse res,
                           java.util.Hashtable formData)
                    throws ServletException,
                    NamingException,
                    IOException
{

        String username[] =
                (String[])formData.get(USER_NAME);

        String password[] =
                (String[])formData.get(PASSWORD);

        if((username.length <= 0) ||
           (password.length <= 0))
        {
          res.sendError(res.SC_BAD_REQUEST,
                        "could not find user_name "+
                        "or password in form data");
        }
        else
        {


            /**
             *   Some people may try to login several times.
             *   We don't want to create a session and
             *   connection to the ldap server for each
             *   attempt, so we check to see if there is
             *   a valid session.
             */

          if(!isValidSession(req))
          {
             HttpSession session = req.getSession(true);
             InitialDirContext idc = login(ijs, username[0],
                                          password[0], res);
             session.putValue(DIR_CONTEXT,
                        new SessionInitialDirContext(idc));
          }

           res.sendRedirect(getHostURL(req) + REDIRECT_TO);
        }
```

```
}

public InitialDirContext login(IjndiSession ijs,
                               String usr,
                               String pwd,
                               HttpServletResponse res)
                       throws NamingException,
                               IOException
{

  Hashtable env = new Hashtable(5, 0.75f);
  env.put(DirContext.INITIAL_CONTEXT_FACTORY,
          ijs.getContextFactory());
  env.put(DirContext.PROVIDER_URL, ijs.getURL());
  env.put(DirContext.SECURITY_AUTHENTICATION,
          RESTRICTION);
  env.put(DirContext.SECURITY_PRINCIPAL,
          "uid=" + usr + ", ou=People, " +
          ijs.getSearchbase());
  env.put(DirContext.SECURITY_CREDENTIALS, pwd);

  try
  {
    return new InitialDirContext(env);
  }
  catch(Exception e)
  {
    e.printStackTrace();
    res.sendError(res.SC_BAD_REQUEST,
                  "could not log in, invalid " +
                  "username or password.");
    return null;
  }

}

}
```

After a new `InitialDirContext` is created, it is stored in a `SessionInitialDirContext` object, which is then bound to the application-layer data of the `HttpSession`.

So, what is the difference between the `UserLoginCommand` class the `AnonymousLoginCommand` class? We could have put logic into a single class to determine the login type:

```
if(login is "user login")
      get the username and password
      log the user in
else //anonymous login
      log the user in as anonymous
```

Instead (keeping the state design pattern in mind) we factor out two classes—
`UserLoginCommand` and `AnonymousLoginCommand`—to handle each case
separately, thus making the code much more readable and weeding out those ugly
conditional statements that are frowned upon by the OO community. The main difference between a user login and an anonymous user login is that a user is required
to supply a username and password. This also changes the login method (for
user and anonymous), because we must set up the environment differently
before attempting to log into the LDAP server. The complete source for the
`AnonymousLoginCommand` class is presented in Listing 11-7.

Listing 11-7   AnonymousLoginCommand

```
import javax.servlet.*;
import javax.naming.directory.*;
import javax.naming.*;
import javax.servlet.http.*;
import java.util.*;
import java.io.*;


public class AnonymousLoginCommand extends JndiCommand
{

    //redirect the user to this URL
    //if he successfully logs in
  public static final String REDIRECT_TO =
                              "jndi/search_jndi.html";

  public void processCommand(IjndiSession ijs,
                      HttpServletRequest req,
                      HttpServletResponse res,
                      java.util.Hashtable formData)
                      throws ServletException,
                      NamingException,
                      IOException
    {
        if(!isValidSession(req))
        {
          InitialDirContext idc = login(ijs, res);
          HttpSession session = req.getSession(true);
```

```
            session.putValue(DIR_CONTEXT,
                        new SessionInitialDirContext(idc));
        }

      res.sendRedirect(getHostURL(req) + REDIRECT_TO);


  }

  public InitialDirContext login(IjndiSession ijs,
                                  HttpServletResponse res)
                                  throws NamingException,
                                  IOException
  {
    Hashtable env = new Hashtable(5, 0.75f);
    env.put(Context.INITIAL_CONTEXT_FACTORY,
                        ijs.getContextFactory());
    env.put(Context.PROVIDER_URL, ijs.getURL());
    env.put(Context.SECURITY_AUTHENTICATION, RESTRICTION);

    try
    {
      return new InitialDirContext(env);
    }
    catch(Exception e)
    {
      e.printStackTrace();
      res.sendError(res.SC_BAD_REQUEST,
                      "could not log you in " +
                      "please file an error report " +
                      "to the system administrator.");
      return null;
    }
  }
}
```

The `SessionInitialDirContext` class implements the `HttpSession BindingListener` interface so that it can be notified when an `HttpSession BindingEvent` occurs. It is mainly interested when the `InitialDirContext` is unbound from the application layer, in which case the handle to the `InitialDirContext` can be nullified to allow the garbage collector to reclaim its resources. The source for the `SessionInitialDirContext` class is presented in Listing 11-8.

Listing 11-8   SessionInitialDirContext

```
import javax.naming.directory.*;
import javax.naming.*;
import javax.servlet.http.*;

public class SessionInitialDirContext extends InitialDirContext
          implements HttpSessionBindingListener
{
  private InitialDirContext theDirContext;

  public SessionInitialDirContext(InitialDirContext dirContext)
          throws NamingException
  {
    theDirContext = dirContext;
  }

  public InitialDirContext getInitialDirContext()
  {
    return theDirContext;
  }

  public void valueBound(HttpSessionBindingEvent hsbe)
  {
    //do nothing for now
  }

  public void valueUnbound(HttpSessionBindingEvent hsbe)
  {
    theDirContext = null;   //nullify this handle
  }
}
```

SearchCommand

The SearchCommand class provides the needed functionality to search the directory tree given a root to start the search from (o=foobar.com). Its processCommand method uses the following logic:

```
if(the session is valid)
      perform the search;
  else(redirect to jndi/invalid_session.html)
```

A client who submits a search request, but has an expired session, is redirected to a page which has a link to the login page, as shown in Figure 11-18.

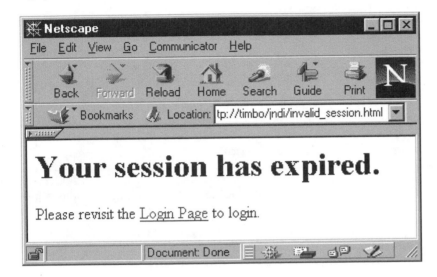

Figure 11-18 Performing a search with an invalid session.

Figure 11-11 shows the form that is used to search the directory tree. The processCommand method will look for the following parameters in the request:

```
search_attribute
attribute_value
[attribute, attribute, ...]
```

As an example, consider the FORM in Figure 11-11, which would POST the following form data to JndiSessionServlet:

```
search_attribute="cn"
attribute_value="C*"
attribute="mail"
attribute="telephonenumber"
attribute="ou"
attribute="cn"
```

The search_attribute and attribute_value parameters are used as input to the doSearch method. In this case, we would search for all people having a common name (cn) starting with the letter c:

```
cn="c*"
```

The doSearch method also allows you to ask for what you expect back from the search results by specifying multiple attribute names in the request. The `search_jndi.html` file has multiple hidden input types that are used to specify the attribute names:

```
<INPUT TYPE=hidden NAME=attribute value="mail">
<INPUT TYPE=hidden NAME=attribute value="telephonenumber">
<INPUT TYPE=hidden NAME=attribute value="ou">
<INPUT TYPE=hidden NAME=attribute value="cn">
```

Core Note

You will not always get everything you ask for in the search results. For example, if you are logged in as an anonymous user, you may not have access to the telephonenumber attribute, even though you requested it.

We could have also specified the following attributes in addition to those just listed:

```
<INPUT TYPE=hidden NAME=attribute value="sn">
<INPUT TYPE=hidden NAME=attribute value="uid">
<INPUT TYPE=hidden NAME=attribute value="userpassword">
```

Parsing these from the request is straight forward:

```
attrs = (String[])formData.get("attribute");
```

The `doSearch` method takes the following arguments:

searchbase	A place in the directory tree to start the search
idc	The InitialDirContext (stored in the application layer)
theCriteria	The criteria to be used in the search (i.e. cn="c*")
attrs	An array of values to be returned as a result of the search (i.e., "mail," "telephonenumber," "ou," "cn")

The `doSearch` method will perform a search beginning at the searchbase. In our case the searchbase is o=foobar.com, the root of the directory tree (see Figure 11-9). `SearchControls` (a class in the JNDI API) is used to specify a set of controls to be used in the search:

```
SearchControls srch_controls = new SearchControls();
srch_controls.setSearchScope(
                        SearchControls.SUBTREE_SCOPE);
srch_controls.setReturningAttributes(attrs);
```

First, we set the search scope to the SUBTREE_SCOPE, which will cause the LDAP server to search the entire tree, starting at the given root. The `setReturningAttributes` method allows you to specify what attributes to return as a result of the search. The `doSearch` method returns a `NamingEnumeration` which contains the results from the search. The `makeTable` method is used to loop through the search results and create a set of HTML tables reflecting these results. Finally, the `sendResponse` method in the `SearchCommand` class is invoked to send the search results to the client.

Figures 11-12 and 11-13 show the results from a user and an anonymous search. Notice that these searches produce different results, based on the login type (anonymous or user). These rules are enforced at the database level (using ACIs), not by the `SearchCommand`. Listing 11-9 shows the complete source for `SearchCommand.java`.

Listing 11-9   SearchCommand.java

```
import javax.servlet.*;
import javax.naming.directory.*;
import javax.naming.*;
import javax.servlet.http.*;
import java.util.*;
import java.io.*;

public class SearchCommand extends JndiCommand
{

    //a user who attempts to search with
    //an invalid session will be redirected
    //to this path on the server
    public static final String REDIRECT_TO =
                        "jndi/invalid_session.html";

    //the attribute (i.e. "cn", "mail", "ou")
    //this is retrieved from the form data that is
    //passed into processCommand
    public static final String ATTRIBUTE =
                        "search_attribute";

    //the attribute value
    //(i.e. "cn", "mail", "telephonenumber")
    //this is retrieved from the form data that is
    //passed into processCommand
    public static final String VALUE =
                        "attribute_value";

    public void processCommand(IjndiSession ijs,
                        HttpServletRequest req,
                        HttpServletResponse res,
```

continued

```
                               java.util.Hashtable formData)
                               throws ServletException,
                               NamingException,
                               IOException
        {

          synchronized(req)
          {
            HttpSession session = req.getSession(false);

            if(isValidSession(req))
            {
              String att[] = (String[])formData.get(ATTRIBUTE);
              String val[] = (String[])formData.get(VALUE);
              String theCriteria = att[0] + "=" + val[0];

              SessionInitialDirContext sidc =
                    (SessionInitialDirContext)
                    session.getValue(DIR_CONTEXT);

              InitialDirContext idc =
                    sidc.getInitialDirContext();

              String searchbase = ijs.getSearchbase();

              String attrs[];

              if((String[])formData.get("attribute") != null)
              {
                attrs = (String[])formData.get("attribute");
              }
              else //specify some defaults
              {
                attrs = new String[4];
                attrs[0] = "cn";
                attrs[1] = "ou";
                attrs[2] = "uid";
                attrs[3] = "mail";
              }

              NamingEnumeration ne =
                    doSearch(searchbase, idc, theCriteria, attrs);
              StringBuffer table = makeTable(ne);
              sendResponse(req, res, table);

            }
            else
```

```
      {
        res.sendRedirect(getHostURL(req) + REDIRECT_TO);
      }
    }
  }


public synchronized NamingEnumeration
              doSearch(String searchbase,
                       DirContext context,
                       String theCriteria,
                       String attrs[])
                       throws NamingException
{
  SearchControls srch_controls = new SearchControls();
  srch_controls.setSearchScope(
                         SearchControls.SUBTREE_SCOPE);

    /**
     *  Note: just because you request these attributes
     *  does NOT mean that you will get every one of
     *  them back! That depends on what ACIs were set
     *  in the database. You may not have access to all
     *  of them.
     */

  srch_controls.setReturningAttributes(attrs);
  String search_criteria = "(" + theCriteria + ")";
  NamingEnumeration ne;
  ne = context.search(searchbase,
                       search_criteria,
                       srch_controls);
  return ne;
}


public StringBuffer makeTable(NamingEnumeration ne)
                              throws NamingException
{
  StringBuffer tbl = new StringBuffer();

  if(ne != null)
  {
   while(ne.hasMore())
   {
     SearchResult sr = (SearchResult)ne.next();
```

```
        Attributes attribs = (Attributes)sr.getAttributes();
        tbl.append("<table bgcolor=\"FFFF00\" border=0>");

        for(Enumeration e = attribs.getIDs();
                        e.hasMoreElements();)
        {
          String id = (String)e.nextElement();
          NamingEnumeration a_ne;

          for(a_ne = attribs.get(id).getAll();
                              a_ne.hasMore();)
          {
            tbl.append("<TR><TD>");
            tbl.append(id);
            tbl.append(" <TD>");
            tbl.append(a_ne.next().toString());
            tbl.append("</TR>");
          }
        }
          tbl.append("</table><P>");
      }
    }
    return tbl;
  }


  public void sendResponse(HttpServletRequest req,
                           HttpServletResponse res,
                           StringBuffer table)
                           throws IOException
  {
    res.setContentType("text/html");
    PrintWriter pw = res.getWriter();
    pw.println("<html><body>");
    pw.println("<h1>Search Results</h1>");
    pw.println(table.toString());
    pw.println("</body></html>");
    pw.close();
  }
}
```

In order to run this servlet you will need to grab the JNDI API from Sun (visit www.java.sun.com/jndi) and set your classpath variable so the Java Web Server can locate the needed JNDI classes. For more on using extension classes with the Java Web Server, see Chapter 4, "Administrating the Java Web Server."

Summary

In this chapter we covered the core classes involved in session management. We showed you how the cookie class is used as a mechanism for passing unique session Ids between a client and the Java Web Server. We focused on the event-driven architecture used by the Java Web Server to manage session-specific events and on the way in which these events can communicate with Java objects stored in the application layer of the `HttpSession`. Finally, in a more advanced servlet, we showed how JNDI can be paired with the Java Web Server to produce a Web-based directory server. Up to this point, we've been coding servlets which are used for a specific purpose. As a servlet developer, you should be thinking more on the lines of reusable components, which can be tested separately and later combined to form a complete application. This next chapter will focus on the component architecture supported by the Java Web Server.

SERVLET BEANS

Chapter 12

U p to this point you've programmed some industrial-strength servlets, several consisting of multiple source files. These servlets have focused on filling a specific function in the Web server. This approach answers specific needs but lacks the flexibility of a generic solution.

Now the time has come to produce components, or *software nuggets,* that group together related code into one customizable module. As an example, consider a JDBCServlet that utilizes the Java Database Connectivity (JDBC) API to provide access to a database. For this servlet some properties are necessary: the JDBC URL, the logon name and password required for the connection, and the name of the JDBC driver implementation class.

Forcing a user to completely customize this servlet, using the servlet configuration panel, for every Java Web Server installation would be like digging a trench with a dinner spoon. (The servlet configuration panel was covered in Chapter 4, "Administrating the Java Web Server.") A component architecture provides a way to preconfigure the module before it is distributed.

Of course, you could do the same thing by providing hard-coded defaults. But changing those defaults would require a recompile of the source code (hardly a flexible alternative!).

No, what's required is a way to capture the state of a component and distribute this frozen state along with the module's code. Fortunately, JavaSoft has provided an API called Java Beans that handles all of this work transparently for you. The Java Beans architecture provides a set of guidelines and utility classes for producing Java-based components. These guidelines and their application to the Java Web Server is the focus of this chapter.

Your exploration begins with a tour of various design patterns exploited by Java Beans, followed by a thorough explanation of how servlets can be made into Beans. Finally, you'll discover how to bundle your servlets in neat, byte-sized (excuse the pun!) packages called JAR (Java Archive) files.

Understanding the Java Beans Architecture

When Java hit the software development scene in 1995, there was no standardized method of creating components. Microsoft, however, had a component model based on their Component Object Model (COM) specifications, which made the task of assembling programs simpler. When Microsoft licensed Java from Sun Microsystems in 1996, they immediately implemented COM-based components written in Java.

There was a problem with using COM-based components—they only worked on operating systems supporting COM. With one clever stroke, Microsoft tied anyone who wrote for their component model onto the Windows platform!

To keep Java (and components written in Java) cross-platform, Sun produced a rivaling specification called "the JavaBeans component model." Beans, as these components are called, are 100% Pure Java modules that work on any Java virtual machine (not just those running Windows).

Beans, unlike ActiveX controls (which is yet *another* name for COM components), are Java classes that follow a short list of requirements:

- They support JDK 1.1 Serialization.
- They utilize the get/set method-naming convention.

That's all folks! Serialization is a JDK 1.1 feature that allows a class's state to be captured to an output stream. You can make a Java class serializable by implementing the `java.io.Serializable` interface. The get/set method-naming convention is a fancy way of saying that any method starting with the three letters 'g', 'e', and 't' is expected to return a property, and any method starting with 's', 'e', and 't' is expected to set a property. Properties are a formal name for accessible (read, configurable) member variables. So, if a Bean named `FooBar` had a String property called `Name`, and it wanted to make that property accessible to other components, `FooBar` would need two methods like those shown in Listing 12-1.

Listing 12-1   FooBar Bean

```
class FooBar implements java.io.Serializable
{
  private String m_name;

  public String getName ()
  {
    return m_name;
  }

  public void setName (String newname)
  {
    m_name = newname;
  }
}
```

Now, any Beans-aware program (such a Java GUI interface builder) can use Java introspection to find out what properties can be changed for class `FooBar` by looking at the method signatures defined by the class. A user of the GUI interface builder can specify initial values for these properties, and this configured state can be saved and reloaded on demand.

The saving and loading of state for JavaBeans is handled by Java Serialization. Did you notice that the `FooBar` class implements the `Serializable` interface? It could have implemented the `java.io.Externalizable` interface just as easily.

Core Note

The `Externalizable` *and* `Serializable` *interfaces are fully explained in* Core Java *by Cay Horstmann and Gary Cornell. If you want to know more about how Java Serialization works, check this book out.*

The code in Listing 12-2 illustrates Serialization in a small example. The program stores a `FooBar` instance in a file named `FooBar.ser` by using an `ObjectOutputStream`:

Listing 12-2   Serializing the `FooBar` object to disk

```java
import java.io.*;

public class SerializationTest
{
  public static void main (String[] args)
  {
    FooBar theInstance = new FooBar();
    theInstance.setName("Tim");

    try
    {
      FileOutputStream fos =
        .new FileOutputStream("FooBar.ser");
      ObjectOutputStream oos = new ObjectOutputStream(fos);
      oos.writeObject(theInstance);
      oos.close();
    }
    catch(IOException ioe)
    {
      ioe.printStackTrace();
    }
  }
}
```

If theInstance had not been a Serializable object, when you attempted to flatten it through a call to an `ObjectOutputStream`'s `writeObject` method you'd be handed a `java.io.NotSerializableException` exception. Similarly, you can raise theInstance from its file-system grave by using an `ObjectInputStream` and making a call to its `readObject` method, as shown in Listing 12-3.

Listing 12-3   Retrieving theInstance from the file system

```java
import java.io.*;

public class DeSerializationTest
{
  public static void main (String[] args)
  {
    FileInputStream fis = null;
    ObjectInputStream ois = null;

    try
```

```
   {
     fis = new FileInputStream("Foo.ser");
     ois = new ObjectInputStream(fis);
     FooBar theInstance = (FooBar)ois.readObject();
     System.out.println("theInstance.name= " +
     theInstance.getName());
   }
   catch(IOException ioe)
   {
     ioe.printStackTrace();
   }
   catch(ClassNotFoundException cnfe)
   {
     cnfe.printStackTrace();
   }
 }
}
```

Of course, class isn't Serializable if one of its member variables isn't Serializable. Some important Java classes (`java.lang.Thread`, `java.io.File`, `java.sql.Statement`, etc.) aren't Serializable objects. The only way to make a class using these troublemakers Serializable is to mark them as *transient* objects. Transient objects are ignored during the Serialization process.

Core Note

There are some caveats for using the transient keyword on a member variable. When an object is deserialized, these variables will be set to `null`*. You'll need to override the* `readObject` *method in your class so that you can rebuild these variables. Check out* Core Java *for more information.*

Whew! After all that, it should be clear that a JavaBean is a component. Then what the heck is a ServletBean?

Server-Side JavaBeans = ServletBeans

Just as the formula says, ServletBeans are JavaBeans that run on the server (as opposed to the client). In more precise language, ServletBeans are Serializable objects that implement the `javax.servlet.Servlet` interface. If you've already read Chapter 5 "Generic Servlets," you know that the most common way to write a servlet is to derive it from the `javax.servlet.GenericServlet` class or one of its children (such as `javax.servlet.http.HttpServlet`).

So here's a little secret: all servlets deriving from the `GenericServlet` class are already ServletBeans. All that is left for you to do is to define your properties (using the get/set method-naming convention) and handle the packaging.

Let's see this in action with a little ServletBean example.

Your First ServletBean

If you've read any of the servlet programming chapters so far, you know that servlets provide dynamic control of Web content. You can configure a servlet to change its background color, the content of the generated page, or anything else—the possibilities are endless. With a ServletBean, configuration becomes a snap compared to regular servlets. Figure 12-1 shows a Web page generated by the `CoreBeanServlet`.

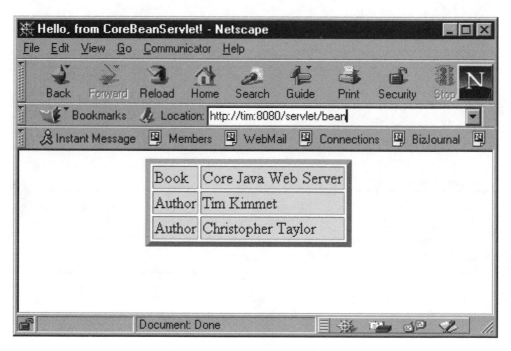

Figure 12-1   The Web page generated by CoreBeanServlet.

The data tabulated in Figure 12-1 could be the result of a database search. That is, the `CoreBeanServlet` used JDBC or some other database interface to retrieve data with a query and present the data using HTML. This servlet would be flexible if you could dynamically change the appearance of the Web page through some property at run time, instead of having to manipulate and recompile the source code for the servlet. Some standard content changes are:

- Change the title of the Web page.
- Change the background color of the Web page.
- Change the background color of the HTML table.
- Change the border of the HTML table.

You could use the `ServletConfig` to grab configuration parameters to initialize `CoreBeanServlet`, just as you've seen in past chapters:

```
public void init(ServletConfig config) throws ServletException
{
    super.init(config);

    html_bgcolor   = config.getInitParameter("html_bgcolor");
    html_title     = config.getInitParameter("html_title");
    table_bgcolor  = config.getInitParameter("table_bgcolor");
    table_border   = config.getInitParameter("table_border");
    ...

}
```

Then you could use the admin tool to configure the parameters, as shown in Figure 12-2:

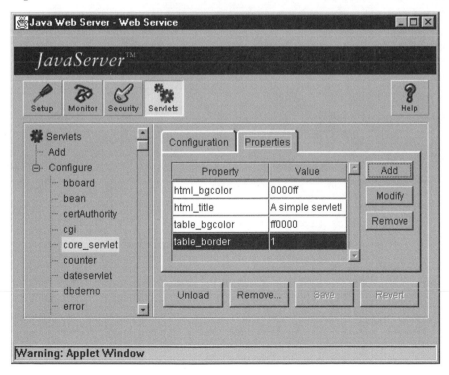

Figure 12-2   Using the admin tool to configure CoreBeanServlet.

Configuring a servlet through the `ServletConfig` interface has two important drawbacks:

- There is no automatic mapping between properties in the servlet and the properties shown in the configuration dialog (so that anyone who uses the servlet must remember the names of the properties).

- You must restart the servlet before changes take effect.

Although you could get past the first hurdle by supplying documentation with your servlet, the second hurdle is unacceptable.

ServletBeans, on the other hand, don't require a restart when properties are changed. The `CoreBeanServlet` servlet does not introduce any new servlet API features that we haven't covered up to this point—it uses the get/set method-naming convention and implements the `Serializable` interface automatically by sub-classing the `javax.servlet.http.HttpServlet` class (as discussed in the previous section). The complete source for `CoreBeanServlet` is presented in Listing 12-4.

Listing 12-4   CoreBeanServlet

```
import javax.servlet.*;
import java.io.*;
import javax.servlet.http.*;
public class CoreBeanServlet extends HttpServlet
{

  private String html_title    = "Hello, from CoreBeanServlet!";
  private String html_bgcolor  = "ffffff";

  private String table_bgcolor = "ffff55";
  private String table_border  = "5";


  public void doGet(HttpServletRequest req,
                    HttpServletResponse res)
                         throws ServletException, IOException
  {
    res.setContentType("text/html");

    PrintWriter pw = res.getWriter();

    pw.println("<html>");
    pw.print  ("<head><title>");
```

```
pw.print   (html_title);
pw.println("</title></head>");
pw.print   ("<body bgcolor=\"");
pw.print   (html_bgcolor);
pw.println("\">");

//an HTML table
pw.println("<CENTER>");
pw.print   ("<table bgcolor=\"");
pw.print   (table_bgcolor);
pw.print   ("\"");
pw.print   (" border=\"");
pw.print   (table_border);
pw.println("\">");
pw.println("<TR>");
pw.println("<TD>Book</TD>");
pw.println("<TD>Core Java Web Server</TD>");
pw.println("</TR>");
pw.println("<TR>");
pw.println("<TD>Author</TD>");
pw.println("<TD>Tim Kimmet</TD>");
pw.println("</TR>");
pw.println("<TR>");
pw.println("<TD>Author</TD>");
pw.println("<TD>Christopher Taylor</TD>");
pw.println("</TR>");
pw.println("</table>");
pw.println("</CENTER>");

pw.println("</body>");
pw.println("</html>");

pw.close();

}

public String getHtml_title()
{
   return html_title;
}

public void setHtml_title(String aTitle)
{
   this.html_title = aTitle;
}

public String getHtml_bgcolor()
```

continued

```
    {
        return html_bgcolor;
    }

    public void setHtml_bgcolor(String aColor)
    {
        this.html_bgcolor = aColor;
    }

    public String getTable_bgcolor()
    {
        return table_bgcolor;
    }

    public void setTable_bgcolor(String aColor)
    {
        this.table_bgcolor = aColor;
    }

    public String getTable_border()
    {
        return table_border;
    }

    public void setTable_border(String aBorderSize)
    {
        this.table_border = aBorderSize;
    }
}
```

Notice that CoreBeanServlet does not make use of the ServletConfig interface, so how is it able to retrieve its configuration parameters? As we said before, JavaBeans are typically configured with GUI interface builders that utilize Java introspection to retrieve a Bean's properties. Since ServletBeans aren't GUI components, using a GUI interface builder may not make sense, but the same principles apply. Furthermore, the fact that JavaBeans are usually associated with graphical applications is merely a historical artifact of their beginnings. GUI builders such as the BeanBox (it comes with the JavaSoft Beans Development Kit) can be used to configure ServletBeans. In a little while you'll learn how to use the BeanBox to configure your servlets.

Of course there is that little matter of installing your ServletBean components...

Packaging Your Beans

Before you can make use of ServletBeans, you'll need to know how to package them into a JAR (Java Archive) file. The Java Developer's Kit comes with a utility conveniently named `jar` for packaging a set of classes into a JAR file. This section covers only the basic features of the `jar` utility required for successfully packaging your ServletBeans. In the next section you'll use the JAR file we create in this one to configure the `CoreBeanServlet` with the Java Web Server's servlet configuration panel.

The syntax of the `jar` utility should feel familiar to `tar` aficionados, as the two programs share the same command-line parameters (`tar` is short for <u>t</u>ape <u>ar</u>chive). To place the `CoreBeanServlet` Bean into a JAR file, invoke the `jar` utility and use the `cvf` option to create a new JAR file that contains the `CoreBeanServlet` class:

```
jar cvf bean.jar CoreBeanServlet.class
```

Similarly, if you want to archive a group of files, you can specify the wildcard character to add all of them at once:

```
jar cvf bean.jar *.class
```

Or, you can specify a directory:

```
jar cvf bean.jar directory_name
```

Now you can use the servlet configuration panel to add the CoreBeanServlet to the current list of servlets in the usual way (check out Chapter 4 for more details). This time, however, you'll need to check Yes to specify that this servlet entry is a ServletBean and add its JAR file (`bean.jar` in this case) to the text box. as shown in Figure 12-3.

If you click on the Add button in the servlet configuration panel, the Java Web Server will add the `CoreBeanServlet` to the list of servlets and display the `Configuration` and `Properties` tabs. Click on the `properties` tab, and you should see a table similar to the one shown in Figure 12-4.

Notice that the unlike a regular servlet, the servlet configuration panel automagically knows every property advertised by the `CoreBeanServlet`. How did the magic work? Recall the definition of the four data fields in the `CoreBeanServlet` class:

```
private String html_title    = "Hello, from CoreBeanServlet!";
private String html_bgcolor  = "ffffff";
private String table_bgcolor = "ffff55";
private String table_border  = "5";
```

and the four corresponding accessor methods:

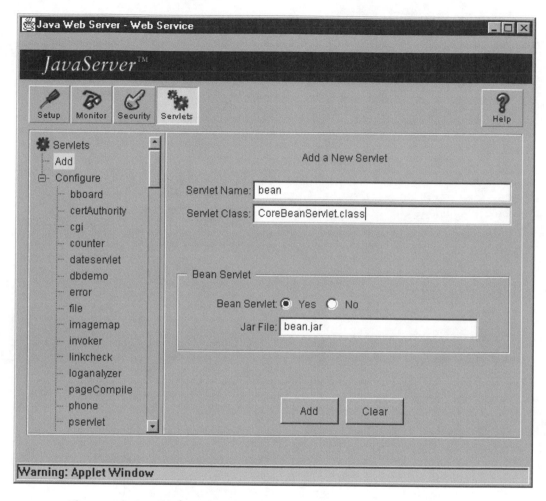

Figure 12-3   Configuring CoreBeanServlet with the Java Web Server's servlet configuration panel.

```
public String getHtml_title()
{...}
public String getHtml_bgcolor()
{...}
public String getTable_bgcolor()
{...}
public String getTable_border()
{...}
```

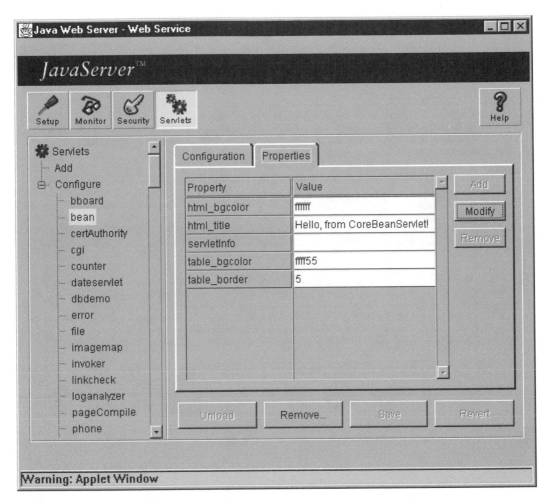

Figure 12-4   Changing the CoreBeanServlet's properties.

Just like a GUI interface builder, the servlet configuration panel can figure out through introspection which properties are available. Once it knows the names and the types returned by all of the available public methods, gaining access to the properties offered by `CoreBeanServlet` is only a method call away. This architecture is far superior to the standard method of configuring servlets (using `ServletConfig`) because it solves the two problems mentioned earlier:

- You aren't required to memorize the names of a ServletBean's properties, as they will be automatically provided for you in the servlet configuration panel.

- Any property changes at run time take effect immediately, without requiring a restart of the servlet.

Now, activate the `CoreBeanServlet`, just as you would any other servlet. Figure 12-5 shows `CoreBeanServlet` in action.

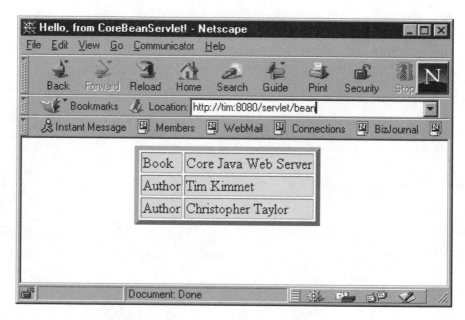

Book	Core Java Web Server
Author	Tim Kimmet
Author	Christopher Taylor

Figure 12-5   CoreBeanServlet in action.

A ServletBean added through a JAR file is considered an *installed* ServletBean.

Core Alert

Just as servlets are stored in a subdirectory named `servlets`*, ServletBeans are stored in a subdirectory named* `servletbeans`*. If you want the dynamic loading features that are enjoyed by servlets (the Java Web Server will reload a servlet's class file if it's been updated), you must not put your ServletBean JAR files into the system* `classpath`*.*

Figure 12-6 shows the results of changes made to the `CoreBeanServlet`.

If you take a look at the `servletbeans` directory, you will notice that the Java Web Server saved the new configuration for the `CoreBeanServlet` in a file called `bean.ser`. This file holds a serialized instance of a CoreBeanServlet, containing the newly configured version of the `CoreBeanServlet`, and takes precedence over the uninitialized class file in the `bean.jar` file.

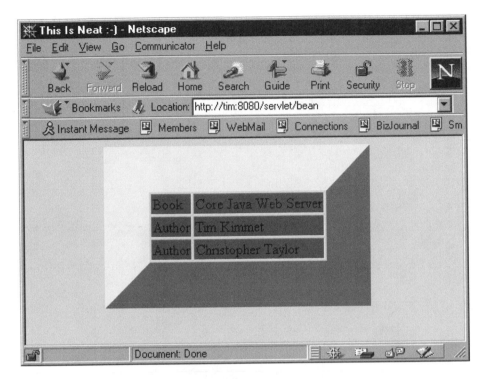

Figure 12-6 Watching those changes in action!

Serialized files containing the state of a servlet bean that are dropped into the `servletbeans` directory are classified as *uninstalled* files (in comparison to *installed* files in JAR format), as discussed below.

Installed versus Uninstalled Files

Once you've packaged your ServletBean's class file into a JAR file and added it to the list of servlets using the servlet configuration panel, it is classified as an *installed* ServletBean. As mentioned earlier, an *uninstalled* ServletBean lives outside of a JAR file (for example, a .class or .ser file). The major difference here is that you cannot use the Java Web Server to configure parameters of uninstalled files, since they do not live in a JAR file, and thus the servlet configuration panel cannot use introspection to recognize properties advertised by the servlet's class file.

Servlet Bean Configuration with the BeanBox

Here is the brief tutorial we promised on how to configure your ServletBeans with the Beans Development Kit BeanBox. Since a ServletBean is a JavaBean, you aren't forced to use the Java Web Server to configure it. Instead, you have a whole host of choices, ranging from free tools like the BeanBox to commercial products like Sun Microsystem's Java Workshop. This is just one more added feature you get by using ServletBeans, making it particularly attractive to your customers not using the Java Web Server as a regular Web server.

The BeanBox is used to drag JavaBeans on a form and manipulate their properties. In order to use it to configure ServletBeans you'll need to add a few sections to a *manifest* file. This special file, created automatically by the `jar` utility, contains a listing of all of the files available in the JAR. It also contains other information about the files, such as boolean flags hinting that this class should be treated as a JavaBean and security information that makes the file tamperproof. You can extract the manifest file by using the `xf` option with the `jar` utility:

```
jar xf bean.jar META-INF
```

This will create a directory called **META-INF**, which contains the **MANIFEST.MF** manifest file.

Let's have a look at the manifest file that was automatically generated by the `jar` utility:

```
Manifest-Version: 1.0

Name: CoreBeanServlet.class
Digest-Algorithms: SHA MD5
SHA-Digest: LgK/4ieq7YenIiwY/IvlaXLgtcw=
MD5-Digest: 5i7SETM9GQX3nEpyQ2jxXg==
```

This manifest file is missing the boolean flag for hinting that your servlet is a JavaBean. By specifying the `Java-Bean` tag in the manifest file, you can tag your class as a Bean. As an alternative, you can create a simple manifest file before you use the `jar` utility on your files, creating a `Java-Bean` tag for each Bean in the JAR. In the case of the `CoreBeanServlet`, create a `beans.mf` file and tag the `CoreBeanServlet.class` as a Bean by including the `Java-Bean` tag and setting it to `True`:

```
Name: CoreBeanServlet.class
Java-Bean: True
```

Now you can create the JAR file in the usual way, but this time specify the m option, which tells the `jar` utility to use your manifest file instead of generating a new one:

```
jar cfm CoreBeanServlet.jar CoreBeanServlet.mf CoreBeanServlet.class
```

If you extract the `manifest.mf` file from the `CoreBeansServlet.jar` file and look at the results, you'll see that it added the `Java-Bean` tag:

```
Manifest-Version: 1.0

Name: CoreBeanServlet.class
Java-Bean: True
Digest-Algorithms: SHA MD5
SHA-Digest: LgK/4ieq7YenIiwY/IvlaXLgtcw=
MD5-Digest: 5i7SETM9GQX3nEpyQ2jxXg==
```

The `jar` utility created a `manifest.mf` file that looks very similar to the one shown earlier, but this time it included the `Java-Bean: True` tag that you specified in the `CoreBeanServlet.mf` file. Now, your servlet is ready for the BeanBox. If you downloaded and installed the Beans Development Kit (BDK), you will find a subdirectory named `jars` under its root directory (typically `c:\bdk` by default on Windows). Copy the `CoreBeansServlet.jar` JAR file to the `jars` directory—the BeanBox looks in the `jars` directory for automatically loading beans into the BeanBox environment when the BeanBox is started.

Using the BeanBox

The BDK is packaged with some batch files (`run.sh` for UNIX and `run.bat` for Windows) meant for running the BeanBox. These batch files are located in the `beanbox` subdirectory. These batch files will not work automatically with your ServletBeans, since they override the current `classpath` settings and don't include the needed servlet packages. The `run.bat` batch file packaged with the BDK sets the `classpath` and runs the BeanBox:

```
if "%OS%" == "Windows NT" setlocal
set CLASSPATH=classes
java sun.beanbox.BeanBoxFrame
```

To configure the `run.bat` file to run with your servlets, you can append the location of classes needed to by the BDK to your current classpath by using the `%CLASSPATH%` directive on Windows machines or **$CLASSPATH** on UNIX:

```
if "%OS%" == "Windows NT" setlocal
set CLASSPATH% CLASSPATH %;classes
java sun.beanbox.BeanBoxFrame
```

Configuring Your ServletBeans in the BeanBox

Now that you have fixed the BeanBox's startup script to work with your ServletBeans, and you've placed your JAR file into the `jars` directory, you can use the BeanBox to configure your own ServletBeans. Figure 12-7 shows the BeanBox in action. Notice that the CoreBeanServlet was automatically included in the list of available beans in the ToolBox.

To configure a CoreBeanServlet, click on its icon in the Toolbox and drop it onto the BeanBox's form. The BeanBox frame should look like Figure 12-7.

When you drop the CoreBeanServlet onto the BeanBox frame, the properties for CoreBeanServlet should appear on the properties sheet, similar to the one shown in Figure 12-8.

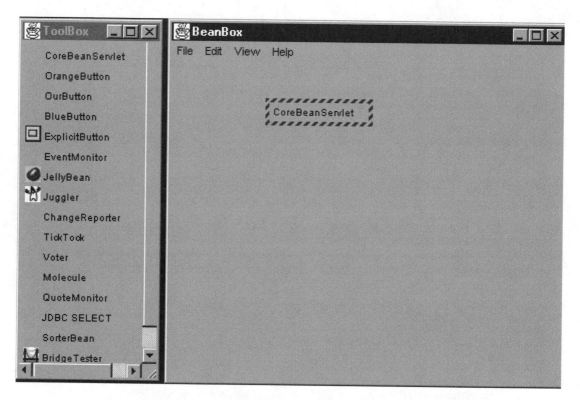

Figure 12-7   Dragging the CoreBeanServlet onto the BeanBox frame.

The BeanBox automatically displays the default settings for the `CoreBeanServlet`. You can change these settings and save them as dropped-in files in the Serialized (.ser) format, just as you did with the Java Web Server.

Figure 12-8   Configuring CoreBeanServlet's properties.

Summary

This chapter focused on the concepts you need in order to start developing ServletBeans. You were introduced to the two primary requirements for ServletBeans: Serialization and the get/set method-naming convention. Then you developed a simple ServletBean, the `CoreBeanServlet`, and you learned how to configure its properties both with the servlet configuration panel and with the BeanBox program from the JavaBeans Development Kit.

Of course, not everything about ServletBeans was covered in this chapter. ServletBeans, like JavaBeans, can be signed using cryptographic keys for security purposes. This topic is covered in Chapter 13, "Security." If you are planning to sell the components you develop, you should give that chapter a look.

Finally, ServletBeans can be accessed via a new Java Web Server technology called "Java Server Pages" (more commonly known as "JSP"). Based on their previous work on page compilation, the Java Web Server development team have really outdone themselves this time with this hot new technology, and we proudly feature it as the *almost* last (but certainly not the least) topic of *Core Java Web Server*.

GENERATING HTML WITH TEMPLATES, SERVER-SIDE INCLUDE, AND JSP

Topics in This Chapter

- Why use tools for generating HTML?

- Rolling it the old way with Server-Side Include scripts

- Separating content from appearance with Presentation Templates

- The future of content-generation: JavaServer Pages

Chapter 13

U p until now, you've been writing servlets for every bit of customized data you need to wring from the Java Web Server. While whipping together a servlet isn't a tough task, sometimes it's overkill for a particular need. For example, take the case of the standard "last modified" date placed at the bottom of a Web page: writing a `last-modified` servlet just for tracking the modification dates of accessed pages requires the servlet to be consulted on each request. As if that weren't enough, how do you get the text inserted into the right spot on the Web page without having the servlet generate the entire document?

This document-merging problem requires tools that can read an existing HTML document and extract scripting directives for on-the-fly processing. Fortunately, you won't need to write your own tools, since some that already come with the Java Web Server can give you what you want in three different ways:

- Server-Side Include files (`.shtml`)
- Presentation Template files (`.template`)
- JavaServer Pages files (`.jsp`)

But before you dive into using these tools, let's step back and ask: "Why do I need these tools at all?"

Why Do I Need These Tools at All?

We're glad you asked! What JSP, Presentation Templates, and Server-Side Include provide is a *second-level* API, meaning that each is built atop the servlet API.

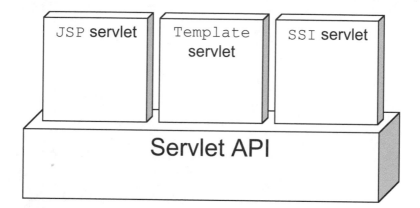

Figure 13-1   Tools built on the servlet API.

While all of these modules mix static and dynamic content, they do so in different ways. The Server-Side Include module supports the NCSA SSI scripting language, while JavaServer Pages takes server-side scripting to the next level by supporting Java code directly in HTML content. On the other hand, presentation templates provide a way to support a consistent look-and-feel across all documents in a site without forcing each to be altered for a style update.

These tools also allow nonprogrammers to build dynamic Web applications. You can take advantage of servlets in SSI and JSP documents, adding a degree of flexibility to your Web-site design. It's no surprise that other Web servers have similar server-side scripting capabilities (Netscape Server's Javascript, Microsoft IIS Active Server Pages, etc.).

Convinced? Maybe you'd like to see these tools in action first. Let's start with Server-Side Include (since it is the oldest and most widely used server-side scripting language).

Server-Side Include

Server-Side Include has been around since the early days of the NCSA Web server. Originally designed to paste documents together (working much as the #include preprocessor directive does in the "C" programming language), SSI was expanded to support several commands. Table 13-1 lists the directives and their descriptions.

Table 13-1	Server-Side Include Directives

Directive Name	Description
config	Configures how the Server-Side Include module will respond to certain requests. The config directive can change what message is returned if an error occurs during processing (the errmsg tag), the time format used when presenting dates (the timefmt tag), and how file sizes will be represented (the sizefmt tag).
include	Inserts text from another file (just like the #include directive in C). Data can be returned via URI (absolute or relative) using the virtual tag or from a file (but only with a relative physical pathname not containing "../") using the file tag.
echo	Echoes the value of an include variable (defined in Table 13-2) into the document. You specify the desired variable with the var tag.
fsize	Inserts the size of a file in either bytes or an approximate number of kilobytes/megabytes (depending on whether the config directive has specified a sizefmt tag). The file to interrogate is referred by either a URI or a relative physical pathname using the same notation as the include directive.
flastmod	Pastes the last modification date of a file (once again using the include directive's tag notation). The date format is subject to the value of the config directive's timefmt tag.
exec	Inserts the output of either a program or a CGI script into the document. Programs are invoked if the cmd tag is utilized, and CGI scripts are specified using the cgi tag. Unlike the include or the fsize directives, Server-Side Include lets you execute any program on the computer (so be careful!).

Server-Side Include directives are placed within SGML comment tags. (SGML = Standard Generalized Markup Language—see Appendix A for details.) So, if you wanted to print the last modification date of the file "foo.txt," residing in the same directory as the script file, you would write:

```
<!- #flastmod file="foo.txt" ->
```

As you can see, all directives (just like those in C) are prefixed with the pound ('#') character. In order to be processed properly, Server-Side Include directives must be placed in files ending with the extension ".shtml".

Now that you're familiar with the various SSI directives, what about a short example? Listing 13-1 has a short shtml document that displays the last modification date in the footer.

Listing 13-1   Your first shtml document

```
<html>
<body>
This is a Server-Side Include example document<br>
<i>Last Modified on <!-#echo var="LAST_MODIFIED" -></i>
</body>
</html>
```

Save the contents of the example in a file (the name "first.shtml" would be a good choice) beneath the Java Web Server's `public_html` directory. Next, open up your Web browser, connect to the server, and see the results. Your browser should look similar to the output in Figure 13-2.

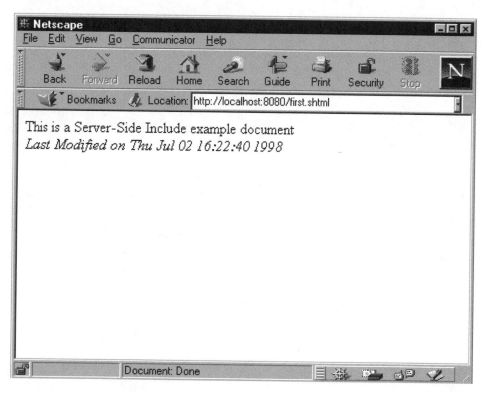

Figure 13-2   Your first shtml file.

See how you used the #echo directive in the example? The LAST_MODIFIED variable pastes in the last modification date of the document. Table 13-2 lists this and the rest of the SSI environment variables, any of which can be used with the #echo directive.

Table 13-2	SSI Environment Variables

Environment Variable	Description
DATE_GMT	The server's date represented in Greenwich Mean Time. The results of this field are subject to the timefmt tag of the config directive.
DATE_LOCAL	The server's date represented in Local Time. Just like DATE_GMT, this variable's representation depends on the option directive's timefmt tag.
DOCUMENT_NAME	The current filename.
DOCUMENT_URI	The virtual path to the current document.
LAST_MODIFIED	The time that the current document was last modified. The representation depends on the value of the option directive's timefmt tag.
QUERY_STRING_UNESCAPED	The client's query string.

Core Bug

When we were playing with Server-Side Include in the Java Web Server, we noticed that the #[directive name] must be presented directly after the open comment tag. Any white space will cause the directive to be ignored by the SSI processing engine.

While Server-Side Include scripting is important if you're moving an *existing* site to the Java Web Server, its lack of useful features makes it a poor choice for server-side programming. SSI was used primarily to change the look of a Web site by #include-ing the documents' header and footer tags. Listing 13-2 shows an example.

Listing 13-2 Using SSI to alter look-and-feel

```
[- somefile.shtml -]
<html>
<!-#include file="header.shtml"->
<b>Content is placed here</b>
<!-#include file="footer.shtml"->
</html>

[- header.shtml -]
<body bgcolor="#FFFFFF" text="#0000FF">
<img src="banner.gif">
<hr>

[- footer.shtml -]
<br><i>Page Last Modified on <!-#echo var="LAST_MODIFIED"-></i>
</body>
```

So, when `somefile.shtml` is requested, it will pull in the contents of the header and footer files and place them in the page.

Of course, if you're familiar with the way SSI works, you should see the problem already. The LAST_MODIFIED variable won't do what we've expected; instead, it will report the last modification date of the footer.shtml file, *not* the file that is including it.

As it turns out, SSI isn't that great for creating headers and footers. First of all, you have to make all of your pages .shtml files. A more difficult task is making sure that all of the documents have the right #include directives. Sounds like an administrative nightmare!

Or, you could just use Presentation Templates.

Core Note

Before moving on to Presentation Templates, you should know that the Java Web Server team added a non-standard feature to SSI: the `<servlet>` *tag. It acts like its client-side cousin: the* `<applet>` *tag. The opening* `<servlet>` *tag has several attributes: an optional name, the class name, the optional codebase, and optional initialization parameters. Furthermore, it can contain* `<param>` *child elements containing request parameters (like those used on an HTML form POST, for instance). If a servlet tag registers a name for the target servlet, it will exist beyond the confines of the page request; however, if the name is not specified, the servlet is shut down after the page is loaded. More information can be found in the on-line documentation, but you should know that the power of JSP overshadows this single dynamic feature of SSI.*

Presentation Templates

Presentation templates provide a way of cleanly separating header and footer data from the rest of a site's content. Unlike using Server-Side Include, templates add the right information regardless of the content in the source pages (no #include's required!). Templates are applied to directories of content, where subdirectories may override their parent's behavior (just as in object-oriented programming) while inheriting everything else that hasn't changed.

There are three steps to adding presentation templates to your site:

- Create the `default.template` file.
- Add the optional `default.definitions` file.
- Enable Presentation Template processing for the directory (and its child directories).

Creating the default.template File

The `default.template` file contains the header and footer information that will be injected into all Web pages. It contains regular HTML content, plus an additional HTML tag named subst that's used for merging data over from the source HTML file. Figure 13-3 illustrates how the template servlet merges the two documents together.

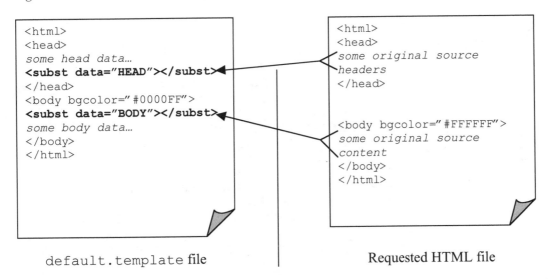

default.template file   Requested HTML file

Figure 13-3   The magic of Presentation Templates...explained!

Listing 13-3 shows a sample template file with a simple information area at the top of the page.

Listing 13-3   Your first default.template file

```
<html>
<body>
<subst data="BODY"></subst>
</body>
</html>
```

Do you notice the use of the subst element tag in the body section of the template? The body content of the requested page will replace this element (as illustrated in Figure 13-3). Notice that the subst element's value "BODY" was specified in uppercase letters. This value *is* case-sensitive. If you had replaced the text with "body," the template servlet would ignore the tag, and no body content would be displayed.

Also, notice that the example had no subst tag for the head area. This means that no header information from a requested document will reach the client. While this might be desirable in some cases, most likely it will be seen as a bug. The moral: at the least place a subst tag for both the body and the head HTML elements, and make sure that the two are specified in uppercase letters.

Core Note

HTML Frames are not currently supported by the template servlet (which might be more of a blessing than a missing feature!).

Adding an Optional default.definitions File

While the default.template file lets you add additional text to a document transparently, it forces you to place literal strings into the document's structure. Think of it this way: the template enforces a *structure* on the content, such as BANNER BODY CONTENT FOOTER or BANNER NAVIGATION CONTENT EMAIL. If the content of the banner and the footer or the navigation and e-mail are placed directly into the template text, it requires a new template for new information. Wouldn't it be nice if those fields could be variables themselves, where the values are pulled in at run time from some other source?

Well, you *can* get that, if you use a definitions file. A definitions file is a Java properties file (basically, name=value pairs in a simple text file) where variable names are mapped to the text that replaces them. Listing 13-4 shows a simple example of a definition file and the template file that uses it.

Listing 13-4   A sample default.definitions file and its template

```
[- default.definitions -]
BANNER=<img src="banner.gif" border=0>
EMAIL=<a href="mailto:webmaster@somesite.com">Feedback?</a>

[- default.template -]
<html>
<head>
<subst data="HEAD"></subst>
</head>
<body>
<subst data="BANNER"></subst>
<subst data="BODY"></subst>
<subst data="EMAIL"></subst>
</body>
</html>
```

Now the structure of the page has been cleanly separated from its content. Like template files, definition files in subdirectories inherit all of the parent's variables, so you could vary the value of the `BANNER` variable in a subdirectory's `default.definitions` file to visually reflect the change of the user's location on the site, all without changing the page's structure.

Core Note

Once a `default.properties` *file is accessed by the* `template` *servlet, it cannot be deleted (but it can be altered!) unless the* `template` *servlet is restarted. This is a side effect of the* `template` *servlet's implementation, so this restriction may disappear in a future release.*

Enable Presentation Template Processing for the Directory

This is the final step in setting up presentation templates processing for a family of directories. You'll need to make a servlet alias between the virtual path of the directory and the `template` servlet. Refer to Chapter 5 "Administrating the Java Web Server," for more details.

As you can see, Presentation Templates are a neat method for separating content from structure on your Web site, but they don't have any truly *dynamic* properties. You're going to need JavaServer Pages for that.

Java + HTML = JavaServer Pages

As the equation suggests, JavaServer Pages provides the key to combining the power of Java with the flexibility of HTML's presentation capabilities. It's simple: Java code is interspersed within the HTML. Yet in its simplicity lies its strength, as you can mix in the Java code right where you need it.

Like the other HTML-generation tools, the JSP (JavaServer Pages) engine is packaged as a servlet. It receives requests for `.jsp` documents due to a preconfigured servlet alias (servlet aliases are covered in detail in Chapter 5 "Administrating the Java Web Server"). Upon receiving a request, the JSP servlet opens the requested file and parses it. From the processed information the JSP servlet produces a temporary Java source file, which is passed to the JDK's Java compiler! The final result is a servlet built on-the-fly and loaded dynamically into the Java Web Server. Figure 13-4 illustrates this parsing/compiling/loading process in greater detail.

Let's see this in action. Listing 13-5 shows the source code for a "Hello JSP World" program.

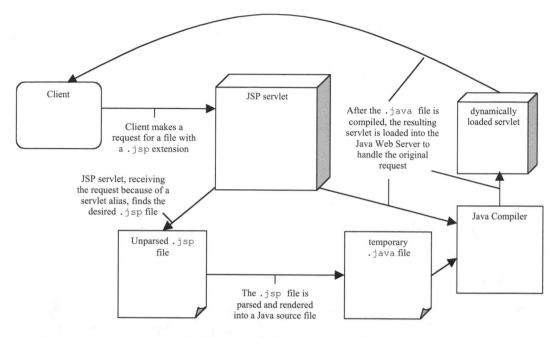

Figure 13-4   The JSP servlet handles a request.

Listing 13-5   HelloWorld.jsp

```
<html>
<body>
<%@ content_type="text/html;charset=UTF-8" %>
<% out.println("Hello JSP World!"); %>
</body>
</html>
```

What's with the "<%" stuff? That tag is used by JSP to denote special content. When it is detected in the Web page, the JSP servlet will interpret it as Java code and place it into the generated source code.

Save this file as `helloworld.jsp`, and access it via your Web browser. You should see something that looks like Figure 13-5.

Core Bug

If the plain text of the `.jsp` *page appears instead of the output shown in Figure 13-5, another servlet may be interfering with the request. As we said in Chapter 4 "Administrating the Java Web Server," if two servlet aliases conflict, the more specific alias takes precedence. As wildcard aliases are the least-specific kind of alias, they will always lose out to a servlet that has control of a specific URI.*

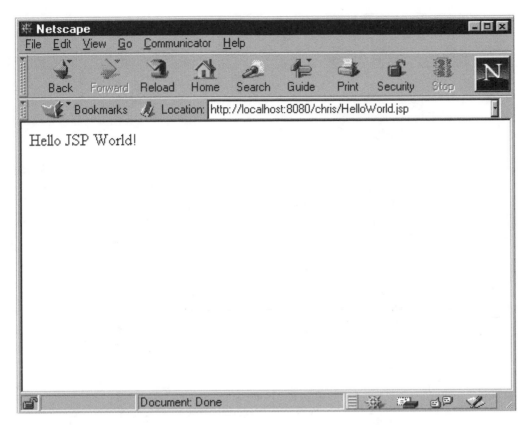

Figure 13-5   HelloJSPWorld!

If you paid close attention to Figure 13-4, you're probably wondering about the source code which represents the servlet that produced the output displayed in Figure 13-5. That source code is kept in the pagecompile subdirectory of the Java Web Server. From there, the directory structure mirrors the URI of the request made to access the .jsp page.

Huh?

Okay, use the HelloJSPWorld as an example. Do you see the URL request line in Figure 13-5? Our test used the URI /chris/HelloWorld.jsp. If you were to look in our pagecompile directory, you would see a child directory named _chris. That's how it works: it takes each subdirectory of the URI and maps it to a directory in the pagecompile directory (prepending a "_" to each directory name).

Navigate into the _chris directory, and you'll find two files: _HelloWorld_xjsp.java and _HelloWorld_xjsp.class. This is the temporary Java source code shown in Figure 13-4. If you inspect the source code with an editor, you should see something similar to Listing 13-6.

Listing 13-6   JSP-generated source code

```java
package pagecompile._chris;

import java.io.*;
import java.util.*;
import javax.servlet.*;
import javax.servlet.http.*;
import java.beans.Beans;
import com.sun.server.http.pagecompile.ParamsHttpServletRequest;
import com.sun.server.http.pagecompile.ServletUtil;
import com.sun.server.http.pagecompile.filecache.CharFileData;
import com.sun.server.http.pagecompile.NCSAUtil;


public class _HelloWorld_xjsp extends
javax.servlet.http.HttpServlet {
    private static final String sources[] = new String[] {
    "D:\\JSP-test\\bin\\..\\public_html\\"+
    "chris\\HelloWorld.jsp",
    };

    private static final long lastModified[] = 899572481000L,
    };

    public void service(HttpServletRequest request,
                                HttpServletResponse response)
    throws IOException, ServletException
    {
        PrintWriter out = response.getWriter();
        CharFileData data[] = new CharFileData[sources.length];
        try {
            for (int i = 0 ; i < data.length ; i++)
            data[i] = ServletUtil.getJHtmlSource(this,
                            sources[i],
                            "8859_1",
                            lastModified[i]);
        } catch (Exception ex) {
            ex.printStackTrace();
            throw new ServletException("fileData");
        }
    // com.sun.server.http.pagecompile.jsp.CharArrayChunk
    // D:\JSP-test\bin\..\public_html\chris\HelloWorld.jsp
    // 1,1-D:\JSP-test\bin\..\public_html\chris\HelloWorld.jsp 3,1
        data[0].writeChars(0, 16, out);
    // com.sun.server.http.pagecompile.jsp.CharArrayChunk D:\JSP-
    // test\bin\..\public_html\chris\HelloWorld.jsp 3,46-D:\JSP-
```

```
// test\bin\..\public_html\chris\HelloWorld.jsp 4,1
    data[0].writeChars(61, 2, out);
// com.sun.server.http.pagecompile.jsp.ScriptletChunk D:\JSP-
// test\bin\..\public_html\chris\HelloWorld.jsp 4,1-D:\JSP-
// test\bin\..\public_html\chris\HelloWorld.jsp 4,39
    out.println("Hello JSP World!");
// com.sun.server.http.pagecompile.jsp.CharArrayChunk D:\JSP-
// test\bin\..\public_html\chris\HelloWorld.jsp 4,39-D:\JSP-
// test\bin\..\public_html\chris\HelloWorld.jsp 7,0
    data[0].writeChars(101, 20, out);
  }

}
```

Whew! That's a lot of code for such a simple little Web page! What is it doing? The key to the answer lies within the JSP-generated comments before each write to the `java.io.PrintWriter` (there are four of them). Each comment says:

- What kind of element am I?
- Where was I found in the source `.jsp` document?

Just from our simple `HelloJSPWorld` example, you can see that there are two different kinds of chunks:

- `com.sun.server.http.pagecompile.jsp.CharArrayChunk`
- `com.sun.server.http.pagecompile.jsp.ScriptletChunk`

A `CharArrayChunk` is just a group of Java characters—raw HTML extracted from the source `.jsp` file. A `ScriptletChunk` is the Java source code that was written directly into the document:

```
out.println ("Hello JSP World!");
```

This code was extracted by the JSP servlet and placed into the source code `_HelloWorld_xjsp.java`.

After each chunk-type description are two filename/cursor-position pairs describing where the chunk was found in the source document. In the case of the `CharArrayChunks` this data is used to pull the appropriate HTML out of the source `.jsp` document and output it to the client through the `PrintWriter`. In the case of the ScriptletChunk, the position is used simply for documentation purposes.

Did you notice the package declaration at the top of the source file? JSP uses the directory hierarchy as the package name of the servlet. This makes it easy to tell the difference between JSP pages with the same name, because they can't be in the same directory.

Now that you've had your first taste of JSP scripting, let's move on to a complete description of the syntax. According to the JavaServer Pages specification document, the syntax is split into five different parts:

- Directives
- Declarations
- Scriptlets (you've seen these!)
- Expressions
- Beans

Directives

Directives alter how the code within the .jsp file is interpreted by the JSP servlet. They work much as preprocessor directives work in the "C" language. There are six kinds of directives:

- Scripting language
- Method name
- Imported packages
- Content type of the returned data
- Interfaces implemented
- The Java class the generated servlet extends from

By the way: you can always recognize a JSP directive by its characteristic signature: "<%@."

Scripting Language

Even though the first implementation of JSP supports only the Java language, the Java Web Server team haven't ruled out other languages (such as TCL or Perl). By including a scripting-language directive in the specification, they've allowed for other languages to be supported in the future. A scripting-language directive looks like this:

```
<%@ language="java" %>
```

Core Note

It's a good idea to place a language directive in your .jsp files now, so that nothing funny happens when other scripting languages are introduced later. Be aware, also, that multiple language tags can be in a document, but only the first one encountered is honored (so once you choose the language, there's no going back!).

Method Name

All of the Java code strewn throughout the `.jsp` file needs to go *somewhere* into the generated servlet. By default, this code goes into the `service` method. You can change the target method, if you specify a method directive. A method directive looks like this:

```
<%@ method="doGet" %>
```

So, all of the code will go into the `doGet` method of the class and not the `service` method. As with the scripting-language directive, multiple tags are permitted, but only the first one encountered is honored.

Imported Packages

At some point you'll want to dip into classes that aren't already imported into the generated servlet's namespace (for example, `java.sql.*`). An import directive's value is a comma-delimited list of package (or object) names. An import directive pulling in JDBC and Java Security packages would look like this:

```
<%@ import="java.sql.*,java.security.*" %>
```

Multiple import directives are supported, and each of them is honored during code generation.

Content Type of the Returned Data

Specifying the content-type directive is akin to using the ServletResponse class's `setContentType` method. For example, if you wanted the data to be interpreted as plain text, the content-type directive would look like this:

```
<@% content_type="text/plain" %>
```

Core Note

According to the JSP draft specification, the content-type directive is the right way to specify the MIME type of the returned data. In the JavaServer Pages preview release, this didn't work. If you find that your implementation fails to work properly, try placing this scriptlet before any output:

```
<% response.setContentType(content-type); %>
```

You can also specify the character set used for the response (after all, Java *does* support international applications!) by appending it to the content type. For example, to specify UTF-8 encoding for the output text, the content type directive would look like this:

```
<@% content_type="text/plain;charset=UTF-8" %>
```

Interfaces Implemented

Although your generated servlet supports the javax.servlet.Servlet interface by default, you may want to take advantage of other interfaces in your JSP code. Imagine iterating over the contents of a JDBCServlet response. If the servlet supported the java.util.Enumeration interface, you could request an Enumeration from your servlet and walk through the contents. An implements directive looks like this:

```
<%@ implements="java.util.Enumeration" %>
```

Like the imports directive, the implements directive is a comma-delimited list of supported interfaces. Multiple tags can be used as well, and all of them will be honored in the source code.

Core Note

As you'll see in the Declaration syntax section, methods besides the pagewide default (remember the method directive?) can be defined. You'll need to take advantage of that feature when supporting other interfaces (such as java.util.Enumeration).

Extending from a Class

Up to this point, we've assumed that the generated class is a servlet. Looking at the source code in Listing 13-6, you see that the object is a derivative of the HttpServlet class. The extends directive lets you change the superclass of the generated servlet. For example, if you wanted it to derive from the GenericServlet class instead of the HTTP-specific HttpServlet, the extends directive would look like this:

```
<%@ extends="javax.servlet.GenericServlet" %>
```

Of course, you'll run into problems when you try to run a .jsp page that wants to extend from the GenericServlet class. That's because the parameters to the generated function will *always* be the HttpServletRequest and HttpServletResponse classes (as the current JSP specification doesn't give a directive for changing those parameters!), so unless you define the proper service method (taking ServletRequest and ServletResponse objects instead) the compilation will fail with an "abstract class" error.

In our own experiences with JSP, we've noticed that it's much easier to extend from the HttpServlet class (or one of its derivatives) than to implement the right interfaces and get the code added in the declaration area.

And speaking of declaration area...

Declarations

The declaration area is where you can place member variables and support functions necessary for the generated servlet's operation. Everything in the declaration area is dumped directly into the body of the class. So, if you wanted your servlet to have a `java.util.Random` number generator as a member variable, the declaration area would be defined as:

```
<script runat=server>
private java.util.Random m_rand = new java.util.Random();
</script>
```

Declaration areas are easily distinguished by the telltale `<script>` element. Its `runat` attribute informs the JSP servlet that the content should be used on the server side, instead of as a hint to the browser.

Multiple `SCRIPT` tags are possible, with all of the server-side declarations merged into the generated source file.

As we mentioned earlier, you can use declaration areas to implement interfaces (or extend methods defined by a base class). For example, if you wanted to implement the `java.util.Enumeration` interface after you gave the appropriate implements directive, you would write:

```
<SCRIPT runat="server">
public Object nextElement()
{
...
}

public boolean hasMoreElements()
{
...
}
</SCRIPT>
```

Scriptlets

As you saw in the `HelloJSPWorld` example, scriptlets are little blobs of Java code. These blobs can do whatever regular Java code can do, such as declare local variables, call internal methods, invoke methods on other classes, and alter the flow of execution. In our opinion, changing the flow of execution in the `.jsp` file is the most powerful feature of a scriptlet, as you can defer until run time which HTML will be sent to the client. Listing 13-7 has a revised version of `HelloJSPWorld` called `HelloJSPWorld2` that will change what it says depending on what browser has activated it.

Listing 13-7   HelloJSPWorld2.jsp

```
<html>
<body>
<% String agent = request.getHeader("USER-AGENT");
    if (agent.indexOf("IE") == -1)
    {
    %>
    That's a cool browser!
    <%
    }
    else
    {
    %>
    Oh.  Well, at least it was free!
    <% } %>
</body>
</html>
```

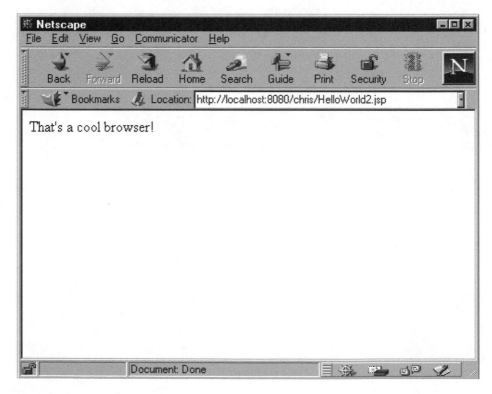

Figure 13-6   Communicator says hello to HelloJSPWorld2.

Figures 13-6 and 13-7 show the results of HelloJSPWorld2 when activated from Netscape Communicator and Microsoft Internet Explorer, respectively.

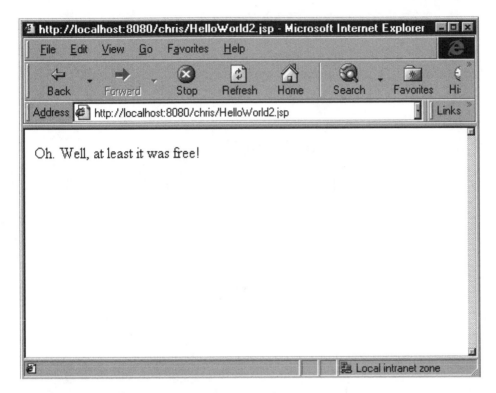

Figure 13-7   Internet Explorer gets insulted by HelloJSPWorld2.

Of course, there are much better uses for scriptlets than insulting your clients. You can use them to send alternate content from one source, instead of separating the site into different duplicated areas that support different browser versions. For example, there is a bug with Communicator 4.04 that will call start/stop on any applets if the page is resized (definitely a problem!). You can use a scriptlet to send an additional PARAM to the applet that says "enable a Communicator 4.04 workaround."

Listing 13-8   Workaround.jsp

```
<html>
<body>
<SCRIPT runat="server">
private static final String COMM_404 = "Mozilla/4.04";
</SCRIPT>
<applet code="someapplet.class" codebase="somecodebase"
```

continued

```
width=300 height=300>
<param name="param1" value="value1">
<param name="param2" value="value2">
<% String agent = request.getHeader("USER-AGENT");
   if (agent.indexOf(COMM_404) != -1)
   {
%>
<param name="enable_workaround" value="true">
<% } %>
</applet>
</body>
</html>
```

Besides any local variables declared within a scriptlet and member variables declared within a SCRIPT tag, four other variables are automatically made available within a .jsp file:

- request
- response
- in
- out

The request variable is an instance of an object implementing the javax.servlet.http.HttpServletRequest interface. As we said about the extends directive, the pagewide function *always* has an HttpServletRequest and HttpServletResponse objects as its parameters. So, response is naturally a HttpServletResponse object. The out variable is a java.io.PrintWriter object. When the code for the generated servlet is produced, there is a line that reads:

```
PrintWriter out = response.getWriter();
```

Likewise, in is an instance of the java.io.BufferedReader class. It is initialized with a call to:

```
BufferedReader in = request.getReader();
```

Core Bug

According to the JSP draft specification, the in variable should be automatically defined when the generated servlet is created. In the JavaServer Pages preview release, it wasn't. If you find that your implementation fails to work properly, try placing this scriptlet before any output:

```
<% BufferedReader in = request.getReader(); %>
```

`Writers` and `Readers` are great for implementing multilanguage applications. (Their JDK1.0.2 cousins, `OutputStreams` and `InputStreams`, were byte oriented, making it difficult to write programs for multibyte character sets such as Japanese). If you need to return byte-oriented data (like a graphic or a sound file), you can retrieve an `OutputStream` from the `response` object and use that to return the data.

```
<% byte[] sound_buffer = …;
OutputStream os = response.getOutputStream();
os.write(sound_buffer);
os.flush();
%>
```

Likewise, you can still get an `InputStream` from the `request` object by calling `getInputStream`. More information on how to use the `request` and `response` objects can be found in Chapter 6, "Generic Servlets."

Expressions

Expressions are *very* similar to scriptlets, except they contain a single expression and not a group of statements. You can use expressions to dynamically fill-in attribute values in your HTML, which comes in handy when generating forms from JSP. Listing 13-9 shows a small HTML form that displays the value of the User-Agent in the text field, which is automatically sized, depending on the length of the value.

Listing 13-9   DynamicForm.jsp

```
<html>
<body>
<form method=post action="/servlet/FormHandler">
Browser <input type="text" name="browser"
      value="<%= request.getHeader("USER-AGENT") %>"
      size="<%= request.getHeader("USER-AGENT").length() %>">
<input type=submit value="Your favorite browser!">
</form>
</body>
</html>
```

Expressions are easily recognized by their characteristic "<%=" open tag.

When this code gets generated, the value of an expression is turned into a character string. In the case of the input element's `value`, it already is a string, but in the case of the `size` attribute, the integer is turned into a string before it is sent.

Core Note

The difference between an expression tag and a scriptlet tag is that an expression is a single expression that evaluates to some value (one of the Java intrinsic types, or a derivative of `java.lang.Object`, *basically anything but a* `void` *type) without the standard semicolon. You'll get a nasty error from the JSP page compiler if you tack on a semicolon at the end of an expression.*

Beans

If you've read Chapter 12 "ServletBeans," you're familiar with the JavaBeans architecture. If you haven't read it yet, a JavaBean is a Java class that has methods with special names. (OK, there *is* more to JavaBeans than that. For a rigorous review, check out Chapter 12.) Because of these method names, any Java program can manipulate bean objects. This comes in handy in a scripting environment like JSP.

Frankly, bean support is the *coup d'état* for JSP. Rival scripting systems (such as Microsoft's ASP) offer component scripting, but JSP takes the cake for maintaining portability without sacrificing functionality (say that ten times fast!). In a nutshell, you get the power of JSP/beans without being tied to a single Web server on a single platform (can you say "IIS"?).

OK, enough with the pompoms already! Using JavaBeans with JSP is a *big* topic (it takes eleven of the eighteen pages in the JSP specification!), so let's start by writing a simple JavaBean and using it in a simple JSP file.

Except, you can't. There are some unspoken rules about using JavaBeans with JSP that you need to know *before* you can do any examples. For instance, all JavaBeans *must* be stored in the system `CLASSPATH` to be used with JSP. If you've read the chapter on ServletBeans, this seems odd; if the beans are in the `CLASSPATH`, they can't be dynamically reloaded, right?

Yep.

This means that once a JavaBean's class is loaded into the Java Web Server via JSP, you'll need to restart the server to update it. This is a side effect of the code-generation/compiling process, a topic that will be covered later in the chapter.

So, in the meantime, you can stick whatever beans you create into the `<server_root>/classes` directory for now, and they'll be automatically added to the system `CLASSPATH`.

There are other rules that will uncover themselves in later examples, but for now you're ready to run the first example. Listing 13-10 shows `SimpleJSPBean.java`, the source code for a JavaBean, and Listing 13-11 shows the JSP code that uses it.

Listing 13-10   SimpleJSPBean

```java
package test;

import java.io.*;
import javax.servlet.http.*;
import javax.servlet.*;

public class SimpleJSPBean extends HttpServlet
implements Serializable
{
  private long m_counter = 0L;

  public long getCounter ()
  {
    return m_counter;
  }

  public void service (HttpServletRequest req,
              HttpServletResponse res)
  throws IOException, ServletException
  {
    m_counter++;
  }
}
```

Listing 13-11   SimpleJSPBean.jsp

```jsp
<html>
<body>
<BEAN name="counter" scope="session"
 type="test.SimpleJSPBean" create="yes"
 introspect="yes">
</BEAN>

You've accessed this page
<%= counter.getCounter() %> times
</body>
</html>
```

If you open up your Web browser and navigate to `SimpleJSPBean.jsp`, you should see something similar to Figure 13-8. Reloading the JSP page multiple times should increment the counter (just as a good page counter should!).

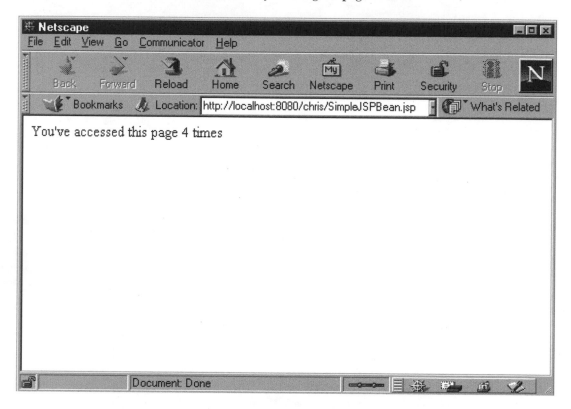

Figure 13-8   The SimpleJSPBean in action!

The Java source code for the `SimpleJSPBean` looks pretty standard, except for the package definition—up until now none of the examples have been members of packages. With JSP, your beans *must* belong to a package. This requirement is a side effect of the JSP page compiler—when a JSP page is generated, its code is placed in a package corresponding to the source's directory structure. At that point, no classes from the "default" package can be referenced from the code, which goes for the JSP beans, since they are referenced in the JSP code.

Another interesting feature of the `SimpleJSPBean` is its parent class: `HttpServlet`. According to the JSP specification, any bean supporting the `Servlet` interface will have its `service` method invoked when its host JSP page is accessed.

Core Bug

According to the JSP draft specification, the `service` *method should be automatically called whenever the page is accessed. In the JavaServer Pages preview release, this didn't work. If you find that your implementation fails to work properly, try placing this scriptlet in your JSP page:*

```
<% [Bean name].service(request,response); %>
```

The JSP page looks pretty standard, except for the new <BEAN> tag. This tag acts like the <SERVLET> tag from Server Side Include, but with some additional properties, as listed in Table 13-3.

Table 13-3   The Attributes of the BEAN Tag

Attribute Name	Description
name	The "handle" of the bean. Think of it like a hashtable: the handle is the key by which the bean will be retrieved. For Beans that exist beyond the lifetime of a single page (either as a session-level bean or from JSP page chaining), you can use the name attribute for retrieving the bean.
varname	The variable name of the bean within the JSP code. This name is relevant (scoped) only within the JSP page. If this optional attribute is not specified, the varname defaults to the value of the name attribute.
type	The Java type of the bean. This can be the actual type of the bean instance, or one of its superclasses. When this optional attribute is not specified, its default value is java.lang.Object. The values of the type and varname attributes are used together for defining the bean within the JSP page: `[type value] [varname value];`
introspect	This tells the JSP page generator to write code that takes incoming HTTP query parameters (sent via either a GET or a POST request) and sets the values of the bean's properties to these values. Values are either "yes" or "no."
create	Specifies whether a bean should be created if it doesn't already exist. Values are either "yes" or "no."
scope	Informs the JSP code generator whether this bean should be a transitory object living only for the lifetime of a single request, or if it should be persistently placed within a session object.
beanName	An optional attribute that can be used to specify a serialized bean instance rather than just a class name.

Core Bug

According to the JSP draft specification, the `create` *and* `introspect` *attributes should default to the "yes" value. In the JavaServer Pages preview release, both of these attributes' values defaulted to "no." If you find that your implementation fails to work properly, just place those optional attributes explicitly within the* `<BEAN>` *tag to ensure the right behavior. In the same vein, the* `type` *attribute is ignored—you may have to use the older* `class` *attribute (left over from the days of page compilation) with earlier JSP implementations.*

The next example relies on introspection to supply the right parameters to the bean—a bean that calculates the quadratic formula! The source code in Listing 13-12 shows how any JSP bean can take advantage of introspection (even a boring math one!), and Listing 13-13 gives the JSP file that uses it.

Core Note

This is the first and last of the worthless examples we'll show to illustrate JSP capabilities. Would that all computer science textbooks showed such restraint!

Listing 13-12   Solving some basic mathematics

```
package stupidmath;

import java.io.*;

public class QuadraticBean implements Serializable
{
  private double m_a = 0.0;
  private double m_b = 0.0;
  private double m_c = 0.0;

  public String getQuadratic ()
  {
    return "The solution to Ax^2+Bx+C for"+
    " A="+m_a+" B="+m_b+" C="+m_c+" is "+
    ((-m_b)+Math.sqrt(Math.pow(m_b,2)-4*m_a*m_c))/2*m_a+
    ","+(m_b+Math.sqrt(Math.pow(m_b,2)-4*m_a*m_c))/2*m_a;
  }

  public void setA (String A)
  {
    try
```

```
     {
       m_a = new Double(A).doubleValue();
     }
     catch (NumberFormatException oops)
     {
       }
     }
  public void setB (String B)
  {
     try
     {
       m_b = new Double(B).doubleValue();
     }
     catch (NumberFormatException oops)
     {
     }
  }

  public void setC (String C)
  {
     try
     {
       m_c = new Double(C).doubleValue();
     }
     catch (NumberFormatException oops)
     {
     }
  }
}
```

Listing 13-13   Solving math with JSP

```
<html>
<body>
<BEAN class="stupidmath.QuadraticBean" create="yes"
 scope="session" introspect="yes" name="calc">
</BEAN>

<%= calc.getQuadratic() %>
</body>
</html>
```

Now, point your browser to the URL

```
http://localhost:8080/stupidmath.jsp?a=1&b=4&c=3
```

and you should see something like Figure 13-9.

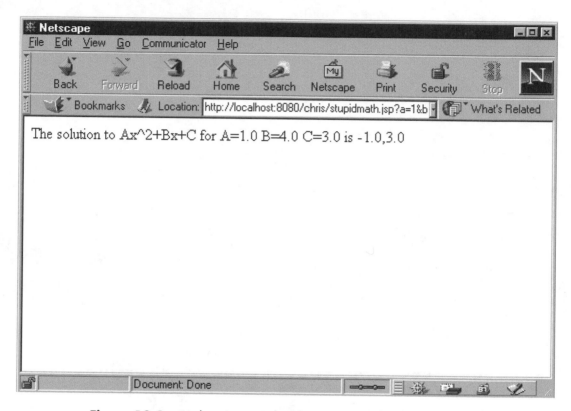

Figure 13-9   *"At least it wasn't the Fibonacci sequence."*

Kidding aside, the power of introspection is subtle in this example. The JSP servlet casts some magic by reading the name/value pairs from the query string, then uses those pairs to set the bean properties A, B, and C. (Readable variable names like these are another wonderful by-product of math-based examples!) When the method getQuadratic is called, the bean uses those set properties to calculate both roots of a second-degree polynomial equation.

Remember—these properties are case sensitive! If we had specified A=1 instead of a=1, the A property would never have been set. Also, a query string isn't the only way to get the properties of a bean set; they could have been passed in via a form POST as well.

Summary

All of these services—JSP, SSI, and Presentation Templates—provide automated ways of generating HTML on-the-fly. While the SSI and Templates pieces have become a tested part of the Java Web Server, the Java Server Pages specification is still in limbo. At the time this text was written, the JSP specification was only in a first draft from the Java Web Server team (the 0.9 JSP specification). Team members say that a revised edition of the specification will be available by the time this book has hit the streets. Check out the *Core Java Web Server* site at www.phptr.com for more details as this technology story unfolds.

SECURITY

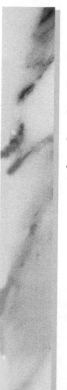

Topics in This Chapter

- Why security?
- Web authentication: Basic, Digest, and SSL
- Realms, users, and ACLs
- Accessing Realms from servlets
- Writing custom Realms

Chapter 14

Computer security shouldn't be a new topic to anyone by now. Hollywood movies like *WarGames* and *Hackers* have glorified computer break-ins, while the media circus surrounding the Kevin Mitnick affair has ingrained into our minds that unprotected computers are open to misuse. Like a trusting child, a computer will do what it is told, even if that means turning over secrets like credit card numbers or bank-account information to whoever knows the right buttons to push.

These break-ins can take place on the victim machine itself, or they can reach the victim across the network from a remote workstation. Kevin Mitnick, for example, supposedly used TCP SYN flooding (a technique that allows a machine to masquerade as another computer) from computers he had compromised to break into yet others and acquire their secrets. The approach taken by viruses such as the Internet Worm was to use unsafe programs on the server on a host to gain access to its local secrets. (One such unsafe program is the finger daemon, a program that reports information about a given user on a machine.) These attacks fall roughly into two categories: host security breaches and network security breaches.

As a server application, the Java Web Server needs to protect its resources from prying eyes, insure that sensitive information (such as addresses and credit card numbers) isn't readable by everyone with a network sniffer, and at the same time protect its host machine against intrusions through its own code (avoiding security holes like the finger daemon's). This chapter discusses these aspects of Java Web Server security from technical, administrative, and programming perspectives. Here, we'll be covering the following:

- HTTP authentication
- Securing your Web resources
- Managing groups, users, and ACLs with Realms
- Using SSL to protect your customer's data

So without further ado…

HTTP Authentication

Have you ever been snooping out on the Web with your browser and come across a password dialog that looks like Figure 14-1?

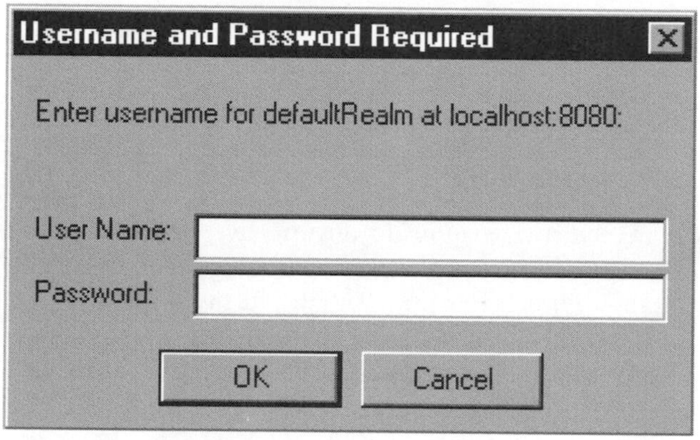

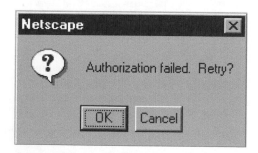

Figure 14-1   "Halt! Who goes there?"

Curious, you enter a name and password ("guest" and "guest" might be good guesses), and the Web server responds by slamming the drawbridge gate, as in Figure 14-2.

Figure 14-2   No password, no entrance.

You've just been shut out by a Web authorization procedure! But how was this accomplished?

Check the Spec...

According to the HTTP/1.1 specification, when a Web browser makes a request for a protected resource, the server responds with an authentication request header. This header is titled WWW-Authenticate, and it contains enough pertinent information to carry out a challenge-and-response session between the user and the server. Figure 14-3 illustrates this interaction.

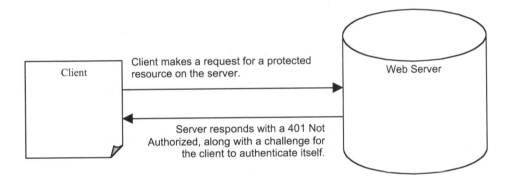

Figure 14-3 Requesting a protected resource.

But don't take our word for it! Just try it yourself by playing the "Man in the Middle" between your Web browser and the Java Web Server.

Core Note

The term "Man in the Middle" is used to describe a specific type of security attack, where an unauthorized, interloping third person pretends to be the opposite member of a two-person conversation. In this chapter you'll use the same concept to "capture" the conversation between the Web browser and the Java Web Server.

Playing Both Sides as the Man in the Middle

For our own "Man in the Middle" testing, we wrote a tool called SimpleServer that acts as a simplified Web server. It's designed to load behavior from special classes called ServerModules, which implement a single method: processInputText. Modules can override this method to simulate certain scenarios with clients.

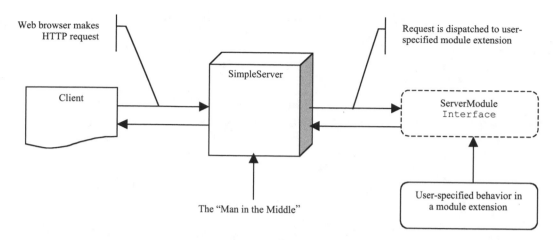

Figure 14-4   The SimpleServer architecture.

Listing 14-1 shows the source code for SimpleServer, and Listing 14.2 that for the ServerModule interface.

Listing 14-1   The SimpleServer test harness

```
import java.net.*;
import java.io.*;

public class SimpleServer implements Runnable
{

   public static final int DEFAULT_PORT = 4040;
   private static final int PAGE_SIZE   = 4096;
   private static final String USAGE =
      "Usage: SimpleServer [module-class] [port]";

   private ServerModule m_module = null;
   private int m_port = DEFAULT_PORT;

   public SimpleServer (int
   port, String classname)
   throws IllegalArgumentException
   {
      m_port = port;

      try
      {
         Class tempClass = Class.forName(classname);
```

```
        m_module =
          (ServerModule)tempClass.newInstance();
    }
    catch (Exception e)
    {
        throw new IllegalArgumentException ("Class "
          +classname+" is having some problems");
    }
}

public void run ()
{
    try
    {
      ServerSocket server = new ServerSocket(m_port);
      boolean shouldContinue = true;
      byte[] buffer = new byte[4096];

      while (shouldContinue)
      {
        Socket client = server.accept();
        InputStream is = client.getInputStream();
        int readCount = is.read(buffer);
          OutputStream os = client.getOutputStream();

        String output =
          m_module.processInputText(new
          String(buffer,0,readCount));

        os.write(output.getBytes());
        os.close();
        client.close();
      }
    }
    catch (Exception e)
    {
      e.printStackTrace();
    }
}

public static void main (String[] args)
{
    int port = DEFAULT_PORT;
    String className = null;

    switch (args.length)
    {
```

continued

```
        case 0 :        System.err.println(USAGE);
            System.exit(0);
            break;
        case 1 :        className = args[0]; break;
        default:        className = args[0];
            try
            {
            port = Integer.parseInt(args[1]);
            }
            catch (NumberFormatException nfe)
        {
            }
            break;
    }
    try
    {
      SimpleServer theServer = new
        SimpleServer(port,className);
      new Thread(theServer).start();
    }
    catch (Exception e)
    {
      e.printStackTrace();
    }
  }
}
```

Listing 14-2   The ServerModule interface

```
public interface ServerModule
{
  public String processInputText (String input);
}
```

When the SimpleServer is activated, it requires the fully qualified package name of the ServerModule to use for handling client requests, followed by the optional port (the default port is '4040') to listen on. If you had put together a sample module named SampleModule, and you wanted the SimpleServer tool to listen on port 80 (the default HTTP port), you would type:

```
java SimpleServer SampleModule 80
```

As you can see, `SimpleServer` takes care of the server side of the test, but who will impersonate the client when accessing the Java Web Server? You'll need a second tool for the second half of the MITM analysis, which we'll call `SimpleClient`.

The `SimpleClient` works just like the `SimpleServer`: it uses modules called `ClientModules` supplied at run time. By creating new modules, you can test specific HTTP messages against the Java Web Server and see the results.

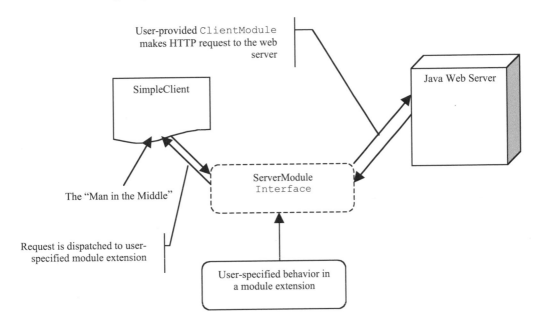

Figure 14-5   Introducing the SimpleClient.

The source code for the `SimpleClient` is given in Listing 14-3, and that for the `ClientModule` interface in Listing 14-4.

Listing 14-3   The SimpleClient class

```java
import java.net.*;
import java.io.*;

public class SimpleClient implements Runnable
{
  private static final String DEFAULT_URL
                      = "http://localhost";
  private static final String USAGE =
    "Usage: SimpleClient [classname] [URL]";
```

continued

```java
private ClientModule m_client = null;
private URL     m_theURL = null;

public SimpleClient (ClientModule client, String url)
throws IllegalArgumentException
{
  if (client == null)
  {
    throw
    new IllegalArgumentException ("Client is null");
  }
  m_client = client;
  try
  {
    m_theURL = new URL(url);
  }
  catch (MalformedURLException murle)
  {
    throw
    new IllegalArgumentException ("Bad URL "+url);
  }
}

public void run ()
{
  try
  {
    m_client.connect(m_theURL.openConnection());
  }
  catch (Exception e)
  {
    e.printStackTrace();
  }
}

public static void main (String[] args)
{
  String theURL    = DEFAULT_URL;
  String klassName = null;

  switch (args.length)
  {
    case 0 : System.err.println (USAGE);
            break;
    case 1 : klassName = args[0]; break;
    default: klassName = args[0];
          theURL = args[1]; break;
  }
```

```
     try
     {
        Class theClass = Class.forName(klassName);
        ClientModule client =
           (ClientModule)theClass.newInstance();

        SimpleClient theClient = new
           SimpleClient(client,theURL);

        new Thread(theClient).start();
     }
     catch (Exception e)
     {
        e.printStackTrace();
        System.exit(0);
     }
  }
}
```

Listing 14-4   The ClientModule interface

```
import java.net.*;
import java.io.*;

public interface ClientModule
{
   public void connect (URLConnection conxion)
   throws IOException;

}
```

You run the `SimpleClient` by passing the name of the `ClientModule` to use and the module's connection URL. In this manner, a module can be reused for multiple URLs without forcing each implementation of the `ClientModule` interface to come up with its own discovery scheme.

Now, consider an example where you want to test the connection to a Web server running locally on port 8080, using a module named `SampleClientModule`. Just type the following command to activate the `SimpleClient`:

```
java SimpleClient SampleClientModule http://localhost:8080
```

That's all there is to it! We suggest that you get familiar with these tools, as you'll be relying on them for answers throughout the rest of this chapter.

Exploring HTTP Authentication with the SimpleClient

Before you start your expedition, you'll need to make a protected resource (Chapter 4, "Administrating the Java Web Server," will show you how) for testing purposes. You'll want to start by protecting the root resource (the "/" document) with the Basic authentication scheme. This scheme lets you unlock protected resources with any Web browser (which isn't true of more sophisticated authentication schemes). Owing to its simple nature, the Basic scheme also provides a backdrop for understanding the entire process of authenticating a client's identity to the Web server.

After you have the resource protected, you'll want to write a customized `ClientModule` that retrieves all of the content sent by the server. We've written one called `SimpleConnectionModule` for you, and the code is shown in Listing 14-5.

Listing 14-5   SimpleConnectionModule for displaying a server's content

```java
import java.net.*;
import java.io.*;

public class SimpleConnectionModule implements ClientModule
{
   public void connect (URLConnection conxion)
   throws IOException
   {
     conxion.connect();
     InputStream is = conxion.getInputStream();

     try
     {
       while (is.available() == 0)
       {
         Thread.sleep(250);
       }
     }
     catch (InterruptedException ie)
     {
       ie.printStackTrace();
     }
     byte[] buffer = new byte[is.available()];
     int count = is.read(buffer);
     String output = new String(buffer,0,count);
     boolean stop = false;

     System.out.println ("—-Headers—-\n");
     for (int number = 1; !stop; number++)
     {
```

```
    String key = conxion.getHeaderFieldKey(number);
    if (key == null)
    {
      stop = true;
    }
    else
    {
      System.out.println (key+" = "+
        conxion.getHeaderField(key));
    }
  }

  System.out.println ("\n--Content--");
  System.out.println (output);
  }
}
```

Next, run the `SimpleClient` program with the `SimpleConnectionModule`, and you should receive output similar to that found in Figure 14-6.

Figure 14-6 Using the SimpleClient to masquerade as a Web client.

See the line starting with the word WWW-Authenticate in the header section? That's the server's authentication challenge to the client. The WWW-Authenticate header contains two important tokens:

- The authentication type.
- Parameters specific to the given authentication type.

Furthermore, the server can return multiple choices for the client to choose from. According to the HTTP/1.1 specification (page 139), the options must be returned in most secure to least secure order:

```
WWW-Authentication:     [most secure type] [parameters...]
                        [less secure type] [parameters...]
```

So, what are these possible authentication types?

Basic Authentication

The mostly widely used (and supported!) authentication scheme is Basic authentication. As fate would have it, it's also the least secure! It works by passing the name and password of the client, encoded using the Base64 encoding scheme. We can see this in action by creating a special ServerModule that repeats the conversation sent by the Java Web Server. We called this BasicAuthModule, and the code is presented in Listing 14-6.

Listing 14-6   BasicAuthModule

```java
import sun.misc.*;
import java.io.*;

public class BasicAuthModule implements ServerModule
{
  private static final String s_pretext =
    "HTTP/1.1 401 Unauthorized\n" +
    "WWW-Authenticate: Basic realm=\"";
  private static final String s_postText = "\"\n" +
    "Content-Type: text/html\n\n" +
    "<HTML><HEAD><TITLE>Unauthorized(401)</TITLE>" +
    "</HEAD></HTML>";

  private java.util.Random rand = new java.util.Random();

  public String processInputText (String input)
  {
```

```
String finalOutput = null;
int pos = input.indexOf("Authorization");
if (pos == -1)
{
   return s_pretext+"Realm"+rand.nextInt()+
        s_postText;
}

String Authorization = input.substring(pos);
String encoded = Authorization.substring(
   Authorization.indexOf("Basic ")+
   "Basic ".length());

BASE64Decoder decodeMe = new BASE64Decoder();
try
{
   finalOutput =
      new String(decodeMe.decodeBuffer(encoded));
}
catch (IOException ioe)
{
   finalOutput = "Failed to decode authentication";
}

return "HTTP/1.1 200 OK\nContent-Type:"+
      "text/plain\n\nName:Password\n"+finalOutput+
      "\nencoded:"+encoded;


   }

}
```

Compile the module, and load it up with the `SimpleServer`. Next, use your Web browser and navigate to `http://localhost:4040` (the `SimpleServer`'s default URL). You should see a logon screen like that shown in Figure 14-7.

Type in any name and password, and press the OK button. The browser displays the name and password of the user, along with the Base64-encoded data that was sent by the browser to the server (Figure 14-8).

This module retrieves the `Authorization` header from the client's response. Like the `WWW-Authentication` header, the `Authorization` header contains two important tokens:

- The authentication scheme used by the client.
- The scheme-specific authentication information (like the Base64-encoded name and password!).

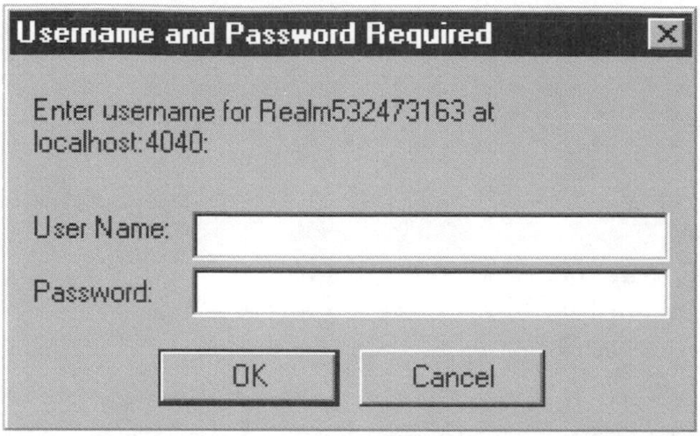

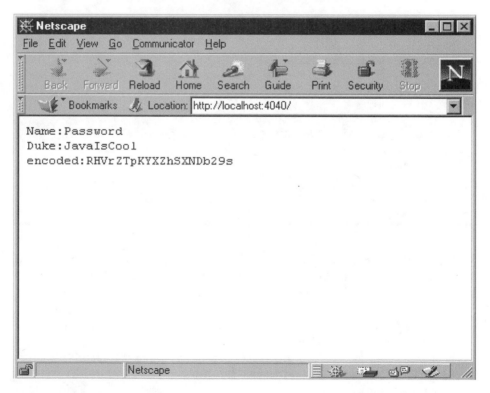

Figure 14-7   Password dialog.

Figure 14-8   The decoded name and password sent by the client.

By using the utility class, `sun.misc.BASE64Decoder`, you've successfully broken the Basic encoding scheme (and not a tough hack, at that!). Armed with this information, you can use the pilfered logon name and password to get at the user's other protected resources.

What?

Well, if *you* can put together a small Java class for decoding logon information tucked away in an HTTP request, can't someone else on the network do the same? Rogue programs masquerading as Web servers can use false authentication requests (just like the `BasicAuthModule`'s response) to harvest logon names and passwords from gullible users. This kind of threat is called an MITM attack, as the rogue program pretends to be the "real" Web server to a client, steals the logon information, then uses this information to attack the "real" server.

Core Note

A second kind of threat, called a "passive attack," can be launched from a computer on the same physical network as the packets passed from the browser to the Web server. This attack uses a special "promiscuous mode" in the networking hardware called that lets an application read all of the Ethernet frames broadcast around the network. The "passive attack" threat is insidious, because there isn't any evidence that an attack has been launched.

Basic authentication also presents another problem if a user has the same logon name and password at another site. Once one of the logon name/password combinations is stolen, the thief can access protected resources using the stolen credentials. Although this seems more of an administrative question about security policies ("Duplicate user names/passwords are forbidden!"), the fact that Basic authentication doesn't obfuscate the logon with server-specific data doesn't help the situation!

Oh! Cleartext logon + security breach / number of shared site accounts = disaster? Exactly.

Core Note

In reality, you didn't even have to decode the Base64-encoded name/password pair to use it to break into the system. The `Basic` *authentication scheme is susceptible to a* replay attack, *where a malicious person can reuse the encoded* `Authorization` *blob, and the receiving server can't tell the difference. Replay attacks are a very serious topic in security, as a cracker could replay a certain transaction (such as "credit my account a $1000.00 deposit") without knowing exactly what it says or the server knowing that the request is invalid.*

`Basic` authentication isn't much better than plain text transmission; in fact, it's worse, because it lulls uninformed users into a false sense of security that their data is protected from prying eyes. According to the HTTP/1.1 specification, "because Basic authentication involves the clear text transmission of passwords, it should never be used (without enhancements) to protect sensitive or valuable information," which means that it shouldn't be used at all (who would protect useless information with a password?).

Fortunately, the HTTP/1.1 specification offers a replacement for Basic called *Digest* authentication, which is documented in RFC 2069.

Digest Authentication

As you've seen through several programming examples, Basic authentication has too many problems to be an acceptable means of verifying a user. Its two fatal flaws are:

- It sends the name and password in the clear.
- It's susceptible to a replay attack.

Digest authentication attempts to meet these shortcomings. First, unlike the Basic scheme, it doesn't send the user's logon information; instead, it uses the name and password as input to a mathematical calculation, then sends the result of the calculation to the server for verification. You can think of it this way: the server and the client share a secret, so if the client gives the server something that uses the secret (but not the secret itself!), the server can use this information as if the name and password had been sent. Yet, as long as the function can't be reversed into revealing the username and password that generated it, no MITM can discover the secret!

Second, Digest authentication permutes the mathematical calculation with an additional parameter called a *nonce*. A nonce is described in RFC 2069 as "a server-specified data string," which can help stymie replay attacks. For every new nonce generated by a server, responses for the same username and password will be different. Using a new nonce each time effectively makes the response a one-time password.

But how does Digest authentication *really* work? Why not rerun the same experiment you used in looking at Basic authentication? First, you'll need to change the authentication scheme on your protected resource from Basic to Digest (Chapter 5, "Administrating the Java Web Server," will show you how), then whip out the `SimpleClient` and connect to the server. Your server's response should look similar to Figure 14-9.

See the `WWW-Authenticate` header? This time it contains a whole group of parameters, which we've placed into Table 14-1 for reference.

Table 14-1   Digest Authentication Parameters

Parameter Name	Description
realm	The realm used for authenticating the client. The user agent (the browser) can use this when prompting for logon information.
nonce	A server-specified data string used as a part of the response. The contents of the nonce are server specific; the client treats the nonce as a piece of opaque (not to be confused with the opaque parameter) data added to the digest.

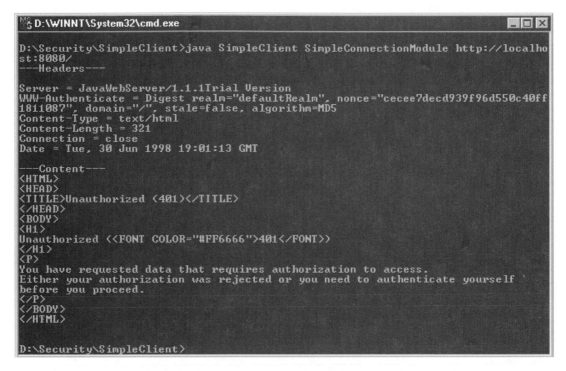

Figure 14-9   SimpleClient receives a Digest authentication request.

Parameter Name	Description
domain	A comma-separated list of URIs (Universal Resource Identifiers) that correlate to this authentication request. This lets a client cache its response as long as the nonce is the same.
opaque	Another server-specified string, except that the opaque data should be returned unchanged by the client. Information about the request can be placed here.
stale	A boolean flag hinting at the reason for an authentication failure. If this flag is specified as true, the authentication request was denied because the nonce value was "stale" (old). The client should attempt to retry the request using the new nonce value (if it has stored the name and password in the client's memory) without prompting the user. This flag will be specified only if the client response is correct for the stale nonce.
algorithm	A pair of strings describing the algorithms used to produce the digest and checksum. If this parameter is missing, the default is "MD5" for creating the digest and checksum.

Wow! Talk about information overload! And you're going to need almost all of this data to properly calculate the Digest, too!

Which raises the next obvious question: what's this "Digest" we keep talking about? Earlier, we referred to it as the result of a "mathematical function" of some input data. How does this function work?

In cryptography, a function that calculates a message digest is usually a *one-way function*, which in nonmathematical terms means "I can't reverse-engineer the inputs from the output." Somehow, the results of the function are completely dependent on the contents of the data, but if you have the results, you can't figure out the contents that created them. The most commonly used one-way functions are one-way hashing algorithms like MD5 (MessageDigest 5) and SHA-1 (Secure Hashing Algorithm 1). Knowing what abbreviations mean is as far as we'll get into the internals of either MD5 or SHA-1. If you're interested in knowing how these algorithms work, we suggest Bruce Schneier's *Applied Cryptography* (if it's about cryptography, it's in there!).

Fortunately for you and me, the JDK 1.1 comes with implementations for both hashing algorithms in its `java.security.MessageDigest` class. With an instance of a `MessageDigest` object, you can calculate the digest value using the update and `digest` methods:

```
MessageDigest md = MessageDigest.getInstance("MD5");
md.update(some_data);
byte[] digest_value = md.digest();
```

And that's it! The `digest_value` variable contains . . . well, the digest value! All that's left to do is make that array palatable with a simple Base16 encoder:

```
Base16Encoder encoder = new Base16Encoder();
String base16value = encoder.encode(digest_value);
```

Of course, nothing can be *that* easy (not if it wants to survive as an Internet specification!), and RFC 2069 is no different. Instead of calculating the hash of the username and the password, the client must follow a complicated formula. This formula is described in section 2.1.2 of the RFC, but a short paraphrase here should suffice:

```
A1 = User-Password Hash = username:realm:password
A2 = Request Hash = request method:digest-request URI
request digest = Hash(Hash(A1):nonce:Hash(A2))
```

Okay, so the `Hash` function is that MD5 (or SHA-1, or whatever was specified in the *algorithm* parameter) one-way function. From the equations, you'll have to apply the hash three times: once for A1, once for A2, and once for the final result.

Core Note

A1 *and* A2 *are the names used in the Digest Authentication specification. For completeness, we've used their names here (even though they're about as descriptive as BASIC variable names).*

Listing 14-7 contains a utility program that calculates the request digest and returns it as an Base16-encoded string.

Listing 14-7   The DigestAuthUtility class

```java
import java.security.*;
import java.math.*;
import java.io.*;

public class DigestAuthUtility
{
  public static final String GET_METHOD = "GET";

  private String m_username;
  private String m_password;
  private String m_realm;
  private String m_nonce;
  private String m_digestType;
  private String m_method = GET_METHOD;
  private String m_path = "\"/\"";

  public DigestAuthUtility (String login, String passwd,
                     String realm, String nonce,
                     String digestType)
  {
    m_username = login;
    m_password = passwd;
    m_realm     = realm;
    m_nonce     = nonce;
    m_digestType = digestType;
  }

  public String getPath ()
  {
    return m_path;
  }

  public String getMethod()
  {
    return m_method;
  }

  public String getName ()
  {
    return m_username;
  }
```

continued

```
public String getRealm ()
{
  return m_realm;
}

public String getNonce()
{
  return m_nonce;
}

public String getDigestType ()
{
  return m_digestType;
}

public void setPath (String path)
{
  m_path = path;
}

public void setMethod (String method)
{
  m_method = method;
}

public void setName (String name)
{
  m_username = name;
}

public void setPassword (String password)
{
  m_password = password;
}

public void setRealm (String realm)
{
  m_realm = realm;
}

public void setNonce (String nonce)
{
  m_nonce = nonce;
}

public void setDigestType (String type)
```

```
  {
    m_digestType = type;
  }

  public String getDigest ()
  throws NoSuchAlgorithmException
  {
    MessageDigest md =
      MessageDigest.getInstance(m_digestType);

    byte[] A1 =
      new String (m_username+":"+m_realm+":"
            +m_password).getBytes();
    byte[] A2 = new String (m_method+":"
                      +m_path).getBytes();

    byte[] H_A1 = md.digest(A1);
    byte[] H_A2 = md.digest(A2);

    byte[] H_A1_nonce_H_A2 =
    String.valueOf(Encoder.encode(H_A1)+":"+
            m_nonce+":"+
            Encoder.encode(H_A2)).getBytes();

    byte[] KD = md.digest(H_A1_nonce_H_A2);

    return Encoder.encode(KD);
  }

  public String toString ()
  {
    return "Name: "+m_username+"\nPassword: "+
        m_password+"\nRealm: "+m_realm+
        "\nNonce: "+m_nonce+"\nDigestType: "
        +m_digestType+"\nMethod: "+m_method+
        "\nURI: "+m_path;
  }
}

class Encoder
{
  private static final char[] encodeArray=
  {
    '0','1','2','3','4','5','6','7','8','9',
    'a','b','c','d','e','f'
  };
```

continued

```
    public static String encode (byte[] buffer)
    {
      int length = buffer.length;
      StringBuffer sb = new StringBuffer();
      byte current;
      for (int loop = 0; loop < length; loop++)
      {
        current = buffer[loop];
        sb.append(encodeArray[(current & 0xF0) >> 4]);
        sb.append(encodeArray[current & 0x0F]);
      }
      return sb.toString();
    }
  }
```

Unfortunately, at the time this section was written, the current versions of Netscape Communicator (4.05) and Microsoft Internet Explorer (4.0) do not support Digest authentication, which makes it difficult to replay a conversation between the client and the server in an example. This bears repeating:

Core Note

NO BROWSER SUPPORT FOR DIGEST AUTHENTICATION!

So what does that mean? It means Digest Authentication is *useless* as an authentication scheme for your clients surfing a site via their Web browser. Now bring Java to the rescue! The fact that the host browser doesn't support Digest authentication doesn't stop Java applets running within the browser from using it! As an example, Listing 14-8 contains a simple Web-browsing applet that will pop up a logon dialog if it encounters a WWW-Authenticate HTTP response header. (Check out Chapter 7 "Introduction to HTTP," for more information on the HTTP protocol.)

Listing 14-8   A DigestApplet

```
import java.awt.*;
import java.applet.*;
import java.net.*;
import java.util.*;
import java.awt.event.*;
import java.io.*;

public class DigestApplet extends Applet
implements ActionListener
{
```

```
private TextField m_URL;
private TextArea  m_area;

public void init ()
{
  setLayout(new BorderLayout());
  add("North",m_URL = new TextField(30));
  add("Center",m_area = new TextArea());
  m_URL.addActionListener(this);
}

private String[] _parseParam (String token)
{
  String[] retVal = null;
  if (token != null)
  {
    StringTokenizer eachItem =
      new StringTokenizer(token,"=");
    if (eachItem.countTokens() > 1)
    {
      String paramName =eachItem.nextToken();
      String paramValue=eachItem.nextToken()
                        .replace('\"',' ')
                        .replace(',',' ').trim();
      retVal = new String[2];
      retVal[0] = paramName;
      retVal[1] = paramValue;
    }
  }
  return retVal;
}

private String _createAuthHeader (String username,
                                  String password,
                                  String URI,
                                  String authField)
{
  StringTokenizer st =
    new StringTokenizer(authField);
  String nonce = null;
  String realm = null;
  String algorithm = "MD5";

  while (st.hasMoreTokens())
  {
    String token = st.nextToken();
    if (!token.startsWith("Digest"))
    {
      String[] params = _parseParam(token);
      if (params != null)
```

continued

```
        {
          if (params[0].equals("realm"))
          {
            realm = params[1];
          }
          else
          if (params[0].equals("nonce"))
          {
            nonce = params[1];
          }
          else
          if (params[0].equals("algorithm"))
          {
            algorithm = params[1];
          }
        }
      }
    }

    try
    {
      DigestAuthUtility dau =
        new DigestAuthUtility(username,
                                  password,
                                  realm,
                                  nonce,
                                  algorithm);
      dau.setPath(URI);
      String digest = dau.getDigest();
        return "Digest username=\""+username+
             "\", realm=\""+realm+"\", nonce=\""+
             nonce+"\", uri=\""+URI+
             "\", response=\""+digest+"\"";
    }
    catch (java.security.NoSuchAlgorithmException oops)
    {
      oops.printStackTrace();
    }
    return null;
  }


  protected URLConnection doUnauthorized
  (URLConnection connection)
  {
    PasswordDialog diag = new PasswordDialog();
    diag.setSize(200,200);
    diag.setVisible(true);
    String username = diag.getName();
    String password = diag.getPassword();
```

```
  String AuthHeader =
    connection.getHeaderField("WWW-Authenticate");

  URL theURL = connection.getURL();

  try
  {
    connection = theURL.openConnection();
    connection.setRequestProperty("Authorization",
      _createAuthHeader(username,
                        password,
                        theURL.getFile(),
                        AuthHeader));
    connection.connect();
  }
  catch (IOException ioe)
  {
    ioe.printStackTrace();
  }
  return connection;
}


protected URLConnection doOK (URLConnection connection)
{
  InputStream is = null;
  try
  {
    is = connection.getInputStream();
    while (is.available() == 0)
    {
      Thread.sleep(250);
    }
  }
  catch (InterruptedException ie)
  {
    ie.printStackTrace();
  }
  catch (IOException ioe)
  {
    ioe.printStackTrace();
  }
  try
  {
    byte[] buffer = new byte[is.available()];
    int count = is.read(buffer);
    String output = new String(buffer,0,count);
    m_area.setText(output);
  }
  catch (IOException ioe)
```

continued

```
    {
      ioe.printStackTrace();
    }
    return null;
  }


  public void actionPerformed (ActionEvent ae)
  {
    if (ae.getSource() == m_URL)
    {
      try
      {
        URL theURL =
          new URL(getDocumentBase(),
                  m_URL.getText());

        URLConnection urlconnect =
          theURL.openConnection();

        urlconnect.connect();

        if (urlconnect instanceof
          HttpURLConnection)
        {
          boolean done = false;
          while (urlconnect != null)
          {
              HttpURLConnection h_conn =
                  (HttpURLConnection)urlconnect;

            switch (h_conn.getResponseCode())
            {
                case h_conn.HTTP_UNAUTHORIZED:
                urlconnect =
                    doUnauthorized(h_conn);
                break;

                case httpconnect.HTTP_OK:
                urlconnect = doOK (h_conn);
                break;
            }
          }
        }
      }
      catch (Exception e)
      {
        e.printStackTrace();
      }
  }
```

```
    }
}

class PasswordDialog extends Dialog
implements ActionListener
{
    private TextField m_name;
    private TextField m_password;
    private Button    m_ok;

    public PasswordDialog ()
    {
        super(new Frame(),"Digest Authentication",true);
        m_name = new TextField(20);
        m_password = new TextField(20);
        m_password.setEchoChar('*');
        setLayout(new GridLayout(3,1));
        Panel p = new Panel();
        p.add(new Label("Name"));
        p.add(m_name);
        add(p);
        p = new Panel();
        p.add(new Label("Password"));
        p.add(m_password);
        add(p);
        p = new Panel();
        p.add(m_ok = new Button("OK"));
        add(p);
        m_ok.addActionListener(this);
    }

    public String getName ()
    {
        return m_name.getText().trim();
    }

    public String getPassword ()
    {
        return m_password.getText().trim();
    }

    public void actionPerformed (ActionEvent ae)
    {
        dispose();
    }
}
```

It's a long program, but it's worth it! You can use the `DigestAuthUtility` class and the code from the `doOK` and `doUnauthorized` methods in your own programs to add Digest authentication between clients and resources on the Java Web Server.

Check out Figure 14-10 to see the `DigestApplet` in action.

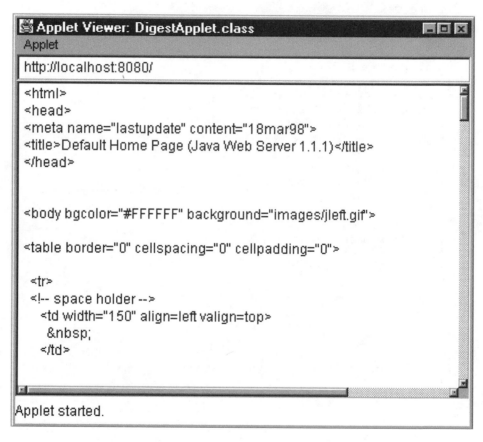

Figure 14-10   The DigestApplet in action.

In this example, we secured the `Snoop` servlet with Digest authentication from the administrative GUI's security panel. (Administrative help can be found in Chapter 4 "Administrating the Java Web Server.") When we point the `DigestApplet` at the `Snoop` servlet, a password dialog gets displayed, so we can type in the appropriate credentials (shown in Figure 14-11).

With the right name and password (for example, "Chris" and "Chris") you get your hands on the fruits of the `Snoop` servlet's labor.

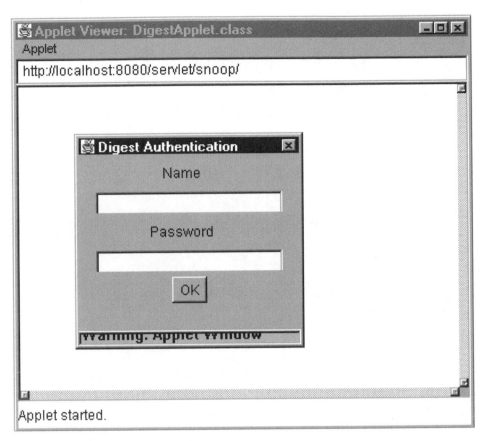

Figure 14-11   Prompted for the right username and password.

There is a *slight* problem with our example. If you remember from the chapter on HTTP caching, the HttpURLConnection class isn't supported on Internet Explorer or Netscape Communicator, making the use of the switch statement in the meat of the DigestApplet a more difficult task. All that the example uses the HttpURLConnection for is its capability to distinguish status codes sent by the server; it is left as an "exercise for the reader" (don't you just hate those?) to make it work on Netscape Communicator and Internet Explorer.

Digest authentication is a great replacement for Basic authentication, but it's not the last word in security. It doesn't protect the data sent by the server from prying eyes intent on sniffing tasty bits of information like credit card numbers or Social Security account information. If you want to use the Java Web Server to do business over the net, you're going to need a way to make that data secure.

And that way is called SSL.

SSL Keeps Your Data Safe!

SSL is an acronym for Secure Sockets Layer, but as with every other acronym, the full name is quickly forgotten. That's too bad, because SSL lives up to its name.

Understanding how SSL works requires that you know how sockets work, so a little refresher course might be helpful. If you're familiar with sockets and socket programming, you can skip the next section and move on to the SSL-specific material.

A Brief Introduction to Network Programming

When network programming is taught, the first thing thrown at you is a diagram of the OSI reference model.

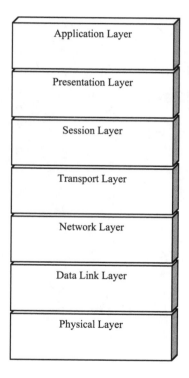

Figure 14-12   The OSI Reference Model...boring!

The way it works is that data flows from one layer to the next, moving down on a send and up on a read. Each layer communicates with the same layer on another machine (so the Transport layer on machine 'A' needs to know only what the Transport layer on machine 'B' wants). Owing to its modular nature, the OSI model lets a layer replace its protocol without affecting the rest of the layers in the stack

But before you start worrying about the number of layers or what they all mean, take heart that no one has actually *used* the OSI model—they just talk about it like it's the most important part of networking you'll ever need to learn.

Core Note

Okay, people have *implemented and used the OSI model. It just never caught on as much as the original designers had hoped. Important tools like ASN.1 and BER encoding have come from the same standards group that produced the OSI model.*

Instead of the OSI model becoming *the* way to implement network protocols, pieces of it were borrowed and used in other networking systems such as TCP/IP. The socket API is a good example of "applying the OSI model to the real world."

Sockets are the most popular way of programming on a TCP/IP network. Although the socket API allows for other protocol types (like Xerox's XNS or Novell's IPX/SPX), you'll see it most often used in Internet applications. Like the OSI model's `session` layer, the socket API provides some context for data flowing through a TCP/IP connection. For example, a socket connects a source machine's IP address (the network address of a machine) and a port number (a special cubbyhole on the IP-specified machine) with a destination machine's IP address and port number.

Using sockets is easy—when you need information from a server, your client creates a socket to the server and receives data across it. In this way, sockets earn their name, because they act like wall sockets, providing standardized access to an important resource (electricity!). As long as the wire is plugged into the socket, power will flow. As soon as the socket is closed, the power stops moving. Fortunately, there aren't separate standards for sockets in Europe, so your Internet apps will work around the world.

So what does this have to do with SSL? SSL sits atop the socket API and it encrypts or decrypts data passing through it. If SSL were placed into the OSI reference model, it would squeeze into the `session` layer above the socket API. A programmer using SSL makes calls to functions such as `SSLInitContext`, `SSLHandshake`, `SSLRead`, `SSLWrite`, `SSLClose`, and `SSLDeleteContext` (to name a few). Each of these functions may make socket API calls like `socket`, `bind`, `gethostbyname`, `read`, `write`, and `close`. Eventually the data is received by the destination machine, where its SSL module will follow the appropriate actions and use the socket API to send data back to the source machine. This communication continues until one of the two parties closes the connection.

And that's about it for the brief network programming section! More on network programming can be found in Core Java, and SSL documentation can be found on Netscape's Web site (`http://test-drive.netscape.com/tdrive-new/sslref.html`).

Back to SSL...

Okay, SSL sits on top of the socket API. So, how does it know how to encrypt data? Time for another digression!

A Brief Introduction to Cryptography

As we said earlier when discussing Digest authentication, cryptography is a broad and complex topic that cannot be given the complete coverage it deserves here (wonderful books like *Applied Cryptography* already fill that need). Instead, this introduction focuses on the ideas behind the practices, and on the way SSL uses those ideas.

The essential element of a public encryption algorithm (an algorithm that doesn't depend on no one's knowing how it works) is the *key*. The key is usually a string of bits that act as input, modifying what the encryption output will be. When the same key is used for encrypting and decrypting data, the algorithm is known as a *symmetric key cipher*. With it, both parties (the sender and the receiver) must know the key's value. A famous example of a symmetric key cipher is the DES (Data Encryption Standard) cipher. Figure 14-13 illustrates how data is encrypted by the source application and sent to the destination for decryption.

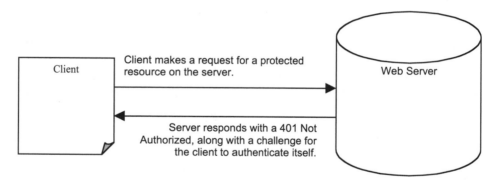

Figure 14-13   Protecting data with a symmetric cipher.

Two new ideas are introduced in Figure 14-13. *Plaintext* is the cryptographers' word for unencrypted text, and *ciphertext* is what the plaintext becomes when encrypted by a specific cipher with a specific key. The ciphertext may be transmitted over insecure lines, as an eavesdropper cannot easily reduce it back into plaintext without knowing the symmetric key.

Did you notice how we made the requirement that both applications share an encryption key seem trivial? In fact it is not a trivial problem. Typically, one side (usually the source) generates a symmetric key and gives it to the destination application. But how does that key get there without an outsider stealing it? Once someone besides the source or the destination has the key, the data encrypted with that key is compromised.

This is where *public key cryptography* comes into play. Unlike that for a symmetric key, the algorithm for a public key (also known as an *asymmetric key*) uses different key values for encrypting and decrypting data. The two values are related mathematically in some way, but with the strict requirement that having one key doesn't let someone who knows its value guess the value of the second key. The most famous public-key cipher algorithm is the RSA algorithm, whose keys are two prime factors of a large (1024-bit) number. One key, known as the *public key*, is freely distributed to anyone who wants to send encrypted data to the owner of the key. The other key, known as the *private key*, is kept secret by the owner for decrypting data sent by others.

By using public-key cryptography, a generated symmetric key can be sent safely to the destination application by encrypting it with the destination application's public key. Figure 14-14 illustrates how this works.

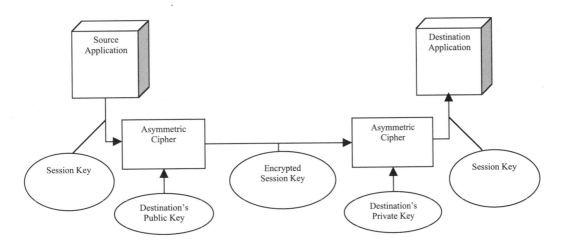

Figure 14-14 Encrypting the session key.

Figure 14-14 introduces yet another term into the mix: *session key*. This is a symmetric key that is generated for use during a specific period of time. The session key is encrypted with the destination's public key and sent as ciphertext to the destination application. Since the latter can read the session key only if it has access to the private key, the source application is guaranteed that the right application receives the session key.

There are still holes in the system, though. How does the source application get a copy of the destination's public key? If it asks the destination application for its public key, a sophisticated interloper could return its own public key back to the source. Since the source application has no way to verify if the public key belongs to the destination, it can be fooled into giving up the session key without knowing that it has been compromised.

This is where the concept of a *digital certificate* enters the picture. A digital certificate is a computer's version of a passport or driver's license. When someone electronically presents a digital certificate, its authenticity is guaranteed if it has been created by a trusted third party. Just as a liquor store trusts the DMV to issue licenses with proper ages marked on them, or a customs officer trusts the United States government to issue passports to American citizens, an application can trust that a certain *certificate authority* (CA) verifies a user's identity before issuing a digital certificate.

Digital certificates have an additional level of security because the contents are *signed* by the CA. Signing is the analog of encrypting: the data is encrypted with a private key, and the signature is verified by decrypting the encrypted data with the public key. Typically, these *keypairs* (encryption and signature) are different.

As well as verifying an identity, the certificate contains the public encryption key of the owner along with the signature verification key. Once the authenticity of the certificate is verified ("Do we trust this CA?"), these keys can be used for sending data to the owner and verifying the owner's response.

Finally! You're up to speed on all of the cryptography-related concepts used by SSL, so without further ado…

Back to SSL, Again …

So, digital certificates contain the public keys of an identity. This comes in handy during the initialization of a secure session between the source and destination applications. When the source initiates a connection, it can request the destination application's certificate. The certificate, being signed by a trusted third party, can be passed in the clear, since any modifications will corrupt the certificate (kind of like trying to modify your age on a driver's license with a magic marker!). Once the source application is happy with the certificate's authenticity, it can use the public key embedded within the certificate to encrypt the generated session key for protecting the conversation between the source and the destination application.

Why all this work to secure the session key? Why not forgo the symmetric and use the asymmetric cipher for all encryption? The main reason is performance: symmetric ciphers are faster than their asymmetric brothers. The expensive encryption is done on a small amount of data (the session key) once, and the bulk of the encryption is done using the computationally cheaper symmetric encryption.

Now, here is where the Java Web Server comes into play. Replacing the words "source application" and "destination application" with "Web browser" and "Java Web Server" in the previous discussion should give you a clearer view of how SSL works with the JWS.

But don't take our word for it, let's see this in action!

Configuring SSL on the Java Web Server

After all this talk about secure transmission and protocol handshaking, it would be a terrible letdown to say that not all versions of the Java Web Server support SSL.

Sorry to disappoint you, but yes, not all versions of the Java Web Server can use SSL! Specifically, only Solaris and Win32 platforms support SSL, so if you're running on a Macintosh or Linux, you might be out of luck.

With that out of the way, let's explore how to get the Java Web Server SSL-enabled on the Windows NT platform. Most of what you'll see here applies to the Solaris version of the Java Web Server, except for some NT-related topics such as Services. (See Chapter 2 "Installing the Java Web Server" for more information on Windows NT.)

Introducing the AuthStore Utility

AuthStore is an additional utility for creating and adding certificates for the Java Web Server. You can find it in the bin subdirectory of the Java Web Server. Running AuthStore should bring up a window like the one shown in Figure 14-15.

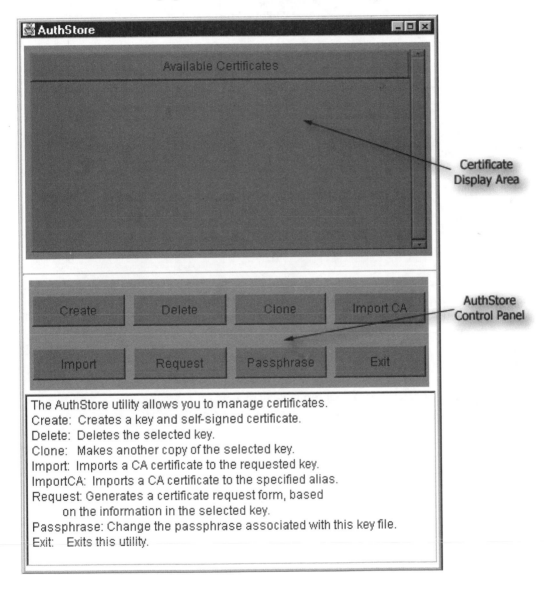

Figure 14-15 Running the AuthStore utility.

The `AuthStore` is logically separated into two pieces: the Certificate Display Area and the Authstore Control Panel. The display area shows the configured certificates. As you can see in Figure 14-15, no certificates have been configured yet.

When you add certificates to the Java Web Server, the private key sets are protected in a stored file called the *keystore* file. This file is named `keys`, and it's kept in the server's installation directory. Deleting the keys file will remove all of the configured certificates from the server, so you should protect that file and keep a backup around in case someone accidentally erases it.

Core Note

If you abort a certificate creation, sometimes the `AuthStore` utility has already created an empty keystore. A zero-length keystore should be erased (as it will confuse the Java Web Server into not starting) and the `AuthStore` utility should be rerun.

There are two kinds of certificates used by the Java Web Server:

- Self-signed certificates
- CA-signed certificates

Self-signed certificates are the easiest and least expensive option for enabling SSL. They are perfect for Intranets that want to handle their own security, or for servlet developers wanting to take advantage of SSL authentication from their servlets (we'll be covering this later in the chapter) without shelling out a ton of cash for a digital identity. Creating a self-signed certificate is simple: just click on the `create` button on the control panel.

After you press the `create` button, you should see the Certificate Display Area disappear, replaced with an informational dialog.

Ignoring the first option (the `key alias` cannot be changed), you have three other configurable options on this dialog. The `key size` determines the strength of the cryptography. The bigger the number, the better the encryption strength, so we picked 1024.

Core Note

The `key size` field is the number of bits used in the key. The more bits in the key, the more possible keys must be checked in a brute-force attack on the key's value. (A brute-force attack occurs when someone who doesn't know the key tries every possible key value until the right one is found.) More information on key strength can be found in Bruce Schneier's Applied Cryptography.

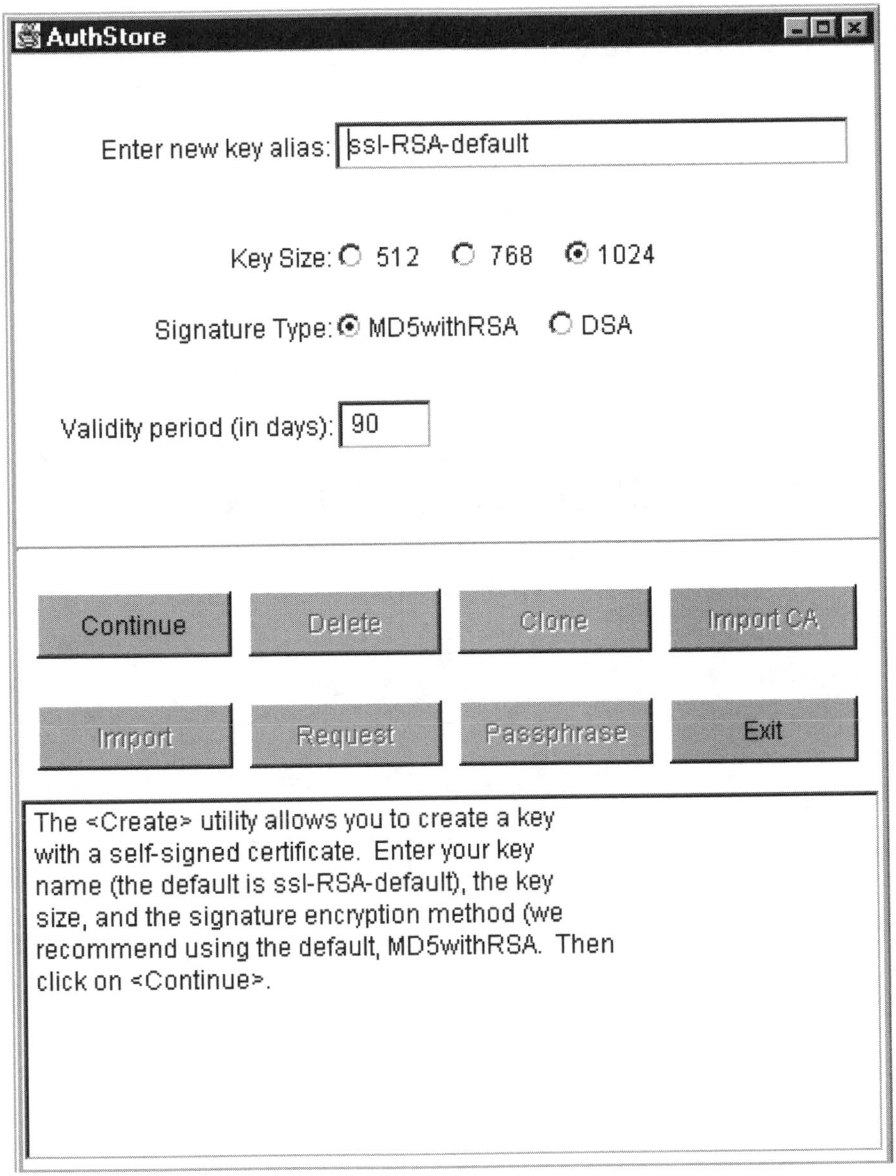

Figure 14-16   Creating a self-signed certificate.

The signature type field describes the keys used to generate digital signatures (verifying that data hasn't been altered in transit from the Java Web Server). RSA is the key type, with MD5 added as the one-way hash algorithm (to verify that the signature hasn't been tampered with), so we chose MD5withRSA for our signature type. The `validity period` contains the lifetime of the certificate. Once that lifetime has been reached, the certificate is no longer valid. This is nothing new, as you see lifetimes on other types of certificates—driver's licenses expire, credit cards have expiration dates, and so on. Also, certificates can be revoked at any time. (As real-world examples, a credit card may be stolen, or a driver be convicted of reckless driving.) As on a bad-check list, revoked digital certificates are stored on a *Certificate Revocation List* (CRL). Programs can refer to a CRL when validating that a certificate is good (first, check whether it has expired, then check whether it has been revoked).

Clicking the `Continue` button will change the informational dialog with a second dialog. This dialog is prompting the user for information to store within the self-signed certificate. Figure 14-17 shows this new informational dialog (along with our own test data).

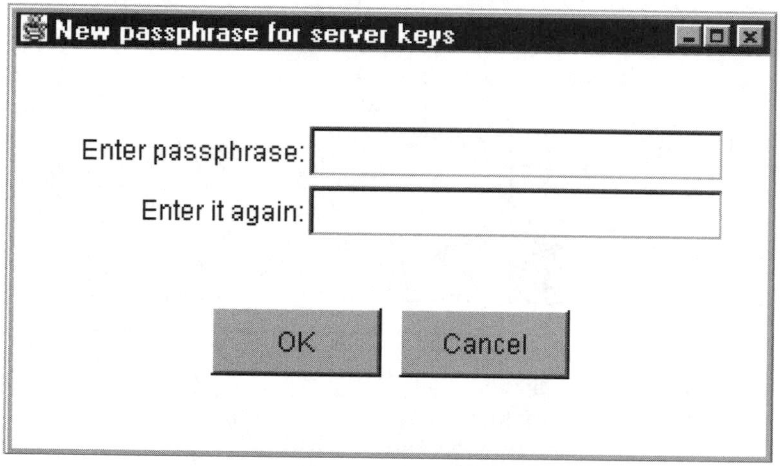

New passphrase for server keys _ □ ✕

Enter passphrase: [   ]

Enter it again: [   ]

[OK   ]   [Cancel]

Figure 14-17   Continuing the certification process.

Pressing the OK button sends you to the passphrase dialog. The bytes of the passphrase string are used as a symmetric key for encrypting the key store. Whenever the Java Web Server starts up, it will need this passphrase to open up it up.

Core Note

Make sure you don't forget your passphrase! Without it, your certificate data is useless, and you'll have to install a new certificate!

After you've entered the passphrase, the `AuthStore` utility will use the information to generate a certificate, then sign it with its own keys (hence the term "self-signed"). With the certificate successfully installed, you'll need to restart the Java Web Server, then use the Admin applet's service management panel to start the Secure Web Service. Once the service is running, use your Web browser and connect to port 7070 using an HTTPS (not an HTTP!) URL.

When your browser reaches the Java Web Server, it should pop up a "unrecognized certificate" dialog. This dialog will let you add the certificate to a list of trusted ones. Figure 14-18 shows the dialog.

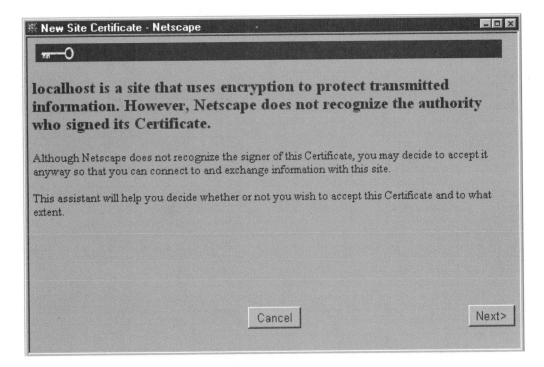

Figure 14-18   Adding a new site certificate from Netscape Communicator.

Having added yours to the browser's list of trusted certificates, your applications on the Java Web Server can communicate securely with the browser. Remember the handshake process between the client and the server from the explanation on SSL basics? During that handshake, a *cipher suite* is agreed on. A cipher suite is a set of encryption algorithms used for encrypting the data. You can configure which cipher suites you'd like your server to support using the service configuration panel. (See Chapter 4 "Administrating the Java Web Server," for more details on configuring the Java Web Server). If you open up the Secure Web Service's security section, you should see a new option on the tree control. Figure 14-19 shows this new option.

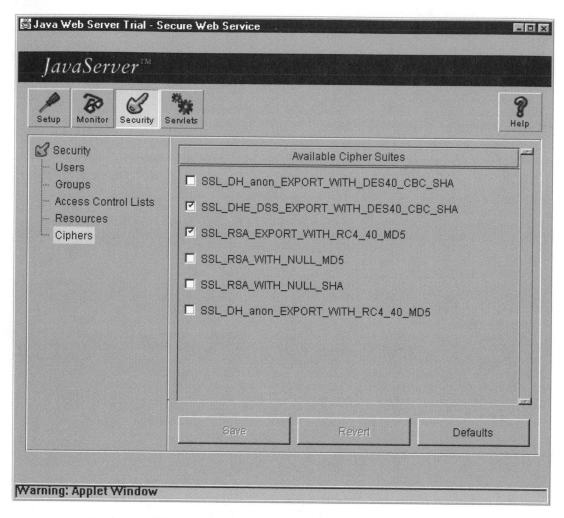

Figure 14-19 Configuring the Java Web Server's SSL cipher suites.

It's best to leave these options as they are, but at least now you know where you can change them if you want to. If you read the names of the ciphers carefully, you can figure our whether you're running an international version of the Java Web Server or a domestic version. Owing to U.S. regulations on exporting products using cryptography, customers outside the United States and Canada only get 40-bit symmetric keys. This makes it relatively easy to launch a brute-force attack on the key, so if you're planning to use SSL to protect business transactions, make sure you're using the strongest cryptography that you can legally obtain. If you're in the United States or Canada, get the domestic version so you can support a larger key size.

You've added a self-signed certificate to the Java Web Server. It works great. So, what's the benefit of a certificate signed by someone else?

The Benefits of a CA-Signed Certificate

When a certificate is self-signed, users of that certificate must trust the server. In an intranet application, that trust might be warranted, but on the Internet you have no idea about the identity on the other side of that network connection. What you really need is a certificate that's signed by someone trusted by both the client and the server. This trusted third party is called a *certificate authority*.

One of the most popular certificate authorities is Verisign (`http://www.verisign.com`). We'll be using Verisign as the CA in our CA-signed certificate examples, but it's not the only commercial CA out there. Furthermore, if you have your own CA (such as Tandem's CSS product) running on your network, you can use it to issue certificates for both your browser clients and your Java Web Server.

You'll need to use the `AuthStore` utility and your Web browser to obtain a Verisign certificate. The first step is opening up the `AuthStore` utility and clicking the Request button on the control panel. This will generate a *CSR*, or Certificate Signing Request, that you'll submit to Verisign (or whatever CA you're using) to get your certificate.

Okay, we've glossed over something important here. Remember when we said that a certificate contains a signature key (for verification) and an encryption key (for sending data)? Somehow the public versions of these keys must be sent to the CA when a certificate is generated. So, when you make a CSR, you need to put your keys inside it. Fortunately, the `AuthStore` utility handles that automatically for you. All you need to do is select the key you generated for the self-signed certificate example, then press the Request button to generate the CSR.

Once you've pressed the Request button, you should see an informational dialog pop up within the `Certificate Display Area`. Figure 14-20 shows this dialog, complete with our test information.

Most of the information is self-explanatory. The `File to Save to` field specifies the path and filename where the CSR will be saved. As you can see in Figure 14-20, our CSR will be saved to a file named `output` in the root of the `D:` directory. The CSR is a Base64 encoded text file, and its content is beyond the scope of this text. (Interested readers should check out the PKCS specification documents at RSA's Web site, `http://www.rsa.com`.)

With the CSR file in hand, you'll need to log on to Verisign's Web site and request a new server certificate. At one point during the request process you'll be asked to attach the content of the CSR on a form. At this point, Verisign (or whatever certificate authority you're using) will send you the server certificate and the root CA certificate for the CA that has signed your server certificate. Before you can import your server certificate into the Java Web Server, you'll need to import the root CA certificate using the `AuthStore`.

Why do you need to import the CA certificate? The Java Web Server uses this information to import server certificates, as each root certificate acts like a template to interpret the data. Use the `AuthStore`'s Import CA button to incorporate the template into the key store. Once the template is installed, the server certificate can be imported using the Import button.

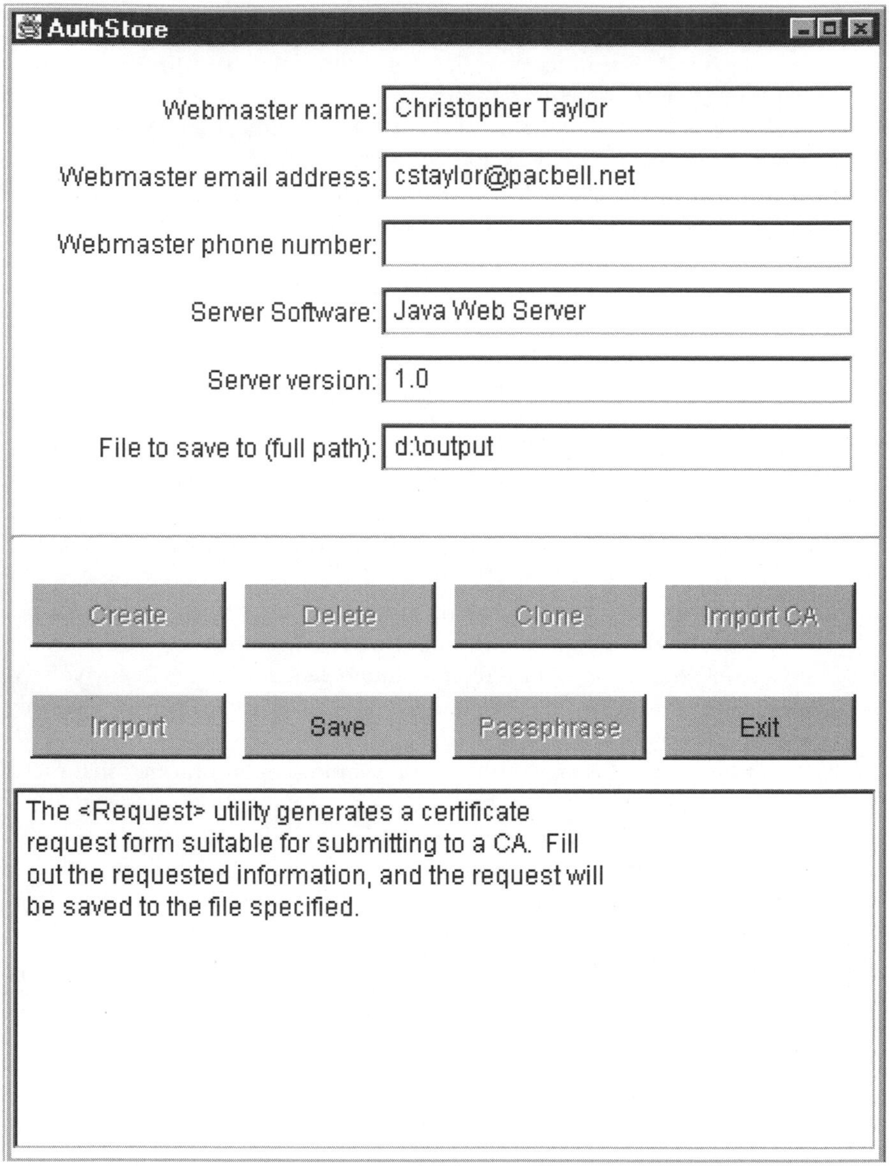

AuthStore [_][□][✕]

Webmaster name:	Christopher Taylor
Webmaster email address:	cstaylor@pacbell.net
Webmaster phone number:	
Server Software:	Java Web Server
Server version:	1.0
File to save to (full path):	d:\output

[Create]   [Delete]   [Clone]   [Import CA]

[Import]   [Save]   [Passphrase]   [Exit]

The <Request> utility generates a certificate
request form suitable for submitting to a CA. Fill
out the requested information, and the request will
be saved to the file specified.

Figure 14-20   Filling out the Certificate Signing Request.

Core Note

*Using the Import CA button is an essential step for getting your server certificate
installed properly. Failure to do this will cause the* AuthStore *utility to fail
when loading your server certificate!*

With the server certificate installed, you can now operate with SSL using a CA-signed certificate.

Using the Default HTTPS Port

Web servers using SSL don't usually run on port 7070. As a convenience to your clients, you should change the port number of the Secure Web Service to 443. Refer to Chapter 4 "Administrating the Java Web Server" for information on how to change the port number of a service.

Automatically Opening the Key Store

You've learned about SSL and how to make it work with the Java Web Server, yet every time you need to get your hands into the key store's goodies you're forced to enter the passphrase. In examples like those in this chapter, entering the passphrase is a reasonable request, but it may not be convenient in a production environment. Since servers can go up and down automatically (periodic reboots, remote administration, etc.), it would be a great feature if the passphrase were placed in a file that the Java Web Server could read on startup.

Core Note

Although it's great for automatic startup, placing your passphrase in a file has serious security consequences. Before taking this step, make sure you understand the risks involved.

Fortunately, the Java Web Server development team made this step easy to accomplish. All you need to do is place the passphrase in a file named `keys.passphrase` in the Java Web Server's base directory, then specify the additional parameter `-passfile` when starting the server:

```
echo "Some Passphrase" > c:\javawebserver1.1\keys.passphrase
httpd -passfile
```

Authentication Summary

Whew! Who would have thought that HTTP-based authorization would be so complicated! Starting with the clear-text Basic authentication, you learned how a client validates its identity to a server. You continued on to implement Digest authentication, a more complex protocol that attempts to address the failings of Basic authentication. Finally, you survived a crash course on the Secure Socket Layer, and how to configure the Java Web Server to use it.

Of course, getting an identity to the server is only the first inning of the security game. Somehow, somewhere, you've got to do something with that identity.

Putting Authentication to Work with Realms

The "somehow" of doing something with an identity brings us to Realms. You've already seen Realms in action in our discussions of the Basic and Digest authentication schemes. Realms in client contexts like those provide *scope* to a logon request. Yet, that's only one of many tasks a Realm handles.

In the most conceptual sense, a Realm is a body holding all the other parts of the security puzzle, including:

- Users
- Groups
- Access Control Lists

Furthermore, User, Group, or ACL names can be duplicated in separate Realms. For example, you may have a user named 'Chris' within a Realm called "LDAP users" and within a Realm called "NT users." An authorization request for Chris is ambiguous, then, *unless* the Realm is an explicit part of the request.

Another constraint requires any users and groups in ACL entries to exist within the same Realm. This makes sense if you think of the Realm as a closed container—it only knows about what lies inside of it, so its ACLs have no way to know about users and groups from other enclosed Realms.

The administrative side of applying ACLs to server resources is covered in Chapter 4 "Administrating the Java Web Server," so when you see some hand-waving about "securing a resource with an ACL," you can refer to that chapter's security section for more information. The present section will focus on working with Users, Groups, and Realms from code.

And with that introduction, Listing 14-9 shows you how to add users to a Realm from a servlet.

Listing 14-9   Adding Users to SharedPasswordRealms from HTML forms

---

```
import com.sun.server.realm.*;
import java.security.acl.*;
import javax.servlet.*;
import javax.servlet.http.*;
import java.io.*;
import java.util.*;
import com.sun.server.realm.sharedpassword.*;

public class RealmServlet extends HttpServlet
{
  protected void doGet (HttpServletRequest req,
  HttpServletResponse res)
```

```
throws IOException, ServletException
{
  res.setContentType("text/html");
  PrintWriter pw = res.getWriter();
  pw.print ("<html><body><table>");
  pw.print ("<form method=post action=\"");
  pw.print (req.getRequestURI()+"\">");
  pw.print ("<tr><td>Realm</td><td><select");
  pw.print (" name=\"realm\">");

  for (Enumeration e = Realm.getRealmNames();
     e.hasMoreElements();)
  {
    String realmName = (String)e.nextElement();
    try
    {
      Realm realm = Realm.get(realmName);
      if (realm instanceof SharedPasswordRealm)
      {
        pw.print ("<option>"+realmName);
      }
    }
    catch (BadRealmException oops)
    {
      oops.printStackTrace();
    }
    catch (NoSuchRealmException oops)
    {
      oops.printStackTrace();
    }
  }
  pw.print ("</select></td></tr><tr><td>User</td>");
  pw.print ("<td><input type=text name=user");
  pw.print (" size=20></td></tr>");
  pw.print ("<tr><td>Password</td><td><input ");
  pw.print ("type=text name=password size=20></td>");
  pw.print ("</tr><tr><td>Confirm Password</td><td>");
  pw.print ("<input type=text name=password2 ");
  pw.print ("size=20></td></tr><tr><td colspan=2>");
  pw.print ("<input type=submit value=\"Create");
  pw.print ("User\"></td></tr></form></table> ");
  pw.print ("</body></html>");
  pw.close();
}

protected void doPost (HttpServletRequest req,
HttpServletResponse res)
throws ServletException, IOException
{
  PrintWriter pw = res.getWriter();
  String[] users = req.getParameterValues("user");
```

continued

```
String[] passw = req.getParameterValues("password");
String[] passw2=
         req.getParameterValues("password2");
String[] realms = req.getParameterValues("realm");

SharedPasswordRealm realm = null;
try
{
  realm =
  (SharedPasswordRealm)Realm.get(realms[0]);
  if (!passw[0].equals(passw2[0]))
  {
    pw.println ("Passwords don't match");
  }
  else
  {
    realm.createUser(users[0],passw[0]);
    pw.println ("User "+users[0]+" created "+
                "successfully in Realm "+
                realms[0]);
  }
}
catch (Exception oops)
{
  oops.printStackTrace();
}
pw.close();
  }
}
```

Compile the `RealmServlet` and throw it into the servlets directory. Next, open up your browser and navigate to `http://localhost:8080/servlet/RealmServlet`. You're browser should look like Figure 14-21.

This code can be broken up into two sections:

- Enumerating Realms
- Adding users to a special kind of Realm called a `SharedPasswordRealm`

You can see the Realm enumeration in the `RealmServlet`'s doGet method. The `com.sun.server.realm.Realm` class has a static method called `getRealmNames` that retrieves an enumeration of String objects containing all of the names of the configured Realms. This method is key when accessing the rest of the Realm API calls, because you'll use those Strings to get (another `Realm` method!) a specific Realm instance.

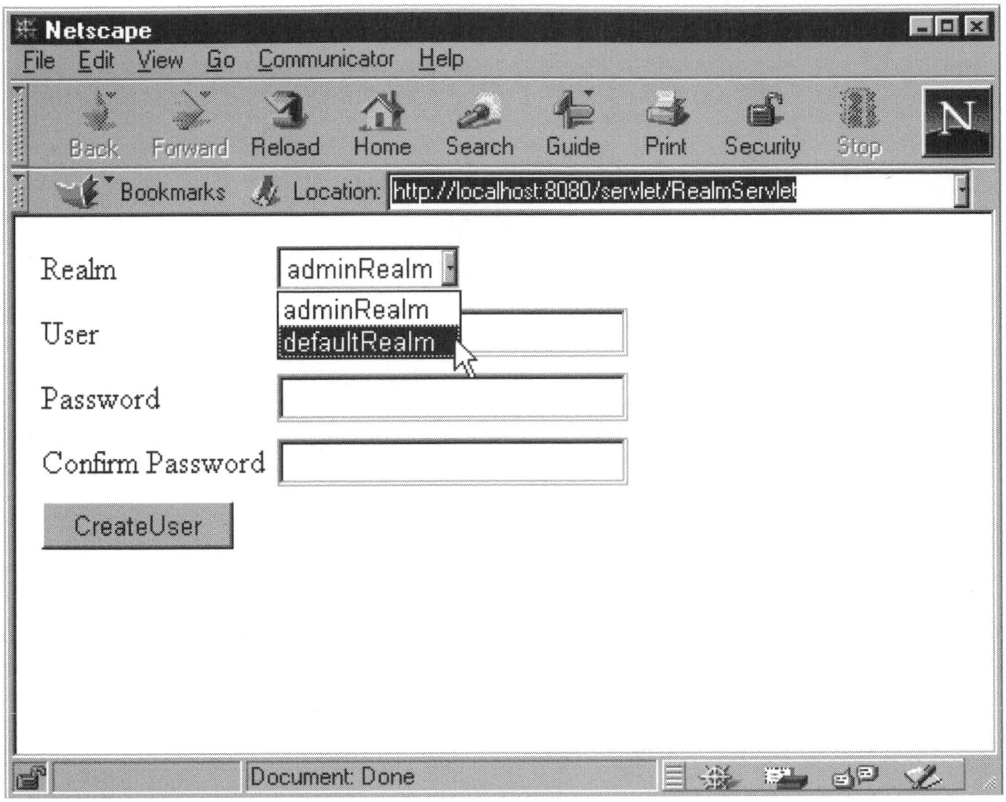

Figure 14-21   A simple user creation form.

REALM CLASS

```
public static Enumeration getRealmNames()
```

Returns an Enumeration of Strings, where each String is the name of a configured Realm. These Strings can be used with the get method to retrieve a Realm instance.

```
public static Realm get (String RealmName)
```

Throws NoSuchRealmException.

```
BadRealmException
```

Returns the Realm instance associated with the parameter RealmName. If no Realm can be found by that name, a NoSuchRealmException is thrown.

So why did we cast the Realm instance into a `SharedPasswordRealm` object? We wanted to create a new user. If you look carefully at the methods supported by the `Realm` class, you'll notice that one is missing: `addUser`. There are APIs for adding groups (`addGroup`) and adding ACLs (`addAcl`), but not for users.

This glaring omission was puzzling at first, but then it made perfect sense: not all Realms would use names and passwords to authenticate their users! For example, users that authenticate with digital certificates (within the certificateRealm) don't have a name and a password. Adding an overloaded `addUser(X509Cert)` method to Realm would be out of place, since not all Realms use certificates, either. Furthermore, any additional `addUser` methods in the `Realm` base class would require a priori knowledge of how all cases of authentication would work—and that would just be bad OOP!

A `SharedPasswordRealm` is a subclass of `Realm` that supports the creation of users with simple names and passwords. It provides this support through the `createUser` method. In the previous example, the `doPost` method in the `RealmServlet` class uses this additional API for creating a user from information submitted through an HTML form submission.

SHAREDPASSWORDREALM

`public void createUser (String name, String password)`

Throws InUseException.

`BadRealmException`

Creates a new user within this Realm using the name and password parameters. If a name clash occurs between the new user and an existing user or group, an InUseException is thrown.

`public void changePassword (String name, String old_password)`

Throws NoSuchUserException.

`BadRealmException`

Changes an existing user's password. If the user specified by the name parameter cannot be found, a NoSuchUserException is thrown.

Other than creating users or changing their attributes (such as their passwords), all of the essential methods for using Realms can be found in the `Realm` base class. You can use its APIs to provide programmatic access to security.

You might wonder here, "Will I even want to do this?"

Maybe. We've never used it for more than a few toy examples, but your mileage may vary. For us, what's more interesting is writing a custom Realm.

Writing Your Own Realms

As we said in the introduction to the section, a Realm encapsulates users, groups, and ACLs. There are several situations in which you might want to add your own Realm implementation to the Java Web Server:

- Bridging an existing logon facility
- Using a different object for identifying users
- Adding a second storage type

In English, bridging an existing logon facility means relying on someone else for authenticating a user. A good example is the Windows NT `Winlogon` facilities. NT already supports the concept of users and groups on a computer, so you could write a Realm that takes advantage of this with some choice native code. Fortunately, the Java Web Server development team already wrote a Realm for handling NT logons, but it requires some minor tweaking to get it to work (as it contains native code libraries).

The `NTRealm` class depends on the existence of a library named `server.dll`. Some releases of the demonstration version of the Java Web Server don't come with that native library (it should be in the Java Web Server's `lib` subdirectory), so trying to use the NT realm in the `security` section of the administrative GUI will cause error dialogs to appear.

So, what's going on? The `server.dll` native library contains the code of four methods:

```
getNextUserName
setpwent
checkCrypt
loadFromPasswd
```

They're all private methods for tying into Windows NT. Without getting too far into the plumbing of NT, the NTRealm gets a collection of user's names with the `NetUserEnum` API call within `NETAPI32.dll` and validates user names and passwords with the `LoginUser` API call from `ADVAPI32.dll`.

Core Note

How did we figure this out? Although having the source code would have made it easier, a tool called dumpbin *from the Microsoft SDK let us peer into the import/export tables of the* server.dll *file. Armed with that information, we could decipher what Java classes and methods were involved with which NT system calls. Anyone interested in doing JNI (Java Native Interface) programming— tying Java into the underlying operating system in a portable way—should check out* Essential JNI *by Robert Gordon and Alan McClellan from Prentice Hall.*

The Solaris version of the Java Web Server supports NIS logons. It works in a similar way, using native code (but since neither of us is a Solaris developer, we don't have the foggiest idea of how it *really* works!).

Although tying into the operating system is a nice touch for user authentication, most companies have a wider base of user information stored within a *directory system* called X.500. Applications can tap into this user base with a special protocol called *LDAP* (which was covered in Chapter 11 "Session Management"). Creating a Realm that could get at these user accounts would be a tremendous help to overworked system administrators.

Core Note

Instead of writing directly to LDAP, the next example will use JNDI (which was also explained in Chapter 11) to abstract the type of directory system in use.

With over ten abstract methods left to implement, deriving from the `Realm` class could turn the `JNDIRealm` class into an example nightmare. Fortunately, the Java Web Server development team comes to the rescue! To make this task easier, they developed a "Custom Realm Cookbook," which is a set of prewritten classes that handle some of the tedious aspects of handling Realm service requests. Just like the basic `Realm` class, the crux for using the cookbook is the class `CustomRealm`. `CustomRealm` provides hooks for three new support classes:

```
AclEntity
GroupEntity
UserEntity
```

In reality, these are interfaces and not classes, but the idea is the same. `AclEntity` handles Access Control Lists, `GroupEntity` handles group management, and `UserEntity` handles user authentication. For the `JNDIRealm` you'll need to implement only the `UserEntity` interface, leaving the other two to use file-based classes for storing their information (which also comes with the cookbook).

Well, the team reduced the job of implementing abstract methods from double digits down to four. But they didn't stop there! They've created a convenience class called `UserEntityImpl`, which implements the `UserEntity` interface by throwing simple "I don't support this function" exceptions. By extending this class, you can just override the methods that you'd like to support (like `getUser`, `authenticate`, and `getUserNames`) and leave out the ones you don't want (like `delete`).

As promised, Listing 14-10 is an implementation of a `JNDIRealm` that makes some assumptions about the directory server being accessed (you can modify it to your own taste). Listing 14-11 contains the code for the `JNDIUserEntity` class, and Listing 14-12 contains the code for the supporting class `JndiBean`.

Listing 14-10   JNDIRealm

```java
import com.sun.server.realm.*;
import com.sun.server.realm.util.*;
import java.io.*;
import java.util.*;

public class JNDIRealm extends CustomRealm
{
  public synchronized void init(Properties props)
  throws BadRealmException, NoSuchRealmException
  {
    try
    {
      super.init(props);
      setAclEntity(new FileAclEntity(this));
      setGroupEntity(new FileGroupEntity(this));
      setUserEntity(new JNDIUserEntity(this));
    }
    catch(Exception e)
    {
      throw new BadRealmException(e.getMessage());
    }
  }
}
```

Listing 14-11   JNDIUserEntity

```java
import java.util.*;
import java.io.*;
import com.sun.server.realm.*;
import com.sun.server.realm.util.*;

public class JNDIUserEntity extends UserEntityImpl
{
  private JndiBean m_accessBean;

  public JNDIUserEntity(CustomRealm aRealm)
  throws IOException
  {
    super(aRealm);
    m_accessBean = new JndiBean();
```

continued

```
    }

    public Enumeration getUserNames()
    {
      try
      {
        return m_accessBean.getPeople().elements();
      }
      catch (Exception e)
      {
        return null;
      }

    }

    public boolean authenticate(String userName,
                        String password)
    throws NoSuchUserException
    {
      try
      {
        return
        m_accessBean.isValidUser(userName,password);
      }
      catch (Exception e)
      {
        return false;
      }
    }

    public User getUser(String name)
    throws NoSuchUserException, BadRealmException
    {
      return  new RealmUser(name, getRealm());
    }
}
```

Listing 14-12   JndiBean

```
import javax.servlet.*;
import javax.servlet.http.*;

import javax.naming.*;
```

```java
import javax.naming.directory.*;

import java.io.*;
import java.util.*;


public class JndiBean implements java.io.Serializable
{
  private String jndi_context_factory =
    "com.sun.jndi.ldap.LdapCtxFactory";
  private String jndi_provider_url    =
    "ldap://taylor-pc2:389";
  private String jndi_searchbase      = "o=Airius.com";
  private String security_level       = "simple";

  public String getJndi_context_factory()
  {
    return this.jndi_context_factory;
  }

  public void setJndi_context_factory(String aFactory)
  {
    this.jndi_context_factory = aFactory;
  }

  public String getJndi_provider_url()
  {
    return this.jndi_provider_url;
  }

  public void setJndi_provider_url(String aProvider)
  {
    this.jndi_provider_url = aProvider;
  }

  public String getJndi_searchbase()
  {
    return this.jndi_searchbase;
  }

  public void setJndi_searchbase(String aSearchbase)
  {
    this.jndi_searchbase = aSearchbase;
  }

  public String getSecurity_level()
  {
```

continued

```
    return this.security_level;
}

public void setSecurity_level(String aLevel)
{
    this.security_level = aLevel;
}

public boolean isValidUser(String usr, String pwd)
throws NameNotFoundException, NamingException
{

    Hashtable env = new Hashtable(5, 0.75f);
    env.put(DirContext.INITIAL_CONTEXT_FACTORY,
        this.jndi_context_factory);
    env.put(DirContext.PROVIDER_URL,
        this.jndi_provider_url);
    env.put(DirContext.SECURITY_AUTHENTICATION,
        this.security_level);
    env.put(DirContext.SECURITY_PRINCIPAL,
        "uid=" + usr +", ou=People, " +
        this.jndi_searchbase);
    env.put(DirContext.SECURITY_CREDENTIALS, pwd);

    try
    {
        DirContext context = new InitialDirContext(env);
    }
    catch(javax.naming.AuthenticationException ae)
    {
        //return false because authentication failed
        return false;
    }

    //if here, user's password is valid
    return true;
}


public DirContext login() throws NamingException,
IOException
{
    Hashtable env = new Hashtable(5, 0.75f);
    env.put(Context.INITIAL_CONTEXT_FACTORY,
        this.jndi_context_factory);
    env.put(Context.PROVIDER_URL,
        this.jndi_provider_url);
```

```java
      env.put(Context.SECURITY_AUTHENTICATION,
        this.security_level);

      try
      {
        return new InitialDirContext(env);

      }
      catch(Exception e)
      {
        e.printStackTrace();
      }
       System.out.println("returning null in login()");
      return null;
}



public NamingEnumeration doSearch(DirContext dir_context,
                      String theCriteria,
                      String attrs[])
throws NamingException
{
    SearchControls srch_controls = new SearchControls();
    srch_controls.setSearchScope(
          SearchControls.SUBTREE_SCOPE);

    srch_controls.setReturningAttributes(attrs);
    String search_criteria = "(" + theCriteria + ")";

    return dir_context.search(this.jndi_searchbase,
                      search_criteria,
                      srch_controls);
}

public java.util.Vector getPeople()
throws NamingException, IOException
{

    java.util.Vector names = new java.util.Vector();
    String attrs[] = {"uid"};
    NamingEnumeration ne = doSearch(login(),"ou=People",
                          attrs);

    if(ne != null)
    {
     while(ne.hasMore())
```

continued

```
      {
        SearchResult sr = (SearchResult)ne.next();
        Attributes attribs = (Attributes)sr.getAttributes();

        for(Enumeration e = attribs.getIDs();
            e.hasMoreElements();)
        {
          String id = (String)e.nextElement();
          NamingEnumeration a_ne;

          for(a_ne = attribs.get(id).getAll(); a_ne.hasMore();)
          {
            names.addElement(a_ne.next().toString());
          }
        }
      }
    }
    return names;
  }
}
```

Once you've got these three classes compiled, you'll need to move them and the rest of the Realm cookbook classes into the `classes` subdirectory of the Java Web Server. For your convenience, the cookbook classes are on the CD-ROM (so you won't have to go get them from the Java Web Server site at `http://jserv.javasoft.com`).

Next, you'll need to configure the Java Web Server to use the JNDIRealm. When the Java Web Server starts up, the security module looks for a directory called `realms`. If it finds that directory, it opens up each file in it and treats it as a properties file. Each file needs two entries:

```
classname
directory
```

The `classname` entry is the package-qualified name of the Realm class that gets instantiated. The object, when it is created, must be a subclass of the `com.sun.server.realm.Realm` class.

The `directory` entry is where all of the Realm's private data gets stored. When the directory is specified as a separate parameter, a Realm can work with any directory (adding another level of flexibility!).

The `JNDIRealm` configuration file should look like Listing 14-13.

Listing 14-13   JNDIRealm configuration file

```
classname=JNDIRealm
directory=realms/data/JNDI
```

Save the configuration file, then make the directory you specified in the configuration file.

```
mkdir realms/data/JNDI
```

The final step for getting the Java Web Server to use the `JNDIRealm` is to restart the server (the security module initializes itself only at startup time!). Once the server is restarted, use the administrative GUI's security panel and look at the users in the `JNDIRealm`. Hopefully, if all went well (and a lot could go wrong—check out Chapter 11 "Session Management," for more details on JNDI), you should see a full dialog of UIDs loaded from the directory server, just like that in Figure 14-22.

Adding support for an existing authentication system (like an X.500 server) will be the most common reason to create a custom Realm. While it *is* possible to support different methods of authentication, most Web browsers support only username/password schemes and digital certificates, so creating a custom Realm for a new authentication device makes sense only for non-browser-based clients (like a Java application with its own authentication scheme—Smart cards anyone?). Making custom Realms for different storage types might be a useful exercise, especially if the medium was designed for concurrent access (like a JDBC datasource). Yet, the value added by substituting a database for a flat file may not warrant the effort, while making existing legacy authentication systems (with Java bigots like us, anything that was around before 1995 is "legacy") available for protecting Web resources is a big win.

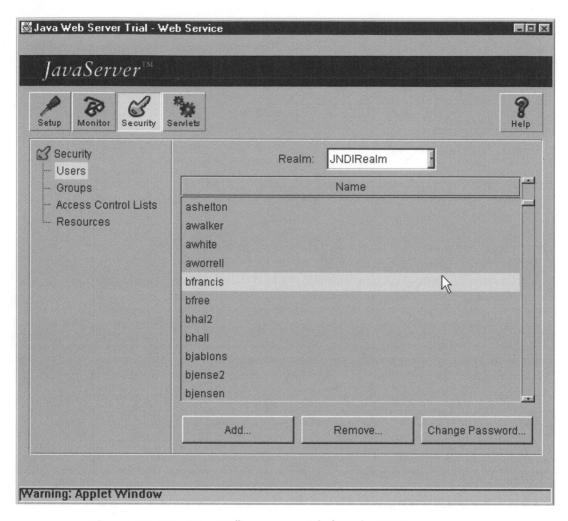

Figure 14-22   Wow! Pulling users straight from the LDAP server!

Summary

Addressing security is a tough task—it's a broad field filled with land mines. Any one hole in your network protection can be the Achilles heel of system integrity. Unfortunately, the Web doesn't make security any easier—in many ways, it makes security almost impossible! That point was made crystal clear in our discussion of Basic authentication (which, unfortunately, is *still* the most widely used form of "security" out on the Web). Digest authentication tries to patch up Basic authentication's gaping wounds. Without introducing encryption into the equation, however, the data is still publicly accessible (even if it can't be forged!) on a broadcast network like Ethernet. SSL comes to the rescue by encrypting the data stream between the client and the server, effectively putting an end to eavesdropping on Web surfers.

You also saw how authentication lies as the first stone on the road to a secure site. Once the identities have been obtained, they must be used somewhere. The HTTP specification calls this "somewhere" a Realm. You learned how to massage existing Realms, enumerating the user names into HTML. Finally, you created your own custom Realm, tying the Java Web Server's security to a popular piece of business equipment called an X.500 directory server (speaking LDAP). To accomplish this heady goal you used pieces of the Java Web Server development team's Realm cookbook. Once it was complete you saw how powerful a combination an LDAP-based Web authentication is.

HTML, SGML, AND XML

Topics in This Appendix

- XML and its most popular product: HTML

- Elements, attributes, and content

- HTML editors

- The Microsoft XML Parser for Java

- Channel definition format

- Making it work: the CDFServlet

Appendix A

It seems everybody and his dog has a home page these days, and all of these Web pages are written in HTML (HyperText Markup Language). HTML has become a "household word" synonymous with the Internet. A Web-savvy developer should have a good working knowledge of HTML, but that knowledge may not include why and how HTML works. Since this information isn't *vital* to writing Web pages or creating Web sites, we've decided to offer it in an appendix, where interested readers can learn more about the most common publishing format on the Web today.

A Brief History of HTML

HTML was born at the CERN laboratories in the early 1990s as a way to facilitate the distribution of scientific data among researchers. Tim Berners-Lee, the primary developer behind the system, utilized a text-processing technology called SGML to produce HTML.

Core Note

Standard Generalized Markup Language (SGML) was made an ISO standard in 1986 as a system- and device-independent method for representing electronic text (ISO 8879: Information processing). An excellent primer called "A Gentle Introduction to SGML" is included on the CD-ROM.

Based on ideas from hypertext information processing, early Web browsers at the CERN laboratories could navigate through a "web" of documents by activating text that had been "marked up." This linking capability allowed them to connect together groups of documents from different sites. For example, a paper on supercolliders (a topic of typical reading for the CERN scientists) could connect to a supplemental document at a different research center with a hyperlink reference. Someone reading the document could access these other papers by activating the link. Users thereby could peruse a world of information from one client, one link at a time.

But HTML on the Internet didn't really take off until the NCSA released Mosaic, its graphical Web browser, to the world in 1993. Instead of simply indenting or repositioning text, as did the early UNIX-shell-based Web browsers, Mosaic rendered the HTML documents with fonts and point sizes and retrieved graphical images for viewing along with the text. It was this capability to do crude document publishing with Mosaic that caught the public eye. Information was no longer set in dry, shapeless ASCII text but rendered in bold faces and full-color images.

When the popularity and success of Mosaic became evident, some of the developers left the NCSA to form Mosaic Communications Corporation, later renamed Netscape Communications Corporation. Netscape quickly gained control of the browser market with its "Navigator" product by introducing new (but nonstandard) HTML extensions such as tables and frames.

Over the years since its inception, HTML has gone through several revisions. Some were produced by Netscape and other vendors by the use of nonstandard tags, but these proprietary additions to HTML imposed difficulties on the Web developer. With no guarantee of what browsers would be visiting a site, a Web developer had to choose from a minimal subset of all the available features in order to support all browsers, or else create multiple pages customized with tags specific to each browser. Fortunately, the most popular features have been rolled back into standard HTML in version 4, but unfortunately, the percentage of users using HTML 4 compliant Web browsers is very small.

The Difference Between SGML and HTML

A typical misconception is that HTML is "based" on SGML. Actually, HTML is an *application* of SGML, similar to the computer-science concept of metalanguages (languages that define other languages), where SGML would be a metalanguage that describes HTML. For example, if you used the Scheme programming language to create the Haskell language, you would be defining Haskell in terms of Scheme (even if the Haskell language had different semantics, such as lazy evaluation of parameters). Similarly, while HTML provides facilities for more than just text processing, these features are presented in terms of an SGML document.

SGML provides a structural definition for applications such as HTML; therefore, an HTML document could be checked for proper syntax (a process similar to parsing by a compiler). This process is called *validation*. The rules for what makes a proper document are described in an SGML construction called a DTD (Document Type Definition), which the SGML parser uses during validation. The DTD is chosen depending on the document type (which in the case of a Web page is the HTML document type). Figure A-1 shows how an SGML Document, along with its appropriate DTD, is parsed, ending with either a good document or a list of errors.

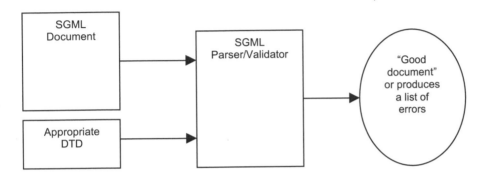

Figure A-1   Validating an SGML document.

So, if a Web page is an SGML document, what does its DTD look like? A DTD defines SGML objects called *elements*. You've seen elements when you've written Web pages, but in HTML-speak they're called "tags." A tag differs from an element. Consider, for example, the following HTML:

```
<BODY><H1>Hello Web!</H1></BODY>
```

The BODY *tag* ends at the greater-than symbol (<BODY≥), while the *element* ends at the greater-than symbol of the closing tag (</BODY≥). This is important, as an element can have zero, one, or two tags that define its boundaries. For example, the following HTML is valid:

```
<HTML><TITLE>My Home Page</TITLE></HTML>
```

A TITLE element is not a child of the HTML element, but a child of a HEAD element. Even though there are no tags defining the HEAD element in this document, its existence is implied by the TITLE element.

Also, consider the use of the IMG tag:

```
<BODY>...<IMG SRC="http://localhost/images/intro.gif">...</BODY>
```

In this case the IMG element is defined by the starting tag.

There are five parts of an element definition in the DTD:

- Element name
- Start tag

- End tag
- Attribute list
- Content model

The element definition looks like this:

```
<!ELEMENT [element name] [start tag] [end tag] [content model]>
```

The attribute list for an element looks like this:

```
<!ATTLIST [element name] {attribute definitions} >
```

Element Name

The name corresponds to the tag used in the SGML document. For example, in HTML there is the familiar HEAD tag, which would correspond to the HEAD element in the DTD.

Start and End Tags

The start- and end-tag fields tell the parser whether a tag is required in the document or should be inferred (leaving the parser to detect the end of the element in the SGML document). The HTML IMG tag is an example of an element that doesn't require an end tag. These fields are boolean fields marked with a dash ('-') if the tag is required, or with an o ('o') if the tag is optional.

Attribute Lists

The attribute-definition list describes the attributes an element may have. Attributes are name/value pairs that provide a way to customize a specific element. Let us take an HTML IMG tag as an example:

```
<IMG SRC="http://www.ptr.com/java/CoreJavaWebServer.gif" ALT=
                                    "The Coolest Book on the Planet!">
```

Two attributes are defined for this IMG element: SRC and ALT. The SRC attribute stores the URL of the image's data, and the ALT attribute contains display text for nongraphical browsers to use instead of loading the image:

Attribute lists are defined using a special DTD construction called an ATTLIST. For example, the IMG element's ATTLIST is shown in Listing A-1.

Listing A-1   IMG element's DTD

```
<!ATTLIST IMG
  %attrs;
  src    %URL        #REQUIRED — URL of image to embed
  alt    CDATA       #IMPLIED  — for display in place of image
  align   %IAlign     #IMPLIED  — vertical or horizontal
  alignment
  height %Pixels     #IMPLIED   — suggested height in pixels
  width %Pixels      #IMPLIED   — suggested width in pixels
  border  %Pixels     #IMPLIED   — suggested link border width —
  hspace  %Pixels     #IMPLIED   — suggested horizontal gutter —
  vspace  %Pixels     #IMPLIED   — suggested vertical gutter —
  usemap  %URL        #IMPLIED   — use client-side image map —
  ismap (ismap)       #IMPLIED   — use server image map —
  dynsrc  %URL        #IMPLIED   — URL of image to embed —
  start  NAMES       #IMPLIED
  loop NMTOKEN       #IMPLIED
  controls(controls) #IMPLIED

  vrml CDATA                     #IMPLIED>
```

Each entry in the ATTLIST corresponds to a single attribute. An attribute definition includes the attribute's name, its type, and whether the attribute is required for a valid document. Attribute data types are beyond the scope of this chapter. For more information, interested readers should refer to either the XML or SGML specifications.

Like attribute data types, this field can do more than what our simple explanation describes. Check out the SGML specification for more information (`http://www.iso.ch`).

Taking the SRC attribute as an example, the name of the attribute is SRC, the type of the attribute is %URL, and the attribute is required in a valid document. The SRC is the IMG element's only required attribute.

Content Model

The most interesting part of the element definition, however, is the content model. It provides a set of rules used by the SGML parser when a document is checked for proper structure (Figure A-2). A content model describes the parent-child relationship that can exist between elements. This relationship forms a tree structure, where one element contains a group of child elements, much like a file system.

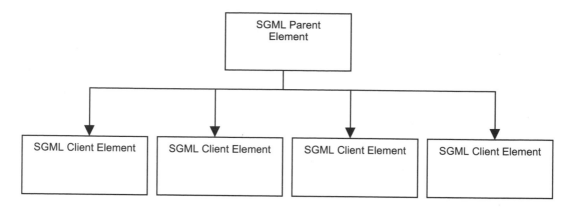

Figure A-2 The SGML content model.

A content model tells the parser what should and should not be in a valid document, but except for the simplest examples it does not dictate what will actually be in an SGML document. In the HTML DTD, for example, the element description of the HEAD element is:

```
<!ELEMENT HEAD O O   (TITLE & ISINDEX? & BASE?)  +(META|LINK)>
```

So, the HEAD element doesn't require a start or end tag and has a relatively simple content model consisting of a TITLE element, an optional ISINDEX element, an optional BASE element, and zero or more META and LINK elements. A DTD tree that corresponds to this entry looks like that shown in Figure A-3.

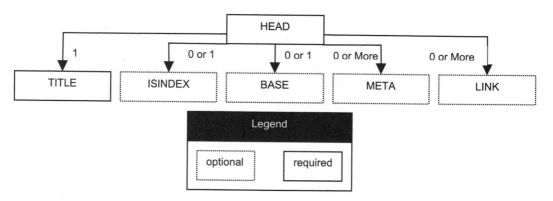

Figure A-3 Optional and required content model.

Now that you know what elements can be contained by a HEAD element, how do you represent these relationships in an SGML document? Imagine that the HEAD element's tags in a document act as the bottom and lid of a box: anything between the two tags must be contained inside it, as in a box. Using a snippet of HTML as an example, you can see how the HEAD element contains a TITLE element as content:

```
<HEAD><TITLE>Welcome to my home page!</TITLE></HEAD>
```

Using the content-model diagram for the HEAD element, the parsed HTML would look like that in Figure A-4.

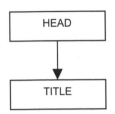

Figure A-4   The actual content-model diagram.

Since only the TITLE element is required as content for the HEAD element, this HTML passes the validation step successfully. If the TITLE element is a child of the HEAD element, what children does TITLE contain? It's another type of content: character data.

Character data is textual information contained in an element. As an example, if our SGML document were representing a book and the element hierarchy were structured: Book, Chapter, Section, and Paragraph, the DTD would look like:

```
<!ELEMENT BOOK - - CHAPTER*>
<!ELEMENT CHAPTER - - SECTION*>
<!ELEMENT SECTION - - PARAGRAPH*>
<!ELEMENT PARAGRAPH - - #CDATA>
```

and a sample document could be similar to the one shown in Listing A-2.

Listing A-2   A sample SGML document

```
<BOOK>
<CHAPTER>
<SECTION>
<PARAGRAPH>
Writing Java programs is fun!
</PARAGRAPH>
<PARAGRAPH>
Please refer to HelloWorld.java for more information
</PARAGRAPH>
</SECTION>
</CHAPTER>
</BOOK>
```

According to the DTD, only the PARAGRAPH element may contain character data. If you placed text in any of the three other elements, the parser would return an error during validation.

Of course, what's a book without authors? To get the authors' names into the book, let's introduce a fifth element called Author:

```
<!ELEMENT AUTHOR - O EMPTY>
```

An author really doesn't need any content, just some attributes (name, e-mail address, and s on). This kind of element is called *empty*, because all its information is stored in the opening tag.

Let's see this in action! Listing A-3 shows the revised BOOK document with the AUTHOR tags.

Listing A-3   A sample SGML document with AUTHORs

```
<BOOK>
<AUTHOR name="Christopher Taylor" email="cstaylor@pacbell.net">
<AUTHOR name="Tim Kimmet" email="tkimmet@seagull.com">
<CHAPTER>
<SECTION>
<PARAGRAPH>
Writing Java programs is fun!
</PARAGRAPH>
<PARAGRAPH>
Please refer to HelloWorld.java for more information
</PARAGRAPH>
</SECTION>
</CHAPTER>
</BOOK>
```

If you already know HTML, you should see the similarity between the AUTHOR tag and HTML's IMG tag (as both have no content).

"But the Browser Liked It!"

With all of this talk about validation, DTDs, valid documents, and structural rules, you would think that Web browsers would be among the strictest set of validating SGML parsers around. Unfortunately, this is far from the truth. Most commercial browsers will accept and display any HTML (within reason) that you throw at them, although with varying results. For example, Netscape Navigator 1.1 renders multiple BODY elements like a slide show, even though a document with this kind of structure is invalid according to the HTML 2.0 DTD.

So, how do you deal with all of these complicated DTDs and still produce valid HTML documents? Using a validating parser is a good way to check if your HTML is correct. A large number of parsers are available on the Internet, both commercial and freeware (visit www.infoseek.com or www.yahoo.com and search for "HTML Parser" to get a list of them).

An alternative solution, however, is never to produce incorrect HTML at all, and the best way to accomplish this is by using an HTML editor.

Choosing the Right Editor

While a good Web developer can efficiently write HTML with a common text editor, most of us mortals aren't quite as lucky. For us, tools are available to create the perfect Web site. These tools vary in price and quality, appealing to a wide range of technical experience levels. But hands down, our favorite is Macromedia's Dreamweaver, a recently released Web-development environment that provides just the right amount of "meddling" without too much interference for the experienced HTML author. It approaches the creation and use of cascading style sheets in an intuitive fashion, and it also comes with a program database for checking your HTML pages against different browser versions (currently Netscape Navigator versions 2.0, 3.0, and 4.0, and Internet Explorer versions 2.0, 3.0, and 4.0). When the check is complete, a report detailing which features won't work on certain browser versions is produced. Since testing a Web site with different browser versions is a tedious yet necessary task, this feature is worth the money. But most of all, the editor is *fast*, and it allows for responsive two-way editing between the GUI and the HTML. Changes to either part are immediately reflected in its peer—a feature that all HTML editors should have had a long time ago.

Hacking Web Pages on 50 Cents-a-Day

Not everyone is ready to invest in a full development system quite yet, and some would be happier with a "notepad on steroids," or an editor integrated with some HTML niceties such as syntax coloring and built-in viewer support. A decent editor for the right price (read "free") is FrontPage Express from Microsoft. It comes as an add-on to Internet Explorer 4.0 and runs on the Windows platform (Windows 95 and Windows NT). Although not as feature rich or user friendly as Dreamweaver, Frontpage makes as attractive alternative to Notepad.

If you are among the die-hard Netscape users who refuse to run IE on their machines, you can always use Netscape Composer for creating Web pages. It has features similar to those of FrontPage Express, and it comes with the same attractive pricing (read again "free").

However, HTML isn't the only game in town. XML, the latest markup language to hit the net, is taking the Web by storm.

XML: The Future of the Web

XML, or eXtensible Markup Language, is a new SGML-like document-definition language. XML contains many of the features provided by SGML, but it removes those that are less-frequently used. (This reduction of features should be a familiar story to RISC microprocessor aficionados.) This "slimming" makes writing a validating XML parser a simpler task, which explains the plethora of XML parsers currently available for use (both freeware and commercial).

Why should you care about XML? Learning HTML makes sense if you are already using the Web, and knowing how SGML operates deepens your HTML knowledge. But how will XML affect you? Well, if you've tried to use HTML for more than home pages, you are probably aware of its limitations for handling anything other than documents. The only way to create new features is to make your own proprietary tags. For example, Javasoft uses a nonstandard <JAVA> tag in its jhtml files for structuring Java source code, and it takes the content of these tags as compiler input to produce classes that generate dynamic content for Web pages .(See Chapter 13 for more details on page compilation.) Trying to validate a document that uses <JAVA> tags requires changes to the HTML DTD, which may not be a possibility for some SGML parsers. Instead of splintering HTML into several proprietary dialects, why not use XML as a data-definition language? By defining your application-specific information in XML, you can validate it with an XML-compliant parser before using it.

XML differs enough from SGML to warrant a comparison. For example, element definitions no longer contain the start/end tag required fields, because XML has stiffened the rules by requiring all tags with content to have an end tag, and empty tags to be ended with a '/>':

```
<img src="foo.gif" />
```

In addition, XML defines two types of documents: well formed and valid. Well-formed documents aren't required to have a DTD, but they do adhere to several rules:

- If there is no DTD in use, the document must start with a Standalone Document Declaration (SDD) saying so:

  ```
  <?XML version="1.0" standalone="yes"?>
  <foo>
  <bar>...<blort/>...</bar>
  </foo>
  ```

- All tags must be balanced: that is, all elements which may contain character data must have both start-tags and end-tags present (omission is not allowed except for empty elements).

- All attribute values must be in quotes [the single-quote character (the apostrophe) may be used if the value contains a double-quote character, and vice versa; if you need both, use ' and "].

- Any EMPTY element tags (e.g., those with no end tag like HTML's <IMG>, <HR>, and <BR>, and others) must end with `/>` or else you have to make them non-EMPTY by adding a real end-tag.

  Example: <BR> would become either <BR/> or
</BR>.

- There must not be any isolated markup characters (< or &) in your text data (i.e., they must be given as < and &), and the sequence]]> must be given as]]> if it does not occur as the end of a CDATA marked section.

- Elements must nest inside each other properly (no overlapping markup, same rule as for all SGML).

- Well-formed files with no DTD may use attributes on any element, but the attributes must all be of type CDATA by default.

Valid documents are also well-formed documents (which means that all XML documents must be well formed), but they are required to have a DTD. A DTD is referenced in an XML document just as in SGML:

```
<?XML version="1.0"?>
<!DOCTYPE book SYSTEM "book.dtd">
<book> … </book>
```

The previous example used an "external" DTD (the contents of the DTD are not found in this document). An XML document may also have an internal DTD, as shown in Listing A-4.

Listing A-4   A sample XML document

```
<?XML version="1.0"?>
<!DOCTYPE book [
<!ELEMENT book (author+,chapter*)>
<!ATTLIST book title CDATA #REQUIRED>
<!ELEMENT author EMPTY>
<!ATTLIST author name CDATA #REQUIRED>
<!ELEMENT chapter (paragraph)*>
<!ATTLIST chapter title CDATA #REQUIRED>
<!ELEMENT paragraph (#PCDATA)>
]>
<book title="Core Java Web Server">
<author name="Chris Taylor" />
<author name="Tim Kimmet" />
<chapter title="Introduction">
<paragraph>Here is some text!</paragraph>
<paragraph>Here is some more text!</paragraph>
</chapter>
</book>
```

Notice how the `<!DOCTYPE>` entity includes the contents of the DTD. "Internal" means the DTD is defined inside the body of the document.

XML is also a case-sensitive language, meaning that the names of attributes and elements must match the case specified in the DTD. This applies only for valid XML documents, because they have a DTD. For well-formed documents without DTDs, differently cased elements and attributes will be treated as different types by the parser. In the previous example, replacing

```
<book title="Core Java Web Server">
```

with

```
<BOOK Title="Core Java Web Server">
```

would cause an error. The parser wouldn't recognize the BOOK tag as a valid element because it didn't exist in the DTD.

Finally, the current version of XML is experimenting with *namespaces*, where data is qualified by a namespace name separated by a colon. This is similar to a feature that exists in Java (as packages) and in C++ (as namespaces). One use of namespaces would be to allow multiple DTDs to be used in a document, where an element or entity name can be qualified with an appropriate namespace. For example, the following processing instruction creates a namespace for a book.dtd:

```
<?XML:NAMESPACE HREF="http://www.prenticehall.com/book.dtd"
                                            AS="book"?>
```

and this XML uses that declared namespace:

```
<book:chapter title="Introduction"></book:chapter>
```

The namespace `xml` is reserved by the XML draft standard for future use, and one of the attributes it contains is `lang`, which is used to denote the language of an element's (and its children's) content:

```
<paragraph xml:lang="en">This is some English text</paragraph>
<paragraph xml:lang="de">Achtung!</paragraph>
```

Great! So now that you're done with the theory, what parsers are available for you to work with? Although all XML parsers do mostly the same things, the examples shown here will use the Microsoft Java XML parser (which can be freely distributed according to the license agreement).

Introduction to the Microsoft XML Parser

While the XML Working Group was putting together a draft standard, Microsoft wrote an XML parser that conformed to their work. Although they wrote parsers in both C++ and Java, the Java version works on all Java-compatible platforms, a big plus for developers writing "Pure Java" solutions who want to utilize XML in their applications.

The Microsoft XML API is made up of four packages:

- XML Object Model
- XML Parser
- XML Utilities
- XML Data Source

As this Appendix isn't meant to be an entire book on XML, but rather a cursory introduction to this new technology, we will cover in detail only the XML Object Model. Interested readers who want to run the examples in this chapter (and explore the other Microsoft XML API packages) will want to install the parser from the CD-ROM. Installing the Microsoft XML package is described in the readme file on the CD-ROM, so it won't be covered here. We've also included on the CD-ROM a copy of IBM's XML for Java package, which provides objects similar to those in the Microsoft package.

XML Object Model

This package provides an object-oriented interface to an XML document, with the key piece being the Document class. The Document class represents an XML document as a Java object, which can be used to:

- Create new documents
- Load existing documents
- Save documents to a stream
- Add new elements to a document
- Remove elements from a document

As a first example, you'll want to load an XML document off the disk, then print it to the screen, as shown in Listing A-5.

Listing A-5   Loading an XML document in Java

```java
import java.net.*;
import com.ms.xml.om.*;
import com.ms.xml.parser.*;
import com.ms.xml.util.*;
import java.io.*;

public class XMLExample1
{
```

continued

```
public static void main (String[] args)
{
  Document doc = null;
  if (args.length == 0)
  {
    System.err.println ("Usage: XMLExample1 [filename]");
System.exit(0);
  }
  try
  {
    doc = new Document();
doc.load(new FileInputStream(args[0]));
    XMLOutputStream xmlos = new XMLOutputStream(System.out);
doc.save(xmlos);
xmlos.close();
  }
  catch (IOException ioe)
  {
    ioe.printStackTrace();
  }
  catch (ParseException pe)
  {
    doc.reportError(pe, System.out);
  }
}
}
```

```
<?XML version="1.0" standalone="yes"?>
<sample>This is some sample text</sample>
```

Since you're a budding XML developer, you can see right away that the XML we are about to use is a well-formed document (because it doesn't use a DTD). In the Java source, you can see that several new packages have been included (Table A-1), but these are the same packages that were described at the beginning of this section.

Table A-1   XML-Specific Packages

Package Name	Part of Microsoft XML API
com.ms.xml.parser	XML Parser
com.ms.xml.om	XML Object Model
com.ms.xml.util	XML Utilities

The actual work of creating a document in this example consists of the following two lines of code:

```
doc = new Document();
doc.load(new FileInputStream(args[0]));
```

An empty document is created first, then filled with data pulled from a file. The Document class has two constructors, one being the default.

DOCUMENT

```
public Document ()
```

Creates an empty document using the default element factory (an element factory specifies how the elements of a document are linked together).

```
public Document (ElementFactory ef)
```

Creates an empty document using the specified element factory (ef). Certain types of programs (such as validating parsers) can use their own element factories for performance reasons. For example, the Microsoft XML parser (msxml) uses a NullElementFactory, which does nothing but return when an element-creation message is sent to the factory. Information on how to create your own ElementFactories is beyond the scope of this chapter, but it can be found in the Microsoft API documentation included with the XML package.

Saving a document takes a stunning three lines of code (21–23):

```
XMLOutputStream xmlos = new XMLOutputStream(System.out);
doc.save(xmlos);
xmlos.close();
```

consisting of creating a special type of output stream (XMLOutputStream), then saving the contents of the document object onto that stream.

XMLOUTPUTSTREAM

```
public XMLOuputStream (OutputStream)
```

Creates an XMLOutputStream object from the OutputStream parameter to the constructor. This object is typically used in the Document objects's save method.

XMLOUTPUTSTREAM

```
public void save (XMLOutputStream)
```

Writes the contents of an XML document to the XMLOutputStream.

To test your first example program, name the XML file as "first.xml" and run the Java interpreter with "java XMLExample1 first.xml." You'll get output similar to that in Figure A-5.

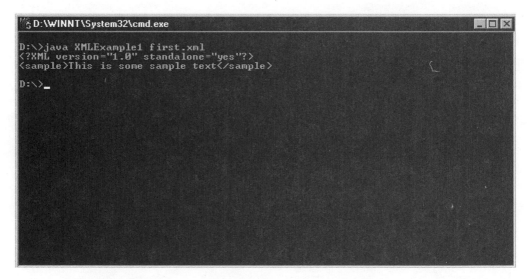

Figure A-5   Parsing a well-formed XML document from Java.

Hey! All the example program did was spit out the same XML file! Well, it did a little bit more than that, but since you wrote *perfect* XML, you didn't receive any ParseExceptions. All this first example does is load a document with the XML file specified as an argument on the command line, then save that same document out to System.out using an XMLOutputStream.

Can you do the same thing with a valid document? Alter the XML file to use an internal DTD, and call this altered file "second.xml":

```
<?XML version="1.0"?>
<!DOCTYPE sample [
<!ELEMENT sample (#PCDATA)>
]>
<sample>This is some sample text</sample>
```

Now run the XMLExample1 program again, except this time you'll use second.xml instead of first.xml (see Figure A-6 for sample output).

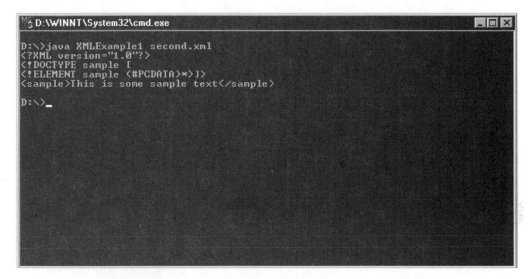

```
D:\>java XMLExample1 second.xml
<?XML version="1.0"?>
<!DOCTYPE sample [
<!ELEMENT sample (#PCDATA)*>]>
<sample>This is some sample text</sample>

D:\>_
```

Figure A-6   Parsing a valid XML document from Java.

Well, it looks like you were successful again! The example works with well-formed documents and valid documents using internal DTDs. Now for the big test using external DTDs! This time, put the DTD information in a separate file called "sample.dtd" and reference the DTD externally in your XML document, "third.xml":

```
<?XML version="1.0"?>
<!DOCTYPE sample SYSTEM "sample.dtd">
<sample>This is some sample text</sample>
```

Uh-oh! What happened to the XML document? Instead of seeing some friendly text printed out to the screen, you got the results of a ParseException as illustrated in Figure A-7.

Core Alert

Although it isn't documented in the Microsoft XML Java API, there is a problem using InputStreams to load valid XML documents with external references. Hyperlinks have base URLs for loading other documents. InputStreams, being streams of bytes, aren't related to any source. This becomes a problem when the DTD is referenced in the XML DOCTYPE declaration without a source. In this case, the onus is on the XML parser to locate the DTD relative to the document's location. Since there isn't a source for InputStreams, this proves to be an impossible task for the parser, which gives up and throws a ParseException.

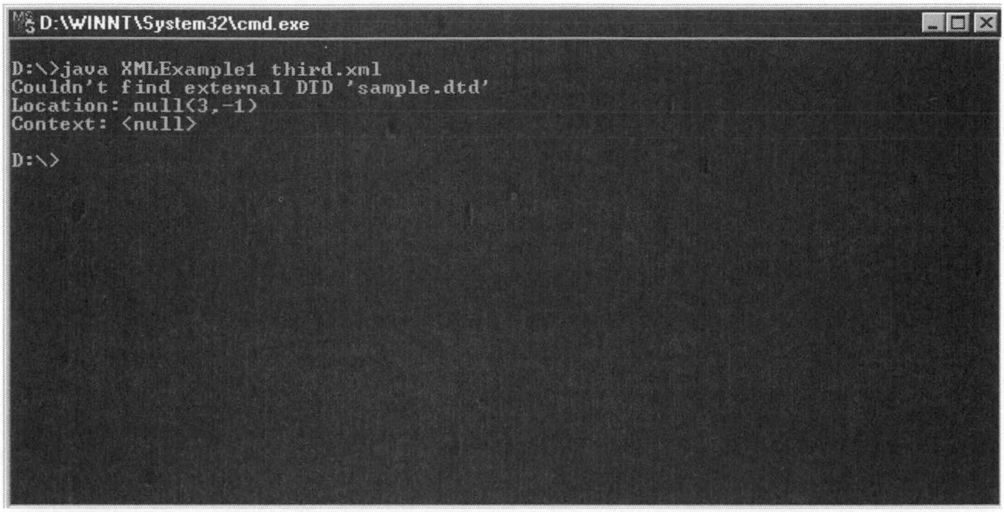

Figure A-7   Oops! ParseException during XML file loading in Java.

So, the ParseException occurred because the system wasn't able to locate a DTD in the InputStream. Someone at Microsoft must have run into this problem when designing the Document class, because they provided three methods for loading an XML document:

DOCUMENT

`public void load (String urlstring) throws ParseException`

Uses the String to internally create a URL object for retrieving the document data, thereby saving the caller the trouble of creating a URL object.

`public void load (URL url) throws ParseException`

Uses the URL to retrieve the document data.

`public void load (InputStream is) throws ParseException`

Reads the document data from the InputStream.

Of the three, using a URL seems to be best choice for loading the document. While you could change the code in the example program to use a URL, you could also specify the source of the DTD in the XML document and let the parser automatically find the DTD.

```
<?XML version="1.0"?>
<!DOCTYPE sample SYSTEM "file:///sample.dtd">
<sample>This is some sample text</sample>
```

Cool! As Figure A-8 suggests, this time the example program worked, because the source of the DTD was defined in the XML DOCTYPE declaration. As Figure A-9 shows, specifying a DTD's location has the same implications as other types of hyperlink references (HREFs).

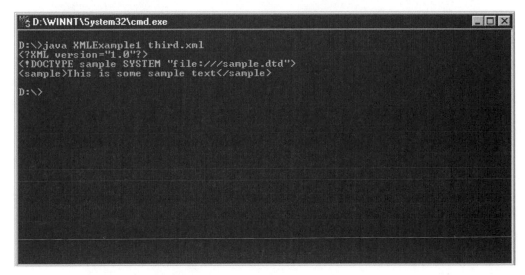

Figure A-8   Solving the problem by specifying the DTD.

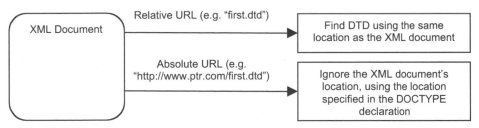

Figure A-9   How a DTD's location affects its parsing.

Core Tip

Using the `file` *URL isn't the best idea for anything but sample programs. When you want to release documents onto the Internet, and you don't want to embed the DTD inside the XML document, use an* `HTTP` *URL so users can access the DTD over the network (e.g.,* `<!DOCTYPE sample SYSTEM "http://www.ptr.com/xml/sample.dtd">`*).*

Now that you're comfortable with loading and saving document objects, what about changing the XML document and then saving those changes? The Document class provides that capability with the createElement method. You'll use this method in the next example by finding all XML files in the current directory and adding a comment to the header of each document found, as shown in Listing A-6.

Listing A-6   Creating an XML document

```
import java.io.*;
import java.util.*;
import com.ms.xml.om.*;
import com.ms.xml.parser.*;
import com.ms.xml.util.*;

public class XMLExample2
{
  private static final String _text =
       "Authored by: Christopher Taylor & Tim Kimmet";
  public static void main (String[] args)
  {
     File current = new File(".");
  String[] filelist = current.list(new XMLFileFilter());
  for (int loop=0;loop<filelist.length;loop++)
  {
    System.out.println ("Commenting XML file"+filelist[loop]);
    Document d = new Document();
    try
    {
      d.load(new FileInputStream(filelist[loop]));
         d.createElement(d.getRoot(),Element.COMMENT, null,text);
      d.save(new XMLOutputStream(new FileOutputStream(filelist[loop])));
    }
    catch (Exception e)
    {
      e.printStackTrace();
    }
  }
  }
}

class XMLFileFilter implements FilenameFilter
{
  public boolean accept (File root, String name)
  {
    if (name.toUpperCase().endsWith(".XML"))
    {
      return true;
    }
    return false;
  }
}
```

All XMLExample2 does is walk through an array of files in the current directory (restricting the search to files that end with the XML extension by using a FilenameFilter), add a Comment type element to the open document, and then save that document back to disk. Table A-2 lists several types of elements in the Microsoft XML Object Model (specified as constants in the Element interface class).

Table A-2   Elements in the Microsoft XML Object Model

Element Type	Constant
CDATA (Raw character data created with the <!CDATA[..]> construction. Not to be confused with PCDATA contained as an element's content.)	Element.CDATA
Comment	Element.COMMENT
Document (The root of the tree and document type.)	Element.DOCUMENT
DTD (Can only be a child of the Document element.)	Element.DTD
Element	Element.ELEMENT
Element Declaration (Found as a child of a DTD element, this type represents the content model and attributes of an element.)	Element. ELEMENTDECL
Entity	Element.ENTITY
Entity Reference	Element.ENTITYREF
Ignore Section (A conditional section of data in an XML document. Defined as a parameterized entity, a conditional section works much like a #ifdef in the C language. For example, if you wanted to mark an entity named "draft" to be ignored, the entity declaration would look like: <!ENTITY % draft "This is some ignored text" 'IGNORE'>. More information about IgnoreSections can be found in section 3.4 of the XML 1.0 Specification.)	Element. IGNORESECTION
Include Section (Same concept as Ignore Section. Refer to section 3.4 of the XML 1.0 Specification for more information.)	Element. INCLUDESECTION
Namespace (A namespace definition.)	Element.NAMESPACE
Notation (Used to name the format of an unparsed entity, so that an interested application can interpret the data for use with an external program. More information can be found in section 4.7 of the XML 1.0 Specification.)	Element.NOTATION
Parsed character data (content found within an element). For example, the title element in HTML contains character data used to represent the title of the document (e.g., <title>Welcome to my home page!</title> contains a PCDATA element with the content "Welcome to my home page!").	Element.PCDATA

continued

Table A-2 Elements in the Microsoft XML Object Model *(continued)*	
Element Type	*Constant*
Processing Instruction. (A PI element is used to pass information to the application without the data becoming part of the document. A C programmer familiar with the #pragma preprocessor directive should understand the use of a PI element.)	Element.PI
Whitespace. An XML parser can be configured not to ignore whitespace but to pass it on to the application.	Element.WHITESPACE

So in the case of the XMLExample2 class, an element of type Element.COM-MENT is created with the content "Authored by: Christopher Taylor & Tim Kimmet" as a child of the document element.

DOCUMENT

```
public Element createElement (Element parent,
                int elementType, Name tag, String text)
```

Creates an element of type `elementType` (one of the types found in Table A-2) with content in the string `text` as a child element of the `parent` element.

```
public Element createElement (int elementType, String tag)
```

Creates an element of type `elementType` but doesn't add it as a child to another element. The element can later be added as an element's child using the Element.addChild method.

```
public Element createElement (int elementType)
```

Creates an element of type `elementType` without a tag.

Wow! You've just flown through the basics of using the Microsoft XML parser and its object model to manage XML documents. Although many more classes are included in the package, most of them perform supporting roles for the main object model, and so we leave it as an exercise for the reader to investigate (unless we want to retitle the book *Core XML!*).

Kidding aside, you might be wondering how to use your new knowledge of XML beyond writing your own documents. Are there any mainstream applications that use XML?

Channel Definition Format: an XML Vocabulary

When Microsoft was developing Internet Explorer 4.0, they wanted to enhance the way the client could receive information from a server. They wanted something that worked like a remote control, allowing the user to flip easily through Web content like channels on a television. Figure A-10 represents a channel bar included with Microsoft's Internet Explorer.

Figure A-10   Flipping the channels using the Explorer remote control.

Other companies such as Pointcast and Marimba had spearheaded this new form of data distribution called *Push* content, but these solutions were based on proprietary data formats. Instead of introducing yet another file format, Microsoft created an XML *vocabulary* called Channel Definition Format to describe a Web channel.

Core Note

An XML vocabulary is a fancy way of saying document type. For example, your previous example of the book document type would be a very simple XML vocabulary.

The architecture of CDF itself is relatively simple. However, writing a CDF document isn't quite so easy. To make the learning curve a little less steep, the discussion on CDF will start with an introduction to the XML elements involved in a channel document. Once you feel aquatinted with the CDF element family, you'll create a few sample channels for Internet Explorer. Finally, since tediously writing CDF documents isn't fun, you'll automate the process with some Java code that will wring CDF files from your own Web site.

The Magnificent Sixteen

The CDF vocabulary defines sixteen elements that can show up in a CDF document. These elements are listed in Table A-3.

Table 2-1: The Standard Toolbar Icons			
A	ABSTRACT	CHANNEL	EARLIESTTIME
HTTP-EQUIV	INTERVALTIME	ITEM	LATESTTIME
LOG	LOGIN	LOGO	LOGTARGET
PURGETIME	SCHEDULE	TITLE	USAGE

Channel

The leader of this gang is the `channel` element. The channel is the document element for a channel-definition file, and it provides some basic information about the site being described. Channel has five attributes that are used to describe a site. They are summarized in Table A-4.

Table A-4	Channel Attributes Used to Describe a Web Site	

Attribute	Value Type	Description
BASE	URL	Similar to the HTML BASE element, this attribute provides a URL that is used to resolve all relative URLs in the channel document. The URL must end with a trailing slash ("/") or the last portion of the URL will be stripped off.
HREF	URL	The URL to the site being described by the channel. When the channel is activated by the remote control, this URL is used to load the site.
LASTMOD	DATE	Gives the date of the last modification to the channel in Greenwich Mean Time format. This is used to enhance performance with site caching.
LEVEL	NUMBER	Specifies how deep the channel should be cached by the client. The default number is 0 (which means no site caching). This feature is ignored if the PRECACHE attribute is false.
PRECACHE	"YES" | "NO"	Toggles whether a channel should be preloaded before it is viewed. The default value is "YES," and when it is used with the LEVEL attribute, a client can download a large portion of a site before it is viewed.

So, a valid CDF file could be as simple as:

```
<?XML version="1.0"?>
<CHANNEL HREF="http://localhost/">
</CHANNEL>
```

Before you move on to a more strenuous example, you'll want to test this simple one with the remote control. In Windows NT, all of your channels are stored in the `favorites/channels` directory of your user profile. Although that's the official location of channel files, it's easier to let Windows install them in the remote automatically. Just right-click on the CDF file and select `subscribe` from the option menu, as illustrated in Figure A-11.

If the CDF file was parsed properly, you'll be asked to name the channel, as illustrated in Figure A-12.

Change the name to "First Sample" and press the OK button. Now open Internet Explorer and use the Channel button to see your "First Sample" channel, as shown in Figure A-13.

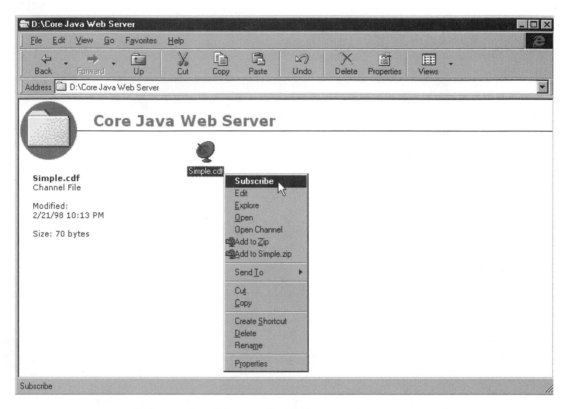

Figure A-11 Subscribing to a channel.

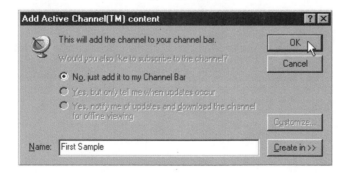

Figure A-12 Name the channel!

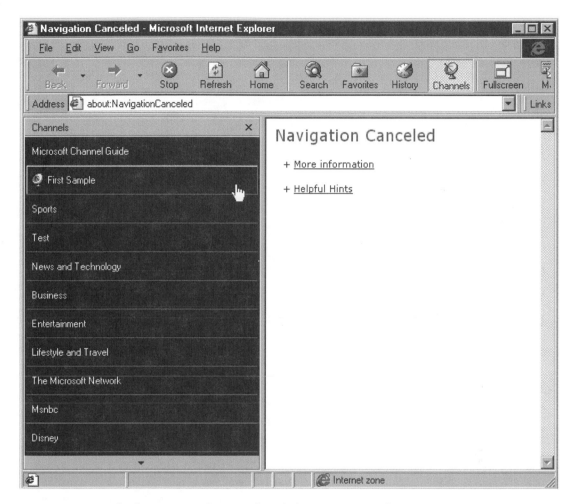

Figure A-13 Checking out your first sample with the Remote Control.

This display is a "docked" version of the remote control in Internet Explorer 4.0. Each entry in the display lists a separate channel available for viewing. A channel element by itself is usually not enough for anything but the simplest sites, so a few more elements are usually required. A good channel should have a few amenities, such as a logo that shows up on the remote control, an abstract that describes the site, and a title for the channel.

Logo

Three different logo images are used when displaying channels. Table A-5 summarizes these three image types.

Table A-5: Summary of the Three Channel Logo Images		
Image Type	*Size in Pixels (Width × Height)*	*When Used*
ICON	16 × 16	Used to represent the channel in an explorer window or on the channels bar
IMAGE	80 × 32	Used on the channel remote control on the desktop
IMAGE-WIDE	194 × 32	Used to provide a link to the channel site in the explorer window

Each of these logos is specified in the CDF file as a child element to the CHANNEL element. The latter, appropriately called LOGO, is an empty element with two attributes, which are summarized in Table A-6.

Table A-6 The Two LOGO Element Attributes		
Attribute	*Value Type*	*Description*
HREF	URL	The URL that locates the image to use as an icon
STYLE	"ICON"	"IMAGE"	"IMAGE-WIDE"	Specifies whether this icon is to be used as an icon, an image, or a wide-image

You'll need to make some images before you can use them in your channel. We've included ours on the CD-ROM, but you can make your own (just use the right pixel sizes!) as we've done (see Figure A-14).

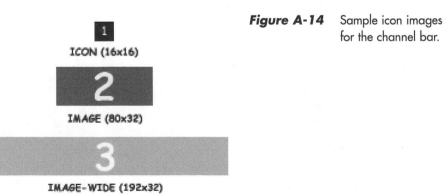

ICON (16x16)

IMAGE (80x32)

IMAGE-WIDE (192x32)

Figure A-14   Sample icon images for the channel bar.

For this example, why not make the files accessible from the Java Web Server? Make a subdirectory under the public_html directory called "channel" and add the three graphics to the new directory. Now reopen the first CDF file and edit the contents to look like Listing A-7.

Listing A-7   Channel file with appropriate icon images

```xml
<?xml version="1.0"?>
<CHANNEL HREF="http://localhost/">
<LOGO HREF="http://localhost/channel/small.gif" STYLE="ICON"/>
<LOGO HREF="http://localhost/channel/medium.gif" STYLE="IMAGE"/>
<LOGO HREF="http://localhost/channel/large.gif" STYLE="IMAGE-WIDE"/>
</CHANNEL>
```

To see the logos brighten up our channel, bring up Internet Explorer, right-click on the `First Channel` entry, and select `refresh`, as illustrated in Figure A-15.

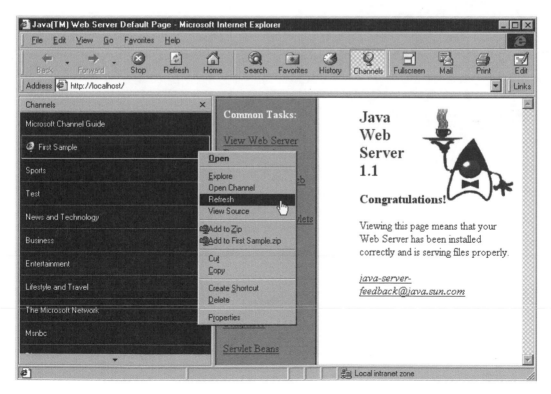

Figure A-15   Where are the changes?

For some reason, Internet Explorer doesn't refresh the display, even if the CDF file has changed. (You can verify that the source has changed by right-clicking on the channel and selecting `view source`.) In order to see the new graphics, you'll need to restart Internet Explorer and click the channels button, as shown in Figure A-16.

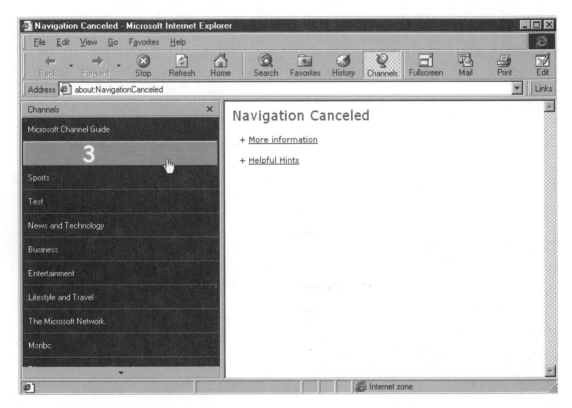

Figure A-16   Our channel is looking good!

Now that you've added some color to your channel, what about adding a title?

Title

The title element in a CDF file is just like an HTML title element, and it has no attributes. The CDF file with a title element for your sample channel looks like Listing A-8.

Listing A-8   A title! A title for my channel!

```
<?xml version="1.0"?>
<CHANNEL HREF="http://localhost/">
<TITLE>Our Sample Channel!</TITLE>
<LOGO HREF="http://localhost/channel/small.gif" STYLE="ICON"/>
<LOGO HREF="http://localhost/channel/medium.gif" STYLE="IMAGE"/>
<LOGO HREF="http://localhost/channel/large.gif" STYLE="IMAGE-WIDE"/>
</CHANNEL>
```

Besides the title, another element called "abstract" allows for a longer textual description of the channel.

Abstract

Like the title tag, the abstract element has no attributes. The abstract is displayed as a tooltip in Windows, providing more information than a simple title. The adding of an abstract to the sample channel is shown in Listing A-9.

Listing A-9   Describing a channel through an abstract

```
<?xml version="1.0"?>
<CHANNEL HREF="http://localhost/">
<TITLE>Our Sample Channel!</TITLE>
<ABSTRACT>Wow! I'm sure glad I bought Core Java Web Server!
Look at all of the neat things I learned about XML!</ABSTRACT>
<LOGO HREF="http://localhost/channel/small.gif" STYLE="ICON"/>
<LOGO HREF="http://localhost/channel/medium.gif" STYLE="IMAGE"/>
<LOGO HREF="http://localhost/channel/large.gif" STYLE="IMAGE-WIDE"/>
</CHANNEL>
```

After refreshing the channel through the channel explorer, move your mouse over the sample and read the tooltip text as shown in Figure A-17.

Now the channel is starting to look more professional! Typically, a channel should have at the least a set of icons, a title, and an abstract. But you shouldn't stop there, as a channel acts as a "face" for your Web site. A pretty face will attract more hits, while a sloppy channel tells surfers that the site isn't organized (and no one likes surfing through a disorganized site). As most Web sites are broken up into sections, give your channel a face-lift by expressing this organization in CDF through the ITEM element.

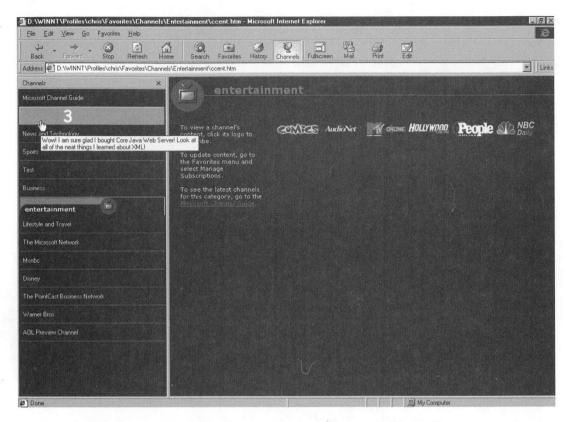

Figure A-17   Reading the description of a channel.

Item

Items separate areas of a channel into "points of interest" like a tourist map. Browsing through items begins by selecting the channel in the channel explorer. A channel that contains items will expand to show a drop-down list as illustrated in Figure A-18.

Items have the same attributes as a channel, except they can't contain other channels or items. Item elements are like files in a file system, where channels are the directories that contain other channels and items. Items, like channels, need to have logos, titles, and abstracts to look professional. Let's add two items to your sample channel in Listing A-10. The first takes the surfer to the Java Web Server documentation page, while the second sends the surfer down to the administrative applet.

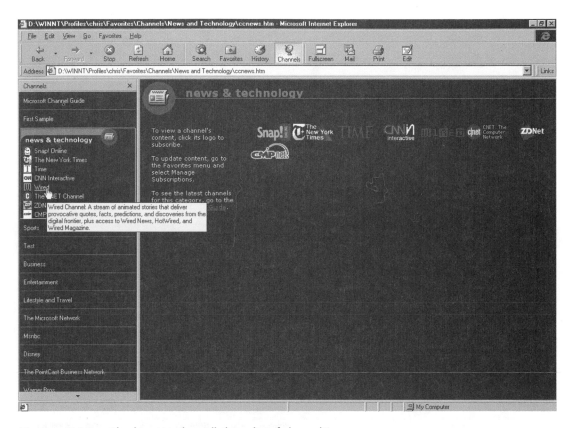

Figure A-18   Checking out the pull-down list of channel items.

Listing A-10   Adding items to your channel

```
<?xml version="1.0"?>
<CHANNEL HREF="http://localhost/">
<TITLE>Our Sample Channel!</TITLE>
<ABSTRACT>Wow! I'm sure glad I bought Core Java Web Server!
Look at all of
the neat things I learned about XML!</ABSTRACT>
<LOGO HREF="http://localhost/channel/small.gif" STYLE="ICON"/>
<LOGO HREF="http://localhost/channel/medium.gif" STYLE="IMAGE"/>
<LOGO HREF="http://localhost/channel/large.gif" STYLE="IMAGE-WIDE"/>
<ITEM HREF="http://localhost/system/doc/index.html">
<LOGO HREF="http://localhost/channel/item1.gif" STYLE="ICON"/>
<TITLE>Java Web Server Documentation</TITLE>
```

continued

```
<ABSTRACT>This is the documentation page for the Java Web
Server.  It contains useful information on how to install,
administrate, and develop applications for the Java Web
Server</ABSTRACT>
</ITEM>
<ITEM HREF="http://localhost:9090/">
<LOGO HREF="http://localhost/channel/item2.gif" STYLE="ICON"/>
<TITLE>Administrate the Java Web Server </TITLE>
<ABSTRACT>Opens the administration applet for the Java Web
Server.  You can edit servlet entries, add or remove security
restrictions, create virtual directories, and more!  Don't
wait! Click here NOW!</ABSTRACT>
</ITEM>

</CHANNEL>
```

Refresh the sample channel, then select it to view the drop-down list of items as shown in Figure A-19.

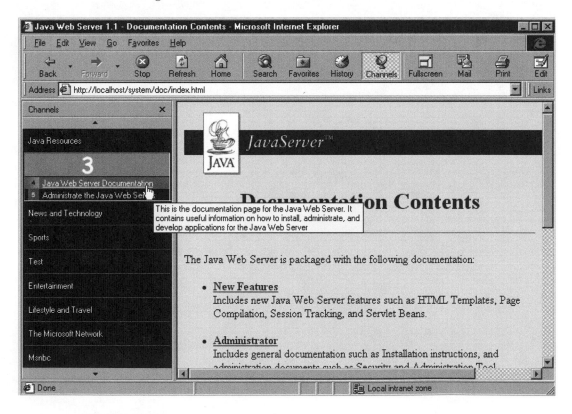

Figure A-19   Now we've got subitems.

Voila! Your channel now has two items floating in it.

Is there anything more you need to know about channels? After all, you've mastered the channel, item, logo, abstract, and title elements, so what do the other eleven elements provide for your site? They can be grouped around two goals:

- Automatically updating channel information
- Logging usage of a cached channel

Since this chapter isn't meant to be a complete CDF tutorial, we'll briefly introduce the rest of the elements but leave interested readers to experiment with their own examples. More information and examples can be found in the Microsoft Internet Client SDK (`http://www.microsoft.com`) and at the W3 Web site (`http://www.w3.org`).

Automating Channel Updates

Just like television channels, Web channels don't stay the same over time. Different programs come and go, seasons end, and page information becomes stale. How can a channel developer ensure that surfers are kept up to date with the latest information about a site? Regular television viewers can receive copies of *TV Guide* in the mail to stay current on the latest shows. CDF uses a similar process called *subscription updates* for their viewers.

Remember when you subscribed to your own channel by right-clicking on the sample CDF file earlier in the chapter? You should have seen a dialog that looked like the one in Figure A-20.

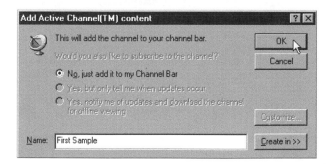

Figure A-20   Naming a subscription.

This dialog had several pieces grayed out. They were grayed out because your channel had no update information stored in the CDF file. This information comes from several different elements in a CDF file, as represented in Table A-7.

Table A-7 CDF Elements and Descriptions	
Element Name	*Description*
SCHEDULE	Describes a schedule for updating the channel
EARLIESTTIME	Optional element describing the earliest time a channel can be updated
INTERVALTIME	Describes how often a subscription should be updated
LATESTTIME	Optional element describing the latest time a channel can be updated

Basically, a channel has one SCHEDULE element describing when the subscription was created and when it expires (just like your subscription to *TV Guide*). A schedule contains an INTERVAL element specifying how often the subscription should be delivered (e.g., once a week for *TV Guide*), and optionally it contains EARLIESTTIME and LATESTTIME elements that set boundaries on when an update must occur.

Who's Reading Those Subscriptions, Anyway?

Having channel subscriptions automatically sent to your desktop is great for users. But caching also limits a Web master's ability to know what parts of her Web site are "hot." Every access to a subscription site doesn't make it home to the server, which results in inaccurate access logs for our Web master to sift through.

Fortunately, the designers of CDF understood this limitation, because they designed a way for clients to report cached page hits back to the server. When this logging feature is used, page hits are stored in a file kept in the `%userpro-file%\history\log directory` in Windows (but these files are hidden, so if you want to look at them you'll need to change some folder options in Explorer). The log file is sent back to the server in an HTTP POST message during the next channel update.

The logging mechanism is enabled with the LOG, LOGTARGET, PURGETIME, and HTTP-EQUIV CDF log elements, which are summarized in Table A-8.

Table A-8 CDF Log Elements	
Element Name	*Description*
LOG	Enables logging for a specific ITEM.
LOGTARGET	Specifies the URL where logged hits will be sent via a form POST.
PURGETIME	Specifies the number of hours for valid log data.
HTTP-EQUIV	Allows a logging system to specify HTTP-specific information in the log file upload.

The access logs are structured in Extended Log File Format according to the draft standard found at `http://www.w3.org/TR/WD-logfile.html`.

It's OK to Be a Cheater

Not everyone wants to chew up a Web site and spit out raw CDF by hand, but what are the alternatives? Taking time to sit down and master XML before providing channel support is too much to ask of overworked Web masters. Is there any way to leverage their experience with HTML editing tools for generating CDF?

This is where Microsoft comes in. After writing the XML parsers, the IE development team put together the "CDF Generator," a Windows program for creating CDF documents with a few mouse clicks and dialog entries. The program is a free download from Site Builder Network (`http://www.microsoft.com/sbn-member/download/download.asp`), and it is included in the Platform SDK or available as a separate file.

While the CDF Generator shares a similar look and feel with FrontPage (Microsoft's HTML editor), it features "dual editing." This works like Macromedia's Dreamweaver, as a CDF author can either use the GUI or edit the CDF directly to create a channel. Another "Dreamweaver" feature keeps both views (the GUI tree view and the XML text) updated, where the results of one action are reflected in the other, providing a useful tool for newbie and expert XML developers alike (see Figure A-21).

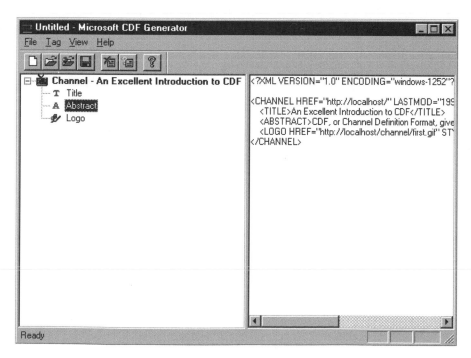

Figure A-21 Introducing the Microsoft CDF editor

You can use the CDF Generator to learn CDF by making changes with the GUI and inspecting the resulting XML. We found out about the CDF Generator after we had spend many hours poring over the CDF and XML specifications, and in hindsight we wished we had used this tool to help lower the learning curve.

Let Your Site Build Your Channels

When the Web came on line in the early 1990s, one of the first applications to make an impact on surfing was the search engine. The World Wide Web Worm was one of the first search tools available on line. The Worm "crawled" across the Web and created an index of sites by parsing the HTML and assigning "hit" values depending on certain criteria. This criteria depended on the context in which the word was found. For example, if I were searching for the word "XML," documents that had XML in their <TITLE>...</TITLE> tags would be assigned a higher hit value than if XML appeared only in the page content. This automatic generation of priority-based indices has proven invaluable for getting the right information to the right people.

The same search technology can be applied to your own Web site. With a little servlet magic, you can take the burden off an already overworked Web master by letting the site create its own channels. This accomplishment requires an XML API, which you already have with the Microsoft XML package.

The steps involved are:

1. Walking the directory tree
2. Parsing HTML files for certain elements
3. Producing the appropriate CDF elements from the parsed HTML
4. Send the completed CDF file back to the caller on a GET request

Core Note

The CDFServlet can be modified to use other XML parsers. In fact, the code for generating CDF files was taken from the IBM XML for Java package (http://www.alphaworks.ibm.com) and modified for the Microsoft API.

Listing A-11 is a simple version (simple in concept, but long in code!) of a servlet-based CDF generator:

Listing A-11   Generating CDF automagically with the CDFServlet

```java
import java.io.*;
import javax.servlet.*;
import javax.servlet.http.*;
import com.ms.xml.om.*;
import com.ms.xml.util.*;

public class CDFServlet extends HttpServlet
{
  // Constants
  public  static final String CDF_CONTENT_TYPE =
    "application/x-netcdf";

  private String    m_path;
  private String    m_url;
  private CDFAgent m_agent       = null;
  private Thread    m_thread     = null;
  private boolean   m_bIsShutdown = true;

  private static final String PATH = "path";
  private static final String URL  = "url";
  private static final int    WAIT = 500;


  public CDFServlet ()
  {
    System.out.println ("Constructing CDF Servlet");
  }

  public void init (ServletConfig config)
  throws ServletException
  {
    if (m_bIsShutdown)
    {
      super.init(config);
      System.out.println ("init() called");
      m_path = config.getInitParameter(PATH);
      m_url  = config.getInitParameter(URL);
      if (m_path == null || m_url == null)
      {
        throw new ServletException (PATH+" and "+
          URL+" parameters must be specified");
      }
      try
      {
        new java.net.URL(m_url);
```

continued

```
      }
      catch (java.net.MalformedURLException murle)
      {
        throw new ServletException (m_url+
                  " isn't a proper URL");
      }

      java.io.File file = new java.io.File(m_path);
      if (!file.exists() || !file.isDirectory())
      {
        throw new ServletException (m_path+
                        " isn't a directory");
      }
      m_agent = new CDFAgent(m_path,m_url);
      m_thread = new Thread(m_agent,
                        "CDFAgent for "+m_path);
      m_thread.start();
    }

  }

  protected void doGet (HttpServletRequest req,
              HttpServletResponse res)
  throws IOException, ServletException
  {
    try
    {
      m_thread.join(WAIT);
    }
    catch (InterruptedException ie)
    {
    }
    if (m_thread.isAlive())
    {
      res.sendError(
        HttpServletResponse.SC_SERVICE_UNAVAILABLE);
    }
    else
    {
      m_agent.sendCDF(res);
    }
  }

  public void destroy ()
  {
    if (m_thread != null)
    {
```

```
      m_thread.stop();
    }
    m_thread = null;
    m_agent  = null;
    System.out.println ("Shutting Down!");

  }
}

class CDFAgent implements Runnable
{
  private boolean m_done = false;
  private File m_directory = null;
  private String m_url     = null;
  private Document m_cdf    = null;

  private static final String TITLE = "<title>";
  private static final String END_TITLE = "</title>";
  private static final int TITLE_LENGTH = TITLE.length();
  private static final int END_TITLE_LENGTH =
                            END_TITLE.length();

  public void run ()
  {
    // do nothing now
    m_cdf = new Document();
    m_cdf.setStandalone("yes");
    Element root =
      m_cdf.createElement(m_cdf,
                      Element.ELEMENT,
                      Name.create("CHANNEL"),
                      null);
    System.out.println (m_cdf.getRoot());

    parseCDF (root,m_directory,m_url);
    m_done = true;
  }

  public CDFAgent (String path, String url)
  {
    m_directory = new File(path);
    m_url = url;
    // do nothing now
  }

  private void parseCDF (Element root,
                File dir,
```

continued

```
                    String prefix)
{
  File f = null;
  try
  {
    String[] fileNameList = dir.list();
    if (fileNameList != null)
    {
      for (int i=0;i<fileNameList.length; i++)
      {
        f = new File(dir,fileNameList[i]);
        String url =
          prefix+"/"+fileNameList[i];
        if (f.isDirectory())
        {
          Element newChannel =
          m_cdf.createElement(root,
                  Element.ELEMENT,
                  Name.create("CHANNEL"),
                  null);
          parseCDF(newChannel,f,url);
        }
        else
        if (f.getName().toUpperCase()
              .endsWith(".HTML"))
        {
          Element newItem =
          m_cdf.createElement(root,
                  Element.ELEMENT,
                  Name.create("ITEM"),
                  null);
          newItem.setAttribute("HREF",url);
          processItem(newItem,f);
        }
      }
    }
    root.setAttribute("HREF",prefix);
  }
  catch (Throwable th)
  {
    System.err.println ("Error parsing CDF");
  }

}

private void processItem (Element el, File f)
{
```

```
  Element elem = m_cdf.createElement(el,
            Element.ELEMENT,
            Name.create("TITLE"),
            null);
  String title = getTitle(f);
  if (title == null)
  {
    title = "no title";
  }
  Element text = m_cdf.createElement(elem,
                  Element.PCDATA,
                  null,
                  null);
  text.setText(title);
}

private String getTitle (File f)
{
    String title = "";
    String total_file;
  try
  {
      FileReader fr = new FileReader(f);
      char[] buffer = new char[(int)f.length()];
    fr.read(buffer);
      total_file = new String(buffer);

      int indexStart = total_file.indexOf("<t");
    indexStart = (indexStart == -1) ?
            total_file.indexOf("<T") :
            indexStart;
    while (indexStart >= 0)
    {
      if (total_file.regionMatches(true,
                      indexStart,
                      TITLE,
                      0,
                      TITLE_LENGTH))
      {
        break;
      }
      indexStart =
        total_file.indexOf("<t",indexStart);
      indexStart = (indexStart == -1) ?
          total_file.indexOf("<T",indexStart)
          : indexStart;
    }
```

continued

```
      int indexEnd = total_file.indexOf("</t");
  indexEnd = (indexEnd == -1) ?
        total_file.indexOf("</t") :
        indexEnd;
  while (indexEnd >= 0)
  {
    if (total_file.regionMatches(true,
                    indexEnd, END_TITLE,
                    0, END_TITLE_LENGTH))
    {
      break; // We found the end of the title
    }
    indexEnd =
      total_file.indexOf("</t",indexEnd);
    indexEnd =
        (indexEnd == -1) ?
      total_file.indexOf("</T",indexEnd) :
      indexEnd;
  }

  if (indexStart != -1 && indexEnd != -1)
  {
    title = total_file.substring(indexStart+
                    TITLE_LENGTH,
                    indexEnd);
  }
}
catch (Exception e)
{
  e.printStackTrace();
    return "Title could not be processed";
}
if (title.length()==0) return null;
return title;
}

public void sendCDF (HttpServletResponse res)
{
  if (m_done)
  {
    try
    {
      res.setContentType(
        CDFServlet.CDF_CONTENT_TYPE);

      ByteArrayOutputStream baos =
```

```
      new ByteArrayOutputStream();
   XMLOutputStream xmlos =
      new XMLOutputStream(baos);
   xmlos.setOutputStyle(
      XMLOutputStream.PRETTY);
   m_cdf.save(xmlos);
   xmlos.close();
   byte[] data = baos.toByteArray();
   res.setContentLength(data.length);
   ServletOutputStream sos =
      res.getOutputStream();
   sos.write(data);
   sos.close();
   }
   catch (IOException ioe)
   {
      ioe.printStackTrace();
   }
   }
  }
}
```

After compiling the CDFServlet, copy the CDFServlet.class and CDFAgent.class files to the servlets directory of your Web server. Now open up the Admin applet and configure the CDFServlet (in our example we map the name "cdf" to the CDFServlet) as shown in Figure A-22.

You'll want the servlet to start when the Java Web Server is loaded, so that the CDF is ready before the first request comes in. Set the servlet to "load at startup" to make this happen.

You'll also need to give the CDFServlet two parameters from the Java Web Server (or an equivalent servlet system): path and url. The path points to a directory acting as the "root" of the channel (i.e., "/javawebserver1.1/public_html/mysite/"). The CDFAgent runs in a background thread and walks down the directory tree starting from this point. The url parameter provides the "base" URL used in the HREF attribute of the CHANNEL and ITEM elements in the CDF file. Using the Admin applet, our parameters are set to use "http://local-host/" and "d:\jeeves\public_html" for the url and path (see Figure A-23).

Inspecting the code reveals that the CDFAgent class handles all of the real XML work. As it walks the directory tree, it opens all HTML files that it finds. It uses the TITLE tag and the name of the file to create appropriate ITEM and CHANNEL entries for the CDF document. That CDF file is sent to a user when the CDFServlet handles a Web request, because it delegates that request to the CDFAgent through a call to the sendCDF method.

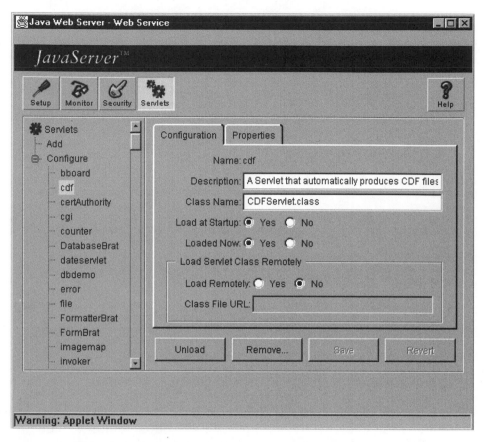

Figure A-22   Making a servlet entry for the CDF servlet.

The CDFServlet is a starting point; you'll want to customize its behavior for your own particular needs. Some good improvements could be:

- Adding LOGO elements
- Rerunning the CDFAgent on a regular basis
- Adding logging support

Fortunately, after reading this appendix you should be able to make these changes without any trouble. Don't forget, though, to run the CDF output through an XML parser (or load it into the CDF Generator) to make sure it's working properly before deployment!

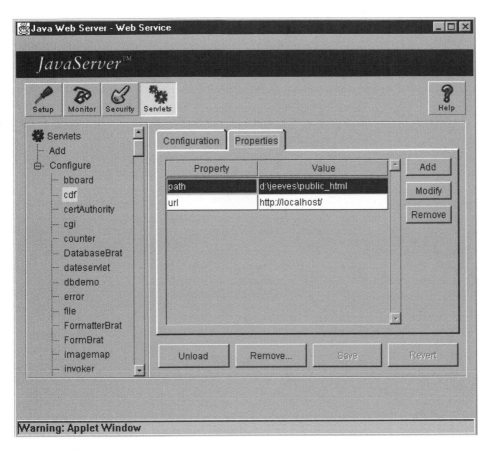

Figure A-23 Creating the appropriate servlet parameters.

Summary

XML, SGML, and HTML are a broad subject that can fill an entire book. Our goal was to present a simple overview of the technology and how it can impact your work as a Web author or Web developer. Hopefully, you've walked away with a deeper sense of how the Web works and how to improve it by using XML in your own projects.

Although we didn't cover it, IBM has an excellent XML package available for use at http://www.alphaworks.ibm.com. It has a cleaner, but slightly more complicated architecture than the Microsoft XML API, and it is worth a look if you plan to write anything substantial in Java using XML.

Also, CDF isn't the only "popular" XML vocabulary around. Two others are XSL and OSD. XSL stands for XML Stylesheet Language, and it's used to transform XML documents into HTML, so that XML developers can leverage Web browsers as a user interface for their programs. OSD is Open Software Description, and it's used to automate software updates. Both of these specifications have been submitted to the W3 (`http://www.w3.org`) for approval, and you can download the specifications from Microsoft's XML Web page (`http://www.microsoft.com/xml`).

Index

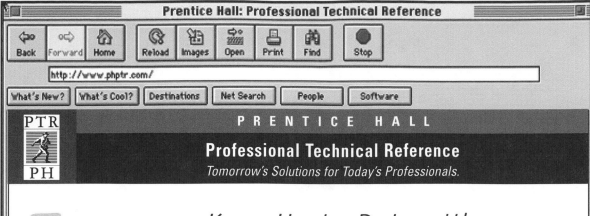

LICENSE AGREEMENT AND LIMITED WARRANTY

READ THE FOLLOWING TERMS AND CONDITIONS CAREFULLY BEFORE OPENING THIS DISK PACKAGE. THIS LEGAL DOCUMENT IS AN AGREEMENT BETWEEN YOU AND PRENTICE-HALL, INC. (THE "COMPANY"). BY OPENING THIS SEALED DISK PACKAGE, YOU ARE AGREEING TO BE BOUND BY THESE TERMS AND CONDITIONS. IF YOU DO NOT AGREE WITH THESE TERMS AND CONDITIONS, DO NOT OPEN THE DISK PACKAGE. PROMPTLY RETURN THE UNOPENED DISK PACKAGE AND ALL ACCOMPANYING ITEMS TO THE PLACE YOU OBTAINED THEM FOR A FULL REFUND OF ANY SUMS YOU HAVE PAID.

1. **GRANT OF LICENSE:** In consideration of your payment of the license fee, which is part of the price you paid for this product, and your agreement to abide by the terms and conditions of this Agreement, the Company grants to you a nonexclusive right to use and display the copy of the enclosed software program (hereinafter the "SOFTWARE") on a single computer (i.e., with a single CPU) at a single location so long as you comply with the terms of this Agreement. The Company reserves all rights not expressly granted to you under this Agreement.

2. **OWNERSHIP OF SOFTWARE:** You own only the magnetic or physical media (the enclosed disks) on which the SOFTWARE is recorded or fixed, but the Company retains all the rights, title, and ownership to the SOFTWARE recorded on the original disk copy(ies) and all subsequent copies of the SOFTWARE, regardless of the form or media on which the original or other copies may exist. This license is not a sale of the original SOFTWARE or any copy to you.

3. **COPY RESTRICTIONS:** This SOFTWARE and the accompanying printed materials and user manual (the "Documentation") are the subject of copyright. You may <u>not</u> copy the Documentation or the SOFTWARE, except that you may make a single copy of the SOFTWARE for backup or archival purposes only. You may be held legally responsible for any copying or copyright infringement which is caused or encouraged by your failure to abide by the terms of this restriction.

4. **USE RESTRICTIONS:** You may <u>not</u> network the SOFTWARE or otherwise use it on more than one computer or computer terminal at the same time. You may physically transfer the SOFTWARE from one computer to another provided that the SOFTWARE is used on only one computer at a time. You may <u>not</u> distribute copies of the SOFTWARE or Documentation to others. You may <u>not</u> reverse engineer, disassemble, decompile, modify, adapt, translate, or create derivative works based on the SOFTWARE or the Documentation without the prior written consent of the Company.

5. **TRANSFER RESTRICTIONS:** The enclosed SOFTWARE is licensed only to you and may <u>not</u> be transferred to any one else without the prior written consent of the Company. Any unauthorized transfer of the SOFT-WARE shall result in the immediate termination of this Agreement.

6. **TERMINATION:** This license is effective until terminated. This license will terminate automatically without notice from the Company and become null and void if you fail to comply with any provisions or limitations of this license. Upon termination, you shall destroy the Documentation and all copies of the SOFTWARE. All provisions of this Agreement as to warranties, limitation of liability, remedies or damages, and our ownership rights shall survive termination.

7. **MISCELLANEOUS:** This Agreement shall be construed in accordance with the laws of the United States of America and the State of New York and shall benefit the Company, its affiliates, and assignees.

8. **LIMITED WARRANTY AND DISCLAIMER OF WARRANTY:** The Company warrants that the SOFTWARE, when properly used in accordance with the Documentation, will operate in substantial conformity with the description of the SOFTWARE set forth in the Documentation. The Company does not warrant that the SOFT-

WARE will meet your requirements or that the operation of the SOFTWARE will be uninterrupted or error-free. The Company warrants that the media on which the SOFTWARE is delivered shall be free from defects in materials and workmanship under normal use for a period of thirty (30) days from the date of your purchase. Your only remedy and the Company's only obligation under these limited warranties is, at the Company's option, return of the warranted item for a refund of any amounts paid by you or replacement of the item. Any replacement of SOFTWARE or media under the warranties shall not extend the original warranty period. The limited warranty set forth above shall not apply to any SOFTWARE which the Company determines in good faith has been subject to misuse, neglect, improper installation, repair, alteration, or damage by you. EXCEPT FOR THE EXPRESSED WARRANTIES SET FORTH ABOVE, THE COMPANY DISCLAIMS ALL WARRANTIES, EXPRESS OR IMPLIED, INCLUDING WITHOUT LIMITATION, THE IMPLIED WARRANTIES OF MERCHANTABILITY AND FITNESS FOR A PARTICULAR PURPOSE. EXCEPT FOR THE EXPRESS WARRANTY SET FORTH ABOVE, THE COMPANY DOES NOT WARRANT, GUARANTEE, OR MAKE ANY REPRESENTATION REGARDING THE USE OR THE RESULTS OF THE USE OF THE SOFTWARE IN TERMS OF ITS CORRECTNESS, ACCURACY, RELIABILITY, CURRENTNESS, OR OTHERWISE.

IN NO EVENT, SHALL THE COMPANY OR ITS EMPLOYEES, AGENTS, SUPPLIERS, OR CONTRACTORS BE LIABLE FOR ANY INCIDENTAL, INDIRECT, SPECIAL, OR CONSEQUENTIAL DAMAGES ARISING OUT OF OR IN CONNECTION WITH THE LICENSE GRANTED UNDER THIS AGREEMENT, OR FOR LOSS OF USE, LOSS OF DATA, LOSS OF INCOME OR PROFIT, OR OTHER LOSSES, SUSTAINED AS A RESULT OF INJURY TO ANY PERSON, OR LOSS OF OR DAMAGE TO PROPERTY, OR CLAIMS OF THIRD PARTIES, EVEN IF THE COMPANY OR AN AUTHORIZED REPRESENTATIVE OF THE COMPANY HAS BEEN ADVISED OF THE POSSIBILITY OF SUCH DAMAGES. IN NO EVENT SHALL LIABILITY OF THE COMPANY FOR DAMAGES WITH RESPECT TO THE SOFTWARE EXCEED THE AMOUNTS ACTUALLY PAID BY YOU, IF ANY, FOR THE SOFTWARE.

SOME JURISDICTIONS DO NOT ALLOW THE LIMITATION OF IMPLIED WARRANTIES OR LIABILITY FOR INCIDENTAL, INDIRECT, SPECIAL, OR CONSEQUENTIAL DAMAGES, SO THE ABOVE LIMITATIONS MAY NOT ALWAYS APPLY. THE WARRANTIES IN THIS AGREEMENT GIVE YOU SPECIFIC LEGAL RIGHTS AND YOU MAY ALSO HAVE OTHER RIGHTS WHICH VARY IN ACCORDANCE WITH LOCAL LAW.

ACKNOWLEDGMENT

YOU ACKNOWLEDGE THAT YOU HAVE READ THIS AGREEMENT, UNDERSTAND IT, AND AGREE TO BE BOUND BY ITS TERMS AND CONDITIONS. YOU ALSO AGREE THAT THIS AGREEMENT IS THE COMPLETE AND EXCLUSIVE STATEMENT OF THE AGREEMENT BETWEEN YOU AND THE COMPANY AND SUPERSEDES ALL PROPOSALS OR PRIOR AGREEMENTS, ORAL, OR WRITTEN, AND ANY OTHER COMMUNICATIONS BETWEEN YOU AND THE COMPANY OR ANY REPRESENTATIVE OF THE COMPANY RELATING TO THE SUBJECT MATTER OF THIS AGREEMENT.

Should you have any questions concerning this Agreement or if you wish to contact the Company for any reason, please contact in writing at the address below.

Robin Short
Prentice Hall PTR
One Lake Street
Upper Saddle River, New Jersey 07458

About the CD

What's Included

The CD-ROM included with *Core Java Web Server* contains:
- all of the source code examples in the book (organized by chapter)
- trial versions of the Java Web Server for Solaris and Windows
- the most current JDK
- a demo version of Macromedia's Dreamweaver
- two XML parsers
- the med editor (used to write all of the code samples in the book)
- two third-party servlet runners
- HTML versions of various standard RFCs referred to in the book

System Requirements

The CD-ROM is a standard ISO 9660 CD formatted with RockRidge and Joliet extensions. The various programs and documents on the CD-ROM are organized into the following directories:

Dreamweaver	Med
IBM's XML for Java	Microsoft XML Parser
Java Web Server Realm Cookbook	ServletExec
Java Web Server Trial	Source Code Examples
JDK116	Standards Documents
JRun	Swing
Jsdk	

Installation instructions, copyright notices, license agreements, and system requirements are provided for each program as appropriate.

Use of the *Core Java Web Server* CD-ROM is subject to the terms of the License Agreement following the index in this book.

Technical Support

Prentice Hall does not offer technical support for any of the programs on the CD-ROM. However, if the CD is damaged, you may obtain a replacement copy be sending an email describing the problem to:

disc_exchange@prenhall.com